KENTUCKY

WILDLIFE ENCYCLOPEDIA

— AN ILLUSTRATED GUIDE TO —

BIRDS, FISH, MAMMALS, REPTILES, AND AMPHIBIANS

SCOTT SHUPE

Skyhorse Publishing

Skyhorse Publishing books may be purchased in bulk at special discounts for sales promotion, corporate gifts, fund-raising, or educational purposes. Special editions can also be created to specifications. For details, contact the Special Sales Department, Skyhorse Publishing, 307 West 36th Street, 11th Floor, New York, NY 10018 or info@skyhorsepublishing.com.

Skyhorse® and Skyhorse Publishing® are registered trademarks of Skyhorse Publishing, Inc.®, a Delaware corporation.

Visit our website at www.skyhorsepublishing.com.

10 9 8 7 6 5 4 3

Library of Congress Cataloging-in-Publication Data is available on file.

Cover design by Rain Saukas
Cover photos courtesy of the author

Print ISBN: 978-1-5107-2882-0
Ebook ISBN: 978-1-5107-2887-5

Printed in China

ACKNOWLEDGMENTS

The author gratefully acknowledges the following individuals who contributed to the completion of this book. In no particular order those individuals are:

Rob Mottice, Senior Aquarist at the Tennessee Aquarium in Chattanooga, TN, for help in identifying freshwater fish species photographed at that facility.

David Wilkins, Curator at the South Carolina Aquarium in Charleston, SC, for his help in identifying freshwater fish species photographed at his facility.

Larry Warner, North Carolina Aquarium on Roanoke Island, NC, for his help in identifying freshwater fish species photographed at his facility.

The staff of the North Carolina Aquarium at Pine Knoll Shores, NC, for help in identifying freshwater fish species photographed at that facility.

The staff at the Georgia Fish Center, for helping identify minnow species photographed at that facility.

The staff at the Texas Fresh Water Fish Center, for help in identifiying minnow species photographed at that facility.

Dave Frymire, for helping the author secure herp specimens for photography and for allowing me to photograph several snake species in his possesion.

John R. MacGregor, KDFWR, for providing a number of amphibian and mammal photographs used in this book and for providing technical information and scientific advice regarding the reptiles and amphibians of Kentucky.

Matthew R. Thomas, KDFWR, for help in identifiying several species of darters and minnows photographed by the author for this book as well as for his technical advice and icthyological expertise; and for providing a large number of fish photographs used in the book.

Amy Berry, Clay Hill Memorial Forest and Nature Center, for providing fish & amphibian specimens for photography.

Dr. Gordon Weddle, Campbellsville University, for providing fish and amphibian specimens for photography.

Dr. Ritchard Kessler, Campbellsville University, for help collecting fish specimens for photography.

Jim Harrison and Kristin Wiley, of the Kentucky Reptile Zoo, for allowing the author to trap on their property mammal and fish specimens for photography.

Clinton Cunningham, for assistance in acquiring and photographing herpetology specimens.

Kathleen Mount, for assistance in acquiring and photographing herpetology specimens.

Judy Tipton, for alerting me to the presence of and allowing me to photograph nesting birds in her yard.

Tim Johnson, for helping secure lizard specimens for photography.

Matt Wagner and John Hardy, from the Mississippi Museum of Natural History, for helping to ID fishes photographed in aquariums at that facility.

Brainard Palmer-Ball, of the Kentucky Ornithological Society, for help identifying fall warblers photographed by the author for this book.

Barbara Graham, for taking the author spelunking in the sandstone caves of eastern Kentucky, searching for bats to photograph.

Candy McNamee, for guiding the author on a search for migratory birds along the Texas coast.

Karen Finch, for guiding the author in a search for migratory birds in south Florida.

Dr. Tim Spier, Murray State University, for his help in collecting fish specimens for photography.

Jennifer Rader, of the Kansas Department of Wildlife, Parks, and Tourism for allowing me to photograph freshwater stream fishes at the Southeast Kansas Nature Center.

John Hewlett, who accompanied the author in the field and helped locate and collect fish and reptile specimens for photography.

James Kiser, for providing several photographs of Kentucky species.

Loren Taylor, KDFWR, for help in locating contributing bird photographers.

Kate Slankard, KDFWR, for her photo contribution and her help in locating contributing bird photographers.

Don Martin, of Don Martin Bird Photography, for contributing several of the more excellent bird photos in the book.

Don Brockmeir, for his photo contribution and also for allowing the author to use his photo blinds in his home state of Nebraska many years ago.

T. Travis Brown, for several photo contributions.

David Speiser, www.lilibirds.com, for several professional-quality bird photo contributions.

Jeffrey Offereman, for his photo contribution.

David Haggard, naturalist with Tennessee Department of Conservation, for his photo contribution of a rare blue morph Green Treefrog.

Kevin Lawson, for his photo contribution.

Phil Myers, University of Michigan, for contribution of several small mammal photos.

Konrad Schmidt, of North America Native Fish Association, for contributions of several fish photos.

Kris Light, for photo contribution.

Uland Thomas, for photo contribution.

Dave Neely, for photo contribution.

Sterling Daniels, TWRA Wildlife Biologist for his photo contribution.

Brian Zimmerman, www.ZimmermansFish.com, for several fish photo contributions.

Cheryl Tanner, for her photo contribution.

And to any others whose names I forgot to include; my thanks—and my sincere apologies for inadverdantly omitting your name!

Last but certainly not least, I would like to thank my publisher, Jason Katzman of Skyhorse Publishing.

In our negotiations Jason has not only shown patience and a willingness to compromise, but also great faith in this author. He has also exhibited extraordinary entrepreneurial courage in taking on a huge project of which this book is but a first step.

Finally, this book is dedicated to author's three sons. Haydn, Denham, and Kyle Shupe. Though now adults, as youngsters their keen eyes, youthful enthusiasm, and unflinching companionship were responsible for the author getting many of the photographs in this book. More importantly, their presence in this world has consistently provided this author with the motivation to repeatedly bite off more than I can chew.

PHOTOGRAPHERS

Most of the over 600 plus wildlife photographs that appear in this book were taken by the author. However, most of the really good photographs were contributed by several other wildlife photographers from around Kentucky and across the USA. Those individuals were critical to the completion of this book and their remarkable photographs add much to its content. The names of those additional photographers and the number of photos each contributed appear below.

Matthew R. Thomas—43
John R MacGregor—23
David Speiser, www.lilibirds.com—12
Don Martin Bird Photography—8
Brian Zimmerman—6
Konrad Schmidt—5
James Kiser—3
T.Travis Brown—3
Phil Myers—2
Kevin Lawson—1
David Haggard—1
Kate Slankard—1
Don Brockmeir—1
Kris Light—1
Uland Thomas—1
Dave Neely—1
Cheryl Tanner—1
Jeffrey Offermann, www.flickr.com/photos/jeff_offerman—1
Sterling Daniels—1

Thanks also to many other photographers who offered their help but whose photographs I was not able to use due to redundancy or timing constraints. A complete list of photo credits appears in the back of this book.

TABLE OF CONTENTS

FOREWORD

Kentucky is fortunate to be located in a global position that provides a temperate climate and moderate amounts of rainfall. This, along with a variable geology, helps create a biological diversity and physiographic composition that is among the most complex in the world. The rainfall and geologic structure here creates thousands of miles of rivers and streams. This provides ample riparian habitats, migratory corridors for mammals and birds, and aquatic habitats for fish and amphibians. These physiographic regions across the state, from mountains to wetlands, include watersheds, vast forests, open grasslands, and micro-habitats within these, that provide a lot of variety. In other words, Kentucky is a great place for wildlife!

Finally, here is a resource book that brings this all together. Not only has naturalist, educator, and author Scott Shupe inventoried all the documented species in Kentucky into one publication, but has also succinctly described the biological and geological composition of the state. This provides for all the beneficial opportunities for our wildlife populations here. While there have been series of books on mammals of Kentucky, reptiles, amphibians, fish, and birds, never before has it been brought all together in this detail. It is aptly named, and is truly an encyclopedia of Wild Kentucky.

I first met Scott thirty years ago, when I was the Park Naturalist at Cumberland Falls State Park. I had asked him to be a part of a special event I had organized, to present a program on wildlife in Kentucky. I learned then, he was a biologist of passion and expertise regarding Kentucky's wildlife. Not only did he want to have this knowledge, but he also had a great desire to share with others what he knew. He especially hoped to inspire our young students to acquire an appreciation of Kentucky's natural world. Scott has spent his entire career doing just that. And to do so well is a rare skill that Scott possesses. His knowledge, coupled with great communication and entertaining programs, has influenced citizens of Kentucky and beyond, young and old alike, to take notice of the world around them. Scott encourages us all to be observant, inquisitive, to explore and immerse ourselves in Kentucky's wild places, recognizing that we are an integral part, connected to those communities.

This book is another step forward for Scott in sharing his wildlife knowledge with us. It will serve as a valuable resource to professional biologists, field naturalists, and resource agencies. It will also be appealing to the general nature lover and wildlife watcher as a great reference book. If you are a wildlife enthusiast, and love Kentucky nature, this book is a must for your professional or personal library. I can't wait to get my copy!

Carey Tichenor
State Naturalist Emeritus

INTRODUCTION

From the earliest European exploration and settlement of Kentucky, the state's wildlife has played and important role. Men like the legendary Daniel Boone were in part lured to Kentucky by the opportunity to hunt Whitetail Deer, Bison, and Elk; and the native Americans living in the region sustained themselves largely by harvesting mammals, birds, and fish. While the state's wildlife is still an important resource for trappers, hunters, and fishermen, wildlife is also increasingly important for its intrinsic, aesthetic value. Though the age-old practice of hunting and fishing is the most obvious example of how wildlife can enrich our lives, for many Kentuckians the opportunity to simply observe wildlife and experience nature also serves to enhance our existence.

In more recent history the pursuit of wildlife has evolved to encompass more benevolent activities such as bird watching, wildlife photography, etc. In fact, the numbers of Americans who enjoy these "non-consumptive" forms of wildlife related recreation today exceed the numbers of those who hunt and fish, and the range of wildlife-related interests and activities has broadened considerably. In addition to the previously mentioned bird watching and wildlife photography can be added the activities of herpetology enthusiasts (reptiles and amphibians), freshwater aquarists, and lepidopterists (moths and butterflies), to name a few.

With interest in wildlife and nature continuing to grow throughout Kentucky, the need for a single, simple reference to the state's wildlife has become evident. There are available a number of excellent books that deal specifically with Kentucky's birds, reptiles, mammals, fishes, etc., but there are none that combine all the state's wildlife into a comprehensive, encyclopedic reference. This volume is intended to fill that niche. It is hoped that this book will find favor with school librarians, life science teachers, students of field biology classes, and professional naturalists as well as with the general populace.

As might be expected with such a broad-spectrum publication, intimate details about the natural history of individual species is omitted in favor of format that provides more basic information. In this sense this volume is not intended for use as a professional reference, but instead as a handy, usable, layman's guide to the state's wildlife. For those who wish to explore the information regarding the state's wildlife more deeply, a list of references for each chapter appears in the back of the book and includes both print and reliable Internet references.

Embracing the old adage that a picture is worth a thousand words, color photographs are used to depict and identify each species. Below each photograph is a table that provides basic information about the biology of each animal. This table includes a state map with shaded area showing the species' presumed range in Kentucky, as well as general information such as size, habitat, abundance, etc. The taxonomic classification of each species is also provided, with the animal's Class, Order, and Family appearing as a heading at the top of the page.

The range maps shown in this book are not intended to be regarded as a strictly accurate representation of the range of any given species. Indeed, the phrase "Presumed range in Kentucky" that accompanies each species range map should be literally interpreted. The ranges of many species in the state are often not well documented. The range maps for some species in this book may be regarded as at best an "educated guess." Furthermore, many wide-ranging species are restricted to regions of suitable habitat. Thus a lowland species like the Beaver, while found statewide, would not be expected to occur on the top of a mountain. Additionally, other species that may have once been found throughout a large geographic area may now have disappeared from much of their former range. The freakishly large and bizarre looking salamander known as the Hellbender is a good example of a species that, due to water quality degradation, is now extirpated from many areas within its former habitats.

Further complicating the issue of species distribution is the fact that animals like birds and bats, possessed with the ability of flight, are capable of traveling great distances. Many species of both birds and bats are migratory and regularly travel hundreds or even thousands of miles annually. It is not uncommon for these migratory species to sometimes appear in areas where they are not typically found. The mechanism of migration and dispersal of many animals is still a bit of a mystery and the exact reason why a bird from another portion of the country (or even from another continent) should suddenly appear where it doesn't belong is often speculation. Sometimes these appearances may represent individuals that are simply wandering. Other times it can be a single bird or an entire flock that has been blown off course by a powerful storm or become otherwise lost and disoriented. Whatever the cause, there are many bird species that have been recorded in the state that are not really a part of Kentucky's native fauna, and their occasional sightings are regarded as "accidental."

On the other hand, some species like the Snowy Owl or Roseatte Spoonbill may appear somewhere in the state once every few years dependant upon weather conditions or availability of prey in its normal habitat. Although these types of "casual species" could be regarded as belonging among Kentucky's native bird fauna, their occurance in the state is so sporadic and unpredictable that deciding which species should be included as a native becomes very subjective. The point is that the reader should be advised that while all the bird species depicted in this volume can be considered to be members of the state's indigenous fauna, not every bird species that has been seen or recorded in Kentucky is depicted in this book.

Likewise, not every one of the state's 267 recorded fish species is individually depicted. Some groups of fishes, such as the darters or the minnows, are represented by dozens or even scores of species that are often remarkably similar in appearance and sometimes have a very limited distribution in the state. The author has determined that to depict individually all of Kentucky's 50-plus species of *Etheostoma* darters would be redundant in a book of this scope. Thus I have chosen in some instances to provide a representative sampling of these large and diverse groups rather than overwhelm the reader with page after page of repetitive species. Again, the decision of which of these species to include has been somewhat subjective. However, the reader can be assured that if a species is widespread, common, or otherwise likely to be encountered or observed, that species has been included in this book; as have most of the rarer and less likely to be seen species.

For readers who wish to delve into more professional and detailed information about the vertebrate zoology of Kentucky, the list of references shown for each chapter should adequately provide that opportunity.

—Scott Shupe, 2017

CHAPTER 1

THE FACE OF THE LAND

— THE NATURAL REGIONS OF KENTUCKY —

Defining and understanding the natural regions of Kentucky is the first step in understanding the natural history of the state. Man-made political boundaries such as county lines and state borders are meaningless to wildlife, whereas mountains or rivers can be important elements in influencing the distribution of the state's wildlife.

The major considerations used in determining and delineating natural regions are such factors such as elevation, relief (topography), drainages, geology, and climate. All these are important elements that can determine the limits of distribution for living organisms. It follows then that some knowledge of these factors is essential when involved in the study of the state's natural history. The study of natural regions is known as Physiography, which means "physical geography" or literally "the face of the land." While the terms geography and physiography are closely related and sometimes used interchangeably, geography is a broader term that includes such things as human culture, resource use, and man's impact on the land, while physiography deals only with elements of geography created by nature.

The term most often used to define a major natural region is "Physiographic Division." There are ten major physiographic divisions across the United States and Canada, and portions of three affect the state of Kentucky. The three major physiographic divisions of Kentucky are the Appalachian Province Division the Interior Plains Division, and the Atlantic Plain Division (see Figure 1). Physiographic divisions are subdivided into smaller units called "Physiographic Provinces." These provinces are then subdivided further into Physiographic Sections (also sometimes called natural regions).

Elevation and topography are the major defining characters of the three main provinces affecting Kentucky. The highest elevations and greatest topographical relief occurs in the mountainous areas of the Appalachian Provinces Division, which occupies most of the easternmost portion of the state. Just to the west of the Appalachian Province Division, the Interior Plains Division covers much of the rest of the state, and farther west a northern extension of the Atlantic Plain Division encompasses the westernmost tip of the state.

The Appalachian Province Division extends from northern Alabama and northern Georgia all the way to Maine, and encompasses approximately the eastern one-third of Kentucky. There are a total of six provinces within this major division, one of which, the Appalachian Plateau Province, occurs in Kentucky.

The Interior Plains Division includes the central portion of Kentucky as well as most of the Great Plains states and most of the American Midwest. This large division extends all the way to the Rocky Mountains.

The Interior Plains Division has three provinces, one of which, the Interior Low Plateau Province, occurs in Kentucky.

Finally, the Atlantic Plain Division occurs mostly offshore (the Continental Shelf) and only the Coastal Plain Province occurs on mainland America. This province includes much of the southeastern United States and encompasses the westernmost tip of Kentucky.

Figure 1 on the following page shows where the major physiographic divisions occur in the Eastern United States.

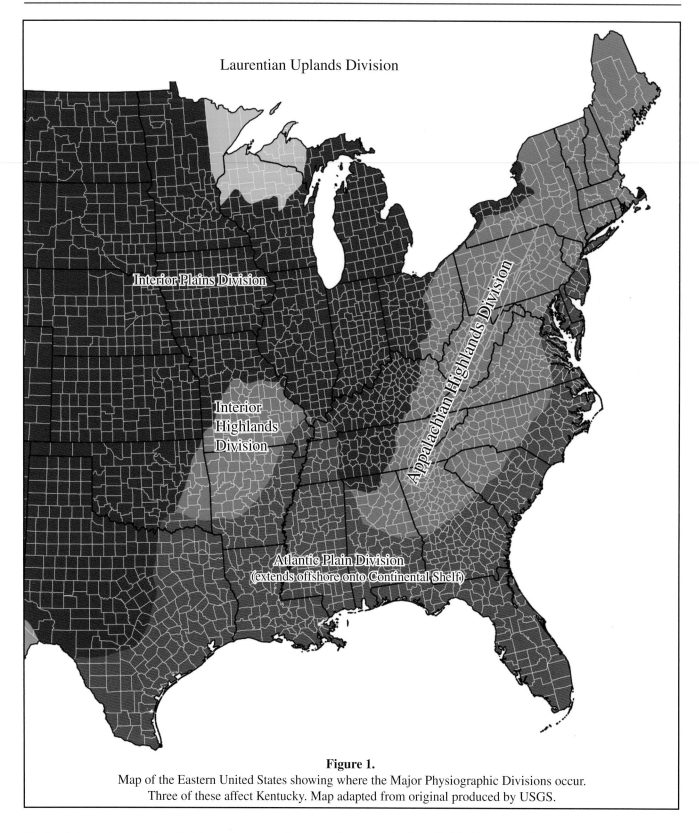

Figure 1.
Map of the Eastern United States showing where the Major Physiographic Divisions occur.
Three of these affect Kentucky. Map adapted from original produced by USGS.

Each of these three major divisions shown on the map above are further divided into smaller provinces.

The map on the following page (Figure 2) shows how these major divisions are divided into smaller provinces.

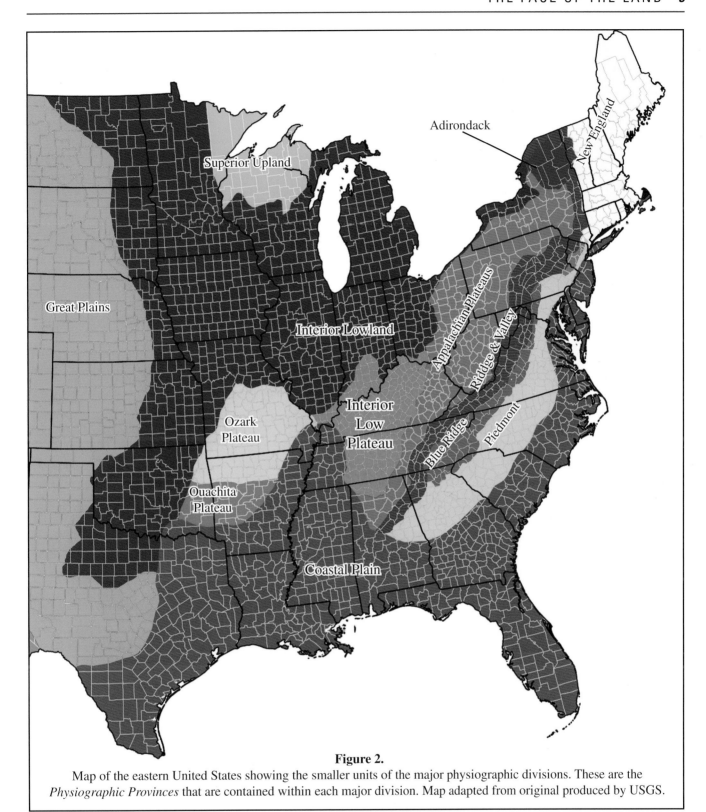

Figure 2.
Map of the eastern United States showing the smaller units of the major physiographic divisions. These are the *Physiographic Provinces* that are contained within each major division. Map adapted from original produced by USGS.

In the Appalachian Highlands Division the Appalachian Plateau Province (which occurs in eastern Kentucky) is shown on the map above in bright green.

In central Kentucky the portion of the Interior Lowlands Division known as the *Interior Low Plateau Province* is shown in purple.

The Coastal Plain Province (brown) constitutes a single large province of the Atlantic Provinces Division. The Coastal Plain Province invades the westernmost tip of Kentucky.

Table 1 below shows the physiographic divisions and their respective provinces that occur in the state of Kentucky. Provinces occurring in Kentucky are highlighted. Below Table 1 is a map of Kentucky (Figure 3) that shows where the three provinces that occur in Kentucky are located within the state.

Table 1. The Physiography of Kentucky.

Appalachian Plateau Division			
Peidmont Plateau Province	Blue Ridge Province	Valley and Ridge Province	Appalachian Plateau Province

Interior Highlands Division		
Interior Low Plateaus Province	Ozark Plateau Province	Quachita Plateau Province

Atlantic Plain Division	
Coastal Plain Province	Continental Shelf

Each of the physiograpic provinces in Kentucky can be subdivided into several smaller units, called Physiograpic Sections. Table 2 below shows how Kentucky's physiograpic provinces are subdivided into physiograpic sections.

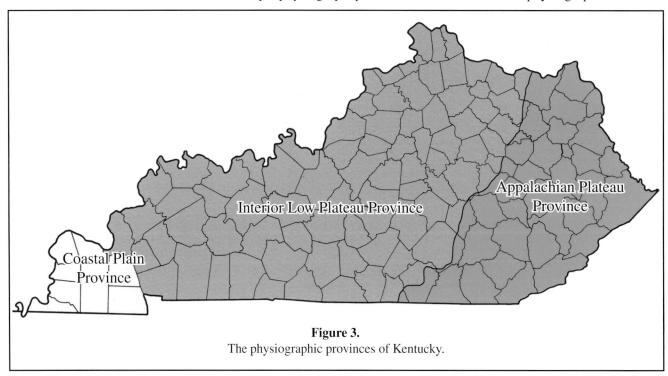

Figure 3.
The physiographic provinces of Kentucky.

Table 2. How Kentucky's Provinces and Sections are Related.

Appalachian Plateau Province		
Cumberland Mountains Section	Cumberland Plateau Section	Allegheny Plateau Section
Interior Low Plateau Province		
Bluegrass Section	Mississippian Plateau Section	Shawnee Hills Section
Coastal Plain Province		
Eastern Gulf Coastal Section	Mississippi Alluvial Plain Section	

Figure 4 on the following page illustrates where the physiograpic sections in Table 2 above occur within the state.

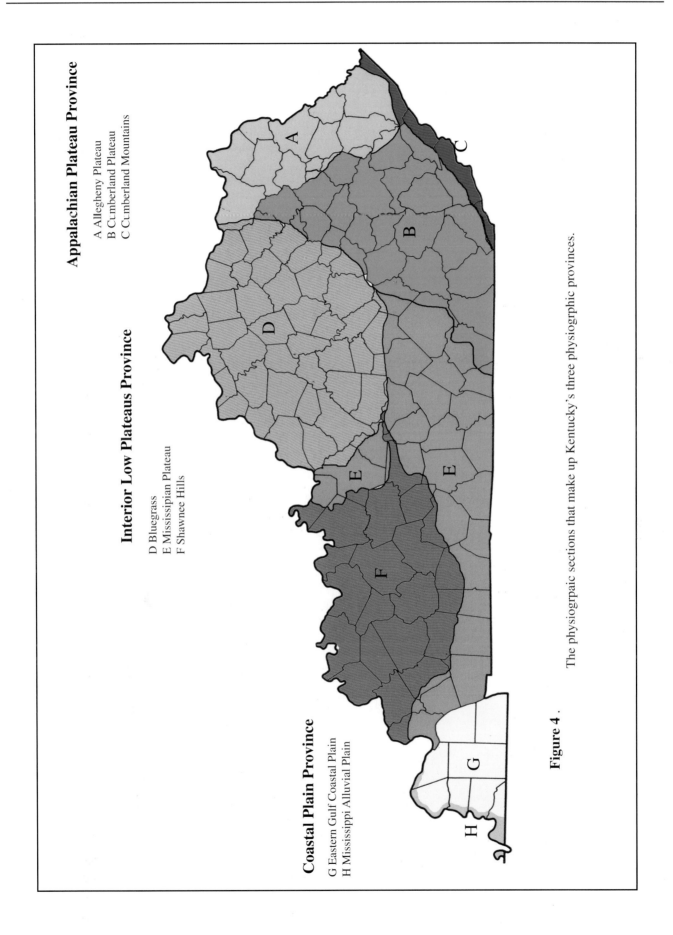

Appalachian Plateau Province

A Allegheny Plateau
B Cumberland Plateau
C Cumberland Mountains

Interior Low Plateaus Province

D Bluegrass
E Mississipian Plateau
F Shawnee Hills

Coastal Plain Province

G Eastern Gulf Coastal Plain
H Mississippi Alluvial Plain

Figure 4 . The physiogrpaic sections that make up Kentucky's three physiogrphic provinces.

A written description of each of Kentucky's physiographic provinces and the respective sections (or natural regions) contained within those provinces is as follows:

The Appalachian Plateau Province

The Appalachian Plateau Province is a subdivision of the Appalachian Highlands Division (Figure 1). This is a region of older mountains that have been heavily eroded over time to produce a high plateau region heavily dissected by rivers and streams. The entire region extends from northern Alabama through Maine. In Kentucky this province is often referred to as the Eastern Kentucky Coal Field. Elevations in Kentucky range from under 2,000 to slightly over 4,000 feet, with the area sloping to lower elevations generally from east to west. While many areas show a pronounced amount of relief, the elevations are much lower and the contours much less pronounced in comparison to the much younger Rocky Mountains in the western United States. Historically this region was nearly completely covered in mature forests (see Figure 12). The area is still the most heavily wooded region of Kentucky and most of the state's remaining forests occur here. The Appalachian Plateau Province is divided into six smaller natural regions (or physiographic sections), three of which—the Cumberland Mountains, the Cumberland Plateau, and the Allegheny Plateaus sections—occur in Kentucky.

A brief description of these two regions follows:

Cumberland / Allegheny Plateaus Regions
The Cumberland / Allegheny Plateaus region of the Appalachian Plateau Province are essentially high, heavily dissected plateaus, but the amount of topographical relief here is pronounced enough to call the area mountainous. Natural Bridge State Park, the Red River Gorge area, the Big South Fork National Recreation Area, and the northern portions of Daniel Boone National Forest are some of the well-known natural landscapes that occur in the Cumberland / Allegheny Plateaus region. Figure 4 shows where the Cumberland / Allegheny Plateaus occurs in Kentucky.

Cumberland Mountains Region
The Cumberland Mountains region of the Appalachian Plateau Province consists of several distinct mountain ridges, the most obvious of which is Pine Mountain, which is barely visible on the satellite image of the state in Figure 5 below. Pine Mountain is a long narrow ridge in the southeastern corner of the state running in a southwest to northeast direction. The highest elevation in the state occurs in the Cumberland Mountains region at the summit of Big Black Mountain on the Virginia Border at 4,150 feet. Other mountains in the region include Little Black Mountain, Cumberland Mountain, and Log Mountain. For a map showing where the Cumberland Mountains region occurs in Kentucky see Figure 4.

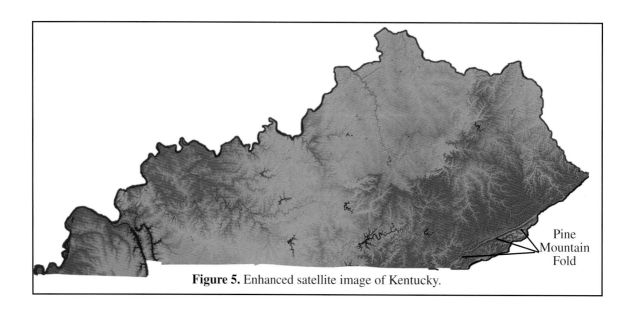

Pine Mountain Fold

Figure 5. Enhanced satellite image of Kentucky.

The Interior Low Plateau Province

The Interior Low Plateau Province is a section of the much larger Interior Plains Division that also includes the Interior Lowlands of the Midwest and the Great Plains farther to the west (see Figure 1). In Kentucky this area is a low, dissected plateau with lower elevations and less relief. Most of the area is under 1,000 feet above sea level, and some areas are less than 500 feet in elevation. It is essentially an area of rolling landscape well dissected by numerous rivers and streams that create areas of moderate relief. The area is more conducive to agriculture than the Appalachian Plateau and today contains less forest than occurs in the mountainous areas of the Appalachian Plateau. The region once contained extensive forests, grasslands, and wetlands. The Interior Low Plateau is subdivided further into the following three natural regions.

The Bluegrass Region

The Bluegrass Region of the Interior Low Plateau is the largest of the states natural regions, occupying nearly one third of the land area of Kentucky and encompassing most of the northern portion of the state. The region is contained mostly within the borders of Kentucky and is characterized by a dominance of limestone substrate (in fact the region is often referred to by geologists by the name "Ordovician Limestone Region"). Topographically the region is characterized by rolling hills deeply dissected by streams and rivers. The area once contained significant amounts of savanna-like open woodlands that supported herds of Elk and the now extinct Eastern Bison. Figure 4 shows where the Blue Grass Region occurs in Kentucky.

The Mississippi Plateau Region

The Mississippi Plateau region is a still lower plateau dissected by drainages that exhibits even more moderate relief. This region extends southward from Kentucky through middle Tennessee. Some areas within this region once contained patches of Tall-grass Prairies. The Land Between the Lakes National Forest is a well-known natural region located on the western edge of the Mississippian Plateau Region. This area is sometimes called the Highland Rim region. In Kentucky it also often goes by the name Pennyrile Region. Figure 4 shows where the Mississippian Plateau occurs in Kentucky.

The Shawnee Hills Region

The Shawnee Hills region is characterized by rolling hills of moderate relief. Upland hardwood forests are common and sandstone is the dominant geologic feature throughout much of the region. There are broad river valleys that once contained significant wetlands. This region extends across the Ohio River to the north/northwest into southern Indiana and southern Illinois. The portion of the Shawnee Hills region occurring in Kentucky is sometimes called the Western Coal Fields. Figure 4 shows where the Shawnee Hills Region occurs in Kentucky.

Coastal Plain Province

A subdivision of the Atlantic Plain Division (Figure 1), the Coastal Plain province occupies a huge swath of the southern and eastern United States from Massachusetts to Texas and includes all the land areas in the eastern United States that are below 500 feet elevation. This province is divided into three sections with two, the Eastern Gulf Coastal Plain and the Mississippi Alluvial Plain, extending into Kentucky. Historically this region boasted extensive wetlands and grasslands as well as forests. Locals often refer to this region of Kentucky as the Jackson Purchase. It is also sometimes called the "Mississippi Embayment" region because the area was once the northernmost extension of the Gulf of Mexico. In Kentucky the Eastern Gulf Coastal Plain is further divided into two natural regions, described below.

The Eastern Gulf Coastal Plain

The Eastern Gulf Coastal Plain section occupies most of the state west of the Tennessee River. It is below 400 feet in elevation and is a gently undulating plain, with minimal topographical relief being created by erosion. Most of the land area today is agricultural, and the region contains the least amount of forest in the state. Historically, some areas contained patches of Tall-grass Prairies, and most of the state's remaining wetlands occur here. Figure 4 shows where the Eastern Gulf Coastal Plain Region occurs in Kentucky.

The Mississippi Alluvial Plain

The Mississippi Alluvial Plain in Kentucky is contained in a narrow strip of land bordering the Mississippi River and the lower Ohio River. This area is subject to inundation during floods and high water and prior to human construction of dikes, dams, and channels it represented the natural floodplain of the Mississippi River. Historically the area was mostly swamp, marsh, and wet woodlands. Reelfoot Lake National Wildlife Refuge in extreme southwestern Kentucky is typical of what much of this region looked like in historic times. The lowest elevation in the state (275 feet) occurs here. Figure 4 shows where the Mississippi Alluvial Plain Region occurs in Kentucky.

CHAPTER 2
ECOREGIONS AND WILDLIFE HABITATS OF KENTUCKY

— PART 1: ECOREGIONS —

First, it should be noted that in ecology, as in the study of most other scientific disciplines, different opinions exist among experts as to the definition of a particular habitat or ecoregion (such as types of forests). Man's understanding of the earth's ecology continues to evolve and not every ecologist adopts the same model or criteria in describing habitats and ecosystems. Moreover, different models may be used by different researchers based on the needs of that research. The ecological model adopted here is derived from the ecoregions used by the Environmental Protection Agency (www.epa.gov/wed/ecoregions).

The Environmental Protection Agency recognizes a total of fourteen "Level I Ecoregions" in the United States and Canada. Each of these Level I Ecoregions consists of several progressively smaller divisions, known respectively as Level II Ecoregions, Level III Ecoregions, and Level IV

Ecoregions. The entire state of Kentucky falls within one of the larger of North America's fourteen Level I Ecoregions, known as Eastern Temperate Forest (see Figure 6 below).

The designation of Kentucky as a forest habitat is based on the state's naturally occurring wildlife habitats, i.e., the historical natural conditions found in Kentucky prior to the changes wrought by European settlers. Obviously, today much of Kentucky is not forested. In fact, the natural habitats of the state have been so altered by man that today less than 1 percent of Kentucky remains in a pristine, natural condition (see Figure 12). Although there is still much forested land in eastern Kentucky, it is virtually all regrowth, and today only a few acres of pristine, "old growth" forest remains in protected enclaves. West of the Appalachian Mountains, most of the state's forests have been cleared and converted to agricultural land, with only small pockets

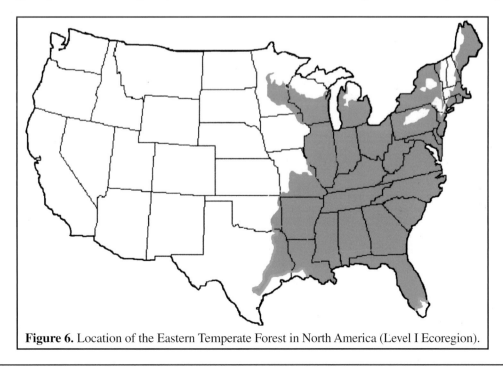

Figure 6. Location of the Eastern Temperate Forest in North America (Level I Ecoregion).

of regrowth woodlands scattered throughout. A notable exception being the Land Between the Lakes National Forest, where 107,000 acres of hardwood forest lie sandwiched between the Cumberland River (Barkley Lake) and the Tennessee River (Kentucky Lake). This woodland represents one of Kentucky's largest tracts of unbroken forest west of the Appalachian Plateau. Like all large forested regions in Kentucky, however, this area is a regenerated woodland, and no virgin forest tracts exist there.

When considering the state's wildlife habitats, it is important to remember that despite the fact that while all of the land area of Kentucky is regarded as a forest habitat,

some areas of grassland, wetland, and savannah habitats also occur in the state. Thus, although the habitat type is designated as forest, Kentucky has always contained a variety of other habitats that were embedded within the boundaries of the Eastern Temperate Forest Ecoregion.

The Eastern Temperate Forest (Level I Ecoregion) consists of five Level II Ecoregions. The Level II Ecoregions of the Eastern Temperate Forest are the Ozark-Ouachita-Appalachian Forest, the Southeast US Plains, the Mississippi Alluvial and Southeast Coastal Plains, Mixed Wood Plains, and Central US Plains. The location of these five Level II Ecoregions are shown in Figure 7 below.

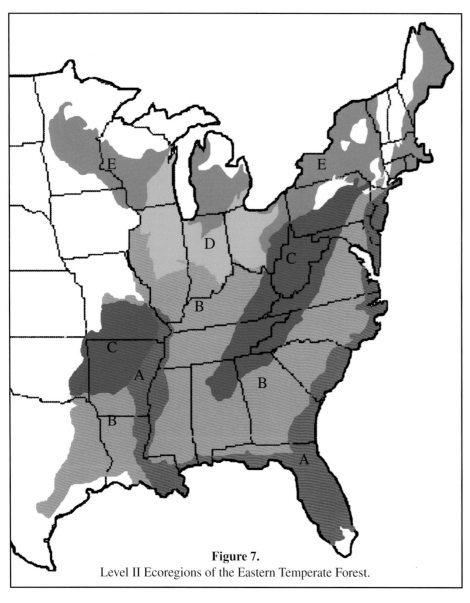

Level II Ecoregions of the Eastern Temperate Forest

A. Mississippi Alluvial and Southeast Coastal Plain
B. Southeast US Plains
C. Ozark-Ouachita-Appalachian Forest
D. Central US Plains
E. Mixed Wood Plains

Figure 7.
Level II Ecoregions of the Eastern Temperate Forest.

Three of the Level II Ecoregions shown above occur in Kentucky. The three Level II Ecoregions that affect Kentucky are the Ozark-Ouachita-Appalachian Ecoregion, the Southeast US Plains Ecoregion, and the Mississippi and Southeast Coastal Plain Ecoregion. Figure 8 shows where the Level II Ecoregions impacting Kentucky are found in the state.

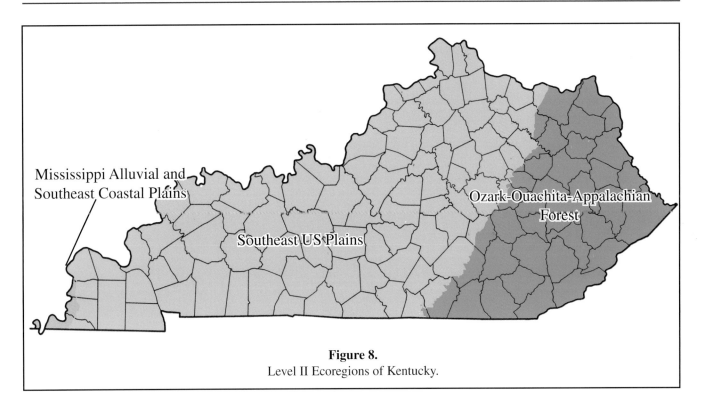

Figure 8.
Level II Ecoregions of Kentucky.

The Level II Ecoregions shown above are often referred to differently by other ecological models. The portion of the Ozark-Ouachita-Appalachian Forest that occurs in Kentucky is often called "Appalachian Mixed Mesophytic Forest." Similarly, the part of the Southeast US Plains found in Kentucky may be referred to as "Central US Hardwood Forests." And finally the portion the Mississippi Alluvial and of Southeast Coastal Plains Ecoregion in Kentucky is also known as "Mississippi Lowland Forest." Note how closely these Level II Ecoregions coincide with the physiographic provinces in Chapter 1 (Figure 4). For instance the Mississippi Alluvial and Southeast Coastal Plains (or Mississippi Lowland Forest) Ecoregions closely approximate the physiographic province known as the Mississippi Alluvial Plain. Similarly, the boundary of the Ozark-Ouchita-Appalachian Forest Ecoregion (or Appalachian Mixed Mesophytic Forest) is virtually identical to the physiographic province known as the Appalachian Plateau Province. A brief description of these three ecoregions is as follows:

Ozark-Ouachita-Appalachian Forest
The portion of this ecoregion that affects Kentucky is also sometimes called *Mixed Mesophytic Forests*. This region encompasses the highland regions of the western slope of the Appalachian Mountains from Pennsylvania, West Virginia, and Ohio south and west to northern Alabama. In Kentucky this ecoregion corresponds closely to the Appalachian Plateau physiographic province (see Figures 2, 3, or 4 in Chapter 1). These forests boast a high diversity of species for a temperate region. They are characterized by being relatively cool and damp forests. They have a wide variety of deciduous trees (oaks, hickories, walnuts, birches, ashes, maples, elms, beech, etc.) as well as a variety of evergreen species such as pines, hemlocks, rhododendron, magnolia, and Mountain Laurel. Within this ecoregion several types of localized habitats occur including mesic (damp) woodland, xeric (dry) woodland, wetlands (seeps and bogs), and open lands (glades, barrens, and some agricultural lands in valleys). Also widespread are ecotone habitats, successional areas, and man-made habitats (see Table 3). As much as 95 percent of this type of forest ecoregion has been altered from its original state, but some large tracts of older growth do exist in Kentucky within the Daniel Boone National Forest, Blanton Forest, Lily Cornett Woods, and in Cumberland Gap National Park. Both Blanton Forest and Lily Cornett Woods contain small tracts of unaltered old growth forest, offering a glimpse of the magnificent forests that once existed throughout the Appalachian Plateau region.

Southeast US Plains

This portion of the forest ecoregion occurring in Kentucky is frequently referred to as *Central U.S. Mixed Hardwood Forests*. In Kentucky this ecoregion roughly corresponds to the physiographic province known as the Interior Low Plateaus (see Figure 2). Hardwoods are dominant in this ecoregion with more drought tolerant species such as oaks and hickories being more common. Pines also occur commonly in much of the region. Grasslands were once sporadic but fairly widespread within this ecoregion, and wetland swamps and marshes dominated river valleys and lowlands. Also widespread are ecotone habitats, successional areas, and most commonly, man made habitats (see Table 3). This ecoregion supports the highest number of herbaceous plants and shrubs in North America (over 2,500 species). Modern agriculture has drastically altered the natural habitats in this region and in fact pristine examples of the original habitat in this region in Kentucky are virtually nonexistent.

Mississippi Alluvial and Southeast Coastal Plain

This ecoregion corresponds to the Coastal Plain physiographic region (see Figure 4). The portion that affects Kentucky also sometimes goes by the name *Mississippi*

Lowland Forests. The original riparian floodplain forests of the Mississippi River floodplain have been devastated by logging and agriculture. Originally stretching from the mouth of the Mississippi to southern Illinois, only a few pockets of this magnificent forest type remain. Wetter areas and river swamps are dominated by Baldcypress, tupelo, and willows. On the higher ground oaks, hickories, gum, Cottonwood, River Birch, Sycamore, Red Maple and pines are the main forest components. Local habitats are now dominated by open lands (mostly agricultural) and ecotones where pockets of swampland, marsh and woodlots remain. In addition to mesic floodplain forests and some dry woodlands, swamps and marshes were a common naturally occurring habitat here. Today all these habitats are but a sliver of what once occurred in the ecoregion. At present human altered habitats (mostly agricultural areas) are the most widespread interspersed with some ecotone habitats and successional areas.

The Level II Ecoregions described above are further divided into Level III Ecoregions. Figure 9 below shows how the each of Kentucky's three Level II Ecoregions are divided into Level III Ecoregions.

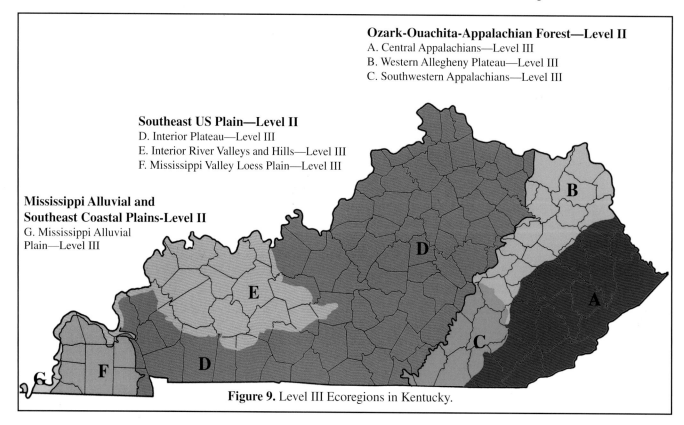

Ozark-Ouachita-Appalachian Forest—Level II
A. Central Appalachians—Level III
B. Western Allegheny Plateau—Level III
C. Southwestern Appalachians—Level III

Southeast US Plain—Level II
D. Interior Plateau—Level III
E. Interior River Valleys and Hills—Level III
F. Mississippi Valley Loess Plain—Level III

Mississippi Alluvial and Southeast Coastal Plains-Level II
G. Mississippi Alluvial Plain—Level III

Figure 9. Level III Ecoregions in Kentucky.

The Level III Ecoregions of Kentucky can be divided even further into Level IV Ecoregions. Ecologist and wildlife biologists can find these finer eco-region divisions useful in the study of the natural history of organisms. Some species are dependent upon a specific habitat or ecoregion for survival. Thus, an understanding of the various ecoregions and what factors are important in the designation of that ecoregion are imperative to wildlife management and conservation efforts. Figures 10 and 11 below show where the Level IV Ecoregions of Kentucky are located in the state.

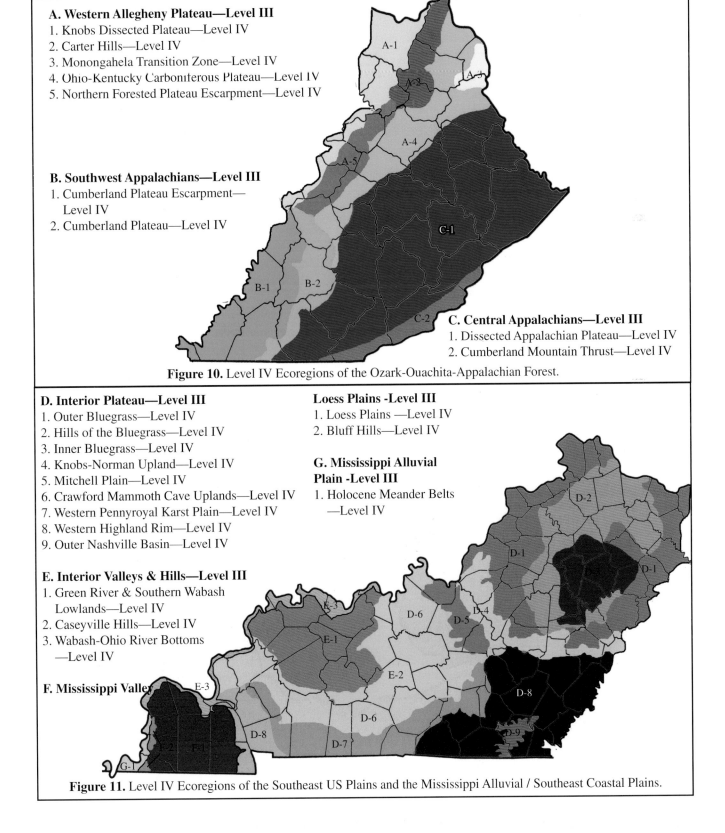

A. Western Allegheny Plateau—Level III
1. Knobs Dissected Plateau—Level IV
2. Carter Hills—Level IV
3. Monongahela Transition Zone—Level IV
4. Ohio-Kentucky Carboniferous Plateau—Level IV
5. Northern Forested Plateau Escarpment—Level IV

B. Southwest Appalachians—Level III
1. Cumberland Plateau Escarpment—Level IV
2. Cumberland Plateau—Level IV

C. Central Appalachians—Level III
1. Dissected Appalachian Plateau—Level IV
2. Cumberland Mountain Thrust—Level IV

Figure 10. Level IV Ecoregions of the Ozark-Ouachita-Appalachian Forest.

D. Interior Plateau—Level III
1. Outer Bluegrass—Level IV
2. Hills of the Bluegrass—Level IV
3. Inner Bluegrass—Level IV
4. Knobs-Norman Upland—Level IV
5. Mitchell Plain—Level IV
6. Crawford Mammoth Cave Uplands—Level IV
7. Western Pennyroyal Karst Plain—Level IV
8. Western Highland Rim—Level IV
9. Outer Nashville Basin—Level IV

E. Interior Valleys & Hills—Level III
1. Green River & Southern Wabash Lowlands—Level IV
2. Caseyville Hills—Level IV
3. Wabash-Ohio River Bottoms—Level IV

F. Mississippi Valley

Loess Plains -Level III
1. Loess Plains —Level IV
2. Bluff Hills—Level IV

G. Mississippi Alluvial Plain -Level III
1. Holocene Meander Belts —Level IV

Figure 11. Level IV Ecoregions of the Southeast US Plains and the Mississippi Alluvial / Southeast Coastal Plains.

Part 2: Habitats

In this book, as in many discussions about the natural environments of America, the terms habitat and ecoregion are frequently used interchangeably. But strictly speaking, there are differences between the two. The term "ecoregion," as defined by the World Wildlife Fund, means "a large unit of land or water containing a geographically distinct assemblage of species, natural communities, and environmental conditions." A habitat meanwhile is usually defined simply as "where an organism lives." Thus, an area of mesic (moist) forest, or xeric (dry) forest, are both habitats that are contained within the larger forest ecoregion. In many publications, the word biome is sometimes used synonymously with both the term habitat and the term ecoregion.

Table 3 below shows the various natural and man-made habitats that are today found within Kentucky's Eastern Temperate Forest Ecoregion. The Table below was created by the author for this book and may not necessarily match the habitat models of other authors.

Table 3. Kentucky Ecoregions and Wildlife Habitats.

Level I Ecoregion											
Eastern Temperate Forests (Temperate Broadleaf and Mixed Forests)											
Level II Ecoregions											
Ozark-Ouachita-Appalachian Forest (Appalachian Mixed Mesophytic Forest)				**Southeast US Plain** (Central U.S. Hardwood Forests)				**Mississippi Alluvial and Southeast Coastal Plains** (Mississippi Lowland Forest)			
Ecoregion Habitats											
Woodlands	Mature	Regenerative	Mesic (moist)	Woodlands	Mature	Regenerative	Mesic (moist)	Woodlands	Mature	Regenerative	Mesic (moist)
			Xeric (dry)				Xeric (dry)				Xeric (dry)
Wetlands			Bog	Wetlands			Swamp	Wetlands			Swamp
			Marsh				Marsh				Marsh
			Springs / Seeps				Springs / Seeps				Springs / Seeps
Forest Openings			Glades & Barrens	Open Land			Savannah	Open Land			Marsh
							Grassland				Sandbars
							Glades / Barrens				
Caves				Caves							
Universal Habitats Occurring throughout all ecoregions.											
Ecotones											
Successional Areas											
Riparian Zones											
Man-made Habitats Occurring sporadically or commonly in all ecoregions.											
Agricultural Areas											
Reclaimed Lands											
Urban Areas											

Definitions of Kentucky Habitats
ECOREGION HABITATS

Woodlands

As the naturally occurring ecoregions of Kentucky are forests, it comes as no surprise that woodlands are the most widespread naturally occurring habitat type in the state. Although professional biologists and ecologists recognize a larger number of different woodland habitat types, in this volume woodland habitats have been simplified and combined into two major types of woodland habitats that can *occur in all of Kentucky's three forest ecoregions.* Nearly all of Kentucky's woodland habitats are regenerative woodlands, i.e. woodlands that have been logged for timber at some time during the last 150 years. A few enclaves of mature woodlands remain in the state, but they are tiny, highly fragmented remnants of what once was a mature forest ecosystem.

Xeric (dry) Woodlands

These woodlands are usually found at the tops of mountains and ridges where the soil is thin and runoff is high. They can also occur on the sides of south or west south facing slopes. Drought tolerant plant species dominate these habitats. In the *Appalachian Mixed Mesophytic Forests* conifers such as Pitch Pine and Virgina Pine are common, with Chestnut Oak being dominant among the greatly reduced variety of deciduous tree species. In some xeric woodlands where trees are widely spaced and shrub growth is reduced, grasses and herbs normally associated with savannas and grasslands can be found on the forest floor. Within the *Central U.S. Mixed Hardwood* ecoregion pines and Red Cedar are the representative conifers while a variety of oaks and hickories dominate the deciduous tree community in dry woodlands. Xeric woodlands in this region occur on ridge-tops and steep, south or west facing slopes subject to a high rate of runoff and extensive sunlight. Dry woodlands are also common in areas where rocky substrate may be near the surface and topsoils are thin or very poor. Many of the tree species are the same as those found in mesic woodlands, but in the xeric woods they are often stunted and gnarly. Xeric woodland is least common in the *Mississippi Lowland Forest*, but can occur in the few upland areas such as the loess bluffs that border the river floodplain, or in highland areas with sandy soils.

Mesic (moist) Woodlands

Within the *Appalachian Mixed Mesophytic Forest* mesic woods are found on north or east facing slopes, at the bottoms of deep gorges, and in protected coves and valleys where prolonged direct sunlight is limited and evaporation is low. Small streams and springs and seeps are common. Hemlocks and White Pine are common conifers, while Tulip Poplar, Sugar Maple, Beech, Basswod, oaks, hickories (and in historical times the American Chestnut) are just a few of the deciduous tree species found in these diverse woodlands. Rhododendron and Mountain Laurel are common shrub species. Within the *Appalachian Mixed Mesophytic Forest* ecoregion, mesic woodlands can often contain plant species that are of a more northern origin. Mesic woodlands here are also a refuge for animal species, especially salamanders, which reach their highest diversity within the moist forests of the Appalachian Plateau.

In the Central United States Hardwood Forests mesic woodlands are typical in low lying areas such as valleys and bottom-lands. Typical tree species here are similar to those found in mesic woodlands elsewhere and Elm, White Oak, Black Oak, Red Oak, Shagbark Hickory, Sweetgum, Sycamore, and Dogwood are among the more common tree species.

Mesic woodland habitats are common in the Mississippi Lowland Forest, but the dominant tree species are different. Cottonwoods, willows, Baldcypress, Red Maple, River Birch, and Sycamore are more common here than in other regions of Kentucky. In historical times, prior to the taming of the mighty Mississippi River, the most significant factor influencing forests here was the degree of inundation by seasonal flooding.

Wetlands

Wetlands were once a very significant part of the wildlife habitat of the western portion of Kentucky and occurred extensively throughout the Coastal Plain Province. Wetland habitats also occupied large areas of the Interior Low Plateau Province along the lower Ohio, lower Green River, and Tradewater River systems (see Figure 12). Wetlands can be areas that are seasonally flooded or contain permanent standing water. In this book, wetlands are characterized by two basic types, swamps and marshes. Both swamps and marshes are very important habitats for many types of wildlife in Kentucky. Today less than one fifth of the original wetland habitats remain in Kentucky (see Figures 12 and 13).

Swamps

A swamp is best defined as a wetland area in which the dominate plants are trees. Most of Kentucky's swamplands have always been found in western third of the state, in low lying areas adjacent to rivers and streams. Baldcypress, willows, Red Maple, and Tupelo are the common tree species of Kentucky swamps. Generally speaking swamps are permanently flooded, but some habitat models may include seasonally flooded bottom-land forest. Swamps are important areas of biodiversity and are critical to the survival of many vertebrate wildlife species in Kentucky. Swamps are sometimes categorized by the dominant tree species present (as in Baldcypress Swamp, Gum-Tupelo Swamp, etc.).

Marshes

Marshes are wetlands in which the main plant species are grasses, sedges, and shrubs. Some small trees like willows may be present, but they are never dominant. Cattails, Pickerel Weed, Buttonbush, Rose Mallow, and Water Lily are common plants in Kentucky marshes. Some marshes may be only seasonally flooded, while others have permanently standing water. As with swamps, marshes enjoy significant diversity and are vital habitats to many of Kentucky's vertebrate wildlife species. As is the case with swamps, most of Kentucky's marshland is located in the western third of the state, but marsh habitat is present in small amounts the eastern portions of the state along stream courses. Most of the marshes occurring in the Ozark-Ouachita-Appalachian Forest were created by the actions of Beavers.

Bogs

Bogs are shallow depression that are permanently moist and often contain standing water. The vegetation usually consists of mosses (especially Sphagnum Moss), ferns, sedges, Jewelweed, and other herbaceous plants. Though bogs are widespread in the boreal forests of the far north, in the southern United States they are rare habitats that are usually an acre or less in size. Appalachian bogs are among the rarest habitats in Kentucky and harbor many rare plant species, but they are too small

and rare to be significant for most vertebrate wildlife. However, they do provide important habitats for some amphibian species, especially in upland areas where standing water may be uncommon.

Springs / Seeps

Springs and seeps are areas where underground water reaches the surface. The main difference between the two is the amount of water emerging. In seeps, the amount of water is usually much less than in a spring, with the water literally "seeping" from the ground. Seeps also may encompass a much larger area than a typical spring where the water emerges from a single point. These are small habitats but they can be very important and their influence can extend far downstream from the point of emergence. Many of Kentucky's amphibian and fish species are tied to these habitats. Although they occur statewide their greatest significance is in Appalachian Plateau Province.

Open Lands

The naturally occurring areas of open land in Kentucky were historically limited to Savanna, Grasslands, and small forest openings known as Glades and Barrens. Obviously today much of Kentucky consists of open land, but present day open lands are the result of changes wrought by man. A description of the state's *naturally occurring* open lands is as follows:

Glades / Barrens

Glades and Barrens are rare and widely scattered throughout Kentucky east of the Coastal Plain Province. They are among the smallest (and subsequently the most endangered) habitats in Kentucky. These habitats are created when underlying rock or gravels reach the surface. The resulting absence of soils creates an opening where the region's usual assemblage of plant species are lacking. *Glades* are usually associated with woodlands, and as there is not enough soil to allow for the growth of large trees, they produce open to semi-open areas within forests. Grasses and herbaceous plants are common within glades, and many glades in the Interior Low Plateau Province of Kentucky are associated with grassland plant communities. Some drought tolerant tree species can occur in these habitats by taking root in deep crevices within the rock. Red Cedar is the most common tree species found in this habitat. *Barrens* are often large slabs of exposed bedrock or underlying gravel and are usually much more "barren" than glades. They are nearly always dominated by grasses, herbaceous plants and small shrubs, and they are sometimes associated with or support grasslands. In some places in the mountains they consist of exposed bedrock with only the smallest amount of vegetation consisting of an occasional tuft of grass, moss or lichen clinging to cracks in the rock. Glades and Barrens usually occupy very small areas of land and are thus extremely vulnerable to human disturbance. Although Barrens and Glades support some very unique and extremely rare plant species, most are too small to be a significant habitat for Kentucky's vertebrate wildlife species.

Savannas

Savanna habitats are best characterized as grasslands with widely spaced trees. In Kentucky, most savanna habitats today are within the Bluegrass Region of the Interior Low Plateaus Province, although some savanna habitats also once occurred in the Mississippian Plateau region (see Figure 9). Burr Oak, Shumard Oak, and Blue Ash were important indigenous tree species in the original Bluegrass Savanna. Original savanna is one of the state's most imperiled habitats and the few remaining remnants of Kentucky's protected savannas are all located in the Bluegrass Region.

Grasslands

It should be no surprise to residents of the "Bluegrass State" to learn that Kentucky's natural habitats included significant swaths of tallgrass prairie. Like many other natural habitats within the state, however, the native tallgrass habitat has all but disappeared from Kentucky. Historically, grasslands occurred in much of Kentucky west of the Appalachian Plateau. Major areas of grassland habitat was found in the Bluegrass Region, portions of the Mississippian Plateau Region, and the Eastern Gulf Coastal Plain Region (see Figure 9). These grasslands were defined by a number of grass species including Big Bluestem, Little Bluestem, Gamagrass, Switchgrass, and Indian Grass. Despite the state's nickname, Bluegrass was introduced from Europe and is not one of the state's native grass species. It is believed that Kentucky's grasslands were enhanced and maintained

in part by regular burns initiated by native Americans to help maintain open areas within an otherwise heavily forested region. In recent decades an interest in recovering some areas of grassland has resulted in the preservation of some of the few naturally remaining grasslands in the state along with the replanting of new grassland habitats on public and private lands. Still, this remains one of Kentucky's rarest natural habitats.

Caves

Perhaps the most unusual category of wildlife habitat in Kentucky is the subterranean habitat of caves. The state of Kentucky is well blessed with caves. Mammoth Cave (the world's largest cave) lies in the heart of the Mississippian Plateau region of the Interior Low Plateau Province, and numerous smaller caves occur in that region. In addition, caves are well represented in the portion of the Appalachian Plateau Province that extends across eastern Kentucky. With the exception of three species of cave fishes, none of Kentucky's vertebrate wildlife species are true troglodytes (full-time cave dwellers). But several species do utilize this habitat for shelter or denning. Caves are a critical habitat for many of the state's bat species, who use caves both as daytime roosts and vital winter hibernacula. Lesser species like salamanders can be common in and around cave openings, and one species, the Cave Salamander, can be quite common in caves within its range.

Universal Habitats

These habitats occur in virtually all ecoregions throughout North America. The term "universal habitat" is not a commonly used scientific denotation, but rather it is a term created by the author for this book as a way to designate those types of habitats that can and do occur almost everywhere. However, three types of universal habitats listed immediately below (ecotones, successional areas, and riparian zones) are scientifically recognized terms.

Ecotones

Ecotones are defined as areas of transition between two or more habitats. The term "edge area" is often used synonymously with ecotone. Classic examples of ecotone areas in Kentucky would be a place were a woodland meets an open field or where a swamp or bottom-land abuts against a ridge of upland woods. Ecotones are universal habitats found in all regions. These are very productive areas for wildlife, as species from varying habitats can often be found together around ecotones.

Successional Areas

This is another type of habitat that can occur anywhere. Nature is never static. Grasslands are always in the process of becoming woodlands unless the successional process is altered by fire or mowing. Woodlands destroyed by fire may become grassland. A lake subject to sedimentation can become a swamp or marsh. In time a marsh can fill and become a meadow. Beavers can create a new wetland where before there was a meadow with a small stream. In Kentucky, the most familiar successional habitat is the regeneration of a woodland following logging or the reversion to a weedy field of a neglected cropland. These last two types of successional areas are favored by wildlife species like the Whitetail Deer and the Eastern Cottontail.

Riparian Zones

A riparian zone is a narrow band of habitat bordering a stream or river. Technically, the term is used to describe the narrow zone of lush growth that accompanies a stream coursing through an otherwise arid landscape (as in the riparian habitats of the desert southwest). In Kentucky, where so much of the natural landscape has disappeared, stream courses through open farmlands with their associated ribbon of trees, shrubs, and forbs are significant zones of natural habitat that can become very important corridors for the movement and dispersal of vertebrate wildlife. Riparian habitats occur throughout the state.

Man-Made Habitats

Man-made Habitats usually receive no attention in most scientific discussions regarding natural habitats. However, humans have so altered the natural condition of the land that much of the wildlife habitat that exists in America today has been created by human activities. Although the loss of natural habitats has contributed to the disappearance of many species and continues

to be the greatest threat to wildlife worldwide, many species been able to adapt to man-made habitats and a few actually thrive in these new habitats.

Agricultural Areas

Although some may find it difficult to envision a harvested soybean field as a wildlife habitat, in truth many of Kentucky's wildlife species have adapted to occupy or use on a part-time basis the state's abundant agricultural areas. In the Coastal Plain of Kentucky, the harvested soybean field in winter is one of the best places to see winter migrant birds like the American Pipit or Lapland Longspur. A cattle pasture in summer is home to the Eastern Meadowlark and flocks of Common Grackles will use both habitats throughout the year. Some species like the White-tailed Deer and the Wild Turkey in part owe their present-day abundance to the ever present food supply provided by grain farmers. In fact, most mammals and many birds found in Kentucky have adapted to include agricultural areas in their habitats.

Reclaimed Lands

Strip mining for coal has destroyed many thousands of acres of naturally occurring wildlife habitat in Kentucky. Many of these lands have undergone *reclamation* and now constitute radically altered but significant wildlife habitats. Although the reclaimed habitats are quite different from the original habitats, and support a much lower species diversity, they are utilized by several vertebrate species. Perhaps the best example of reclaimed habitats are the mountainous areas in the southeastern part of the state that now support re-introduced Elk herds. Sadly, the habitats lost in the mining/reclamation process were many times richer in species diversity than the present-day reclaimed habitats, and those original habitats are now forever gone from the reclaimed areas.

Urban Habitats

As is the case with Agricultural lands, it is sometimes difficult to think of urban landscapes as wildlife habitat. Again, however, many species adapt well to towns and cities and in fact some will thrive there. The Chimney Swift experienced a population boom in the days when every building in Kentucky had a chimney. The Common Nighthawk frequently nests on the flat rooftops of downtown buildings, and everyone is familiar the sight of a Robin plucking worms from a well manicured suburban lawn or a Rock Dove (Pigeon) strolling the sidewalks of a large city.

Today most of Kentucky's land mass is held in private ownership. Very little of these private lands are managed for wildlife or set aside as areas for the conservation of natural habitats. Fortunately, there are a number of agencies that hold land in public trust in Kentucky with the goal of providing and maintaining natural wildlife habitats. The largest single owner of public lands in Kentucky is the federal government. The U.S. Forest Service, the National Park Service, the U.S. Fish and Wildlife Service, and the Department of Defense together own over a million acres in Kentucky. Meanwhile the state of Kentucky holds about a quarter million acres in public trust.

Table 4. Public Lands in Kentucky.

Landowning Agency	Number of Acres
State of Kentucky	**245,155**
Kentucky State Forests	37,696 acres in 6 State Forests
Kentucky State Nature Preserves	21,269 acres in 52 preserves
Kentucky State Parks	38,396 acres in 52 parks
Kentucky Wild Rivers	1,614 acres
Department of Fish & Wildlife Resources	126,507 acres in over 100 WMAs
Universities & Misc.	19,673 acres
U.S. Forest Service	**809,705**
Land Between the Lakes Nat. Rec. Area	106,458
Daniel Boone Nat. Forest (Redbird Unit)	145,458
Daniel Boone Nat. Forest (all other units)	557,789
National Wildlife Refuges	**10,654**
Clark's River National Wildlife Refuge	8,500
Reelfoot Lake National Wildlife Refuge	2,040
Ohio River Islands National Wildlife Refuge	114
National Park Service	**92,891**
Big South Fork Nat. Rec. Area	30,430
Mammoth Cave National Park	51,592
Cumberland Gap National Park	10,869
Military Installations and Corps of Engineers	**161,096**
Total Acreage	**1,308,820**

The maps below (Figures 12 and 13) provide a shocking portrait of just how radically the naturally occurring wildlife habitats in Kentucky have been depleted by human activities.

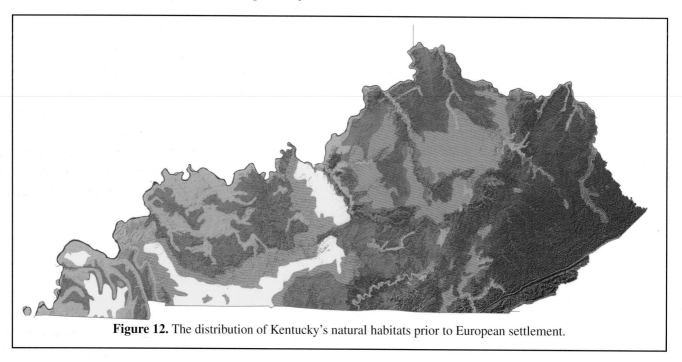

Figure 12. The distribution of Kentucky's natural habitats prior to European settlement.

In Figure 12 above, forests appear as green, savanna as brown, grassland as yellow, and wetland as gray. This is how Kentucky is believed to have looked prior to the arrival of European settlers. Figure 13 below shows how Kentucky's habitats look today.

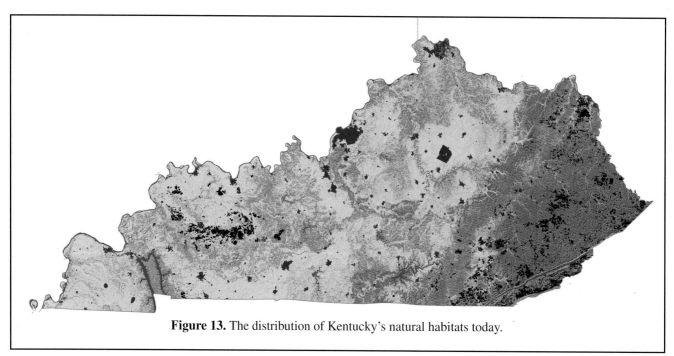

Figure 13. The distribution of Kentucky's natural habitats today.

In Figure 13 above, some forest is still visible as green, red is urban areas, black is strip-mined areas, and the rest is agricultural land or otherwise altered habitats. No significant areas of savanna, wetland, or grassland can be seen on the map above. All but an invisible fraction of the forest land seen is regenerated forest.

Both maps shown here are derived from original maps produced by the Kentucky Natural Heritage Council.

A quick look at the maps in Figures 12 and 13 provides profound picture regarding the scope of the loss of Kentucky's original landscapes. To anyone with an appreciation of wilderness and nature in its pristine condition, Kentucky has become an impoverished place. Many of the state's wildlife species face a perilous and uncertain future. Happily, many species continue to adapt and some to thrive in the commonwealth's new environments. Thankfully, agencies like the Kentucky Department of Fish & Wildlife Resources, the Kentucky Nature Preserves Commission, and the U.S. Fish and Wildlife Service work unceasingly to protect, manage, and enhance the state's wildlife and remaining wild habitats. But there is only so much that these organizations can accomplish. Today less than 1.5 million of the state's roughly 26 million acres is publicly owned. That means that the real responsibility for stewardship of nature in Kentucky falls to individual landowners.

We humans, to a very great degree, have succeeded in altering our natural landscapes so much that we no longer feel an intimate connection to the land. We consider ourselves to be residents of an artificially created locality. We are Kentuckians rather than residents of the formerly great Eastern Deciduous Forest. If asked what part of the state in which our town is located we may say "Graves County" rather than reply that our town is located within gently undulating lowlands of the Gulf Coastal Plain.

To some extent, natural boundaries have always been utilized by man when creating political boundaries. A prime example is the Ohio River that serves as the northern border of Kentucky. Smaller creeks and rivers regularly serve as county lines, and our state's eastern border with Virginia is delineated by the peak of the high ridge formed by Big Black Mountain. But we humans have a strong tendency to create regions and boundaries that ignore natural boundaries and instead serve our serve our personal, social, and political needs.

While this mindset serves our society well in many ways, it often does a disservice to our environment. If we could learn to think of ourselves more as a part of the larger ecosystems, we would perhaps show more concern for the stewardship of those ecosystems. At this stage in human history, with our population topping 7 billion people, our natural resources being pushed to the point of exhaustion, our ocean ecosystems possibly on the verge of collapse, mass extinctions just around the corner, and global climate change the immediate future, a new understanding and appreciation of the natural world by all citizens seems to be the only hope for a promising future.

The pages that follow are intended to introduce Kentuckians to the remarkable diversity, wondrous beauty, and miraculous lives of our state's wildlife species. It is hoped that this introduction will lead to a greater awareness, concern, and appreciation for our natural heritage. It is further hoped that acquiring that awareness and appreciation will lead to a better stewardship of the living things with which we share this planet. And more importantly, the natural ecosystems upon which both they and we ultimately depend.

CHAPTER 3

THE MAMMALS OF KENTUCKY

Class—**Mammalia** (mammals)

Order—**Didelphimorphia** (opossums)

Family	**Didelphidae** (opossum)

Order—**Cingulata** (armadillos, anteaters, sloths)

Family	**Dasypodidae** (armadillos)

Order—**Carnivora** (carnivores)

Family	**Procyonidae** (raccoon family)
Family	**Ursidae** (bears)
Family	**Felidae** (cat family)
Family	**Canidae** (canines)
Family	**Mustelidae** (weasel family)
Family	**Mephitidae** (skunks)

Order—**Artiodactlya** (hoofed mammals)

Family	**Cervidae** (deer family)

Order—**Lagamorpha** (rabbits, hares)

Family	**Leporidae** (rabbits)

Order—**Rodentia** (rodents)

Family	**Sciuridae** (squirrel family)
Family	**Castoridae** (beaver)
Family	**Muridae** (rats, mice)
Family	**Dipodidae** (jumping mice)

Order—**Soricimorpha** (moles, shrews)

Family	**Soricidae** (shrews)
Family	**Talpidae** (moles)

Order—**Chiroptera** (bats)

Family	**Vespertilionidae** (mouse-eared bats)

Table 5.
The Orders and Families of Kentucky Mammals.

Class—**Mammalia** (mammals)

Order—**Didelphimorphia** (opossums)	Order—**Cingulata**
Family—**Didelphidae**	Family—**Dasypodidae** (armadillos)
Virginia Opossum *Didelphis virginiana*	**Nine-banded Armadillo** *Dasypus novemcinctus*

Presumed range in Kentucky

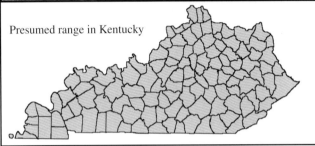

Presumed range in Kentucky

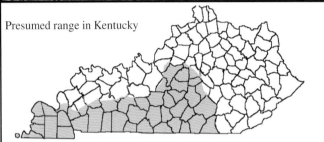

Size: About 2.5 feet from nose to tail tip. Males can weigh up to 14 pounds, females are smaller.	**Size:** About 30 inches from snout to tail tip. Can weigh up to 17 pounds.
Abundance: Very common. In fact, this is one of the most common medium-sized mammals in Kentucky.	**Abundance:** Still fairly rare in Kentucky, but increasing numbers of Armadillos are being seen in the state.
Variation: Opossums are quite variable. In most the fur is grizzled gray (as in photo above). All white or all black individuals can also occur, along with a cinnamon color phase.	**Variation:** There is no significant variation in Armadillos and no subspecies in America. The sexes look alike but males are somewhat larger than females.
Habitat: Virtually all habitats within the state are utilized, including suburban and even urban areas where there is enough vegetative cover. Opossums are more common in areas altered by humans, such as farmlands and the vicinity of small, rural communities. They are less common in areas of true wilderness.	**Habitat:** This wide-ranging animal's habitat includes everything from tropical rain forest to arid semi-desert, grassland, and temperate forests. Moist or sandy soils are preferred as they facilitate easier digging of denning burrows as well as rooting for soil invertebrates. In Kentucky presently restricted mostly to the western and southwestern part of the state.
Breeding: This is America's only member of the mammalian subclass Marsupialia. Young Opossums are born as embryos only twelve days after conception. The newborn babies are just over 0.5 inch in length. At one month they are about the size of a mouse. Litters are large (up to 13) and two litters per year is common.	**Breeding:** Females always give birth to four identical twins, all derived from a single fertilized egg that divides in two, then divides again to form four zygotes before beginning to then develop into individual embryos. The young are well developed at birth, which reduces mortality among immatures. One litter per year is typical.
Natural History: Opossums are one of the most successful medium-size mammals in America, which is somewhat surprising given that they are slow moving, rather dim-witted animals that rarely survive beyond two years in the wild. They are mainly nocturnal and eat most any palatable plant matter (seeds, grains, fruits, berries), and any type of meat they can catch or scavenge. They are known to kill and eat venomous snakes and have a strong resistance to pit viper venoms. They are well known for faking death (playing possum) when stressed. Their greatest enemy today is the automobile. Thousands are killed nightly on highways across America.	**Natural History:** Armadillos first began their northern expansion into the U.S. from Mexico about 150 years ago; 100 years later there were still no records from Kentucky, although they were then found as far north as west Tennessee. Today increasing numbers are being seen in western and southern Kentucky. How far north they will spread is unknown. Cold climates may be a limiting factor to their spread. Surprisingly, Armadillos are capable of swimming and they are also known to hold their breath and "bottom walk" short distance across small streams. They are known to sometimes carry the ancient disease of leprosy and are used in leprosy research.

Class—**Mammalia** (mammals)

Order—**Carnivora** (carnivores)

Family—**Procyonidae** (raccoons)	Family—**Ursidae** (bears)	Family—**Felidae** (cats)
Raccoon *Procyon lotor*	**Black Bear** *Ursus americanus*	**Bobcat** *Lynx rufus*

 Presumed range in Kentucky	 Presumed range in Kentucky	 Presumed range in Kentucky
Size: Up to 3 feet in length. 25 pounds is big for Kentucky specimens.	**Size:** Four to five feet in total length. Males up to 400 pounds, females 200.	**Size:** 30 to 34 inches in total length. Kentucky males may reach 30 pounds.
Abundance: Very common.	**Abundance:** Rare but increasing yearly.	**Abundance:** Fairly common.
Variation: There is little variation in Kentucky specimens. A few black individuals occur occasionally. Most resemble the photo above.	**Variation:** Despite their name Black Bears may be black, cinnamon, blond, blue gray, or even white. Kentucky specimens are invariably black in color.	**Variation:** Some specimens have more pronounced spotting to their fur, but otherwise little variation. Males are about 1/3 larger than females.
Habitat: Found in virtually every habitat in the state, but wetlands, stream courses and lake shores are favorite haunts.	**Habitat:** Kentucky habitat is mixed deciduous forest on higher mountain slopes, especially Pine Mountain and Black Mountain in southeast Kentucky.	**Habitat:** All habitat types in Kentucky are utilized except urban areas. Rugged, remote mountains and impenetrable swamps are sanctuaries.
Breeding: Breeds in late winter with an average of four (maximum of eight) young born two months later.	**Breeding:** Breeds in summer. One to six cubs are born in January or February in the female's winter den.	**Breeding:** Most breeding occurs in winter or spring with an average of three or four young born two months later.
Natural History: Raccoons are omnivores that feed on a wide variety of crustaceans, insects, amphibians, reptiles, small mammals and eggs as well as grains, berries, fruits, acorns, weed seeds, and some vegetables. Although they are mainly nocturnal, they are often active by day, especially in morning and late afternoons. During particularly harsh weather they may den for days at a time. Summer dens are often tree hollows while old groundhog burrows may be used during the winter. In Kentucky the Raccoon is an important game animal harvested for its fur and to a lesser extent as food. More often they are hunted just for sport and released unharmed after being treed by hounds.	**Natural History:** Prior to the European invasion of Kentucky the Black Bear was the most common large carnivore in the state. Over-hunting and deforestation led to their complete disappearance by the mid-1800s. With the resurgence of forests in the eastern part of the state these magnificent animals are re-colonizing many of their former haunts in the mountains of eastern Kentucky. This has been a natural expansion from historic strongholds in the mountains of western Virginia and northwest of Tennessee. A variety of plant and animal matter is eaten. In Kentucky, the annual mast crop (acorns and nuts) is the most important food item in preparing for a winter hibernation that can last five months.	**Natural History:** Strictly a meat eater, the Bobcat's food items range from mice to deer. Cottontail and Swamp Rabbits are a favorite prey as are squirrels, young turkeys, and songbirds. Hunts by ambush or stalking to within close range and making an explosive attack. Although mainly nocturnal, Bobcats can be abroad at any time of day. Their home range can be from one to several square miles and males have larger ranges than females. Scent marking territory with urine and feces is common. In captivity Bobcats have lived for over 20 years, but the estimate for wild cats is 12–14 years. This species has recovered almost completely from very low numbers fifty years ago.

Class—**Mammalia** (mammals)

Order—**Carnivora** (carnivores)

Family—**Canidae** (canines)

Gray Fox *Urocyon cinereoargenteus*	**Red Fox** *Vulpes vulpes*	**Coyote** *Canis latrans*

Presumed range in Kentucky 	Presumed range in Kentucky 	Presumed range in Kentucky 
Size: Length 32 to 45 inches. Weight up to 15 pounds.	**Size:** Length 33 to 43 inches. Weight up to 15 pounds.	**Size:** Length up to 49 inches. Average about 35 pounds.
Abundance: Common.	**Abundance:** Common.	**Abundance:** Common.
Variation: As many as six subspecies range across North America. Only one occurs in Kentucky and no significant color variation occurs.	**Variation:** Red Foxes can occur in several different color phases, the best known of which are red, silver, and cross fox. Kentucky specimens are red.	**Variation:** Very dark individuals and reddish specimens are know to occur in Kentucky. Most resemble the photo above.
Habitat: Primarily a woodland animal that is more common in the forested regions of the eastern third of the state. In western KY it uses small woodlots.	**Habitat:** Although habitat generalists, Red Foxes shows a preference for semi-open country over deep woods. They are most common in western Kentucky.	**Habitat:** Coyotes have adapted to all habitats in Kentucky, but they are more common in the more open agricultural areas in the western half of the state.
Breeding: Dens in a burrow, hollow log or rock cave. Four pups is usual but up to seven is known.	**Breeding:** About four to five young are born underground, often in an old groundhog burrow, but they will dig their own hole.	**Breeding:** Coyotes are able to breed before their first birthday. Litter size (2–10) varies with availability of prey.
Natural History: The Gray Fox is the only American canine with the ability to climb trees. Insects are important food items in summer with mice and rabbits becoming more important in winter. When grapes, persimmons, and other fruits are ripe they will eat them almost exclusively, and in fact this is the most omnivorus canine in America. Home range can vary from a few hundred acres to over a square mile, depending upon habitat quality. Unlike the Red Fox that can be found as far north as the Arctic Circle, the Gray Fox is a more southerly animal and ranges southward into South America. Gray Foxes have lived for up to 14 years in captivity, but the average lifespan in the wild is only a few years.	**Natural History:** The Red Fox is one of the world's most widespread mammals and is found in Europe, Asia, north Africa, and Australia (introduced) as well as throughout North America. They are adaptable, opportunistic omnivores that will eat everything from grasshoppers to grapes. Scavenging carrion is also common. Their fur is such a good insulator that they can sleep atop a snowbank without melting the snow beneath their body. These are important fur-bearing animals and are today often reared in captivity on "fur farms." Red Fox populations in Kentucky have probably increased since European settlement and subsequent clearing of forests for agriculture.	**Natural History:** The Coyote is a relative newcomer to Kentucky, having begun their invasion from the west about a half century ago. Today they range all the way to the Atlantic are the top predator in much of the state, occupying a niche once held by the Red Wolf and the Cougar. They are extremely intelligent, adaptable canines that quickly learn to thrive in almost any environment. In rural areas where hunters abound they are extremely wary, but in urban areas or protected lands they may become quite bold around humans. The characteristic yipping and howling of these vocal canines has become a common nighttime sound in rural Kentucky. Mostly nocturnal, but also active by day.

Class—**Mammalia** (mammals)
Order—**Carnivora** (carnivores)
Family—**Mustelidae** (weasel family)

Mink *Mustela vison*	**Long-tailed Weasel** *Mustela frenata*	**Least Weasel** *Mustela nivalis*

Presumed range in Kentucky 	Presumed range in Kentucky 	Presumed range in Kentucky 
Size: 20 to 27 inches in length. Weighs 2–3 pounds.	**Size:** 12 to 15 inches from snout to tail tip. Weighs 6 to 11 ounces.	**Size:** 7 inches. Weighs about 1.5 ounces.
Abundance: Fairly common.	**Abundance:** Uncommon.	**Abundance:** Rare in Kentucky.
Variation: Males are twice as large as females. Pelage color varies from light brown to very dark brown. Kentucky Mink are usually medium brown.	**Variation:** Males are nearly twice the size of females. Specimens in the far north turn white in winter. No color variation occurs in Kentucky specimens.	**Variation:** Specimens from farther north turn white in winter but there is no variation in individuals in Kentucky. Males are about 1/3 larger than females.
Habitat: Swamps and marshes are the primary habitat. Also frequents creeks, rivers and lake shores.	**Habitat:** Occupies a wide variety of habitats but favors being near stream courses.	**Habitat:** Avoids deep woods and lives mostly in or around the edges of fields and marshes.
Breeding: Three to six young are born in an underground den that is often an old muskrat house. Young begin to hunt with mother at about two months.	**Breeding:** Breeding occurs in mid-summer but embryo development is delayed until the following spring. Four to five young is typical and babies have white fur.	**Breeding:** Breeds throughout the year and can produce two litters per year of one to six young. Young develop quickly and can hunt on their own in six weeks.
Natural History: Mink are well known for their luxurious fur. Most mink fur sold in America today is from captive, farm-raised mink. Mink are excellent swimmers and will catch fish in stream pools. They are strict carnivores that feed heavily on amphibians and crayfish during the summer. In winter their diet turns to mammal prey such as rabbits and rodents. Muskrats are a favorite winter food of the large males who kill their formidable prey with a bite to the back of the neck. As with other members of the Mustelidae family, mink have well developed musk glands that produce a distinct musky odor when the animal is excited, breeding, or marking territory.	**Natural History:** Weasels are known for being, on a pound per pound basis, one of the world's most ferocious predators. Although their prey includes animals as small as insects, they will also take prey the size of a grown Cottontail Rabbit. Mice, voles, and other rodents, along with shrews and small birds make up the bulk of their non-invertebrate diet. They have also been known to scavenge the dead bodies of large animals such as deer. These highly active mammals have a high metabolic rate and they are active by both day and night, consuming up to a third of their body weight in a day. When an animal is killed that is too large to consume at one meal, they will cache the remains.	**Natural History:** This is one of the world's smallest carnivores. Their tiny, elongated bodies allow them to maneuver easily into rodent burrows and mice and voles are their primary prey. They hunt day and night, alternating hunts with short naps. They are active year-round and their rapid metabolism means they must consume one-half of their body weight each day. When the opportunity presents they will kill more than they can eat and store the extra food for later. In the far northen parts of their range the Least Weasel turns white in winter. This is one of the rarest mammals in Kentucky. The range map above is an estimation, their exact range in Kentucky is poorly known.

Class—**Mammalia** (mammals)

Order—**Carnivora** (carnivores)

Family-**Mustelidae** (weasels)	Family - **Mephitidae** (skunks)	
River Otter *Lutra canadensis*	**Striped Skunk** *Mephitis mephitis*	**Eastern Spotted Skunk** *Spilogale putorius*

Presumed range in Kentucky

Presumed range in Kentucky

Presumed range in Kentucky

Size: Length 35–45 inches. Up to 25 pounds.

Size: Length 23–31 inches. Average weight about 8–10 pounds.

Size: 11–24 inches total length. Weighs about 2 pounds as adult.

Abundance: Uncommon.

Abundance: Common.

Abundance: Rare in Kentucky.

Variation: As many as 7 subspecies range across North America. There is very little variation in Kentucky.

Variation: Varies considerably in the amount of white in the dorsal stripes. Can be nearly all white or solid black.

Variation: There is no variation in Kentucky except that males are larger. There are 3 subspecies total in the U.S.

Habitat: Any unpolluted aquatic habitat in the state may be suitable for River Otters. They are always in association with rivers, lakes, swamps, or creeks.

Habitat: Striped Skunks are found in all habitats in Kentucky, but they are most common in mixed, semi-open habitats and edge areas.

Habitat: These little skunks are mostly woodland animals and when they occur in open areas they stick close to areas that offer cover.

Breeding: Two or three young are born in an underground den often dug in a stream bank.

Breeding: Breeding occurs in late winter. Litter size averages three to four but can be as many as ten.

Breeding: Averages about five young. The den is often a natural cavity or small cave but they will also dig underground.

Natural History: River Otters are semi-aquatic mammals that possess fully webbed toes and waterproof fur. They are excellent swimmers that prey on fish, frogs, crayfish, turtles, and small mammals. Their fur is highly valued, a fact that lead to their extirpation from Kentucky and most of the eastern United States by the late 1800s. Restocking programs by the Kentucky Department of Fish and Wildlife Resources have been highly successful and today these endearing animals can once again be found in many areas of the state. Although there are still parts of Kentucky where they may not yet have colonized, it is reasonable to consider their range today as being statewide and otter trapping is now allowed in Kentucky.

Natural History: The Striped Skunk's distinctive black and white color is almost as well known as its primary defense, which of course is to spray an attacker with its pungent, foul-smelling musk. The musk can burn the eyes and membranes and its odor is remarkably persistent. They can effectively project the musk up to about 15 feet and the odor can be detected hundreds of yards away. Skunks dine mainly on invertebrates and as much as three-fourths of their diet consists of insects and grubs. They possess well developed front claws for digging and a powerful sense of smell for locating buried grubs, worms, turtle eggs, etc. Baby mice, eggs, and nestlings of ground-nesting birds are also frequently eaten.

Natural History: These diminutive little skunks are quite agile and are known for the peculiar behavior of doing a "handstand" on the front feet in preparation for spraying their musk. They are also excellent climbers and sometimes climb trees. They are predominantly nocturnal and feed mostly on small animals like insects, bird eggs, and mice. They are rare in Kentucky and their exact range within the state is poorly understood. They may be more widespread than shown on the range map above. Or, they may be absent from many areas within this range. Although they have a fairly large range in North America, their distribution is spotty and they are not common animals in most regions of their range.

Class—**Mammalia** (mammals)
Order—**Artiodactyla** (hoofed mammals)
Family—**Cervidae** (deer family)

Whitetail Deer—*Odocoileus virginianus*

Buck	Doe	Fawn

Size: Males up to 40 inches high at shoulder. Females about 20 percent smaller. Mature males can weigh over 200 pounds, females up to 150, though most are smaller.

Abundance: Very common.

Variation: There are as many as thirteen different subspecies of Whitetail Deer recognized in mainland North America, plus several more island races. The Kentucky subspecies is the Virginia Whitetail Deer, *Odocoileus virginianus virginianus*. Young (fawns) exhibit a pattern of white spots that fade with age. Adults have reddish brown color in the summer and grayish in the fall/winter.

Presumed range in Kentucky

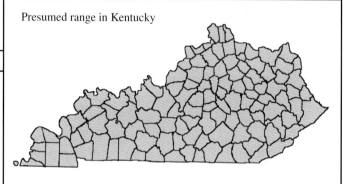

Habitat: Found in virtually every habitat within the state and increasingly common in urban areas. Favorite habitats are a mix of woodland, brushy areas and weedy fields, especially near farmlands. Successional areas, such as regrowth of woodlands after fires or logging is also a prime habitat. In Kentucky, deer are more common in the western end of the state. They are least common in mature, unbroken forests and in areas of intensive agriculture or major urbanization.

Breeding: Breeding begins in early fall and may continue into the winter, with the peak breeding season occurring in November. One to two (rarely three or even four) young are born in the spring or early summer following a six and a half month gestation. Females (does) usually bear their first offspring at two years of age. The first pregnancy typically results in a single fawn, the second pregnancy usually is twins and the third through fifth twins or triplets (rarely quadruplets). Young lie hidden for the first few weeks and are left alone much of the time. The female will visit the hidden fawn about once every four hours to allow nursing, then moves away to avoid attracting predators. At about one month of age the young will begin to follow the mother and stay close through the summer and into the fall.

Natural History: Bucks (males) shed their antlers each year in late winter and regrow a new set by fall. Growing deer antlers are among the fastest growing animal tissue known. While growing the antlers are covered in a spongy, fuzzy skin called "velvet." Antlers grow larger each year up to about six or seven years of age, when they begin a gradual decline. Whitetail Deer are browsers and they feed on a wide variety of forbs, leaves, twigs, buds, crops, and mast (especially acorns). Although they are sometimes destructive to farm crops like corn or soybeans, they are an important game animal in Kentucky with as many as 120,000 harvest annually for food and sport. The maximum life span is 20 years, but most are dead by age 10. In Kentucky and other areas where hunting pressure is high, only the luckiest (or cleverest) males will survive beyond two or three years. The Kentucky Department of Fish and Wildlife Resources, deer management program allows for a liberal harvest of does, but only one buck per hunter per season. This management approach aims to keep the overall population under control while allowing more bucks to reach maturity. This helps both the hunter and the deer population. Hunters have a greater chance at harvesting a mature buck with larger antlers, while the deer population benefits by having more mature bucks in the herd, thus increasing competition among breeding males, which in turn extrapolates into fitter animals doing most of the breeding. This animal represents one of the world's great wildlife conservation stories. Nearly wiped out by the early 1900s, the Whitetail Deer is today as numerous in Kentucky as it was during the time of Daniel Boone. At present, the population in Kentucky numbers nearly a half-million deer—up from a low of only about two thousand a century ago.

Class—**Mammalia** (mammals)
Order—**Artiodactyla** (hoofed mammals)
Family—**Cervidae** (deer family)

Rocky Mountian Elk—*Cervus canadensis*

Bull	Cow	Calf

Size: Males up to five feet high at shoulder. Females about 20 percent smaller. Mature males can weigh up to 800 or 1,000 pounds, females 450 to 550.

Abundance: Uncommon but increasing within their limited distribution in the state.

Variation: There are as many as four subspecies of Elk in North America. Today's Kentucky Elk are transplants of the Rocky Mountain subspecies (*Cervus canadensis nelsoni*). Young are patterned with white spots that fade with age, and of course males have antlers most of the year, otherwise there is no variation in this species in Kentucky

Presumed range in Kentucky

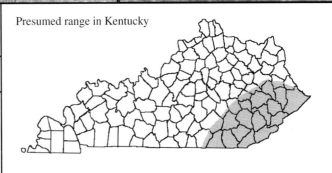

Habitat: Elk are grazers that feed mostly on grasses. Subsequently, they prefer open and semi-open land for feeding. They do use deep woods for cover. Kentucky Elk populations are centered around reclaimed strip mine lands in the mountainous eastern part of the state. Strip mining can remove entire mountaintops, and is thus devastating to the local environment and to the wildlife species that live there. Thanks to federal regulations that require reclamation and re-vegetation with grasses and shrubs, formerly mined lands can become excellent Elk habitat.

Breeding: Breeding begins in September and young are born in late May to early June. One calf is typical with twins being rare. During the breeding season, known as "rut," both males and females find each other by vocalizations. Males at this time gather groups of females called "harems," which they vigorously defend from other males. At this time vicious battles using antlers that can reach five feet in length sometimes result in serious injury or death to combative males.

Natural History: Elk are much more gregarious than their Whitetail Deer cousins and they will often gather in large herds. During the summer the males form bachelor groups apart from the females who are busy rearing young in their own herds. In the fall they come together for breeding and during this time the males are quite vocal, producing a high-pitched call known as a "bugle." Like deer, the enormous antlers of the bull elk are shed every year in late winter and then begin to regrow almost immediately. An Elk's life expectancy can exceed twenty years, though few will reach that ripe old age in the wild. At one time Elk were native to and roamed throughout most of Kentucky, but they quickly disappeared as European settlement progressed. By the early 1800s virtually all Elk east of the Mississippi were gone. The Elk that were originally native to Kentucky represented a distinct form that is now extinct. Restoration in Kentucky with Elk from the Rocky Mountains has been highly successful in the eastern part of the state. Elk re-introduction in Kentucky has been a cooperative effort that involved both the Kentucky Department of Fish and Wildlife Resources and the Rocky Mountain Elk Foundation. Consisting mostly of sportsman and Elk hunters, the Rocky Mountain Elk Foundation, working in conjunction with state wildlife agencies, has been instrumental in helping restore wild Elk to many place across America. Today there are about 10,000 Elk in Kentucky and they have become an important game animal. Over four hundred Elk hunting permits are issued annually. These permits are issued by a lottery type drawing that costs $10 to enter and generates significant funding for wildlife conservation in Kentucky. Thus the Elk in Kentucky provides a wonderful example of wildlife conservation making the best of a bad situation. Mountaintop removal mining for coal is devastating to a myriad of species ranging from frogs and salamanders to insects, snails, woodland wildflowers, fungi, etc. Using these radically altered habitats to re-introduce such a magnificent animal to its former haunts amounts to a "lemons to lemonade" approach to an otherwise environmentally painful land use practice.

Class—**Mammalia** (mammals)

Order—**Lagomorpha** (rabbits, hares, pika)

Family—**Leporidae** (rabbits, hares)

Eastern Cottontail *Sylvilagus floridanus*	Appalachian Cottontail *Sylvilagus obscurus*	Swamp Rabbit *Sylvilagus aquaticus*

Presumed range in Kentucky	Presumed range in Kentucky	Presumed range in Kentucky
Size: Adult length about 17 inches. Weight up to 2.5 pounds.	**Size:** Adult length about 17 inches. Weight up to 2.5 pounds.	**Size:** Adults reach about 20 inches and weigh as much as 5 pounds.
Abundance: Very common.	**Abundance:** Uncommon.	**Abundance:** Uncommon in Kentucky.
Variation: No variation in Kentucky, but at least 12 very similar subspecies are recognized in the United States.	**Variation:** There are no subspecies and no color variation occurs, but females average slightly larger than males.	**Variation:** No variation in Kentucky. There is another subspecies that inhabits the southwestern gulf coastal plain.
Habitat: May be found in virtually any habitat within the state except for permanent wetlands. Most common in overgrown fields and edge areas. Fond of briers, honeysuckle, and tall weeds.	**Habitat:** More woodland oriented than the Eastern Cottontail. Favors second growth areas and can be found at the highest elevations in the Appalachian Mountains.	**Habitat:** Swamps, marshes, and bottom-lands in the western quarter of the state. Most common in the Coastal Plain and the Mississippi Alluvial Plain in the westernmost tip of Kentucky.
Breeding: This is the most prolific of the several rabbit species in America, producing up to seven litters per year with as many as five young per litter.	**Breeding:** Probably very similar in breeding to the eastern species. Young are highly precocious and leave the nest in as little as two weeks.	**Breeding:** Breeds January through August. Three young is typical after a 37-day gestation period. Averages two litters per year.
Natural History: In the spring and summer Eastern Cottontails feed on a wide variety of grasses, legumes and herbaceous weeds. Briers, sapling bark, and other woody materials may make up the bulk of the diet in winter. These rabbits are prey for many predators including foxes, coyotes, bobcats, and hawks and owls, especially the Great Horned Owl. The life expectancy for a Cottontail is not high, and only about one in four will live to see their second birthday. Populations are known to fluctuate and during years when their numbers are highest there may be as many as nine rabbits per acre in good habitat.	**Natural History:** This rabbit is so similar in appearance to the Eastern Cottontail that distinguishing between the two species in the field may be impossible. Even professional biologists rely on examination of the skull to make a positive identification. Unlike the Eastern Cottontail, this species lacks the white spot that is often (but not always) present between the eyes on the Eastern Cottontail. The exact range of this species in Kentucky is poorly known. One study by the KDFWR (Sole, 1999) suggests this species may be much more widespread in Kentucky than the small area that is shown on the map above.	**Natural History:** An excellent swimmer, the Swamp Rabbit will elude hunters' hounds by diving into water and swimming for a long distance. This is the largest of the "true" rabbits in America (not including jackrabbits and hares). They are as much as twice as large as the Eastern and Appalachian Cottontails. The range of this species has diminished with the loss of wetlands both in Kentucky and throughout its range in the southeast. The occurrence of the Swamp Rabbit in wetlands is easily detected by the presence of droppings on floating logs within the swamp. Bobcats are probably their biggest predator in Kentucky.

Class—**Mammalia** (mammals)

Order—**Rodentia** (rodents)

Family—**Sciuridae** (squirrel family)

Eastern Chipmunk *Tamias striatus*	Gray Squirrel *Sciurus carolinensis*	Fox Squirrel *Sciurus niger*

Presumed range in Kentucky 	Presumed range in Kentucky 	Presumed range in Kentucky 
Size: About 10 inches in length and weighing about 4.5 ounces.	**Size:** 19 inches in total and weighing about 18 ounces.	**Size:** 23 inches from snout to tail tip and weighing about 28 ounces.
Abundance: Fairly common.	**Abundance:** Very common.	**Abundance:** Common.
Variation: There are between five and eight subspecies nationwide (experts disagree on the exact number). The differences between the subspecies is very subtle and the single subspecies found in Kentucky (*Tamias striatus striatus*) exhibits very little variation. The photo above is good representative example.	**Variation:** At least six subspecies are recognized and some are quite variable. Melanistic populations can be found in some areas of the northern United States and albino populations occur in a few locations. Some Kentucky specimens may have reddish brown tails but most resemble the specimen pictured above.	**Variation:** There are a total of ten subspecies nationwide and they range in color from solid black to reddish to silver-gray. *S. n. rufiventris* (reddish phase) occurs in Kentucky. Most are like the standing specimen shown above, but a variety of color morphs may be seen in the state (see insets).
Habitat: Deciduous forests in upland areas. Avoids wetlands. Fond of rock outcrops, stone fences, etc. Can be common in urban parks and suburbs.	**Habitat:** Prefers mature deciduous forests but also found in mixed coniferous forests and second growth areas. Can be common in urban parks and lawns.	**Habitat:** Prefers open forests with trees widely spaced. Can be common in swamps. Prefers edge areas, overgrown fence rows, etc., over extensive woods.
Breeding: May breed twice per year, first in February and again in April. Produces four to five young per litter.	**Breeding:** Breeds December through February and again in June/July. Four to six young per litter.	**Breeding:** Produces four to six young twice annually, breeding in winter and again in summer.
Natural History: While they are excellent climbers, chipmunks are true "ground squirrels," sleeping, rearing young, and wintering in an underground burrow, which they dig themselves. They also will use rock crevices or hollow logs. They become less active in winter and will remain below ground living on stored nuts and seeds for long periods during harsh weather. Although Chipmunks are fairly common in much of Kentucky they are mysteriously absent from some areas of the state, including most of the Coastal Plain.	**Natural History:** Feeds on nuts, seeds, fungi, tree buds, and the inner bark of trees as well as bird eggs and hatchlings. May sometimes even eat carrion. Like most rodents they will gnaw bones or shed deer antlers for calcium. Well known for burying and storing nuts. Frequently calls with a raspy "bark," especially when alarmed. Builds summer nests of leaves in tree crotches. Winter dens are in tree hollows. During severe weather may be inactive for several days. Poor mast years may produce mass migrations.	**Natural History:** Fox Squirrels wander frequently into open areas and spend more time on the ground than Gray Squirrels. Their home range may be ten times larger. They are generally less common than the Gray, never reaching the population densities of their smaller cousins. They feed on the same foods of nuts, seeds, buds, berries, etc., but the diet of Fox Squirrels also often includes the seeds of pine cones. Dark morph specimens (inset) sometimes occur in Kentucky in the Coastal Plain and especially in the Mississippi Alluvial Plain.

Class—**Mammalia** (mammals)

Order—**Rodentia** (rodents)

Family—**Sciuridae** (squirrel family)

Southern Flying Squirrel *Glaucomys volans*	**Groundhog** *Marmota monax*

Presumed range in Kentucky	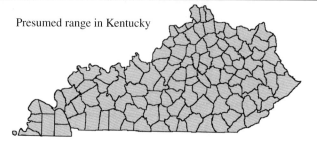Presumed range in Kentucky
Size: 10 inches and 2–3 ounces.	**Size:** Length 16 to 26 inches, and weighs from 6 to 9 pounds.
Abundance: Fairly common.	**Abundance:** Common.
Variation: There is little variation in Kentucky and the sexes are alike. Some biologists recognize as many as eight subspecies nationwide but differences are very subtle and are apparent only upon close examination.	**Variation:** As many as nine subspecies in North America but only one in Kentucky (*M. m. monax*). Individuals vary in color from brown to grayish, reddish, or rarely, nearly black. Most specimens in Kentucky resemble the specimen shown above.
Habitat: These little squirrels are totally dependent upon trees and make their home in woodlands. Primarily hardwoods but also in mixed pine-hardwood forests. They will live in suburbs and urban areas if sufficient mature trees are present.	**Habitat:** Fields and woodland edges. The main habitat requirements are some open ground within the vicinity of the burrow for foraging, as well as some higher ground that is above the floodplain for locating the burrow. They avoid swamps and permanent wetlands.
Breeding: Only one litter per year with up to six young. Nest is usually within a hollow in a tree. Bluebird boxes and other artificial nest sites are also used.	**Breeding:** Mating occurs in March or April with two to four young typical. Only one litter per year. Young are born below ground and remain there until weaned at about six weeks.
Natural History: Lives in tree hollows and old woodpecker holes. Kentucky's only nocturnal squirrel. Leaps from tree to tree and glides using flaps of skin between front and hind legs like a parachute. Flattened tail serves as a rudder while gliding. Feeds on nuts, seeds, fruits, fungi, lichens, tree buds, insects, bird eggs, and nestling birds as well as mice. Flying Squirrels are gregarious animals and several may share a den. Southern Flying Squirrels can live up to ten years and will become quite tame in captivity, making reasonable pets. Wild squirrels in rural areas sometimes invade homes and attics where they can become a noisy nuisance as they scramble about in the wee hours. A much larger version, the Northern Flying Squirrel (*G. sabrinus*), occurs in America the far north and in the higher elevations of the southern Appalachian Mountains. It can be twice as large as its southern cousin.	**Natural History:** These large ground squirrels dig extensive underground burrows where they retreat from danger, spend the night, and overwinter. They accumulate huge deposits of fat during the summer and fall, which sustains them during winter hibernation. During this time their metabolism slows dramatically with as few as four heartbeats per minute. They will sometimes climb small trees and bushes in springtime to eat swelling tree buds, but their primary diet is forbs and grasses. Except during breeding or when rearing young they are solitary animals and typically only one adult occupies a burrow. If too numerous they can become pests in rural gardens or farmers' crops and in Kentucky they can be hunted year-round. They are sometimes eaten by humans and are known to be palatable table fare. Also known by the name "Woodchuck." They are members of a group known to biologists as "Marmots." Their empty burrows are used as dens by a wide variety of animals.

Class—**Mammalia** (mammals)
Order—**Rodentia** (rodents)
Family—**Castoridae** (beaver family)

Beaver — *Castor canadensis*	Beaver dam (top)—Beaver lodge (bottom)

Presumed range in Kentucky

Size: Up to 43 inches in total length. Can weigh up to 65 pounds, though 35 to 50 pounds is average.

Abundance: Most common in western Kentucky and fairly common throughout the rest of the state.

Variation: The American Society of Mammologists recognizes twenty-four subspecies in North America. No variation is known to occur in Kentucky.

Habitat: Beavers are thoroughly aquatic mammals that to a great extent create their own wetland habitats. To construct their ponds and waterways they require the presence of a stream or spring run with constant or near constantly flowing water that can be dammed. Streams that are subject to fierce flooding or with exceptionally powerful flows are avoided in preference for more easily contained water flows. In addition to creating their own habitats they will use lakes, rivers, swamps, marshes, and large, deep creeks. In rivers and lakes the lodge or den is often a burrow into the bank of the lake or river. In dammed streams or swamps and marshes a stick lodge typical of the one pictured above is usual. Although they are found throughout Kentucky, in the eastern mountainous regions they are restricted to river valleys, bottom-lands, and hollows.

Breeding: Mating takes place in mid-winter with the young being born about four months later. There is only one litter per year. Baby beavers are quite precocious and are born with well developed fur and eyes that open immediately. Four or five young, called kits, is typical. In ideal habitats more young may be produced. Young beavers are usually weaned in just two/three weeks, but the young Beavers will remain with the family for up to two years before striking out on their own to find new territories. Adult beavers may mate for life.

Natural History: Beavers are primarily nocturnal in habits, but they may be active at dawn and dusk. In remote locations where human intrusion is absent, they are observed active during the day as well. They feed mostly on the inner bark of trees, with willow being a dietary mainstay. They will also consume sedges and other aquatic vegetation, but in winter live exclusively on bark. The dorsal-ventrally flattened tail is hairless and scaly and along with the webbed hind feet provide these animals with powerful swimming tools. They also possess enlarged incisors which grow continually throughout life and are used to gnaw through trunks and fell trees. Most trees cut by Beavers are small saplings which are used as food, but they will also cut large trees up to two feet in diameter to open the canopy and promote the growth of new food sources. These largest of the North American rodents are famous for their dam building abilities and they will also build elaborate living quarters known as "lodges." After many years of use these lodges may become up to 15 feet across and can house an entire extended family. They have underwater entrances for protection and a hollow "room" that is above the waterline and lined with wood chips or grasses. Other species such as Muskrats and mice may take up residence within these lodges. At one time Beaver fur was one of the most valuable natural resources in America and the pursuit of Beaver fur led to the exploration of much of the continent. Within a few decades they were nearly exterminated by trappers. They can sometimes be a pest when their dam building activities flood farmers' fields, but their wetland creating activities benefit many scores of wetland wildlife species. In fact, the Beaver is one of the most significant players in local ecosystems throughout North America and their value to the overall ecology would be hard to overstate.

Class—**Mammalia** (mammals)		
Order—**Rodentia** (rodents)		
Family—**Muridae** (rats, mice)		
Muskrat *Ondatra zibethicus*	**Hispid Cotton Rat** *Sigmodon hispidus*	**Rice Rat** *Oryzomy palustris*
  Presumed range in Kentucky	  Presumed range in Kentucky	  Presumed range in Kentucky
Size: Adults reach 20 inches total length and weigh about 2.5 pounds.	**Size:** 10 inches in length and about six ounces for adults.	**Size:** Up to 9 inches in length and weighing about 2.5 ounces.
Abundance: Common.	**Abundance:** Common where found.	**Abundance:** Common.
Variation: There is no variation among individuals in Kentucky, but there are several subspecies across the rest of North America.	**Variation:** There are at least a dozen subspecies across the southern U.S. and more in Central America. Shown is *S. h. hispidus*, which is found in Kentucky.	**Variation:** No variation in Kentucky and the sexes are alike. Six other subspecies are found in the southeastern United States.
Habitat: Aquatic. Prefers marshland but also inhabits swamp, ponds, and lakes. Rarely in rivers or large streams.	**Habitat:** Old fields, especially in upland areas. Most common in fields dominated by broom sedge.	**Habitat:** Prefers to be near water. Wet meadow, marsh, and the edges of swamps. Can also be found in uplands.
Breeding: Prolific. Breeds year-round in Kentucky and may produce as many as six young per litter.	**Breeding:** Very prolific. Produces several litters per year (six to eight babies) and young are weaned in less than a week!	**Breeding:** Breeds several time per year. Three to five babies. Young will reach sexual maturity in two months.
Natural History: Primarily nocturnal but often active during daylight hours in the spring. Excellent swimmers, Muskrats feed on a variety of aquatic vegetation. The name comes from the presence of well developed musk glands. These rodents are an important fur-bearer and in the recent past millions were trapped annually across America for their fur. Life span is only three to four years in the wild. The Mink may be the most important predator on muskrats, especially of the young. Adults build lodges similar to the Beaver, but use grasses rather than sticks. The entrance to the Muskrat lodge is below water level while the chamber of the lodge itself is above the high water mark. Sometimes digs a burrow into creek or pond banks.	**Natural History:** Although this species range barely reaches into Kentucky, they are very common farther south and in fact this is perhaps the most common mammal in much of the southern United States. They are active both day and night in their surface runways hidden beneath the grasses and weeds. These are one of the easier to identify of the mouse-like rodents due to the coarse appearance of the fur. Hispid Cotton Rats are a primary prey for a wide variety of predators including snakes, carnivorous mammals, and birds of prey. Their surface runways through overgrown fields are easy to see following a burn, as are the surface nests consisting of a ball of grasses. Populations fluctuate from year to year. Feeds mostly on grasses.	**Natural History:** The name Rice Rat comes from the prevalence of this species in rice fields throughout the southeast. In addition to rice they consume several other types of seeds and plants but also eat large amounts of animal matter. In fact, this is one of the most carnivorous rodents in America. The list of animal prey includes insects, crustaceans, fish, and baby birds and bird eggs to name a few. They are accomplished swimmers and will dive and swim underwater to escape a predator. They are also good climbers. They are strictly nocturnal in habits. As with most other rodents, they are preyed upon by a wide variety of raptors, carnivorous mammals, and especially, snakes.

Class—**Mammalia** (mammals)

Order—**Rodentia** (rodents)

Family—**Muridae** (rats, mice)

Allegheny Woodrat *Neotoma magister*	**Norway Rat** *Rattus norvigicus*	**House Mouse** *Mus musculus*

Presumed range in Kentucky 	Presumed range in Kentucky 	Presumed range in Kentucky 
Size: Adults reach 16 inches and about 12 ounces.	**Size:** Length can be as much as 15 inches and weight up to 12 ounces.	**Size:** Adults reach about 6.5 inches and weigh about 0.75 of an ounce.
Abundance: Uncommon.	**Abundance:** Common.	**Abundance:** Very common.
Variation: The Eastern Woodrat, *N. floridana*, may also occur in Kentucky in the western tip of the state.	**Variation:** None in wild populations. Captives are variable. The well-known lab rat is an albino form of this species.	**Variation:** No variation in wild specimens but domesticate lab mice come in a variety of colors and patterns.
Habitat: Woodrats usually associate with rocks and cliff faces where they make their dens in crevices. They will also use logs, derilict buildings, etc.	**Habitat:** This highly adaptable rodent can live virtually anywhere, including as a stowaway on ships, which is how it immigrated to America from Europe.	**Habitat:** A highly successful rodent that usually associates with human habitations and man-made structures, but can also live in wild environments.
Breeding: No data is available on breeding in KY, but three to four litters per year with two to six young have been recorded.	**Breeding:** The fecundity of the Norway Rat is legendary. From six to eight litters per year with up to a dozen young per litter.	**Breeding:** Broods can number from 5–12. Young females begin breeding at six weeks and produce 14 litters per year.
Natural History: The range of this species in Kentucky is poorly known, and the range map above is an approximation. Woodrats are renowned for their bulky nests (often made on rock ledges or in crevices) and constructed of sticks, cedar boughs, and even human refuse. They are sometimes known as "pack-rats," a name derived from their habit of collecting shiny objects that range from aluminum cans to eating utensils. They cache food in large quantities in what are known as "middens." Ancient woodrat nests in caves can persist for centuries and are studied to gain insight into the historical natural history of a region. Dens are occupied by one adult (and young), but are re-colonized by a new rat when the original owner dies.	**Natural History:** Also called the Brown Rat, this species has followed man to every corner of the globe. They are responsible for an almost unimaginable degree of human suffering. Throughout the history of human civilization these rodents have destroyed crops and stored foods while spreading devastating diseases, most notably Bubonic Plague. Though less of a threat to modern societies, these rats still shadow the human species and are common in both urban and rural settings. The common laboratory rat is a domestic version of this animal that has somewhat redeemed the species for humans, having been used as an experimental animal for medical and scientific research for over a century.	**Natural History:** The House Mouse has adapted to living in close proximity to humans and today they are found wherever there are people throughout the world. As their name implies they regularly enter into houses where they can become both a pest and a health hazard. They live both in cities and farmlands. Like the Norway Rat, the House Mouse originated in Eurasia and traveled around the world as a stowaway on sailing ships, eventually populating the entire globe. These mice are primarily nocturnal and their food includes nearly everything eaten by humans plus insects and fungi. Domestic populations of this species are the familiar laboratory mice or "white mice," so called because most are albinos.

Class—**Mammalia** (mammals)

Order—**Rodentia** (rodents)

Family—**Muridae** (rats, mice)

Cotton Mouse *Peromyscus gossypinus*	Deer Mouse and White-footed Mouse *Peromyscus maniculatus* *Peromyscus leucopus*

White-footed Mouse

Presumed range in Kentucky

Presumed range in Kentucky   Presumed range in Kentucky

Size: About 8.25 inches and 1.5 ounces.

Size: 5–8 inches and 1 ounce.

Size: 7 inches and 1 ounce.

Abundance: Uncommon.

Abundance: Very Common.

Abundance: Common.

Variation: No known variation among Kentucky specimens, but several subspecies are recognized throughout its range in the southeastern U.S. These mice are very similar in appearance to Kentucky's other *Peromyscus* (deer mice) species. As an adult the Cotton Mouse has a larger hind foot (over 22 mm) than the other two deer mice.

Variation: These two species are so similar that most people will not be able to tell them apart. In fact the previous species (Cotton Mouse) is also confusingly similar. The specimen shown above is the White-footed Mouse, but the Deer Mouse is nearly identical. Both have several subspecies nationwide (over a dozen in the White-footed Mouse and over 50 in the Deer Mouse). In the Deer Mouse, short-tailed, small-eared forms are found in open fields and grasslands and a long-tailed, large-eared variant occurs in woodland habits. The woodland form is nearly indistinguishable from the White-footed Mouse. Both species exhibit some age related color variation, with younger mice being darker, more grayish in color.

Habitat: Generally a lowland mammal that enjoys wetlands, wet woodlands, and bottom-land forests. Like other deer mice, may enter both derelict buildings and rural homes.

Habitat: Deer Mice can be found in both woodland habitats and open fields, including agricultural land. This mouse can sometimes be found in wide-open, harvested crop fields.

Habitat: White-footed Mice prefer the woods but may also be found in overgrown fence fields, fence rows, etc. Unlike the previous species these mice avoid open areas.

Breeding: May breed nearly year-round averaging three to four young. Gestation can be as little as 23 days.

Breeding: Both these species are prolific breeders that can breed nearly year-round. A typical litter is four or five young, but can be more. The young mice develop rapidly and are ready to breed themselves when only two months old.

Natural History: In almost every respect the Cotton Mouse is a lowland counterpart of the Deer Mouse and the White-footed Mouse. Most of the range of the Cotton Mouse is to the south of Kentucky, but they do range northward into the western tip of the state. The exact range in Kentucky is not well known, but they are probably restricted to the Coastal Plain and immediately adjoining regions. The name comes from the habit of southern populations to use cotton (pilfered from cotton fields) in the building of their nest.

Natural History: These common mice serve as prey for a variety of predators, from coyotes and bobcats to weasels, snakes, and birds of prey. Both species are primarily nocturnal. They feed on a wide array of seeds, nuts, and grain as well as berries, insects, snails, centipedes, fungi, and occasionally other mice. They will cache large stores of seeds and nuts in the fall and they remain active throughout the winter. Both can become a nuisance as they will regularly enter human dwellings, often nesting in a little used drawer or cupboard. Several species of *Peromyscus* mice are vectors for tick-borne Lyme disease, and in the southwestern United States some Deer Mice can harbor the deadly hantavirus. Humans who experience close contact or prolonged exposure to their feces and urine may be at risk. Both species can be arboreal and they may den or nest well above the ground, or they may live beneath a rotted log or stump. Both are adaptable and successful native rodents. The Deer Mouse is found in every habitat type in America and ranges from near sea level to the high mountains. The White-footed Mouse is nearly as adaptable.

Class—**Mammalia** (mammals)

Order—**Rodentia** (rodents)

Family—**Muridae** (rats, mice)

Golden Mouse *Ochrotomys nuttalli*	**Eastern Harvest Mouse** *Reithrodontomys humulis*	**Southern Red-backed Vole** *Myodes gapperi*

Presumed range in Kentucky	Presumed range in Kentucky	Presumed range in Kentucky
Size: About 6.5 inches. Weight 0.75 oz.	**Size:** Length 4.5 inches. Weight 0.5 oz.	**Size:** Length 5.5 inches. Weight 1 oz.
Abundance: Fairly common.	**Abundance:** Uncommon.	**Abundance:** Uncommon.
Variation: Adults are golden brown. Young mice are slightly grayer in color.	**Variation:** No variation is known to occur in Kentucky.	**Variation:** The race that is found in Kentucky is the subspecies *maurus.*
Habitat: Favors lowland forests and swampy areas in the western end to the state but can be found in highland woods in the Appalachian Mountains of eastern Kentucky.	**Habitat:** Fallow fields, especially areas dominated by Broomsedge. Thickets are also inhabited but absent from large forests. Moist soils and lowlands are primary habitat regions.	**Habitat:** This is a northern species that ranges into Kentucky in the mountains of the southeast corner of the state. Lives in deep, heavily shaded, damp woodlands.
Breeding: Breeds from early spring through fall, producing several litters per year. Two to four young is typical.	**Breeding:** Breeds from early spring through fall. Average litter size is three to four. Several litters per year is possible.	**Breeding:** May breed at any time except deep winter. Litter size varies from two to eight.
Natural History: Mainly nocturnal, Golden mice have strong arboreal tendencies. They use vines and limbs as highways and will forage for seeds both in the trees and on the ground. The nest is usually in a thicket of vines several feet off the ground. Acorns are also eaten as are invertebrates, and these mice are decidedly omnivorous. These are handsome little mice with fine, golden fur. Unlike many other mice species, the Golden Mouse rarely enters human habitations, preferring a more natural habitat. One captive individual was reported to have lived for eight years, a very long life span for a mouse. The average life span in the wild is probably less than a year. Distribution in Kentucky is not well established and the range map shown above is probably not accurate.	**Natural History:** The Harvest Mouse is easily confused with several other mice species that are found in Kentucky. Trained biologists confirm the identity of the Harvest Mouse by examining the upper incisor teeth, which have grooves. These mice are widespread across the southeastern United States but are apparently not common anywhere. Grass seeds and weed seeds are the main food item, but insects may also be eaten. In habits they are mainly nocturnal. Their nests are usually on the surface of the ground (often at the base of a tuft of grass) and consist of a ball of plant fibers and grass. This is one of Kentucky's smallest mouse species. Despite the disdain most humans have for small rodents, they play an important role in nature and are food for many predators.	**Natural History:** Named for the reddish color of the fur on its back. This is the rarest of Kentucky's vole species and its range is restricted to the southeastern corner of the state. Red-backed voles are rodents of the far north and the higher mountain ranges. Although widespread across Canada and much of the northern United States, they are uncommon in Kentucky and are regarded as a species of concern by the Kentucky Department of Fish and Wildlife Resources. There are several subspecies of the Southern Red-backed Vole. The race found in Kentucky is the subspecies *maurus*, the Kentucky Red-backed Vole. Mast, fungi, berries, grasses, ferns, and arthropods are all listed as food items for this omnivorus rodent.

Class—**Mammalia** (mammals)

Order—**Rodentia** (rodents)

Family—**Muridae** (rats, mice)

Meadow Vole *Microtus pennslyvanicus*	**Woodland Vole** *Microtus pinetorum*	**Prairie Vole** *Microtus ochreogaster*

Presumed range in Kentucky	Presumed range in Kentucky	Presumed range in Kentucky
Size: About 6.5 inches and 1.75 oz.	**Size:** Length 5 inches. Weight 1 ounce.	**Size:** 6 inches and 1.5 ounces.
Abundance: Less common in Kentucky than farther north.	**Abundance:** Very common. This is perhaps the state's most common vole.	**Abundance:** Fairly common, but less common than the Woodland Vole.
Variation: None in Kentucky. As many as 25 subspecies are recognized throughout North America.	**Variation:** *M. p. carbonarius* is found in the mountains and *M. p. auricularis* elsewhere in the state.	**Variation:** *M. o. ochrogaster* in the western two-thirds of Kentucky, *M.o. ohionensis* elsewhere in the state.
Habitat: Primarily fields and meadows from the northern U.S. to the Arctic Circle.	**Habitat:** Primarily deciduous woodlands. Widespread from western lowlands to eastern mountains.	**Habitat:** This species generally avoids the woods and prefers open, grassy habitats and overgrown fields.
Breeding: A remarkably fecund animal, young Meadow Voles can breed within four weeks after birth. Litter size is four to six.	**Breeding:** Breeds spring through fall with up to four litters per year. One to four young per litter.	**Breeding:** Unlike most rodents, Prairie Voles are monogamous. Three to five young is typical.
Natural History: Generally regarded as the world's most prolific mammal. Populations in many areas are cyclical and during years of high population density there can be as many as several hundred per acre in prime habitat. Because they can be so common, these voles are an important food source for predatory species ranging from snakes and carnivorous mammals to birds of prey. They can also impact humans by eating crops, garden produce, young trees in orchards, etc. They feed on a wide variety of grasses and plants and will eat seeds, roots, and even bark. The range depiction on the map above may not be entirely accurate. The Kentucky Department of Fish and Wildlife Resources has documented the species from at least 56 counties in Kentucky.	**Natural History:** Woodland Voles create networks of tunnels just below the ground or "runways" that are near the surface but beneath the leaf litter on the forest floor. These tunnel systems are utilized by other small mammals such as shrews. They rarely venture far from these tunnels, but do emerge to glean seeds, grasses, and mast. They also eat roots, especially roots of grasses, and root crops like potatoes are also eaten. Active both day and night. Their subterranean habits render them less vulnerable to many predators, but they are prey for a wide variety of carnivores, raptors, and especially snakes, which are able to enter the burrow systems. Young exhibit a dark gray color. Adults are more chestnut. The two Kentucky subspecies are nearly identical.	**Natural History:** Coarse, grizzled gray fur and shorter tail distinguish this species from the Woodland Vole. Although insects are eaten, these voles feed mostly on vegetation. Including but not limited to grasses, roots, herbaceous weeds, seeds, leaves, stems, etc. Like other voles, creates a system of shallow burrows. The North American range of this species approximates the occurrence of the original American prairies. It is probable less common today than in historical times. The eastern limits of this species' range in Kentucky is poorly known, but it is apparently absent from the higher mountains in the southeastern portion of the state. The two subspecies that occur in Kentucky are indistinguishable to the average observer.

Class—**Mammalia** (mammals)		
Order—**Rodentia** (rodents)		
Family—**Muridae** (rats, mice)	Family—**Dipodidae** (jumping mice)	
Southern Bog Lemming *Synaptomys cooperi*	**Woodland Jumping Mouse** *Napaeozapus insignis*	**Meadow Jumping Mouse** *Zapus hudsonius*

Kentucky's two jumping mice are nearly identical. Pictured here is the Meadow Jumping Mouse. Woodland species is very similar but has a white tail tip.

Presumed range in Kentucky

Presumed range in Kentucky

Presumed range in Kentucky

Size: Adult is 5 inches and 1.25 ounces.

Size: 9 inches (mostly tail) and 1 ounce.

Size: 8 inches (mostly tail) and 0.66 ounce.

Abundance: Uncommon.

Abundance: Rare.

Abundance: Uncommon.

Variation: Seven subspecies. Two occur in Kentucky.

Variation: None in Kentucky. At least five subspecies in North America.

Variation: Two subspecies occur in Kentucky but they are nearly identical.

Habitat: Although they can found in bogs, they occupy nearly all habitat types. The presence of grasses seems to be the only habitat requirement.

Habitat: As their name implies the Woodland Jumping Mouse is a decidedly woodland animal that rarely ventures into open areas.

Habitat: Meadows and fields that contain dense cover. Generally avoids woodlands but may occur in edge areas, treeline fence rows, and stream banks.

Breeding: Breeds most of year except for mid-winter. Typical litter is three with a maximum of eight.

Breeding: Unlike most small rodents, this mouse breeds only once or twice annually producing three to six young.

Breeding: Three to six young are born after an 18-day gestation period. Breeds about three times a year from spring to late summer.

Natural History: Bog Lemmings often use the same burrows as other mice and vole species. Primarily nocturnal and crepuscular, they feed on green plants and berries mainly. They often occur in colonies. Bog Lemmings are mainly northern mammals, and the southern Appalachians represent their southernmost distribution today. As with many small mammal species, the numerous subspecies can be told apart only by expert mammologists. The range map above may not be an accurate depiction of this species distribution in Kentucky. Though older publications show this species occurring in the Coastal Plain of Kentucky, the exact limits of its range in the western end of the state is poorly known, thus the map above should be regarded as a close approximation of this species' range.

Natural History: Another mainly boreal (northern) species that ranges southward through the Appalachian Plateau. These mice hibernate for up to six months in the northern parts of their range. They have very long tails and long hind legs that bestow them a remarkable jumping ability. When startled they can reportedly leap a distance of ten feet! Food is fungi, seeds, berries, and insects. They are mainly nocturnal and they sometimes use the burrows and runways of other small rodent species. Woodland Jumping Mice can be told from the very similar Meadow Jumping Mouse by habitat preference and by the white color on the tail tip. The exact range of this species in Kentucky is difficult to determine, and the map above may not be an accurate reflection of the species distribution in Kentucky.

Natural History: This rodent, along with the preceding species, comprise the North American representatives of the family Dipodidae. This unique family also ranges into the Old World. The Meadow Jumping Mouse is distinguished from the similar Woodland Jumping Mouse by the uniformly dark tail (as opposed to a white tipped tail). As with the previous species they are mainly nocturnal and do not make runways of their own, but frequently use those made by *Microtus* or other small rodents. Food items are similar to the Woodland Jumping Mouse (fungi, insects, seeds, berries). Both species of Jumping Mice put on heavy layers of fat just prior to their long hibernation, but mortality during hibernation is high and as many as two-thirds will not survive their winter sleep.

Class—**Mammalia** (mammals)

Order—**Soricipmorpha** (moles, shrews)

Family—**Soricidae** (shrews)

Least Shrew *Cryptotis parva*	**Short-tailed Shrews** *Blarina carolinensis* (Southern) and *Blarina brevicaudus* (Northern)

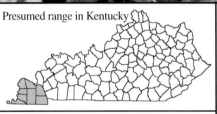

Presumed range in Kentucky

Size: Three inches and 0.2 ounce.

Size: To 4.5 inches and 0.5 ounce. | Maximum 5.5 inches & 1 ounce.

Abundance: Fairly common.

Abundance: Common. | **Abundance:** Common.

Variation: Summer pelage is brownish, turning to slate gray during winter. There is a single subspecies in KY.

Variation: These two species are so much alike that even trained mammologists have difficulty distinguishing between the two in the field and range is the usually the best indicator of species. In winter both have darker, longer fur.

Habitat: Grassy areas and overgrown fields primarily, but also in woodlands.

Habitat: Both species are fond damp woodlands and in fact neither can tolerate excessively dry conditions very well. Both avoid saturated soils, however.

Breeding: Several litters per year is common averaging four to five young per litter.

Breeding: Breeds in spring and fall. Two to six young per litter. | **Breeding:** Breeds in spring and fall. Up to four litters of four to six young annually.

Natural History: Possessing an extremely high metabolism, this tiny mammal can consume its own weight in food daily. Like many other shrews they are known to cache food items. Although these shrews are rarely seen due to their diminutive size and reclusive habits, they are usually a fairly common mammal throughout Kentucky. Owls are a major predator and in fact the presence of these tiny shrews in a given area is often confirmed by examining owl pellets for skeleton remains. Known food items are caterpillars, beetles, other insects, snails, spiders, and earthworms. One other tiny shrew species, the **Pygmy Shrew** (*Sorex hoyi*), also occurs in much of the state, but it is much less common and very rarely observed. The local abundance of the Pygmy Shrew is difficult to determine because they are so tiny they fail to trip the mechanism on most small mammal traps.

Natural History: The Short-tailed shrews are so similar that even experts sometimes resort to lab tests to determine species. Until recently they were regarded as the same species and apparently the only reliable definition of species is obtained by counting chromosomes! Both species are also easily confused with the Least Shrew, from which they can be distinguished by examining the teeth with the aid of a magnifying glass or dissecting microscope (Least Shrews have three visible unicuspids, Short-tail Shrews have four). Both species of Short-tail Shrews are primarily nocturnal animals and both have very high metabolic rates. They are hyperactive animals that will eat as much as one-half their body weight daily! The ferocity of shrews is legendary among mammologists. Many have learned the hard way never to place a shrew in a container with a mouse if you want to keep both alive! The northern species is known to have periods of intense activity followed by periods of lethargy. Food is a variety of insects, snails, earthworms, millipedes, etc., as well as much larger prey including mice that are as large as themselves. The Northern Short-tailed Shrew is known to possess venomous saliva with which it kills its prey. It is presumed that the southern species also possess this ability. Both species have tiny eyes and their vision is quite poor. The northern species is known to utilize echolocation. Some sounds they produce are audible to humans, but others are not. It is believed that these "ultrasonic" sounds act like a form of radar to detect objects in their path, rather like what is known in bats. Except when breeding and rearing young these are solitary animals. They forage beneath the leaf litter in runways and tunnels and will dig their own tunnels or use those of other small rodents. Piebald and leucistic specimens have been reported from Illinois (Hoffmeister, 1989).

Class—**Mammalia** (mammals)		
Order—**Soricimorpha** (shrews, moles)		
Family—**Soricidae** (shrews)		
Southeastern Shrew *Sorex longirostris*	**Masked Shrew** *Sorex cinereus*	**Smokey Shrew** *Sorex fumeus*

Presumed range in Kentucky

Size: 3.5 inches. 0.14 ounce.

Abundance: Fairly common.

Variation: No variation in Kentucky. Three subspecies throughout the southeast.

Habitat: Found in a wide variety of habitats. Woods, fields, thickets, etc.

Breeding: Breeds throughout the summer. At least two litters of four to six annually.

Natural History: As with most tiny vertebrates, the Southeastern Shrew has a remarkable metabolic rate and must eat almost constantly to survive. Another characteristic of tiny mammals is a short life span. The maximum life span for the Southeastern Shrew is reported to be about one and a half years. Spiders are reported as the most important food item, but a wide variety of other invertebrates are also eaten. As the name implies, they are found throughout the southeastern United States. Until recently these shrews were regarded as rare, but increasingly effective trapping/collecting techniques have revealed that they are fairly common in many areas of their range. They can sometimes be discovered beneath cover boards, tin, or other material placed in suitable habitats to attract small, secretive vertebrates.

Presumed range in Kentucky

Size: 3.8 inches. 0.375 ounce.

Abundance: Uncommon.

Variation: Brownish in summer, grayish in winter.

Habitat: Found in virtually all wild habitats. Primarily a northern species.

Breeding: Four to ten tiny (0.5 inch) young are born from spring to fall.

Natural History: Though mainly nocturnal, these shrews are active both day and night. They dart in and out of leaf litter on the forest floor or move rapidly along runways in overgrown fields. They will make chirping noises as they forage and some believe they echo-locate. Known food items are snails/slugs, caterpillars, grubs, spiders, and ants. They will also eat carrion. Shrews do not hibernate, and must forage year-round. For an animal with such high food requirements, survival in winter would seem a daunting task. But dormant insects and other invertebrates are located and eaten in large quantities. In fact, shrews may be quite beneficial to man by consuming enormous quantities of injurious insects and grubs. The Masked Shrew also frequently goes by the name Cinereous Shrew.

Presumed range in Kentucky

Size: Length 4.5 inches. Weight 0.5 ounce.

Abundance: Probably fairly common.

Variation: Winter pelage dark gray, summer pelage browner.

Habitat: Moist woodlands. Especially where there is abundant ground cover.

Breeding: Litter size averages five to six. Two or three litters in warmer months.

Natural History: This is another primarily northern species that invades the southern United States as far south as northern Georgia along the Appalachian Plateau. Like other shrews it does not hibernate and will be active even in the coldest weather. Its diet is mostly insects and other invertebrates, but salamanders are also listed as prey. The Smokey Shrew, along with other shrew species, is undoubtedly a very beneficial species to man due to the large number of larva, pupae, and adult insects consumed daily. Many of these are significant pests to forest trees. The average life span of this species is less than a year and half. The **Rock Shrew** (*Sorex dispar*) is another very similar but quite rare shrew that can be found in the higher mountains in the southeastern corner of Kentucky.

Class—**Mammalia** (mammals)
Order—**Soricimorpha** (shrews, moles)
Family—**Talpidae** (moles)

Eastern Mole *Scalopus aquaticus*	**Hairy-tailed Mole** *Parascalops breweri*

Presumed range in Kentucky 	Presumed range in Kentucky 
Size: 6 inches and 2 ounces.	**Size:** 6.33 inches and 1.8 ounces.
Abundance: Common.	**Abundance:** Uncommon.
Variation: Males are slightly larger.	**Variation:** No variation.
Habitat: Except for wetlands these moles can be found in any habitat where soils are suitable for burrowing.	**Habitat:** Except for wetlands these moles can be found in any habitat where soils are suitable for burrowing.
Breeding: One litter per year in early spring. Two to five young.	**Breeding:** Mating takes place in the spring and four or five young is average.
Natural History: The most wide-ranging mole in America. Although considered a pest in suburban lawns and rural gardens, Eastern Moles actually perform some helpful tasks. The tunnels they dig help to aerate the soil and allow rainfall to penetrate more easily. They also prey heavily upon destructive grubs such as the Japanese Beetle. The pelage of the Eastern Mole is "reversible" and will lie smoothly against the skin whether mole is moving forward or backward in tight tunnels. The powerful forelegs allow this animal to burrow at an astonishing pace, and the webbed toes help move dirt aside. The eyes are tiny and covered with skin, and there are no external ears. This is an animal that is superbly adapted to a subterrean lifestyle, and Eastern Moles will spend 99 percent of their lives below ground.	**Natural History:** Active year-round in both day and night, but in winter utilizes deeper tunnel systems. More shallow tunnels are used in warm weather when it may sometimes leave tunnels at night to forage above ground. Feeding on earthworms and grubs, this mole has been known to consume its own weight in food daily. The tunnels of the Hairy-tail Mole are less obvious above ground than those of the Eastern Mole. Many other small mammals such as shrews and mice are known to use the tunnels constructed by this mole. Life span of four years. The range of this species closely coincides with that northern and central portions of the Appalachian Plateau. In most respects very similar to the Eastern Mole, from which it is easily differntiated by the presence of a furry tail.

Class—**Mammalia** (mammals)
Order—**Chiroptera** (bats)
Family—**Vespertilionidae** (mouse-eared bats)

Eastern Pipistrelle *Pipistrellus subflavus*	**Evening Bat** *Nycticeius humeralis*	**Silver-haired Bat** *Lasionycteris noctivagans*
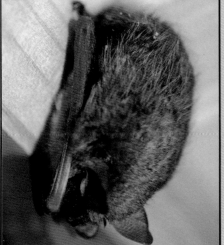		
Presumed range in Kentucky	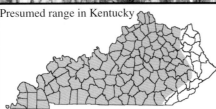Presumed range in Kentucky	Presumed range in Kentucky
Size: 3.5 inches. Weight about 0.25 ounce.	**Size:** 4 inches. Up to 0.5 ounce.	**Size:** 4 inches and 0.33 ounce.
Abundance: Common.	**Abundance:** Uncommon.	**Abundance:** Uncommon.
Variation: None.	**Variation:** None.	**Variation:** None.
Habitat: Woodlands, stream courses, and edges of fields bordering woodlands are favorite hunting areas.	**Habitat:** Swamps, stream corridors, and woodlands as well as woods openings and edge areas are used.	**Habitat:** The Silver Haired Bat is a forest species that hides in tree hollows or beneath peeling bark during daylight.
Breeding: Females give birth to one or two babies (pups) in June.	**Breeding:** One to three young are produced in late spring/early summer.	**Breeding:** Young are born in late spring. Two pups is typical.
Natural History: Eastern Pipistrelles are widespread and common throughout the eastern United States. In fall they will migrate short distances to hibernacula. In Kentucky they are most common during warmer months, but sometimes emerge in warm weather. Food is tiny airborne insects. They will leave the roost before dark and are often seen hunting at dusk. Like many bats the females form maternal colonies where young are reared, often in buildings or sheds. Unlike many other species, however, these maternal colonies are usually small, numbering only one or two dozen individuals. Hibernation begins in late fall (October) and lasts until April or May. Hibernating bats may lose as much as 25–30 percent of their body weight before emerging in the spring.	**Natural History:** Evening Bats in Kentucky are summer residents that winter farther south where hibernation is not necessary. Most leave Kentucky by early fall, but some may stay into late fall. Summer roosts include hollow trees as well as buildings, and they do not seem to utilize caves as is the habit of many bat species. A wide variety of small insects are eaten, including species that are injurious to farm crops. The Evening Bat is a threatened species in Kentucky. Though widespread across much of the southeast, these are lowland and low plateau animals that avoid the higher elevations of the Appalachian Mountains. Most of these bats found in the northern portions of their range in summer are females, with the males apparently staying farther to the south.	**Natural History:** This is a widespread species that ranges from coast to coast in North America. In summer this species ranges as far north as Canada and southeastern Alaska. In fact this species is more common in summer months in northern regions. In Kentucky this is a apparently a migrant species that leaves the state in summer for more northerly forests. It is probably most common in Kentucky in spring and fall and is known to overwinter in the state. Unlike many bat species the Silver-haired Bat is mostly a solitary animal that roosts singly, although some colony activity is reported among females with young. Silver-haireds derive their name from the "frosted" appearance of their pelage, a unique and identifying characteristic among Kentucky bats.

Class—**Mammalia** (mammals)
Order—**Chiroptera** (bats)
Family—**Vespertilionidae** (mouse-eared bats)

Eastern Red Bat *Lasiurus borealis*	**Hoary Bat** *Lasiurus cinereus*

Presumed range in Kentucky 	Presumed range in Kentucky 
Size: Maximum 5 inches. Up to 0.5 ounce.	**Size:** Maximum 5.5 inches. Up to 1 ounce.
Abundance: Common.	**Abundance:** Common.
Variation: Males are conspicuously red, females are chestnut frosted with white.	**Variation:** Females are on average slightly heavier than males.
Habitat: Woodlands and edge areas in both rural and urban regions.	**Habitat:** Another forest species that is seen in both rural and urban areas.
Breeding: Litter size is one to four with the pups born in late May or early June.	**Breeding:** Averages two pups born in mid-May to mid-June.
Natural History: In summer this species usually roosts in trees by hanging from a limb. Usually solitary but sometimes more than one bat will roost together. Roosting bats resemble dead leaves. Trees chosen for roosting are often at the edge of a woodland bordering an open field. This is a migratory species that summers in Kentucky and winters farther to the south. The range is quite large and includes most of the United States east of the Rocky Mountains and much of southeastern Canada. Some hibernation occurs among those few individuals that stay in Kentucky year-round. Hibernation takes place in hollow trees or beneath leaf litter on the forest floor, a very unusual tactic for a bat! Though mainly nocturnal, this species often flies in daylight, especially in late afternoon or early evening. This is one of Kentucky's more handsomely colored bat species.	**Natural History:** This is the largest bat species in Kentucky. The wingspan of the Hoary Bat can be up to 16 inches! Its name comes from the white-tipped hairs of the fur on its back. Hoary Bats have the greatest distribution of any American Bat. They summer as far north as Canada and winter in the coastal plain of the southeastern United States. Most of the Hoary Bats seen in Kentucky are migrating to and from summer / winter residences. A few may summer and breed in the state. Oddly, the sexes segregate themselves following breeding and most of those seen in the eastern U.S. in summer are females. Males summer farther west in the Great Plains, Rocky Mountains, or west coast. A related similar species, the **Seminole Bat** (*L. seminolus*), is a southern bat that has been recorded in Kentucky on a few occasions during summer months.

Class—**Mammalia** (mammals)
Order—**Chiroptera** (bats)
Family—**Vespertilionidae** (mouse-eared bats)

Rafinesque's Big-eared Bat *Corynorhinus rafinesquii*	**Big Brown Bat** *Eptisicus fuscus*

Presumed range in Kentucky 	Presumed range in Kentucky 
Size: 3.75 inches and 0.4 of an ounce.	**Size:** 4.5 inches and nearly an ounce.
Abundance: Uncommon, possibly in decline.	**Abundance:** Common.
Variation: None in Kentucky.	**Variation:** None in Kentucky..
Habitat: Woods, riparian areas. For roosting uses tree hollows, caves, beneath loose bark, and derelict buildings.	**Habitat:** Open fields, vacant lots, rural and urban areas. Sometimes seen hunting insects around suburban streetlights.
Breeding: Breeds in fall and gives birth to a single baby in spring.	**Breeding:** Breeds in fall. Delayed fertilization. Twins born in late spring.
Natural History: Rafinesque's Big-eared Bat hibernates in the state and is thus found here year-round. It may roost communally or singly, and like many bats it will sometimes roost among other species. In the Appalachian region this species shows a preference for sandstone caves. Food is mostly moths (as much as 90 percent). More nocturnal than many bats, these bats do not fly at twilight, instead waiting for full darkness. Females congregate in "nursery roosts" in the spring to give birth. Young bats can fly at about three weeks and may live more than ten years. This bat occurs rather sporadically throughout its range and the map above is an estimation of its range in Kentucky. A similar species known as the **Townsend's Big-eared Bat** (*C. townsendii*) can be seen in Kentucky on rare occasions in the eastern half of the state.	**Natural History:** Stays year-round in Kentucky. Winters in caves or derilect buildings. Summer roosts are usually associated with human structures (buildings, eaves, bridges). Also known to use hollow trees and abondoned mines. The primary food is reported to be beetles. This is perhaps Kentucky's most recognizable bat species. They are the large, brown bats that are common around human habitations and they range throughout the state. Roosting bats seen alone during warm weather are nearly always males. Females congregate into "maternity colonies" of up to several dozen adults to rear their young. These bats seem to tolerate cold fairly well and they remain active well into the fall. They can sometimes even be seen flying around on warm days in winter. This bat is useful consumer of insect pests.

Class—**Mammalia** (mammals)		
Order—**Chiroptera** (bats)		
Family—**Vespertilionidae** (mouse-eared bats)		
Myotis Bats—genus—*Myotis* (6 species in Kentucky, 3 shown below)		
Gray Bat *Myotis grisescens*	**Northern Bat** *Myotis septentrionalis*	**Little Brown Bat** *Myotis lucifugus*

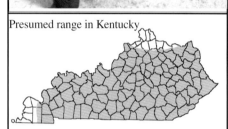Presumed range in Kentucky	Presumed range in Kentucky	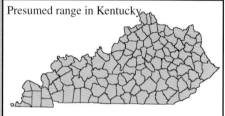Presumed range in Kentucky

Size: All *Myotis* are somewhat small bats, ranging in size from 3 to 3.5 inches and weighing from 0.2 to 0.33 of an ounce. The Gray Bat is are the largest (3.5 inches), with one of the smallest being the Eastern Small-footed Bat.

Abundance: The six species of Myotis Bats found in Kentucky range in abundance from common to rare. The rarer species are the Gray Bat (federally endangered) and the Indiana Bat (not shown, federally endangered). The Southeastern Bat (not shown) is endangered in Kentucky, and the Eastern Small-footed Bat (not shown) is threatened in Kentucky. Both the Little Brown Bat and the Northern Bat are fairly common.

Variation: Most bats present an identification problem for the average person, but the Myotis Bats can be especially confusing. Confirming the exact species usually requires looking very closely and may sometimes mean having the bat in hand. An exception would be the Gray Bats, that can be told from other Myotis Bats by their decidedly grayish coloration.

Habitat: Gray Bats are true cave dwellers, using caves for hibernation, roosting and rearing young. Other *Myotis* species may hibernate in caves but will also use other places such as hollow trees or buildings for summertime roosts. Some species are sometimes seen roosting in clumps by day beneath the shelter of roof overhangs, roofs of picnic pavilions, inside old barns, etc. A wide variety of habitats are utilized by these bats during warmer months. Forests, fields, wetlands, and especially stream courses.

Breeding: Mating occurs in the fall with fertilization delayed until early spring. Young are born in late spring or early summer and all species form "maternity colonies" of females with young which may be in caves, buildings, hollow trees, or other structures. *Myotis* bats produce a single baby annually (except for the Southeastern Bat which can give birth to twins).

Natural History: Virtually the entire population of Gray Bats in America hibernate in a handful of caves scattered across the southeastern United States. Indiana Bats are also known for their huge hibernating colonies that tend to concentrate in only a few select caves during winter. Both species are thus vulnerable to human or natural disturbance of their select hibernating locales. Some Myotis Bats are migratory, moving south during winter months. Most feed in flight on flying insects but one species (Northern Bat) feeds by gleaning insects from leaves while hovering. Some like to forage primarily over water above ponds, creeks, and wetland areas (Little Brown Bat, Gray Bat, Southeastern Bat). Throughout America, many bat species are in steep decline and many once common species have been hard hit by a fungal disease known as "White Nose Syndrome." The Little Brown Bat, once perhaps the most common *Myotis* in Kentucky, has been especially hard hit by this disease. All bats are remarkable little animals that consume untold numbers of injurious insect species, including many millions of mosquitoes, and they are thus extremely useful to man.

CHAPTER 4
THE BIRDS OF KENTUCKY

Class—**Aves** (birds)

Order—**Passeriformes** (songbirds)

Family	**Tyrannidae** (flycatchers)
Family	**Turdidae** (thrushes)
Family	**Mimidae** (thrasher family)
Family	**Lanidae** (shrikes)
Family	**Aluidae** (larks)
Family	**Motacillidae** (wagtails)
Family	**Bombycillidae** (waxwings)
Family	**Corvidae** (crows, jays)
Family	**Paridae** (chickadee family)
Family	**Sittidae** (nuthatches)
Family	**Certhidae** (creepers)
Family	**Regulidae** (kinglets)
Family	**Polioptilidae** (gnatcatchers)
Family	**Troglodytidae** (wrens)
Family	**Vironidae** (vireos)
Family	**Parulidae** (warblers)
Family	**Icteridae** (blackbirds)
Family	**Sturnidae** (starling)
Family	**Thraupidae** (tanagers)
Family	**Emberizidae** (sparrows)
Family	**Passeridae** (european sparrows)
Family	**Cardinalidae** (grosbeaks)
Family	**Fringillidae** (finches)
Family	**Hirundinidae** (swallows)

Order—**Apodiformes**
(swifts, hummingbirds)

Family	**Apodidae** (swifts)
Family	**Trochilidae** (hummingbirds)

Order—**Cuculiformes**

Family	**Cuculidae** (cuckoos)

Order—**Columbiformes**

Family	**Columbidae** (doves)

Table 6.
The Orders and Families of Kentucky Birds.

Order—**Piciformes**

Family	**Picidae** (woodpeckers)

Order—**Coraciiformes**

Family	**Alcedinidae** (kingfishers)

Order—**Galliformes** (chicken-like birds)

Family	**Phasianidae** (grouse)
Family	**Odontophoridae** (quail)

Order—**Caprimulgiformes**

Family	**Caprimulgidae** (nightjars)

Order—**Strigiformes** (owls)

Family	**Strigidae** (typical owls)
Family	**Tytonidae** (barn owl)

Order—**Falconiformes** (raptors)

Family	**Accipitridae** (hawks, eagles, kites)
Family	**Falconidae** (falcons)
Family	**Cathartidae** (vultures)

Order—**Ciconiiformes** (wading birds)

Family	**Ardeidae** (herons)
Family	**Ciconiidae** (storks)
Family	**Threskiornithidae** (ibis)

Order—**Gruiformes** (rails, cranes)

Family	**Rallidae** (rails)
Family	**Gruidae** (cranes)

Order—**Charadriiformes** (shorebirds)

Family	**Charadriidae** (plovers)
Family	**Recurvirostridae** (stilts)
Family	**Scolopacidae** (sandpipers)
Family	**Laridae** (gulls, terns)

Order—**Pelicaniformes**

Family	**Pelecanidae** (pelicans)

Order—**Suliformes**

Family	**Phalacrocoracidae** (cormorants)

Order—**Gaviiformes**

Family	**Gaviidae** (loons)

Order—**Podicipediformes**

Family	**Podicipedidae** (grebes)

Order—**Anseriiformes** (waterfowl)

Family	**Anatidae** (ducks, geese, swans)

Class—**Aves** (birds)

Order—**Passeriformes** (songbirds)

Family—**Tyrannidae** (flycatchers)

Olive-sided Flycatcher *Contopus cooperi*	**Eastern Wood Pewee** *Contopus virens*	**Eastern Phoebe** *Sayornis phoebe*

Presumed range in Kentucky	Presumed range in Kentucky	Presumed range in Kentucky

Olive-sided Flycatcher

Size: 8.5 inches.

Abundance: Uncommon in Kentucky.

Migratory Status: A spring and fall passage migrant. Passes through Kentucky en route to and from the boreal forests of Canada each spring and fall.

Variation: None. Sexes alike.

Habitat: The summer habitat is coniferous forests of the Rocky Mountain region and northern North America where it associates with small forest openings.

Breeding: Nest is typically on a branch of a conifer and built of sticks, lichens, and rootlets. One clutch per year. Three to four eggs per clutch.

Natural History: These flycatchers are quite acrobatic in the air. They feed in typical flycatcher fashion by sallying forth from a high perch to snatch flying insects. Bees and wasps are reportedly a favorite food. This species avoids deep forest in favor of openings such as bogs, meadows, or second growth and may benefit from forest fires or human activities such as logging. Paradoxically, the species has been declining in recent decades. This decline is possibly tied to changes in the winter habitat in tropical America. They are federally listed as Species of Concern by the USFWS. Noted for its habit of perching on the highest point available in a dead tree.

Eastern Wood Pewee

Size: 6.5 inches.

Abundance: Common.

Migratory Status: Wintering in South America, the Eastern Wood Pewee arrives in Kentucky in late spring and stays throughout the summer.

Variation: No variation. Sexes alike.

Habitat: Wood Pewees are forest birds but they favor small openings in the woods or edge areas where marshes or fields border woodlands.

Breeding: Nests are usually built high in trees in a terminal fork. Nest material consists of grasses and lichens. Two to four eggs are laid.

Natural History: These nondescript little brown birds often go unnoticed except for the distinctive call from which they derive their name. Their "pee-a-weee" song is a common summer sound in the woodlands throughout Kentucky. Like other members of the flycatcher family, they hunt flying insects from high perches, swooping out to catch their food on the wing. Very similar to Eastern Pheobe, but note orange lower bill and pale wing bars on the Wood Pewee. These birds can be fairly common summer residents in rural yards that are surrounded by woodlands. They will often become quite tame in those situations.

Eastern Phoebe

Size: 7 inches.

Abundance: Common.

Migratory Status: May be found year-round in westernmost Kentucky. In much of the rest of the state it can be seen from early spring through fall.

Variation: No variation. Sexes alike.

Habitat: Woodlands and woods openings. Also in rural yards or parks in wooded regions. Can be common around rural homesteads.

Breeding: Pheobes are very early nesters in Kentucky. Nesting can occur by early April and there will often be a second nesting later in the summer.

Natural History: The Eastern Pheobe is most easily told from other Flycatchers by its habit of constantly wagging its tail down and up. Its nests are also distinctive, being constructed of mud and lined with mosses. Nests are placed beneath some form of overhang, most often the eaves of buildings. The cup shaped nest is plastered to the surface in the manner of many swallows. These are normally tame little birds that may nest on the back porch and allow humans to approach to within a few yards before flying off only a short distance. Similar to the preceding Wood Pewee but note the dark bill and lack of wing bars on the Eastern Pheobe.

Class—**Aves** (birds)

Order—**Passeriformes** (songbirds)

Family—**Tyrannidae** (flycatchers)

Empid Flycatchers
genus—*Empidonax* (five nearly identical species in Kentucky)

Acadian Flycatcher *Empidonax virescens*	**Willow Flycatcher** *Empidonax traillii*	**Least Flycatcher** *Empidonax minimus*

Alder Flycatcher *Empidonax alnorum*	**Yellow-bellied Flycatcher** *Empidonax flaviventris*	

Presumed combined range of "Empid" Flycatchers in Kentucky.
All five species may been seen statewide.

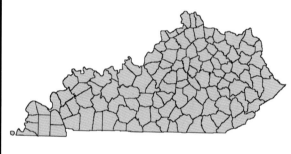

Size: Range in size from 5.25 to 5.75 inches.

Abundance: Least Flycatcher is fairly common in Kentucky in April/May and August/September. Alder Flycatcher may be the least common of the group. Acadian is probably the most common. Willow is an uncommon summer resident. Yellow-bellied is and uncommon species in Kentucky in spring and fall.

Variation: Five species of *Empidonax* flycatchers may be seen in Kentucky. They are the Acadian Flycatcher *(E. virescens)*, the Willow Flycatcher *(E. traillii)*, the Alder Flycatcher *(E. alnorum)*, the Least Flycatcher *(E. minimus)*, and the Yellow-bellied Flycatcher *(E. flaviventris)*. All five species are so similar in appearance that even expert bird watchers have trouble identifying individual species. Most people must content themselves with calling them all "Empid Flycatchers."

Migratory Status: The Acadian and Willow Flycatchers breed in Kentucky. All other species are spring and fall migrants that merely pass through the state. *Empidonax* species return to Kentucky beginning in late April through May. All begin to leave in August and most are gone by mid-September. All winter far to south, some as far as South America.

Habitat: All are woodland species. Acadian and Willow Flycatchers are fond of stream-side habitats, swamps, and marshes. Least Flycatchers prefer regenerative woodlands and edge areas. Alder Flycatchers and Yellow-bellied Flycatchers are both species that summer in the boreal forests of the far north. All five species may be seen throughout Kentucky during migration. Two above pictured species are known to nest in the state.

Breeding: Only two species regularly breed in Kentucky. The Acadian Flycatcher weaves a flimsy nest of grass on a low branch and lays two to four eggs. Willow Flycatchers build their nest in the fork of a low branch or bush and lay two to four eggs.

Natural History: Some species, like the Acadian Flycatcher, may be less numerous in Kentucky today due to the decline in forested habitats. The Willow Flycatcher on the other hand may be helped by the regeneration of successional forests. The other three species are transients in Kentucky. The Least Flycatcher is regarded as an endangered species in Kentucky. Serious bird-watchers find that the most reliable way to identify these small flycatchers is to learn their songs.

Class—**Aves** (birds)

Order—**Passeriformes** (songbirds)

Family—**Tyrannidae** (flycatchers)

Eastern Kingbird *Tyrannus tyrannus*	**Great Crested Flycatcher** *Myiarchus crinitus*

Presumed range in Kentucky

Presumed range in Kentucky

Size: 8.5 inches.

Abundance: Common.

Migratory Status: A summertime resident of Kentucky that winters in South America, some as far south as Argentina. Seen in Kentucky from mid-April to mid-September.

Variation: None. Sexes alike.

Habitat: Prefers open fields and pastures in rural areas. In urban settings it likes open parks and large empty lots. Commonly seen perched on fences.

Breeding: Sturdy nest is placed on limb near the top of large tree. The nest is built of twigs and grass. The average clutch size is three to five eggs. One clutch per year.

Natural History: The name "Kingbird" is derived from this species' aggressive defense of territory against other birds, including even large hawks! They hunt flying insects from an open perch, which is frequently a fence or power line. When flying insect prey is spotted they will launch themselves into an attack that often results in an aerial "dogfight" between bird and insect. Berries are an important food item. These are conspicuous birds. Their charcoal gray upper parts contrast strongly with a whitish breast and belly. The bright reddish-orange blaze on the top of the head is usually not visible to the casual observer. Some populations in the eastern United States have shown declines in the last few decades.

Size: 8.75 inches.

Abundance: Fairly common.

Migratory Status: A summertime resident of Kentucky. Arrives in Kentucky in late April or early May. Winters in Central America, Mexico, or southern Florida.

Variation: None. Sexes alike.

Habitat: Deciduous and mixed woodlands. Favors small woods openings and edge areas. Usually with some large trees present. Winter habitat is tropical forests of many types.

Breeding: Unlike most flycatchers this bird is a cavity nester, often using old woodpecker holes. Three to five eggs, laid in mid-May, is typical.

Natural History: The name comes from the "crested" look of the head, which may not be readily apparent. Reddish underside of the tail and wing primaries along with the distinctly yellowish belly contrasting with gray breast is unique among Kentucky flycatchers. These features plus large size make it one of the more recognizable members of the flycatcher family. Feeds on large insects captured in flight from its perch, which is often high in the canopy. In Kentucky this species is more common in the western end of the state. Returns to Kentucky in late April from wintering grounds in Central America. Forages for insects in treetops and catches flying insects on the wing.

Class—**Aves** (birds)

Order—**Passeriformes** (songbirds)

Family—**Turdidae** (thrush family)

Robin *Turdus migratorius*	**Eastern Bluebird** *Siala sialis*	**Wood Thrush** *Hylocichla mustela*

Presumed range in Kentucky	Presumed range in Kentucky	Presumed range in Kentucky
Size: 10 inches.	**Size:** 7 inches.	**Size:** 7.75 inches.
Abundance: Very common.	**Abundance:** Common.	**Abundance:** Fairly common.
Migratory Status: Robins are most common in spring and summer months but they can be seen year-round in most of the state.	**Migratory Status:** Farther to the north the Bluebird is a summer only resident, but in Kentucky they are often present year-round.	**Migratory Status:** A summer resident that winters in Central America and even as far as south as northern South America.
Variation: Females are less brightly colored with browner backs and paler breasts.	**Variation:** In the Eastern Bluebird the male is more vividly colored than the female (see photos above).	**Variation:** No variation. Sexes alike. The lack of sexual dimorphism is a trait shared with many thrush species.
Habitat: Virtually all habitats in the state may be utilized. Most common in areas of human disturbance, especially older suburbs. They are fond of hunting earthworms in suburban lawns.	**Habitat:** Field edges, woods openings, and open fields, marshes, and pastures. Savanna like habitats, i.e. open spaces interspersed with large trees, are a favorite habitat.	**Habitat:** Woodlands. May be found in both mature forests and successional areas. In both it likes thick undergrowth. The Appalachian Plateau Province offers the most habitat in Kentucky today.
Breeding: The three to four "sky blue" eggs are laid in a nest constructed of mud and grass, often in the crotch of a tree in an urban yard.	**Breeding:** Bluebirds are cavity nesters that readily take to man-made nest boxes. Two broods per summer is common in Kentucky. Three to six eggs per clutch.	**Breeding:** Nest is mud, twigs, and grass similar to that of the Robin. Nest may be in under story or at mid-level. Lays two to five blue-green eggs.
Natural History: Despite the fact that the Robin is a migratory species, individuals are seen in Kentucky year-round. It is likely that the state's summer residents retreat south during winter and are replaced by southward moving individuals that have summered much farther to the north. In winter they are sometimes seen in large migratory flocks numbering over 100 birds. Perhaps the best known of Kentucky's bird species, Robins are commonly seen on both urban and rural lawns throughout the state. Feeds heavily on earthworms.	**Natural History:** The Eastern Bluebirds habit of readily adapting to artificial nest boxes has helped bring them back from alarmingly low numbers decades ago, when rampant logging of eastern forests depleted nest cavities. They are primarily insect eaters and are vulnerable to exceptionally harsh winters. In winter Bluebirds eat many types of berries and will readily eat raisins from feeders. Their popularity among humans has lead to the establishment of the North American Bluebird Society, dedicated to Bluebird conservation.	**Natural History:** The Wood Thrush feeds on insects, spiders, earthworms, and other invertebrates found by foraging beneath leaf mold on the forest floor. They will also feed on berries, which can be an important food during fall migration. Like many songbirds this species is threatened by the fragmentation of forest habitats throughout North America. Smaller forest tracts make it easier for cowbirds to find Wood Thrush nests. Consequently nest predation by cowbirds is increasing and has been noted in Kentucky.

Class—**Aves** (birds)

Order—**Passeriformes** (songbirds)

Family—**Turdidae** (thrush family)

Hermit Thrush *Catharus guttatus*	**Veery** *Catharus fuscescens*	**Swainson's Thrush** *Catharus ustulatus*

Presumed range in Kentucky	Presumed range in Kentucky	Presumed range in Kentucky

Size: 7 inches	**Size:** 7 inches..	**Size:** 7 inches.
Abundance: Fairly common.	**Abundance:** Uncommon.	**Abundance:** Fairly common.
Migratory Status: In reverse from most thrushes, the Hermit Thrush is seen in Kentucky mostly in the winter. It breeds far to the north in summer.	**Migratory Status:** Spring and fall migrant throughout most of the state. A few will summer in the high mountains of southeastern Kentucky.	**Migratory Status:** Spring and fall migrant. Winters in South America and summers far to the north in Canada and even Alaska.
Variation: Individuals will vary slightly from reddish brown to grayish brown. Several subspecies are known.	**Variation:** Kentucky specimens are reddish, those from farther west are duller, more brownish.	**Variation:** Slight variation in eastern vs. western populations. No significant variation occurs in Kentucky.
Habitat: Damp woodlands, thickets, and successional areas with heavy undergrowth.	**Habitat:** Under story of deciduous woodlands. Most common in second growth forest with thick undergrowth.	**Habitat:** Moist to wet woodlands and swamps with heavy underbrush and cool, heavily shaded woods.
Breeding: Three to five bluish-green eggs are laid in a nest built just above ground level. Birds seen in Kentucky in winter nest in the boreal forests of Canada.	**Breeding:** Breeds mostly well to the north of Kentucky. Nest is hidden in thickets on or near the ground. From three to five eggs are laid.	**Breeding:** Builds its moss-lined nest in a coniferous tree in boreal forest far to the north of Kentucky. Lays three to five eggs that are blue with brown spots.
Natural History: Any thrush seen in Kentucky during the winter will be this species. They are rather shy but less so than other *Catharus* and they will sometimes visit feeders. They feed mainly on insects found on the forest floor and beneath leaf mold, but berries are also an important element in the diet, especially in winter. The song of the Hermit Thrush is regarded by many as one of the more beautiful summer sounds in the northern forests. Although secretive their presence during winter makes them more conspicuous. Unlike most other thrush species, populations of the Hermit Thrush appear stable.	**Natural History:** Although the Veery is widespread during migration, they are hard to observe in Kentucky since they are usually just passing through and they migrate mostly at night. One of the more secretive of the thrushes, they stay mostly in thick undergrowth where they feed on a variety of insects, earthworms, spiders, and berries. Bird watchers often confirm this bird's presence by recognizing its distinctive call, which has been described as "hauntingly beautiful." Most Veerys seen in Kentucky are just passing through, but some nesting has been observed in the Cumberland Mountains ecoregion.	**Natural History:** Another secretive, difficult to observe thrush that in migration flies by night and spends its days resting and feeding in heavy undergrowth. As with many of the thrushes, positive identification can be difficult. This species and the Gray-cheeked Thrush are easily confused. The buff colored cheeks are a good identification character. Like others of its kind, the Swainson's Thrush feeds on insects and invertebrates as well as berries. Unlike others of its genus, however, this thrush is known to feed higher in trees (most other thrushes feed mostly on the ground).

Class—**Aves** (birds)

Order—**Passeriformes** (songbirds)

Family—**Turdidae** (thrush family)	Family—**Lanidae** (shrikes)	Family—**Alauidae** (larks)
Gray-cheeked Thrush *Catharus minimus*	**Loggerhead Shrike** *Lanius ludovicianus*	**Horned Lark** *Eremophila alpestris*

 Presumed range in Kentucky	 Presumed range in Kentucky	 Presumed range in Kentucky
Size: 7.25 inches.	**Size:** 9 inches.	**Size:** 7.5 inches.
Abundance: Uncommon.	**Abundance:** Uncommon.	**Abundance:** Fairly common.
Migratory Status: A secretive spring and fall nighttime migrant that is easily missed. Summers as far north as Alaska and Siberia.	**Migratory Status:** A year-round resident in the Coastal Plain of Kentucky. In the rest of the state it may retreat its farther south in harsh winters.	**Migratory Status:** Year-round, but much more common during winter months as resident populations are supplemented by birds from farther north.
Variation: Overall coloration varies from grayish to slightly brownish.	**Variation:** No subspecies in Kentucky and sexes are alike.	**Variation:** Sexes alike, immatures are duller.
Habitat: Summer habitats are boreal forests. Winters in South America. May be seen in woodlands throughout the state during migration.	**Habitat:** Open to semi-open habitats are preferred. In Kentucky this species avoids the Appalachian Plateau in favor of more open habitats to the west.	**Habitat:** This is a prairie species that is seen only in expansive, open fields. Large, harvested crop fields are the primary habitat for this bird in Kentucky.
Breeding: Breeds in remote tundra and taiga in northern Canada and Alaska. Lays three to six eggs.	**Breeding:** Shrikes build a bulky nest of sticks in a thick bush or small tree. Lays up to seven eggs.	**Breeding:** Nests on barren ground. Lays three to five eggs. Most breed far to the north, but some breed in Kentucky.
Natural History: Secretive and uncommon, the biology of the Gray-cheeked Thrush is poorly known. Its summer habitats are dense spruce forests and willow-alder thickets in the far north. Breeding range extends well into the Arctic Circle and winter range is at least as far south as northern South America. Differentiating between the various thrush species can be challenging. The Gray-cheeked Thrush is easily confused with both the Swainson's Thrush and the Hermit Thrush but can be told by the gray color of the cheek. The Bicknell's Thrush of the eastern seaboard was once regarded as a subspecies of this bird.	**Natural History:** These fierce little birds are much like a miniature raptor. They hunt mostly insects, but will also attack and kill lizards, mice, small snakes, and birds as large as themselves. Sometimes called "Butcher Bird," they kill with a powerful beak and have the unusual habit of caching food items by impaling the bodies of prey onto a thorn or fence barb. They will form permanent territories that they defend from other shrikes. An endemic North American bird, Loggerhead Shrikes range from south-central Canada to southern Mexico. Sadly, this unique species is declining throughout its range. Most experts blame agricultural practices.	**Natural History:** This prairie species needs open ground and has probably moved into Kentucky as a result of human habitat alterations. Closely cropped pastures or tilled lands are used almost exclusively within the state. Except during nesting, these are gregarious birds that are nearly always seen in flocks. They feed on small seeds and tiny arthropods gleaned from what may appear to be nearly barren ground. Harvested agricultural fields, gravel bars, and other open lands are utilized. Like the American Pipit with which it sometimes associates, the Horned Lark is a species that is often overlooked by Kentuckians.

Class—**Aves** (birds)		
Order—**Passeriformes** (songbirds)		
Family—**Mimidae** (thrasher family)		
Mockingbird *Mimus polyglotos*	**Gray Catbird** *Dumetella carolinensis*	**Brown Thrasher** *Toxostoma rufum*

Presumed range in Kentucky

Presumed range in Kentucky

Presumed range in Kentucky

Size: 10.5 inches.	**Size:** 8.5 inches.	**Size:** 11.5 inches.
Abundance: Common.	**Abundance:** Fairly common.	**Abundance:** Fairly common.
Migratory Status: A year-round resident that nests in the state. Expanding its range northward into southern Canada.	**Migratory Status:** Spring, summer, and fall only. Winters from southern United States south to Central America.	**Migratory Status:** Found year round in western KY. Birds in the rest of the state retreat farther south in the winter.
Variation: None. Sexes alike.	**Variation:** None. Sexes alike.	**Variation:** No variation. Sexes alike.
Habitat: Prefers semi-open habitats with some cover in the form of bushes and shrubs. Common in both rural and urban environments. During colder months they are usually found in the vicinity of berry producing plants.	**Habitat:** Edge areas, thickets, and overgrown fence rows are this bird's preferred habitat. In urban areas it is often found in older neighborhoods containing landscapes overgrown with large bushes and shrubs.	**Habitat:** Edges of woods, thickets, fence rows, overgrown fields and successional areas. Suburban lawns that have adequate cover in the form of bushes & shrubs may also be used. Avoids deep woods.
Breeding: The nest is made of sticks and is usually in a thick bush or small tree. Three to four eggs are laid and more than one nesting per season is usual.	**Breeding:** The loosely constructed nest is made of sticks, vines, and leaves placed in dense bushes. Three to four eggs is common.	**Breeding:** Builds a stick nest in the heart of a dense shrub, usually within a few feet of the ground. Lays two to five eggs in late spring.
Natural History: The name "Mocking Bird" is derived from this birds habit of mimicking the calls of other birds, and they have a huge repertoire of songs. They are known to mimic the calls of everything from warblers to blue jays and even large hawks. New songs are learned throughout their life and the number of different songs recorded by this species is up to 150. They feed largely on insects, but in the winter will switch to berries and fruits. Mockingbirds have a reputation among rural folk as a useful bird that will chase away other pesky birds such as blackbirds and other species that can be garden pests.	**Natural History:** The Gray Catbird is much more secretive than its relative the Mockingbird. Food includes all manner of insects, spiders, larva, and berries. Named for their call which sounds remarkably like a meowing cat, these shy birds are often heard but unseen as they "meow" from beneath a dense shrub. Like their cousins the Mockingbirds, Catbirds are accomplished mimics of other bird species. In Kentucky they are more common in the eastern part of the state. They winter along the lower coastal plain of the U.S., Florida, the Caribbean, Mexico, and Central America.	**Natural History:** During warm weather the Brown Thrasher feeds on insects and small invertebrates of all types. It uses its long bill to overturn leaves and debris beneath trees and shrubs and also actively hunts in the grass of urban lawns. In winter they will eat berries. During the breeding season males perch atop bushes or small trees and serenade all within earshot with their song. Though the Brown Thrasher lacks the repertoire of its cousin the Mockingbird, it does possess one of the most varied song collections of any bird in America. In Kentucky, these birds are least abundant in the east.

Class—**Aves** (birds)

Order—**Passeriformes** (songbirds)

Family—**Motacillidae** (wagtails)	Family—**Paridae** (chickadee family)	
American Pipit *Anthus rubescens*	**Carolina Chickadee** *Poecile carolinensis*	**Tufted Titmouse** *Baeolophus bicolor*

Presumed range in Kentucky

Presumed range in Kentucky

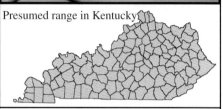
Presumed range in Kentucky

American Pipit	Carolina Chickadee	Tufted Titmouse
Size: 6.5 inches.	**Size:** 4.75 inches.	**Size:** 6 inches.
Abundance: Uncommon.	**Abundance:** Very common.	**Abundance:** Very common.
Migratory Status: Mostly a migrant seen during spring and fall, but also can sometimes be seen in winter.	**Migratory Status:** A year-round resident that is much more conspicuous in winter when it visits feeders for seeds.	**Migratory Status:** A year-round resident. Like the Chickadee this species is common at seed feeders during winter.
Variation: Significant seasonal plumage changes. Winter birds are as above.	**Variation:** No significant variation and the sexes are alike.	**Variation:** No significant variation and the sexes are alike.
Habitat: In Kentucky the American Pipit is usually seen in expansive open areas such as harvested croplands or mudflats.	**Habitat:** Primarily a woodland species but may be found anywhere so long as at least a few trees are present. Found in both urban and rural areas.	**Habitat:** Small woodlots and successional areas. Favors edge habitats. Common in both rural and urban habitats.
Breeding: Breeds in tundra areas and southward into the higher altitudes of the Rocky Mountains. Lays three to seven eggs in a nest on the ground.	**Breeding:** Nests in hollow limbs, rotted fence posts, old woodpecker holes, or man-made nest boxes. Lays four to six eggs in April or May.	**Breeding:** This species is a cavity nester that will utilize natural cavities as well as old woodpecker holes. Average of five eggs.
Natural History: The American Pipit is a hardy species that nests in America's coldest climates. They move south in the winter where they are easily overlooked. Their mottled brown winter plumage is highly cryptic, especially where they usually reside in expansive, open fields or mudflats. In the western end of the state they may be seen throughout the winter, often in company with flocks of Horned Larks or rarely with Lapland Longspurs (another winter migrant from the far north). A small, brownish bird seen in Kentucky in winter on barren ground, that characteristically wags its tail up and down, is likely to be this species.	**Natural History:** One of Kentucky's smallest songbirds, the Carolina Chickadee is a familiar bird at feeders throughout the state. They will become quite acclimated to people and with some patient coaxing they may be induced to land upon an outstretch hand containing sunflower seeds. An acrobatic little bird when searching for insect prey, they can dangle upside down from tiny branches. Their whistling song and their "chick-a-dee-dee-dee" call is distinctive and they can be quite noisy at times. In winter they will form mixed flocks with other small birds. They are hyperactive, tiny birds that have high energy requirements. Winter mortality can be high.	**Natural History:** Primarily a seed eater in winter, the Tufted Titmouse is one of the first birds to find a new bird feeder. Sunflower seeds are favored, but they also love peanuts. Like Chickadees they are sometimes quite bold around humans servicing feeders. In warm months they forage for small insects and spiders among the foliage of trees. They can sometimes be seen hanging upside down on a small branch or leaf as they search for prey. Their familiar song is a melodic "birdy-birdy-birdy." In winter they mix readily with Chickadees and other small birds. Their range corresponds closely to the Eastern Temperate Forest Level I Ecoregion.

Class—**Aves** (birds)

Order—**Passeriformes** (songbirds)

Family—**Bombycillidae** (waxwings)	Family—**Sittidae** (nuthatches)	
Cedar Waxwing *Bombycilla cedrorum*	**White-breasted Nuthatch** *Sitta carolinensis*	**Red-breasted Nuthatch** *Sitta canadensis*

Presumed range in Kentucky

Presumed range in Kentucky

Presumed range in Kentucky

Size: 7 inches.	**Size:** 5.75 inches.	**Size:** 4.5 inches.
Abundance: Uncommon.	**Abundance:** Fairly common.	**Abundance:** Uncommon in Kentucky.
Migratory Status: Can be seen year-round but is probably most common in Kentucky in the spring.	**Migratory Status:** The White-breasted Nuthatch is a year-round resident in Kentucky.	**Migratory Status:** Red-breasted Nuthatches are fall and winter migrants in Kentucky, summering in the far north.
Variation: No variation.	**Variation:** None.	**Variation:** No variation.
Habitat: Found both in forests and semi-open country. May be seen in both rural and urban settings.	**Habitat:** This is a bird of deciduous and mixed woodlands. Mature forests are preferred.	**Habitat:** Summers in the coniferous forests of the north and west. Occupies deciduous woodlands in Kentucky.
Breeding: Builds a nest of grasses. Nest site is typically high on a tree branch. Lays three to five eggs.	**Breeding:** Nests in natural tree cavities or woodpecker holes. Averages six eggs per clutch.	**Breeding:** Cavity nesters that excavate their own nest holes in the manner of woodpeckers. Average of six eggs.
Natural History: Waxwings are named for the peculiar red-colored waxy feathers on their wings. The name "Cedar" Waxwing comes from their propensity for Eastern Red Cedar trees where they consume large quantities of cedar berries. These birds are highly social and are usually seen in large flocks. They feed mostly on berries and wander relentlessly in search of this favored food item. In summer insects, mulberries and serviceberries are important food items. Crabapples and other fruiting trees are also favored. They are highly irregular in occurrence but are frequently seen across the state as they rove around in search of food sources. In Kentucky they are least common in the Coastal Plain. This may be due to a relative lack of Eastern Red Cedar trees.	**Natural History:** Nuthatches are famous for foraging tree trunks in an upside down position. This behavior gives them the opportunity to occupy a different feeding niche from woodpeckers and other bark hunting birds that may miss insects hidden in crevices visible only from an above perspective. In addition to insects they also eat seeds and are regulars at most bird feeders in the state. They will cache seeds in bark crevices and they tend to be quite territorial. Pairs will stake out a territory and typically live within that area throughout the year. One of four species of nuthatch found in North America and the only one that is a full-time inhabitant of deciduous woodlands. Other species occupy boreal forests, southern pine forests, and western pine forests.	**Natural History:** These birds usually appear in Kentucky in large numbers only every second or third winter and the exact mechanism of their irruptive movements remains something of a mystery. It is believed to be related to cone production in northern coniferous forests where this species usually lives. During the spring and summer the Red-breasted Nuthatch feeds entirely on small arthropods. Seeds are the staple food during winter and sunflower seeds are a favorite item at bird feeders. They will wedge seeds into bark crevices to hold them fast while using the beak to hammer open the shell in characteristic "nuthatch" fashion. They will glean insects from bark in the same upside-down manner as their larger cousin the White-breasted Nuthatch.

Class—**Aves** (birds)

Order—**Passeriformes** (songbirds)

Family—**Certhiidae** (creepers)	Family—**Regulidae** (kinglets)	
Brown Creeper *Certhia americana*	**Ruby-crowned Kinglet** *Regulus calendula*	**Golden-crowned Kinglet** *Regulus satrapa*

Presumed range in Kentucky

Presumed range in Kentucky

Presumed range in Kentucky

Size: 5.25 inches.

Size: 4.25 inches.

Size: 4 inches.

Abundance: Uncommon.

Abundance: Uncommon in Kentucky.

Abundance: Fairly common.

Migratory Status: The Brown Creeper is a northern species that migrates southward into Kentucky as part of its winter range. A few have bred in the state.

Migratory Status: Winter migrant. The bulk of the population will winter south of Kentucky, but some can be seen throughout the state each winter.

Migratory Status: Another winter resident in Kentucky that usually arrives from up north in November. May move on farther south if winter is harsh.

Variation: No variation and the sexes are alike.

Variation: Male has red stripe on head that is visible when excited.

Variation: Males have orange crown, females (shown) have yellow crown.

Habitat: This is a forest species that prefers mature woodlands with large trees for breeding. In winter they are also seen in second growth forests, old orchards, swamps, and other habitats.

Habitat: Summer habitat is undisturbed boreal forests. Winter habitats much more generalized to include deciduous and mixed woodlands as well as swamps and lowlands.

Habitat: This species summers in the spruce/fir forests of Canada and winters in a wide variety of habitats across most of the eastern United States. Most common in woodlands.

Breeding: The nest is nearly always built behind a piece of loose bark on the trunk of a large dead tree. Five or six eggs is typical.

Breeding: Breeds in old growth conifers in the far north. Produces enormous clutches of up to 12 eggs. Nest is built near the tops of spruce trees.

Breeding: Builds its nest in the top of a spruce or fir in northern woodlands. Lays a large clutch of up to 11 eggs and may produce two broods per year.

Natural History: Brown Creepers feed on small insects, spiders, etc., found in tree-trunk bark crevices. They have the peculiar foraging habit of landing on the trunk at the base of the tree and "creeping" upward, spiraling around the tree as they go. When they reach a certain height, they fly down to the base of another nearby tree and begin again. In Kentucky, the Brown Creeper is a bit of a loner, and it is rare to see more than two in any one area. The only representative of the creeper family found in North America. A few cases of nesting in Kentucky has been reported.

Natural History: This is one of America's smallest songbird species, smaller even than the Chickadee. The bright red blaze on the top of the head of the male is usually not visible. In summer they prey on arthropods and their eggs. In winter they will also feed on berries and some seeds. They are hyperactive little birds that forage throughout the canopy as well as along lower branches. Flicks wings open and shut while in near constant motion. Hunts mostly along the tips of smaller branches. Some studies suggest this species may be declining in the eastern United States.

Natural History: Even smaller than its cousin the Ruby-crowned Kinglet, the Golden-crowned is a hardier bird that can tolerate colder winter weather. However severe winter conditions can lead to near 100 percent mortality in localized areas. Amazingly, this carnivore manages to find insect prey throughout the winter and does not switch to seeds and berries in colder weather. Hyperactive and always in motion. They often feed by "leaf hawking" (hovering while picking tiny insects from beneath a leaves). In winter they are often seen in small groups or mixed flocks.

Class—**Aves** (birds)

Order—**Passeriformes** (songbirds)

Family—**Troglodytidae** (wrens)

Carolina Wren *Thryothorus ludovicianus*	**Bewick's Wren** *Thryothorus bewickii*	**Marsh Wren** *Cistothorus palustris*

Presumed range in Kentucky	Presumed range in Kentucky	Presumed range in Kentucky
Size: 5.5 inches.	**Size:** 5.25 inches.	**Size:** 5 inches.
Abundance: Common.	**Abundance:** Very rare in Kentucky.	**Abundance:** Uncommon.
Migratory Status: Carolina Wrens are found throughout the year in Kentucky.	**Migratory Status:** Mostly a spring and summer resident.	**Migratory Status:** Mostly a transient species that passes through on migration.
Variation: No variation, sexes alike.	**Variation:** None.	**Variation:** None in Kentucky.
Habitat: Carolina Wrens are very flexible in habitat choices. They can be seen in remote wilderness or in suburban backyards.	**Habitat:** Prefers semi-open lands and human altered habitats. Can be found in both rural and suburban environments. More common to the west of Kentucky.	**Habitat:** Pastures, marshes, and lowland meadows as well as open, grassy edges of wetlands or ponds. Coastal salt marshes are widely used in winter.
Breeding: A nest of fine twigs and grass is built in a sheltered place, often provided by man. Eggs number three to six. Will produce at least two clutches per year.	**Breeding:** Breeding in Kentucky is from April through July with two broods sometimes reported. Nesting is similar to the Carolina Wren with artificial nest sites near human habitations preferred.	**Breeding:** Nest is low in grasses or small bush. Nest is built of grasses woven into a ball with an entrance hole in the side. Several unused "decoy" nests are built. Seven eggs is typical.
Natural History: The most common wren in Kentucky, the Carolina Wren is well known for building its nest in an old pair of shoes or in an vase of flowers left on the back porch for a few days. They will become quite tame around yards and porches and frequently endear themselves to their human neighbors. They are voracious consumers of insects, spiders, and caterpillars and help control insect pests around the home. They are also incessant singers whose musical song serves as a dawn alarm for many residents throughout the state. Although vulnerable to harsh winters, Carolina Wrens are expanding their range northward, perhaps in response to climate change.	**Natural History:** Bewick's Wren was apparently once much more widespread and common but has been in decline for at least the last five decades. The bulk of its range today is west of the Mississippi River. In Kentucky its distribution is very spotty and it is absent from many areas within the range shown on the map above. Most Kentucky birds will leave for warmer climates in the winter, but a few may persist throughout the year. Very similar to the Carolina Wren, from which it may be told by the grayer breast (as opposed to buff) and the white spots on the tail. Like other wrens, the Bewick's Wren actively forages for invertebrate prey and consumes large quantities of arthropod pests.	**Natural History:** Marsh Wrens winter mostly to the south of Kentucky and summer to north of Kentucky. They may be seen anywhere in Kentucky where suitable habitat exists during migration periods. A few birds have been seen in the western tip of the state in winter, mostly in Mississippi Alluvial Plain. Known food items are insects and spiders. A similar wren species, the **Sedge Wren** (*C. palustris*), can also be seen in Kentucky during spring/fall migration. Like the Marsh Wren it winters well to the south of Kentucky and summers to the north, but a few individuals may be seen throughout the summer and some breeding of Sedge Wrens has been recorded in north-central Kentucky.

Class—**Aves** (birds)

Order—**Passeriformes** (songbirds)

Family—**Troglodytidae** (wrens)		Family—**Polioptilidae** (gnatcathers)
House Wren *Troglodytes aedon*	**Winter Wren** *Troglodytes troglodytes*	**Blue-gray Gnatcatcher** *Polioptila caerulea*

Presumed range in Kentucky	Presumed range in Kentucky	Presumed range in Kentucky
Size: 4.75 inches.	**Size:** 4 inches.	**Size:** 4.25 inches.
Abundance: Fairly common.	**Abundance:** Uncommon.	**Abundance:** Fairly common.
Migratory Status: A spring/summer resident that arrives in Kentucky in April.	**Migratory Status:** In Kentucky this is a winter resident. Lingers then moves farther south in harsh winter weather.	**Migratory Status:** One of the earliest returning summer birds, arriving in Kentucky each spring as early as mid-March.
Variation: No variation.	**Variation:** No variation.	**Variation:** No variation. Sexes alike.
Habitat: Prefers open and semi-open habitats. These wrens readily associate with humans and are most common in small towns and suburbs.	**Habitat:** Mature, old growth forests are the primary summer habitat. Deciduous and mixed woodlands are utilized in winter, but conifers are preferred.	**Habitat:** Occupies a wide variety of forested or successional habitats. Most common along wooded streams and bottoms.
Breeding: A cavity nester, the House Wren readily takes to artificial nest boxes. In fact, this species may owe its increase in population to man-made "bird houses." Lays up to eight eggs.	**Breeding:** Breeds well to the north of Kentucky, mainly in the boreal forests of Canada. Nest is often constructed in the root wad of an upturned tree. Lays five to nine eggs.	**Breeding:** Nest is a cup-like structure built with lichens and plant fibers glued together with spiderweb. Nest usually placed at mid-level near the terminus of a branch. Four to five eggs is average.
Natural History: Although the House Wren may be seen anywhere in Kentucky, it is by far most common in the Bluegrass Region of the Interior Low Plateau Province. It is least common in the high mountains of the eastern end of the state. They are more common today than in historical times, as they favor open and semi-open habitats over dense forests. They also have a strong affinity for human altered habitats and settlements. They feed on a wide variety of insects, spiders, snails, caterpillars, etc., and when feeding large broods of young they catch huge quantities daily. House Wrens range from coast to coast across America. The bulk of the population breeds to the north and west of KY.	**Natural History:** Much shyer and more secretive than other wrens, the Winter Wren skulks about under dense bushes and shrubs where it tends to stay close to the ground. This species has likely declined since presettlement times due to the destruction of ancient forests. Like other wrens, these birds are strictly carnivorous and feed on a wide variety of small insects, larva, arachnids, amphipoda, etc. Their stubby, upturned tail makes identification easy, but they are more often heard than seen as they are persistent, loud singers. Winter Wrens are Holarctic in distribution, being found in Europe and northern Asia as well as North America. This is a species that is easily overlooked.	**Natural History:** As their name implies gnatcatchers feed on tiny prey. Any type of small arthropod is probable food item. They hunt the tips of tree branches and sometimes pick off prey while hovering. Despite their small size they will chase away larger birds and will mob predators such as hawks, snakes, or house cats. The gnatcatchers are a unique family that is probably most closely related to the wrens. Like many small songbird species the Blue-gray Gnatcatcher is often the victim of nest parasitism by the Brown-headed Cowbird, which lays its eggs in other birds' nests. Breeding pairs are quite territorial, and males will chase away other small songbirds.

Class—**Aves** (birds)

Order—**Passeriformes** (songbirds)

Family—**Hirundinidae** (Swallows)

Barn Swallow *Hirundo rustica*	**Cliff Swallow** *Petrochelidon pyrrhonota*	**Bank Swallow** *Riparia riparia*

Presumed range in Kentucky 	Presumed range in Kentucky 	Presumed range in Kentucky 
Size: 7 inches.	**Size:** 5.5 inches.	**Size:** 4.75 inches.
Abundance: Common.	**Abundance:** Uncommon in Kentucky.	**Abundance:** Uncommon in Kentucky.
Migratory Status: A summer resident that returns to the state in early April.	**Migratory Status:** Returns to Kentucky from South America around mid-April.	**Migratory Status:** Summer resident that winters in South America.
Variation: Male slightly more vivid.	**Variation:** No variation. Sexes alike.	**Variation:** No variation. Sexes alike.
Habitat: Open and semi-open habitats. Most common in agricultural areas but found virtually everywhere in the state.	**Habitat:** Open areas near large bodies of water are the preferred habitat for this species in Kentucky.	**Habitat:** Open country near large rivers. Cliff banks are a requirement for breeding.
Breeding: Nest is bowl shaped and made of mud and grasses plastered to roof joists of a barn or eaves of buildings, beneath concrete bridges, etc.	**Breeding:** In Kentucky mud nests are plastered beneath sheltered overhangs of concrete structures such as bridges or dams. Four eggs is typical.	**Breeding:** In Kentucky this species nests in banks along major rivers. Nest hole is dug by the parents and may be as much as two to three feet deep. Four to six eggs.
Natural History: A familiar bird to all who grew up on rural farmsteads. Barn Swallows are common throughout most of North America in summer, and birds that summer in the U.S. winter in Central and South America. European breeders winter in the Mediterranean, Africa, and the Middle East while Asian breeding birds winter throughout southeast Asia to Australia. Thus this is one of the most widespread bird species in the world. Its long association with humans throughout the world has led to the invention of many legends. Barn Swallows nesting in your barn was considered by pioneers as good luck, while destroying a nest in the barn would cause the milk cow to go dry. Flying insects are the main food including pesky flies and even wasps.	**Natural History:** The Cliff Swallow is primarily a western species that nested on cliff faces in the Rocky Mountains. They are more numerous in Kentucky today than even a few decades ago. Man-made structures such as dams and bridges have likely helped this species expand its range in the eastern U.S. and in Kentucky. These birds are colony animals that seem to always nest in groups. In Kentucky there seems to be a preference for nesting near water, and colony size varies from a few dozen to a few hundred nests. Farther west, where the species is more common and widespread, colonies consisting of several thousand nests are known. Like other swallows they feed almost entirely upon airborne insects, and they are adept at locating swarms of airborne prey.	**Natural History:** Although widespread across America during migration, this species is rare in Kentucky. Like many swallows the Bank Swallow nests in large communities. Nest colonies are usually associated with large river systems. Despite being somewhat rare in Kentucky, these birds are found throughout the world; in fact they are one of the most widespread bird species on earth. The natural nesting habitat has always been riverbanks and bluffs, but today this species utilizes the banks created by man-made quarries. During migration Bank Swallows can be seen in the company of other species of migrating swallows. Food is exclusively flying insects caught on the wing—mostly flies, flying ants, small beetles, and mayflies.

Class—**Aves** (birds)

Order—**Passeriformes** (songbirds)

Family—**Hirundinidae** (swallows)

Northern Rough-winged Swallow *Stelgidopteryx serripennis*	Tree Swallow *Tachycineta bicolor*	Purple Martin *Progne subis*

Presumed range in Kentucky	Presumed range in Kentucky	Presumed range in Kentucky
Size: 5.5 inches.	**Size:** 5.75 inches.	**Size:** 8 inches.
Abundance: Fairly common.	**Abundance:** Fairly common.	**Abundance:** Fairly common.
Migratory Status: Summer resident wintering in south Florida and Central America.	**Migratory Status:** A warm-weather bird that arrives in Kentucky as early as March after wintering well to the south.	**Migratory Status:** Summer resident. The first arriving birds are males and they may arrive as early as March.
Variation: Sexes alike. No significant variation among individuals.	**Variation:** Sexes alike. Immatures are glossy gray for the first year.	**Variation:** Females are gray-brown and have whitish bellies (above left).
Habitat: Mainly open and semi-open areas, but can be found in forested regions along rivers or cliffs.	**Habitat:** Open and semi-open habitats. Fond of being near water, including small farm ponds and Beaver swamps.	**Habitat:** Inhabits both rural areas and suburbs. Artificial nest boxes near water in open areas are attractants.
Breeding: Nests in crevices in rock faces, cliffs, etc. Today often uses man-made situations such as road cuts, quarries, etc. Not a colony nester. Lays four to eight eggs.	**Breeding:** A cavity nester, Tree Swallows will use old woodpecker holes or tree hollows. They also use artificial nest boxes and sometimes nest in close proximity to Purple Martins.	**Breeding:** Originally nested in natural cavities but today nearly all use artificial nest sites. Three to six eggs is typical but may lay as many as seven or eight. Purple Martins are colony nesters.
Natural History: As with other swallows, the Rough-winged Swallow feeds by catching flying insects in mid-air. All swallows in America are diurnal hunters whose predatory role is replaced at dusk by the bats. Although this swallow is found from coast to coast across America it is not extremely common anywhere. Unlike the similar Bank Swallow, Rough-winged Swallows are not known to dig their own burrow, and availability of nest burrows may be one reason why these swallows tend to be solitary nesters. They will use burrows dug by other species of birds or small mammals as well as natural cavities in cliff faces or even man-made structures.	**Natural History:** Tree Swallows are more numerous in Kentucky today than in historical times and are increasing in numbers in the state. Human activities have benefited this species in Kentucky by creating more open lands and also by creating more ponds and lakes throughout the landscape. The proliferation of artificial nest boxes has also helped and the resurgence of Beaver populations is also credited with helping this and many other species. Flying insects are the primary food items, but this species also eats bayberries during the winter. They are also known to eat snails during the breeding season to obtain calcium for eggshell production.	**Natural History:** Our largest swallow and perhaps the most beloved bird in America. Many people anxiously await the return of Purple Martins each spring to nest boxes erected in their yard. This bird's relationship with humans extends at least as far back as the 18th century and today there are at least two national organizations dedicated to Purple Martin enthusiasts. House Sparrows and Starlings sometimes take over "martin houses" unless the landowner is vigilant. Mainly a warm weather species that is dependent upon flying insect prey, Purple Martins are vulnerable to spring cold fronts in the more northern reaches of the summer range.

Class—**Aves** (birds)

Order—**Passeriformes** (songbirds)

Family—**Corvidae** (crow family)

Blue Jay *Cyanocitta cristata*	**American Crow** *Corvus brachyrhynchos*	**Fish Crow** *Corvus ossifragus*

 Presumed range in Kentucky	 Presumed range in Kentucky	 Presumed range in Kentucky
Size: 11 inches.	**Size:** 19 inches.	**Size:** 17 inches.
Abundance: Common.	**Abundance:** Common.	**Abundance:** Rare.
Migratory Status: A few may move south during the winter, but most Blue Jays are permanent residents in KY.	**Migratory Status:** Many are year-round residents, but numbers are increased in winter by migratory birds from up north.	**Migratory Status:** Summer migrant that winters in the lower coastal plain. Seen in Kentucky spring through fall.
Variation: None. Sexes alike.	**Variation:** No variation.	**Variation:** None.
Habitat: State-wide from dense woodlands to semi-open farmlands. Also suburban and urban neighborhoods. Woodlands are the favored habitat.	**Habitat:** Occurs in virtually all habitats including urban areas. Most common where there is a patchwork of woods and open spaces.	**Habitat:** In Kentucky the Fish Crow is restricted to the floodplains of the Mississippi and Ohio Rivers, as well as near the mouths of tributaries.
Breeding: Builds a stick nest fairly high up on a branch or in a fork. Lays an average of four eggs.	**Breeding:** Crows build a bulky stick nest high in the fork of a tree, well hidden by thick foliage. Four eggs is typical.	**Breeding:** Large stick nest is placed in a tree crotch. Averages about four eggs. A single clutch is produced annually.
Natural History: The Blue Jay's handsome blue, black, and white feathers and distinctive crest make it one of the most recognizable birds in the state. They mainly eat insects, acorns, and grains, but also eat eggs and young of other songbirds. They will aggressively mob much larger birds like hawks and owls, as well as snakes and house cats. Members of this family are relatively long-lived. The record life span for a wild Blue Jay is 18 years, but a captive specimen was reported to have lived for 26 years. Blue Jays are found throughout the eastern half of the United States from about the Rocky Mountains eastward. They also range northward into Canada but well below the Arctic Circle.	**Natural History:** Crows are omnivores that will eat virtually anything, including the young and eggs of other birds. They are among the most intelligent and resourceful of birds. They may be seen in pairs, small groups, or large flocks numbering in the hundreds. Highly adaptable, crows have fared well in human altered habitats and the species is more common today than prior to European settlement. It is almost certain to remain a common species. As a testament to the crow's intelligence, in rural areas where hunting is commonplace, they are extremely wary of humans; while in protected parks and urban regions they will become quite accepting of the presence of humans. Longevity record for a wild bird is 17.5 years.	**Natural History:** Identical to the America Crow but smaller, the Fish Crow occurs in the western-most portion of the state. They are often seen in the company of their larger cousin, and when seen together the Fish Crow can be distinguished by its smaller size. Expert bird watchers can identify this species by its call, which is higher pitched than that of the American Crow. A southern species that historically was found in coastal areas and lowlands of the lower coastal plain, the Fish Crow has expanded its range northward over the last few decades. They were first recorded in Kentucky about fifty years ago in the Mississippi Alluvial Plain. Today they range well up into the lower Ohio River floodplain during summer.

Class—**Aves** (birds)		
Order—**Passeriformes** (songbirds)		
Family—**Corvidae** (crow family)	Family—**Vironidae** (vireos)	
Common Raven *Corvus corax*	**Yellow-throated Vireo** *Vireo flavifrons*	**White-eyed Vireo** *Vireo griseus*
 Presumed range in Kentucky	 Presumed range in Kentucky	 Presumed range in Kentucky
Size: 25 inches.	**Size:** 5.5 inches.	**Size:** 5 inches.
Abundance: Very rare in Kentucky.	**Abundance:** Uncommon in Kentucky.	**Abundance:** Fairly common.
Migratory Status: Although they are year-round residents, Ravens often have very large home ranges.	**Migratory Status:** A long-range migrant that winters as far away as northern South America. Returns to KY in April.	**Migratory Status:** Winters from the lower coastal plain to Mexico. Returns to Kentucky in late March or early April.
Variation: No variation.	**Variation:** No variation, sexes alike.	**Variation:** No variation, sexes alike.
Habitat: In Kentucky these birds are restricted to the higher mountain ranges or areas of steep cliffs bordering deep river gorges.	**Habitat:** A woodland bird that will inhabit a wide variety of forest types excluding stands of pure conifers. Prefers edge areas over interior woodlands.	**Habitat:** Dense thickets and early successional hardwoods are favored. May also be seen in later stage successional deciduous woodlands.
Breeding: Nest consists of sticks and twigs placed in a tall tree or a ledge on a cliff face. Will lay from three to seven eggs per clutch.	**Breeding:** The nest is a woven basket usually suspended from the fork of a small branch at the mid-story level. Four eggs is typical.	**Breeding:** Nest is a woven, hanging basket held together with silk from caterpillars or spiders placed in a fork very low to the ground. Three to five eggs.
Natural History: Like their relatives the crows, the ravens are intelligent, highly adaptable birds. They are found mostly in the western U.S. and in the boreal forests of the far north, but have been recorded from 13 counties in the southeastern portions of Kentucky. They are regarded as a threatened species in Kentucky, but are common and widespread elsewhere within their range. They are consummate opportunist that will consume a wide variety of plant and animal matter ranging from carrion to human garbage. They are also known for their aerial antics and flight maneuvers and for their playful mischievousness. They occupy both remote wilderness and regions of significant human habitation.	**Natural History:** The nest is usually located in a branch overhanging a forest opening such as a lane or a stream. Feeds on a wide variety of arthropods with caterpillars being a mainstay. Also eats small amount of berries and seeds in the fall. The biology of this species is not as well understood as with many other vireos, but it is known that it has decreased in numbers in areas of deforestation. As with many small woodland songbirds, the nest of the Yellow-throated Vireo is subject to parasitism by cowbirds. The summer range of this species coincides closely with the Eastern Temperate Forest Level I Ecoregion. The winter range is from southern Mexico to northern South America. Migrants regularly cross the Gulf of Mexico.	**Natural History:** This is the only vireo with a white iris, making identification easy. Nest parasitism by Brown-headed Cowbirds is estimated to be as high as 50 percent, with no young surviving in parasitized nests. Highly insectivorous. Caterpillars are a favorite food item. Will also eat fruit. White-eyed Vireos winter along the lower coastal plain of the U.S., the Caribbean, and the Yucatan Peninsula. Like the previous species, nest parasitism by Brown-headed Cowbirds posses a potential threat. Deforestation contributes to the problem. *Similar Species:* The **Bell's Vireo** (*V. bellii*) nests rarely in Kentucky. It is a plain "washed out" version of the White-eyed Vireo but has a dark iris and favors more open areas.

Class—**Aves** (birds)

Order—**Passeriformes** (songbirds)

Family—**Vironidae** (vireos)

Blue-headed Vireo *Vireo solitarius*	**Red-eyed Vireo** *Vireo olivaceus*	**Warbling Vireo & Philadelphia Vireo** *Vireo gilvus & Vireo philadelphia*

Presumed range in Kentucky	Presumed range in Kentucky	Presumed combined range of Warbling & Philadelphia Vireos in Kentucky
Size: 5.5 inches.	**Size:** 6 inches.	**Size:** 5.5 inches.
Abundance: Uncommon.	**Abundance:** Very common.	**Abundance:** Uncommon.
Migratory Status: Another summer-only resident that arrives in Kentucky in the early spring. Fall departure probably in September or even October.	**Migratory Status:** A long distance traveler that winters in the Amazon basin of South America. Appears in Kentucky from April to September.	**Migratory Status:** Arrive in Kentucky in late April after wintering in Mexico and Central America. Warbling leaves Kentucky in late summer or early fall.
Variation: No variation in Kentucky.	**Variation:** None.	**Variation:** Little variation of species.
Habitat: This vireo likes expanses of mature forests, and is also partial to conifers. It is thus found as a breeding bird in Kentucky only in the southeast portion of the state.	**Habitat:** Although a woodland species, the Red-eyed Vireo is very generalized in its habitat requirements. Mature forests, regenerating woodlands, and forest fragments are all occupied.	**Habitat:** Warbling Vireo is the found in Kentucky in semi-open habitats. Philadelphia Vireo can be found in large tracts of woodland, including (during migration) the Appalachian Plateau.
Breeding: Nest construction is similar to other vireos. Four eggs is typical.	**Breeding:** Two to four eggs are laid in May. May have two broods per summer.	**Breeding:** Three to four eggs are laid in a basket-like nest attached to a forked limb.
Natural History: Also known as the Solitary Vireo. Most Blue-headed Vireos summer well to the north of Kentucky in New England and in Canada. They do breed in the Appalachian Mountains of Kentucky, however. They winter from the lower coastal plain of the southeastern U.S. all the way to Central America. They are quite common in peninsular Florida throughout the winter. Food is mostly insects, with moths and butterflies and their larva being a major portion of the diet. Most foraging is done in trees well above the forest floor. As is the case with many of America's migrant songbirds, the Blue-headed Vireo is highly dependent upon large tracts of forest.	**Natural History:** This is one of the most common summer songbirds in Kentucky, but it is not readily observed due to its habit of staying high in the forest canopy. It is, however, regularly heard, as it sings incessantly throughout the spring. While on their breeding grounds they are primarily insectivorous feeders, but they do consume some fruits while wintering in the tropics. The population health of the Red-eyed Vireo may be due to its less stringent dependence upon large tracts of forest. This species can subsist happily in small woodlands and regenerative areas. However, in these habitats it is more susceptible to the parasitic nesting of the Brown-headed Cowbird.	**Natural History:** The Warbling Vireo is rare or absent from much of the mountainous eastern portion of the state. They are widespread, however, in most of the rest of Kentucky. Like the similar Red-eyed Vireo, they are persistent singers that are more often heard than seen. They feed by gleaning small insects and other arthropods from canopy foliage. A few seeds and berries are also sometimes eaten. The Philadelphia Vireo migrates through most of Kentucky each spring but it does not nest in the state. They are a somewhat rare bird in Kentucky and are very difficult to distinguish from the more common Warbling Vireo, but they usually have more yellowish wash below.

Class—**Aves** (birds)

Order—**Passeriformes** (songbirds)

Family—**Parulidae** (warblers)

Canada Warbler	Wilson's Warbler	Yellow-breasted Chat
Cardellina canadensis	*Cardellina pusilla*	*Icteria virens*

Presumed range in Kentucky

Presumed range in Kentucky

Presumed range in Kentucky

Size: 5.25 inches.

Abundance: Uncommon. Declining.

Migratory Status: Winters in South America. A few nest in Kentucky in high mountains in the southeast corner of the state. Most are just passing through in route to breeding grounds in Canada.

Variation: Females have less black on face and chest.

Habitat: Kentucky habitat is moist, high mountain forests with understory shrubs such as rhododendron. Farther north it is most abundant in mixed deciduous/coniferous woodlands.

Breeding: Nest is on the ground and hidden amid dense vegetation. In Canada nest is often placed amid carpet of moss. Four or five eggs is typical.

Natural History: A few will nest in the higher elevations in the southeast corner of the state, but they are rarely observed elsewhere in Kentucky, Though they do migrate through most of the state, they do so mostly at night and pass through quickly en route to breeding grounds far to the north. Listed as a Species of Concern, the Canada Warbler has been in decline for several decades. Loss of breeding habitat in North America as well as wintering habitat in South America is probably to blame. Formerly placed in the genus *Wilsonia*.

Size: 4.75 inches.

Abundance: Uncommon in Kentucky.

Migratory Status: A passage migrant in Kentucky. Most spring migrating birds will have passed through the state by late May. Fall migration peaks in mid-September.

Variation: Black "cap" is typically more prominent in mature males.

Habitat: Summer breeding habitat is in the boreal forests of Canada, the Pacific northwest, the northern Rockies, and Alaska. Winter habitat is tropical forests.

Breeding: Nest is on the ground. Uniquely, the nest of this warbler is usually placed in a small depression. From two to seven eggs may be laid.

Natural History: Wilson's Warbler is uncommon in Kentucky. Although they may migrate through any part of the state, the Kentucky Department of Fish and Wildlife web site shows confirmed sightings in only 12 counties. The bulk of this species population occurs and migrates to the west of Kentucky. Some studies indicate that they are declining in the west, due perhaps to loss of riparian habitat. They range as far north as the Arctic Ocean in summer and as far south as Panama in winter. Named for early naturalist Alexander Wilson.

Size: 7.5 inches.

Abundance: Common.

Migratory Status: Summer resident. Winters in southern Mexico and throughout Central America. Arrives in Kentucky for breeding in late April or early May.

Variation: Sexes are alike and there is no significant variation in individuals.

Habitat: This warbler likes overgrown fields, second growth areas and early successional regenerating woodlands. Unlike many warblers, it avoids the deep woods.

Breeding: Nests low to the ground in brier thickets or a dense shrub such as a multiflora rose. Typically lays two to five eggs.

Natural History: The Yellow-breasted Chat is America's largest wood warbler and some question its status in the family Parulidae. They are quite common in suitable habitats in Kentucky in warmer months but are not easily observed due to their secretive nature and preference for dense vegetation. Foods are a wide variety of arthropods with a preference for crickets, grasshoppers, caterpillars, and spiders. They are also known to eat some fruits and berries. These birds are probably more numerous today than prior to deforestation.

Class—**Aves** (birds)

Order—**Passeriformes** (songbirds)

Family—**Parulidae** (warblers)

Black-and-white Warbler *Mniotilta varia*	Hooded Warbler *Setophaga citrina*	Northern Parula *Setophaga americana*
 Presumed range in Kentucky	 Presumed range in Kentucky	 Presumed range in Kentucky
Size: 5.25 inches.	**Size:** 5.25 inches.	**Size:** 4.5 inches.
Abundance: Fairly common.	**Abundance:** Fairly common.	**Abundance:** Fairly common.
Migratory Status: Winters from the southern U.S. to South America, including the Caribbean. Returns to Kentucky in early April. Most birds in the western part of the state are transient migrants.	**Migratory Status:** After wintering in Central America and parts of the Caribbean, the Hooded Warbler returns to Kentucky in late April. Leaves for wintering grounds by September.	**Migratory Status:** Winters from south Florida to Central America. Arrives in Kentucky in April and begins to leave in August or September. All are gone by early October.
Variation: Female very similar but has more white on the face and breast.	**Variation:** Black "hood" on head and face is much reduced in females.	**Variation:** Females lack black on breast but otherwise sexes are similar.
Habitat: Found in a wide variety of forest types, but mature and second-growth deciduous forests are the primary habitat. Mixed conifer-hardwood forests are also used.	**Habitat:** A forest species. Most common in the mountains of the eastern portion of the state but can be found anywhere that there is significant woodlands with dense understory.	**Habitat:** Habitat is forest. Mostly bottomland woods or swamps or along streams and rivers in western Kentucky. Also moist ravines in the mountains in the eastern part of the state.
Breeding: Nest is constructed of dry leaves, dead grasses, and the bark of grapevines. Placed in a depression on the ground at the base of tree or stump. Lays three to five eggs.	**Breeding:** Cup-shaped nest of grasses, bark, and dead leaves is woven into two or more upright limbs of a small bush near the ground. Four eggs. Most nesting in KY is in the Appalachian Plateau.	**Breeding:** Nests high in trees. In Kentucky Sycamores, Baldcypress, and Hemlocks are reported as favorite nest trees. In the deep south nests are often built in Spanish moss. Four or five eggs.
Natural History: Feeds by plucking tiny creatures from tree bark and branches. Its feeding habits are more similar to that of woodpeckers, nuthatches, and creepers than to most warblers. This species is dependent upon deciduous and mixed conifer forests, but apparently it has not been significantly impacted by deforestation. Although this species can be seen throughout the state during migration, it nests only in the eastern mountainous regions.	**Natural History:** Like many small woodland birds the Hooded Warbler is more likely to be heard than seen. On their breeding grounds in the eastern U.S. they require large tracts of woodlands, and they have declined in areas where intensive agriculture or development has resulted in the loss of this habitat. This handsome little warbler is a good example of why the protection of extensive tracts of forest can be so important in the conservation of neotropical migrant songbirds.	**Natural History:** The Northern Parula feeds by gleaning tiny arthropods from tree branches. They tend to feed and spend much time in the middle and upper story of the forest. This habit coupled with their small size make sometimes difficult to observe. These handsome little warblers are most common in Kentucky in the deep forests of the eastern mountains and in the swamps and bottom lands of the western end of the state. In between they are relatively rare in the state.

Class—**Aves** (birds)

Order—**Passeriformes** (songbirds)

Family—**Parulidae** (warblers)

Yellow Warbler *Setophaga petechia*	**Black-throated Blue Warbler** *Setophaga caerulescens*	**Cerulean Warbler** *Setophaga cerulea*
  Presumed range in Kentucky	  Presumed range in Kentucky	  Presumed range in Kentucky
Size: 5 inches.	**Size:** 5 inches.	**Size:** 4.75 inches.
Abundance: Fairly common.	**Abundance:** Rare in Kentucky.	**Abundance:** Fairly common.
Migratory Status: Summer. Winters in Mexico and Central America. Birds nesting in Kentucky arrive in late April.	**Migratory Status:** Summer. Returns to Kentucky in early May after wintering in Central America and the Caribbean.	**Migratory Status:** Winters in the Andes. Flies across the gulf to southeast U.S., arriving in KY by mid-April.
Variation: Male has bright chestnut streaks on breast that are lacking or much reduced on the female.	**Variation:** Strongly sexually dimorphic. Female is olive brown above, drab olive-yellow below.	**Variation:** Male is pale blue above with black streaks on sides; female is blueish green with faded gray streaks.
Habitat: Thickets of willow or buttonbush in wet lowlands are the classic habitat for this species.	**Habitat:** Mature forests with large tracts of unbroken woodlands. Both hardwood and mixed forest.	**Habitat:** Summer habitat is primarily deciduous forests. Both bottomland forest and moist mountain slopes.
Breeding: Nest is built in the upright fork of a sapling and averages four eggs. Most nesting in Kentucky is in the eastern half of the state.	**Breeding:** Nest is strips of bark lined with finer materials such as moss. Usually placed in an upright fork of dense shrub. Clutch size typically four.	**Breeding:** Nest is a tight cup woven around forked branches in the mid to upper canopy level. Average clutch size is three or four to as many as five.
Natural History: This is one of the most wide ranging of the warblers. In fact, some nest north of the Arctic Circle. Their summer breeding range encompasses the entire northern two thirds of North America, from the Atlantic to the Pacific. In Kentucky this species is more common in the eastern half of the state where nesting is common. Throughout most of the rest of Kentucky this species is mostly a transient migrant. Feeds on a variety of insects and other arthropods and uses a variety of foraging techniques including gleaning of leaves and branches, flying from perch to seize airborne prey, and picking insects from leaves and branches while hovering.	**Natural History:** Most of this warbler's summer/breeding habitat is to the north and east of Kentucky. Summers mostly in the high Appalachians, the northeastern U.S. and eastern Canada. In Kentucky it is seen only as a migrant in much of the state. A few nest and spend the summer in the southeastern corner of the state in the vicinity of Pine and Black Mountains, where they are fairly common. Westward from that portion of the state they become increasingly rare and transient. This species forages mostly in shrubs and branches at the mid-story level for caterpillars and other small arthropod prey. Deforestation and forest fragmentation are the greatest threats.	**Natural History:** The Cerulean Warbler hunts high in the canopy, gleaning tiny invertebrates from small branches and leaves. Searches both upper and lower surface of leaves for food. Like many species dependent upon forests, this warbler experienced significant population declines following the European settlement of America. In Kentucky today the species is more common in the eastern portion of the state. Historically it was common in the Mississippi Valley, but is now rare there and Cerulean Warbler populations have declined significantly throughout their range. In fact this is one of the more threatened of our neotropical migrant songbirds.

Class—**Aves** (birds)		

Order—**Passeriformes** (songbirds)		

Family—**Parulidae** (warblers)		

Magnolia Warbler *Setophaga magnolia*	**Yellow-rumped Warbler** *Setophaga coronata*	**Blackpoll Warbler** *Setophaga striata*

Presumed range in Kentucky 	Presumed range in Kentucky 	Presumed range in Kentucky 
Size: 5 inches.	**Size:** 5.5 inches.	**Size:** 5.5 inches.
Abundance: Fairly common.	**Abundance:** Common.	**Abundance:** Uncommon in Kentucky.
Migratory Status: This is a transient species in Kentucky, merely passing through on migration in spring and fall.	**Migratory Status:** Mostly a spring / fall migrant but some will be seen in Kentucky all winter if the weather is mild.	**Migratory Status:** This is a migrant that passes through Kentucky in April and May en route to northern Canada.
Variation: Ontogenetic and sexual variation. Female has dark gray mask (male black); immature has plain gray head.	**Variation:** Sexual and seasonal plumage variations (see above). Winter males, females, and immatures similar.	**Variation:** Sexual, ontogenetic, and seasonal variation. Fall male resembles female.
Habitat: Summer habitat is spruce forests of Canada. Can be seen anywhere during migration. Winters in Mexico, Central America, and Caribbean.	**Habitat:** Outside its breeding range this warbler is a habitat generalist. It can be seen virtually anywhere in the state from late fall through the early spring.	**Habitat:** Summer breeding habitat is taiga and tundra-taiga transition zones; often well above the Arctic Circle. Winter habitat is South American forests.
Breeding: Nests in evergreen trees. The nest is usually well concealed amid dense vegetation. Four eggs laid. Hemlock groves are a favorite nesting habitat.	**Breeding:** Breeds in the boreal forest of Canada and Alaska. Nest is built on the branch of a conifer. Clutch size is usually four or five eggs.	**Breeding:** Nest is an open cup built on a branch near the tree trunk, usually in a spruce. Eggs number three to five. Does not nest in Kentucky.
Natural History: Feeds on insects (including large numbers of caterpillars) that are caught near the ends of branches in dense conifer trees. Known to feed on the Spruce Budworm and may enjoy greater survival of offspring during years of budworm outbreaks. This is an abundant species that appears to be stable in population numbers. Leaves Central American wintering grounds in February and passes through Kentucky in April and May. They are fairly common migrants throughout the state in spring. Fall migration begins in September and may last into October. Fall migration routes generally more easterly than spring.	**Natural History:** There are two morphologically distinct forms of this common warbler, one in the eastern U.S. and one in the western U.S. The form seen in Kentucky is sometimes called the "Myrtle Warbler." In summer feeds mainly on insects, but if bad weather necessitates it is capable of surviving on berries during the winter. Unlike most warblers that winter in the tropics, the Yellow-rumped is a hardy species and in mild winters can be seen as far north as southern IL, IN, and OH in the Midwest and NJ on the east coast. Populations of this bird seem fairly stable and it is probably in less jeopardy than many other warbler species.	**Natural History:** This is one of the great long-distance migrants among America's songbird species. In fall migration some may travel nonstop over the Atlantic Ocean from Newfoundland (Canada) all the way to South America. Considering that this is a bird that weighs less than 0.5 ounce, that is a remarkable feat of endurance. Although some individuals will pass through Kentucky during the spring, they tend to stay hidden high in the forest canopy. The fall migration is mostly along the east coast. Thus this is a rarely seen bird in our state except by those who train themselves to look for it during spring migration.

Class—**Aves** (birds)		
Order—**Passeriformes** (songbirds)		
Family—**Parulidae** (warblers)		
Bay-breasted Warbler *Setophaga castenea*	**Pine Warbler** *Setophaga pinus*	**Black-throated Green Warbler** *Setophaga virens*
		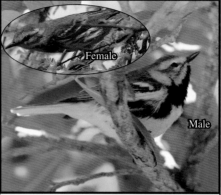
Presumed range in Kentucky	Presumed range in Kentucky	Presumed range in Kentucky
Size: 5.5 inches.	**Size:** 5.5 inches.	**Size:** 5 inches.
Abundance: Uncommon in Kentucky.	**Abundance:** Fairly common.	**Abundance:** Fairly common
Migratory Status: Spring migrant. Passes through Kentucky en route to breeding grounds in Canada. Fall migration is mostly east of the Appalachians.	**Migratory Status:** Mainly a warm weather resident in Kentucky from March through October. However, a few may stay in the state year round.	**Migratory Status:** A spring and fall migrant throughout much of Kentucky. Nests and can be seen all summer in the mountains of the eastern third of the state.
Variation: Pronounced seasonal variation. Chestnut color greatly reduced or lacking on fall birds; head and back greenish. Females typically less vivid.	**Variation:** Males are brighter greenish-yellow. Females and immatures are drabber, more brownish. Pictured above is a mature male.	**Variation:** Sexes similar, but females have less black and more yellow on the throat (see photos above).
Habitat: Summer habitat is spruce/fir woodlands of Canada. During migration through Kentucky it is found in a variety of habitats.	**Habitat:** Pine forests are the primary habitat, but they are also seen in deciduous and mixed woodlands, especially during migration.	**Habitat:** This warbler requires significant tracts of unbroken forests. Except for migration, it is an inhabitant of conifer and mixed conifer/deciduous forests.
Breeding: Nests in dense conifer trees on horizontal limbs. Nest is cup shaped and made of woven twigs, pine needles and grasses. Average clutch size is five or six eggs.	**Breeding:** Builds its nest high in pine trees. This is one of the earliest nesting warblers in Kentucky, with three or four eggs laid by early April. Breeding range is limited to regions where pines occur.	**Breeding:** Breeding populations in Kentucky are restricted to the Appalachian Plateau region. Most nests are in conifers such as hemlock or pine. Only the female incubates the four or five eggs.
Natural History: This long distance migrant is not commonly seen by residents of Kentucky, as they pass through rather quickly. Their primary food in summer is the Spruce Budworm caterpillar, and their populations may rise and fall with the availability of this insect. Populations have declined possibly due to spraying of Canadian forests to control spruce budworms. These birds are less common today than decades ago. They winter from southern Central America to northwestern South America. In winter they will eat fruit.	**Natural History:** As its name implies, this species is always found in association with pine trees. This is the only warbler whose range is contained entirely within the U.S. and Canada. It is also the only one of its kind to regularly change its diet from insects to seeds in the winter, thus it is one of the few warblers seen at bird feeders. These birds can reach high densities in winter in the southern pine forests, when resident populations are supplemented by northern migrants. In Kentucky they are rarest in the Bluegrass Region.	**Natural History:** Like others of its kind, this small, handsome warbler faces many threats. Red Squirrels are reportedly an important nest predator in the boreal forests of Canada and New England. In Kentucky the major threat may come from other birds like the Blue Jay, and from the common and widespread Midland Rat Snake. Sharp-shinned Hawks are always a threat to the adults, while Brown-headed Cowbirds parasitize the nest. Human activities such as forest fragmentation threaten populations as a whole.

Class—**Aves** (birds)

Order—**Passeriformes** (songbirds)

Family—**Parulidae** (warblers)

Blackburnian Warbler *Setophaga fusca*	**Palm Warbler** *Setophaga palmarum*	**Yellow-throated Warbler** *Setophaga dominca*

 Presumed range in Kentucky	 Presumed range in Kentucky	 Presumed range in Kentucky

Size: 5 inches.	**Size:** 5.5 inches.	**Size:** 5.5 inches.
Abundance: Uncommon in Kentucky.	**Abundance:** Fairly common.	**Abundance:** Fairly common.
Migratory Status: Mostly a spring/fall migrant in Kentucky. A few can be seen throughout the summer in southeast KY.	**Migratory Status:** Mainly a spring/fall migrant that is seen in Kentucky briefly during migration. Very rare in winter.	**Migratory Status:** A summertime resident that nests throughout the state. Arrives in April, departs in September.
Variation: Females and immature males are duller.	**Variation:** Does exhibit seasonal variation, but winter plumage not seen in KY.	**Variation:** Sexes similar. No significant variation.
Habitat: Summers mostly in mature coniferous and mixed forests. Migration habitat is highly variable. Birds in the Appalachians favor hemlocks.	**Habitat:** Summer habitat consists of bogs in boreal forests. Transient in a variety of habitats during migration. Winter habitat is mostly open woods.	**Habitat:** In western Kentucky found mostly in bottomland forests and cypress swamps. Elsewhere in the state it favors pine woodlands.
Breeding: Nesting in Kentucky is rare and little is known. Elsewhere nest is usually in a conifer and well concealed amid foliage. Average of four to five eggs.	**Breeding:** Nests of moss is on the ground in a northern bog, usually at the base of a conifer tree. Clutch size is four or five.	**Breeding:** Nesting in Kentucky begins as early as May or as late as July. Nest is high in the canopy. Four or five eggs is typical.
Natural History: The beautiful blaze orange coloration on the head, throat, and breast of the Blackburnian Warbler is unmistakable. However, this is a difficult species to observe due to the fact that it is primarily a treetop dweller. It feeds mostly on caterpillars. Most of these birds seen in Kentucky are merely passing through en route to boreal forests far to the north. Some will nest in the southern Appalachians as far south as Alabama. In Kentucky nesting has been recorded in the extreme southeast corner of the state. Insects (especially caterpillars) are primary food. Forest fragmentation on wintering grounds in South America may pose a threat.	**Natural History:** This species nests in the boreal forests of Canada and winters along the southeastern U.S. coast (including all of Florida). Unlike most warblers that spend most of their time high in the canopy, the Palm Warbler is a decidedly terrestrial species that hunts primarily on the ground or in low shrubs. It is one of the most northerly wintering of the warblers, with many staying in the southeast U.S. or Florida (thus the name Palm Warbler). Some winter in the Caribbean. Summer habitats are far to the north, well into northern Canada. Food is mainly insects caught on the ground (grasshoppers, crickets, flies, butterflies, etc.).	**Natural History:** This warbler species can be seen all summer in Kentucky and a few begin arriving as early as late March. It winters in south Florida and the Caribbean. This is another "treetop" species that spends most of its time high in the canopy. It feeds on diminutive arthropods gleaned in a very deliberate fashion from branches, bark, leaves, and petioles. This species retreated from the northern portions of its breeding range several decades ago, but is now showing a resurgence back into those areas. The cause of this population fluctuation is unknown, but possibly relates to habitat alterations by man, and a subsequent recovery of those habitats. Known to have an affinity to Sycamore trees.

Class—**Aves** (birds)		
Order—**Passeriformes** (songbirds)		
Family—**Parulidae** (warblers)		

Prairie Warbler *Setophaga discolor*	**Chestnut-sided Warbler** *Setophaga pensylvanica*	**American Redstart** *Setophaga ruticilla*

Presumed range in Kentucky	Presumed range in Kentucky	Presumed range in Kentucky
Size: 4.75 inches.	**Size:** 5 inches.	**Size:** 5.75 inches.
Abundance: Common.	**Abundance:** Uncommon in Kentucky.	**Abundance:** Fairly common.
Migratory Status: Summer resident. Arrives in Kentucky in April or May, leaving probably in late August or September.	**Migratory Status:** Mostly a spring/fall migrant. A few summer and breed in the southeastern corner of Kentucky, otherwise quite rare except during migration.	**Migratory Status:** A summer resident that breeds sporadically throughout the state. Arrives in May, leaves in September.
Variation: Sexes similar, but females are less vividly marked, immatures are paler.	**Variation:** Yellow crown and chestnut flanks are reduced on female and immatures.	**Variation:** Male black and orange; female gray and yellow, lacks color on wings and flank. Immature like female.
Habitat: Semi-open habitats. Old overgrown fields, shrubby successional areas. Uses coastal dunes during winter.	**Habitat:** The Chestnut-sided Warbler is a bird of successional areas and shrubby, second-growth.	**Habitat:** Prefers deciduous woodlands over conifers. More common in second growth areas and riparian thickets.
Breeding: Breeds throughout the state. An average of four eggs (three to five) are laid May to June. Sometimes produces two broods.	**Breeding:** Nests fairly low to the ground in thick cover of dense sapling growth. Three or four eggs are laid in late spring or early summer.	**Breeding:** The nest is woven of thin fibers of grass or bark strips and placed in the crotch of an upright branch or trunk. Usually four eggs.
Natural History: Insects, spiders, slugs, and other soft-bodied arthropods are listed as food items. Feeds from the ground all the way up to tree-tops, but mainly gleans lower bushes and shrubs. Tail-bobbing is a common behavior in this species. The Prairie Warbler winters farther north than many warbler species. While some fly as far as the Yucatan Peninsula, others stay in the northern Caribbean or Florida. They can be fairly common in the Florida Everglades during winter. Despite having benefited from clearing of forests the last century, there are unexplained declines in some populations in recent years.	**Natural History:** This is one of the few warbler species that has benefited from deforestation. These birds are more common now than they were in the days prior to the European settlement of America. Despite their overall increase in population, they are negatively impacted by modern agricultural practices. The clearing of fence rows and overgrown field corners, and conversion of successional habitats into cropland is a threat. As with many other warbler species that travel through Kentucky, the Chestnut-sided warbler breeds mostly far to the north in the boreal forests of Canada and New England. Winter range is in Central America.	**Natural History:** The striking bright orange-on-black colors of the male flash like neon in the heavily shaded forests where this species makes its home. They are active little birds that display their bright colors by regularly spreading their tail feathers and drooping their wings. They hunt tiny insects among the foliage and often catch flying insects in mid-air. In Kentucky this species is more common in the mountains of the eastern quarter of the state. Small numbers winter in coastal Louisiana, the lower Rio Grande valley, and the Everglades region of south Florida. Most winter from northwest Mexico to northern South America.

Class—**Aves** (birds)

Order—**Passeriformes** (songbirds)

Family—**Parulidae** (warblers)

Cape May Warbler *Setophaga tigrina*	**Orange-crowned Warbler** *Oreothlypis celata*	**Nashville Warbler** *Oreothlypis ruficapilla*

Presumed range in Kentucky 	Presumed range in Kentucky 	Presumed range in Kentucky 
Size: 5 inches.	**Size:** 5 inches.	**Size:** 4.75 inches.
Abundance: Uncommon.	**Abundance:** Rare in Kentucky.	**Abundance:** Fairly common.
Migratory Status: Transient spring/fall migrant. Spring migration may be statewide while fall migration is generally through and east of the Appalachians.	**Migratory Status:** A spring/fall migrant. Most migrate west of Kentucky in spring, but migration routes are presumed to include all of Kentucky.	**Migratory Status:** A spring and fall migrant that passes through most of the state. Summers in northern U.S. and Canada, winters in Mexico.
Variation: Females and immatures lack chestnut cheek patch and have less yellow on belly.	**Variation:** Sexes very similar. Female slightly duller gray above and slightly less yellow below. Varies regionally.	**Variation:** An eastern and western subspecies. Eastern birds show very little variation and the sexes are alike.
Habitat: Another species that summers in boreal forests, primarily in the vicinity of spruce bogs and other forest openings. Winter habitat is mostly in the West Indies.	**Habitat:** Summers in northern woodlands (Canada and Rocky Mts.) where it prefers habitats with significant understory. Also found old weedy fields, brier thickets, etc., during migration.	**Habitat:** Summer habitat includes tamarack bogs and boreal forests. Prefers second growth and open woodlands with shrubby undergrowth. Avoids the deep woods.
Breeding: Nest is near the trunk in the top of a spruce or fir. Five or six eggs are laid in early to mid-June. One clutch per year.	**Breeding:** Breeds in northern Canada and as far north as Alaska and well into the Arctic Circle. Western subspecies breeds along west coast. Lays four to five eggs.	**Breeding:** Nests on the ground under bushes or in hummocks of grasses or sphagnum moss. Clutch size ranges from three to six.
Natural History: On summer breeding grounds the Cape May Warbler feeds heavily on Spruce Budworm caterpillars. Their breeding cycle corresponds to the timing of maximum availability of budworm caterpillars and the population density of this species is known to be closely tied to the presence of this food source. In years of heavy budworm infestations they will rear large broods. On wintering grounds they are known to feed heavily upon nectar and fruits and they have a specialized tubular tongue for extracting nectar from flowers and juices from fruit.	**Natural History:** Like most warblers, this species is highly insectivorous, but in winter it also eats some fruit and is known to feed at the sap wells created by sapsucker woodpeckers. Feeds deliberately in the lower branches of trees and in bushes. These can be very common birds on their northern breeding grounds, but are seen in Kentucky only briefly during migrations. Orange streak on crown from which it derives its name is not typically visible in the field. Winters across the southern U.S. from the Carolinas to California, and south to northernmost Central America.	**Natural History:** This warbler species has benefited from human alterations to the American landscape (they prefer logged over, second growth habitats). However, some human alterations have also had a very negative effect. As with many other migrant songbirds, they are vulnerable to towers, power lines, and antennas. No one knows exactly how many birds are killed during migration each year by flying into these obstacles, but some estimates are in the millions. Insects are eaten almost exclusively by this warbler. Despite its name it merely passes through the state of Tennessee.

Class—**Aves** (birds)

Order—**Passeriformes** (songbirds)

Family—**Parulidae** (warblers)

Tennessee Warbler *Oreothlypis peregrina*	Blue-winged Warbler *Vermivora cyanoptera*	Golden-winged Warbler *Vermivora chrysoptera*

Presumed range in Kentucky	Presumed range in Kentucky	Presumed range in Kentucky
Size: 4.75 inches.	**Size:** 4.75 inches.	**Size:** 4.75 inches.
Abundance: Common.	**Abundance:** Fairly common.	**Abundance:** Rare in Kentucky.
Migratory Status: Another spring/fall migrant that passes through the state during annual migrations to and from Canada and Central America.	**Migratory Status:** Winters in southern Mexico and Central America. Breeds and summers in much of Kentucky, as well as farther to the north.	**Migratory Status:** A spring and fall migrant through most of the state. A few summer and breed in southeast Kentucky.
Variation: Female's head is not as gray and she is more greenish overall. Fall plumage similar to females.	**Variation:** Seasonal and sexual plumage changes are slight. Females may be slightly duller.	**Variation:** Females and immatures have gray rather than black on face; gold color on crown and wings reduced.
Habitat: Summer habitat is the boreal forest of Canada. Winter habitat in Central America is semi-open forest and forest edges. In migration may be seen anywhere.	**Habitat:** Overgrown weed fields with ample brushy undergrowth and early successional woodlands constitute this bird's habitat in Kentucky. Least common in areas of intensive agriculture.	**Habitat:** Second growth woodlands and overgrown fields. Most of summer range is in boreal forest; a few summer in the higher elevations in southeasternmost Kentucky.
Breeding: Nest is on the ground at the base of a tree or among upturned roots. Clutch size ranges from three to eight.	**Breeding:** Nest is near the ground in or under a low bush. From four to six eggs are laid in May.	**Breeding:** Nests on or near the ground at the base of a bush, hidden in thick grass and weeds. Four to five eggs.
Natural History: The numbers of this species passing through Kentucky each spring and fall fluctuates depending upon the previous year's abundance of its primary summer food, the Spruce Budworm. In the northern forests of Canada in good budworm years, this is one of the most common bird species. In years of diminished budworm populations, the population of these birds also crashes. This relationship provides a valuable insight into the intricate interdependencies of unrelated organisms. Inconspicuous as it feeds high in trees during spring migration.	**Natural History:** A shrub land specialist, the Blue-winged Warbler has experienced an upswing in populations as a result of deforestation by pioneering Europeans settlers of eastern North America. In recent years there has been a decline in their numbers in the northeast as forests have begun recovering from the rampant logging of the last century. These birds sometimes hybridize with the similar Golden-winged Warbler and produce at least two additional forms of difficult to identify hybrid birds. This species is in decline in many areas of its range, including in Kentucky.	**Natural History:** A few individuals nest in the southeastern corner of Kentucky, but they are rare here. Actual sightings of migrant birds are also rare, but they are presumed to pass through most of the state. Hybridization with Blue-winged Warblers, loss of winter habitat, and nest parasitism by the Brown-headed Cowbird are possible reasons for a recent population decline. Winters in a variety of forest habitats in Mexico, Central America, and northern South America from sea level to 7,000 feet. Like many warblers, this species migrates across the Gulf of Mexico.

Class—**Aves** (birds)		
Order—**Passeriformes** (songbirds)		
Family—**Parulidae** (warblers)		
Ovenbird *Seiurus aurocapilla*	**Louisiana Waterthrush** *Parkesia motacilla*	**Worm-eating Warbler** *Helmitheros vermivorus*
 Presumed range in Kentucky	 Presumed range in Kentucky	 Presumed range in Kentucky
Size: 6 inches.	**Size:** 6 inches.	**Size:** 5.5 inches.
Abundance: Fairly common.	**Abundance:** Fairly common.	**Abundance:** Uncommon.
Migratory Status: Winters from south Florida to southern Central America. Summers as far north as northern Canada. Arrives in Kentucky in April, leaves in September or October.	**Migratory Status:** A summertime resident of Kentucky that arrives in KY as early as March and is gone by mid-August. Winters from Mexico and the Caribbean to northernmost South America.	**Migratory Status:** Summer resident that winters in the Caribbean and in Central America. A summertime resident, they are seen in Kentucky from April through August.
Variation: No variation. Sexes alike.	**Variation:** Sexes alike.	**Variation:** No variation, sexes alike.
Habitat: Mature, contiguous forests. Seems to prefer upland woods. A substrate of abundant leaf litter is an important element to this bird's habitat.	**Habitat:** Forested streams are the preferred habitat. In migration they may also be seen along the edges of swamps or small woodland ponds.	**Habitat:** This is a woodland species, but it seems to avoid lowland forests. More common in eastern Kentucky in rugged regions with steep slopes.
Breeding: Nest is on the ground and is constructed of leaves and grass. Nest is unique in that it has a domed roof with an opening in front. Three to six eggs.	**Breeding:** Nesting occurs as early as May in Kentucky. Four to six eggs are laid in a nest placed in tree roots along the banks of a stream.	**Breeding:** Nests are built on the ground in deep woods and are often hidden beneath overhanging vegetation. Four to five eggs is typical.
Natural History: This large warbler is a ground dweller, and is usually observed on the ground or in low foliage. Food is a wide variety of insects and arthropods taken mostly on the ground among the leaf litter. The song of the Ovenbird is distinctive and has been variously described as "emphatic" and "effervescent." Often two nearby birds will sing at once, with their overlapping songs sounding like a single bird. This species has experienced a decline in the last few decades. Forest fragmentation and Brown-headed Cowbird nest parasitism may be to blame. Winter range includes West Indies and Cuba as well as Florida, Mexico, and Central America.	**Natural History:** This species is famous for its incessant "tail bobbing" behavior. The entire rear half of the body constantly wags up and down when foraging in stream side habitats. *Similar Species:* The **Northern Waterthrush** (*P. noveboracensis*) is so similar to the Louisiana Waterthrush that most casual observers will not be able to tell them apart. The Northern merely passes through Kentucky, en route to boreal forest breeding habitats. Meanwhile the Louisiana breeds in most of Kentucky. Northern breeds in bogs and in the vicinity of beaver ponds. Both associate with water and both are usually seen near streams or wetlands.	**Natural History:** Although the Worm-eating Warbler may occur throughout the state, it is much more common in the southeastern part of the state. This is a species that specializes in feeding amid low bushes searching the dead leaf clusters and low hanging foliage for insects, spiders, and primarily, caterpillars. Like many of Kentucky's neotropical migrant songbirds, the Worm-eating Warbler is highly dependent upon deciduous forests for breeding habitat. Winters in Mexico, Central America, and the West Indies. This species is the world's only member of its genus. Its closest relative may be the Swainson's Warbler.

Class—**Aves** (birds)

Order—**Passeriformes** (songbirds)

Family—**Parulidae** (warblers)

Swainson's Warbler *Limnothlypis swainsonii*	**Common Yellowthroat** *Geothlypis trichas*	**Kentucky Warbler** *Geothlypis formosus*

Presumed range in Kentucky	Presumed range in Kentucky	Presumed range in Kentucky
Size: 5.5 inches.	**Size:** 5 inches.	**Size:** 5.25 inches.
Abundance: Rare.	**Abundance:** Common.	**Abundance:** Fairly common.
Migratory Status: Winters on the Yucatan Peninsula and in the northern Caribbean. They may be seen in Kentucky from April through September.	**Migratory Status:** Summer resident. Seen in Kentucky from April through late summer/early fall. Winters from south Florida to Central America.	**Migratory Status:** Arrives in Kentucky by early May. Nests and rears its young before leaving for the tropics in September.
Variation: No variation.	**Variation:** Female lacks black mask.	**Variation:** Sexes very similar.
Habitat: Swainson's Warblers are known to associate with stands of giant cane in the southern U.S. In the Appalachians they frequent Rhododendron thickets. In Kentucky they are most often observed in the eastern mountains.	**Habitat:** Likes thick vegetation in wetland areas. Cattails and sedges in marshes and swamp edges are especially favored. Avoids deep woods but may be seen around edges of woods, especially near streams.	**Habitat:** Throughout its summer range the Kentucky Warbler enjoys deciduous bottomland forests and wooded riparian habitats. Within this macro-habitat it requires a micro-habitat of dense undergrowth.
Breeding: The nest is built on the ground and is made of dead leaves, rendering it quite cryptic and difficult to locate. Lays three to four eggs.	**Breeding:** The nest is woven from wetland grasses among cattails or sedges. Four to six eggs are laid in late May or early June. Cowbird parasitism occurs.	**Breeding:** A ground nester. The nest is constructed of dead leaves and grasses and is usually well hidden. Four to five eggs are laid by mid-May.
Natural History: Kentuckians rarely see this rare and secretive warbler. Very similar in appearance to the previous species, the Swainson's Warbler is primarily a ground dweller. Unlike the Worm-eating Warbler that prefers upland woods, the Swainson's Warbler is more of a lowland species. In Kentucky this species occurs in the two habitat extremes of the state, the lowlands of the Coastal Plain in the far west, and the mountains of the easternmost regions. Although it ranges across much of the southeastern U.S. in summer, it is nowhere common.	**Natural History:** The Common Yellowthroat is one of the more abundant warblers in America and their summer range includes most of North America south of the Arctic. They do avoid the desert southwest and dry southern plains. Not surprising since they are mainly a wetland loving species. They feed low to the ground on almost any type of tiny invertebrate. Their behavior when foraging is rather "wren-like" as they negotiate dense stands of cattails, reeds, and tall grasses. They tend to stick to heavy cover and when flushed make short flights into deep cover.	**Natural History:** Kentucky's namesake warbler is an abundant and widespread bird in suitable habitats throughout the state during summer. Like other small warblers it is easily overlooked. The Cornell Laboratory of Ornithology website reports that this species appears to be in decline. Destruction of mature tropical forests may be to blame. It is also possible that fragmentation of large forests tracts in North America could be a threat. Unlike many warblers whose habitat is high in the canopy, this species feeds low to the ground. It eats a wide variety of invertebrates.

Class—**Aves** (birds)		
Order—**Passeriformes** (songbirds)		
Family—**Parulidae** (warblers)		
Mourning Warbler *Geothlypis philadelphia*	**Connecticut Warbler** *Oporornis agilis*	**Prothonotary Warbler** *Protonotaria citrea*

Presumed range in Kentucky	Presumed range in Kentucky	Presumed range in Kentucky
Size: 5.25 inches.	**Size:** 5.75 inches.	**Size:** 5.5 inches.
Abundance: Uncommon in Kentucky.	**Abundance:** Very rare.	**Abundance:** Fairly common.
Migratory Status: A rarely seen migrant that passes through Kentucky briefly enroute to and from boreal breeding grounds. Migrates later than most.	**Migratory Status:** Moves quickly through the state on spring migration. Fall migration occurs along the Atlantic coast.	**Migratory Status:** A neotropical migrant warbler that winters in mangrove swamps in Central and South America. Summers in Kentucky, April to August.
Variation: Male has gray head, throat, and shoulders with black patch on breast.	**Variation:** Females are duller, without the gray head of the male.	**Variation:** Sexes nearly identical. Female slightly less vivid.
Habitat: The Mourning Warbler's summer/breeding habitat is the boreal forests and bogs of Canada. In Kentucky they are most likely to be seen along the Mississippi and Ohio river valleys.	**Habitat:** Summer / breeding habitat is boreal forest. There it prefers wetland habitats like tamarack bogs and muskeg. Winter habitat is forests in Central and South America.	**Habitat:** Prothonotary Warblers always nest near water. They are most common in swamps and marshes but can also be seen along lake shores, riparian areas, and in the vicinity of small ponds.
Breeding: Nests on the ground in dense vegetation or a clump of grass. Lays on average four eggs.	**Breeding:** Nest is hidden in thick undergrowth on or near the ground. Three to five eggs are laid.	**Breeding:** Unlike other warblers that build a nest, the Prothonotary Warbler nests in tree cavities. Lays four or five eggs.
Natural History: This warbler likes second growth areas with lush undergrowth. It prefers these conditions both in its summer breeding grounds in boreal forests as well as its wintering grounds in tropical forests. Thus it is one of the few neotropical migrant warblers that has actually benefited from man's insatiable appetite for wood products. This is a secretive bird that "skulks" in dense thickets. As is the case with many of Kentucky's neotropical migrant warblers, the summer range of the Mourning Warbler closely coincides with the Level I ecoregion known as the Northern (or Boreal) Forest.	**Natural History:** This shy warbler is rarely observed in Kentucky, in part due to its secretive nature (migrating birds are typically observed low to the ground in dense undergrowth). In addition, it occurs in Kentucky only briefly during the spring migration. Fall migrants follow the Atlantic Coast southward and thus do not return through the state. Despite its name, this species is quite rare in Connecticut, where it may only occasionally be seen during fall migration. Due to its secretive nature and relative rarity, this is one of the least understood and least commonly observed of America's warbler species.	**Natural History:** The dredging and draining of swamplands in the southeastern United States significantly reduced breeding habitat for this warbler in the first half of the 20th century. Loss of wetlands in the U.S. has stabilized somewhat in the last few decades, but the species now faces threats from habitat loss on its wintering grounds in northern South America. In Kentucky this warbler is most common in the western end of the state, becoming increasingly scarce toward the east. In summer feeds on aquatic insects, snails, and tiny crustaceans. In winter they will also eat fruits and nectar.

Class—**Aves** (birds)

Order—**Passeriformes** (songbirds)

Family—**Icteridae** (blackbirds)

Brown-headed Cowbird *Molothrus ater*	**Red-winged Blackbird** *Agelaius phoeniceus*	**Common Grackle** *Quiscalus quiscula*
	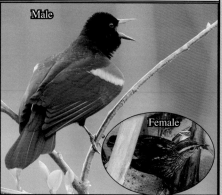	
Presumed range in Kentucky	Presumed range in Kentucky	Presumed range in Kentucky
Size: 7.5 inches.	**Size:** 9 inches.	**Size:** 12.5 inches.
Abundance: Common.	**Abundance:** Common.	**Abundance:** Very common.
Migratory Status: The cowbird can be seen in most of the state year-round, but they are more numerous in spring and summer. Birds that move south for the winter return early, usually by March.	**Migratory Status:** These birds are seen throughout the year in Kentucky, but many summer birds move south in winter to be replaced by birds that have summered farther north.	**Migratory Status:** Grackles are seen year-round in Kentucky, but many do migrate. Some nesting birds may move south in winter, and some that nested farther north may winter in the state.
Variation: Female a uniform drab brownish gray, male shiny black with brown head (see photos above).	**Variation:** Pronounced sexual dimorphism (see photos above). Male's red/yellow epaulets are reduced in winter.	**Variation:** Females are slightly smaller and less iridescent than males. Two color morphs, "bronze" and "purple."
Habitat: Open fields and agricultural areas primarily, but can also be common in towns and suburbs. Inhabits edge areas and woods openings but avoids deep forest.	**Habitat:** The Red-wing Blackbird's favorite habitat is marsh or wet meadows. They are also found along roadside ditches and the edges of ponds in open areas.	**Habitat:** Grackles favor agricultural areas and open fields/croplands. They are also common in urban areas where they inhabit lawns, parks, etc. In winter roosts in large flocks in small woodlots.
Breeding: Female cowbirds lay their eggs in the nest of other bird species, a unique nesting strategy known as "brood parasitism" (see below). As many as 40 eggs may be laid in dozens of songbird nests.	**Breeding:** The nest of the Red-winged Blackbird is a woven basket usually suspended from two or three cattail blades and is most often positioned over water. Two to four eggs are laid. Males will defend the nest against other birds.	**Breeding:** Grackles often nest in groups that may consist of a dozen or more pairs. The nest is built in the upper branches of medium size trees and several nests can be in the same tree, or in adjacent trees.
Natural History: This species is unique among Kentucky birds in that the adults play no role in rearing their young. Instead the female lays an egg in another species' nest and the adoptive parents rear the young cowbird, usually to the detriment of their own offspring. The disappearance of extensive forest tracts has allowed the cowbird to parasitize many more woodland songbirds than was possible prior to settlement.	**Natural History:** In winter Red-winged Blackbirds often join large mixed flocks that can include all the birds shown on this page. Males sing conspicuously in spring. Like the other blackbirds on this page, the Red-winged has benefited from human alterations to Kentucky's natural habitats. Food is almost entirely insects and, along with the Common Grackle, this species plays an important role in insect control.	**Natural History:** Grackles are known for forming large flocks during the winter that will roost communally and can number in the thousands. When these large congregations move into a town or neighborhood they can become a messy nuisance, but their reputation for spreading disease is exaggerated. Throughout most of the year they are busy consuming millions of insect pests. They readily flock with other birds.

Class—**Aves** (birds)

Order—**Passeriformes** (songbirds)

Family—**Icteridae** (blackbirds)

Bobolink *Dolichonyx oryzivorus*	**Rusty Blackbird** *Euphagus carolinus*	**Brewer's Blackbird** *Euphagus cyanocephalus*

Size: 7 inches.	**Size:** 9 inches.	**Size:** 9.5 inches.
Abundance: Uncommon.	**Abundance:** Uncommon.	**Abundance:** Rare in Kentucky.
Migratory Status: Passes through the state in spring and fall.	**Migratory Status:** Seen in Kentucky only during the winter.	**Migratory Status:** A winter migrant visitor from the western United States.
Variation: Pronounced sexual and seasonal changes. Females and winter males are a much drabber brown.	**Variation:** Winter plumage drab gray-brown with rusty highlights, breeding plumage iridescent purplish-black.	**Variation:** Iris of the eye is dark in the female, yellow in male. Females and non-breeding males are duller.
Habitat: Bobolinks are open country birds and in Kentucky they are usually seen in pastures and hayfields. Their original habitats in the state were probably tallgrass prairies, which no longer exist in any significant amount.	**Habitat:** Rusty Blackbirds wintering in Kentucky favor wetland habitats. Floodplain forests, edges of swamps, and woods bordering marshes make up the bulk of this bird's winter habitat in the state.	**Habitat:** Favors open country. In Kentucky it is usually seen in harvested or plowed agricultural fields, pastures, etc. It may also frequent feedlots where it feeds on waste grain. In the bulk of its range out west it inhabits grasslands.
Breeding: Females breed with a number of males and a clutch of five eggs may have several fathers. Nest is woven of grasses and placed on the ground.	**Breeding:** Breeding occurs far to the north (as far as the Arctic). An average of four eggs are laid in a bulky nest of twigs, lichens, and grass.	**Breeding:** As many as eight eggs may be laid, but five or six is probably average. Nests on the ground. No nesting has been recorded in Kentucky.
Natural History: Bobolinks are one of the greatest migrators of any bird seen in Kentucky. They will nest in the northern U.S. and Canada and winter in southern South America in the open grasslands of the Pampas region of Uraguay and Argentina. That's a round trip of nearly 20,000 miles! While most Bobolinks nest farther to the north, a few have been known to nest in the north-central portion of Kentucky. Although most Bobolinks seen in Kentucky are transients, small numbers do breed in the Bluegrass Region of the state. Food items include seeds, grains, and many invertebrates during breeding.	**Natural History:** In the last few years Rusty Blackbirds have garnered the attention of birdwatchers and conservationists concerned about an apparently significant decline in the population of this species. The loss of wet woodlands to agriculture throughout much of the south may be partly to blame. Unlike many blackbirds that regularly intermingle with other species, the Rusty Blackbird seems to remain mostly segregated from the large winter flocks of grackles, cowbirds, starlings, and red-wingeds. These birds summer far to the north and are seen in Kentucky only in winter. Food is insects, seeds, grains, etc.	**Natural History:** The Brewer's Blackbird is a western species that historically inhabited the Great Plains and Rocky Mountian Regions all the way to the Pacific Ocean. With the clearing of land brought on by human activities, the Brewer's Blackbird began to invade the Eastern Temperate Forest Level I Ecoregion in the early 1900s. Although they are still rare in Kentucky, birdwatchers now report sightings nearly every winter. Feeds mostly on grains and seeds of grasses or weeds in winter. Summer diet is largely insects. The stomach of one bird reportedly contain over 50 tiny grasshoppers!

Class—**Aves** (birds)

Order—**Passeriformes** (songbirds)

Family—**Icteridae** (blackbirds)

Eastern Meadowlark	Baltimore Oriole	Orchard Oriole
Sturnella magna	*Icturus galbula*	*Icturus spurius*

Presumed range in Kentucky

Presumed range in Kentucky

Presumed range in Kentucky

Size: 9.25 inches.

Size: 8.75 inches.

Size: 7 inches.

Abundance: Common.

Abundance: Fairly common.

Abundance: Fairly common.

Migratory Status: Meadowlarks live year-round in Kentucky.

Migratory Status: A summer resident that returns in late April or early May.

Migratory Status: Summer resident that breeds throughout Kentucky.

Variation: Females are slightly smaller and duller in color, but differences are barely noticeable.

Variation: Significant sexual dimorphism (see photos above). Immature male less vividly colored (inset photo).

Variation: Significant sexual and ontogenetic plumage variation. Immature males resemble female (see photos).

Habitat: Open, treeless pastures and fields that are kept closely grazed or mowed. They like short grasses and avoid overgrown areas. In winter they are often seen in harvested croplands or emerging wheat fields.

Habitat: Savanna-like habitats are preferred. Pastures with scattered large trees, parks and lawns in urban areas, or farms and ranches in rural areas. During migration may be seen in a variety of habitats.

Habitat: This species shows a preference for semi-open habitats and narrow strips of woodland bordering rivers and streams. Their name comes from the fact that they are fond of orchards and they will often nest in fruit trees.

Breeding: Nest is on the ground and well hidden beneath overhanging grasses or under the edge of a grass tussock. Three to five eggs.

Breeding: The nest is an easily recognizable "hanging basket" woven from grasses and suspended from a tree limb. Four to six eggs is typical.

Breeding: The nest is a rounded basket woven from grasses and suspended from a forked tree branch. Four eggs is typical, but can be as many as six.

Natural History: As might be expected of a bird that loves open spaces, the Eastern Meadowlark is least common in Kentucky in the forested regions of the east. Even in the mountains, however, this bird can be found in areas of open habitat. They feed mostly on insects in warmer months, with grasshoppers and crickets being a dietary mainstay in the summer. During winter they will eat seeds and grain. They tend to occur in small flocks during the winter, but pair off and scatter in the breeding season. A nearly identical species (Western Meadowlark) lives out west and may rarely wander into westernmost Kentucky.

Natural History: These handsome orange and black birds are a favorite with backyard bird watchers. They will come to nectar feeders and fruits such as oranges, and they relish grape jelly. In addition to nectar and fruit they feed heavily on insects. In some areas of their range they have adapted well to human activities. Small town neighborhoods and city parks are among their habitats today. Their appearance in much of the state is sporadic. They may be abundant in a particular area one year and absent for several years thereafter. In Kentucky most nesting occurs in the Bluegrass Region.

Natural History: Like the larger Baltimore Oriole, Orchard Orioles will eat fruit. They also feed on a wide variety of arthropods gleaned from tree branches and leaves, as well as from weedy fields. Immature males resemble females but have a large black throat patch. These birds are somewhat gregarious and they often occur in flocks on tropical wintering grounds. They are also known to nest in small colonies where ideal habitat exists. Spraying for insects in orchards can be dangerous for these insect and fruit eaters as it can be for other bird species, many of which are highly succeptible to insecticides.

Class—**Aves** (birds)

Order—**Passeriformes** (songbirds)

Family—**Thraupidae** (tanagers)

Scarlet Tanager *Piranga ludoviciana*	**Summer Tanager** *Piranga rubra*

 Presumed range in Kentucky	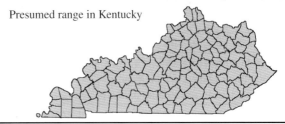 Presumed range in Kentucky
Size: 7 inches.	**Size:** 7.75 inches.
Abundance: Fairly common.	**Abundance:** Common.
Migratory Status: A summer resident that breeds in Kentucky and winters in tropical America. Most arrive in Kentucky in late April.	**Migratory Status:** Well named, this bird is seen in Kentucky only during summer. It winters in the tropics. Spring arrival is usually mid to late April.
Variation: Sexual and ontogenetic plumage variations. Juvenile males resemble females for the first year of their lives. See photos above.	**Variation:** Sexual and ontogenetic dimorphism. See photos above. The mottled yellow-green and bright red of the juvenile male entering its second year can be seen in early spring.
Habitat: The summer habitat for the Scarlet Tanager closely coincides with the Eastern Temperate Forest Level I Ecoregion. It prefers large tracts of unbroken woodlands.	**Habitat:** Like their cousins Scarlet Tanagers, Summer Tanagers are birds of the eastern forests. However, this species is more likely to occupy fragmented forests and edge areas.
Breeding: The thin, saucer-like nest of the Scarlet Tanager is placed on the fork of an outer branch. Four eggs is typical. Only one brood is produced.	**Breeding:** The rather flimsy nest is on a terminal fork of a branch that is usually low over an opening such as a creek bed. The typical clutch size is three to four.
Natural History: The Scarlet Tanager is one of the most strikingly colored birds in Kentucky. Unfortunately, this species' dependence upon larger tracts of forested land means that its future is uncertain. Forest fragmentation leads to vulnerability to cowbird nest parasitism. Throughout much of the Midwest, where deforestation and fragmentation of forests has been rampant, this species is in decline. In Kentucky it is most common in the southeastern mountains where large amounts of woodland remain. Food in summer is mostly insects (including wasps and hornets). Winters from Panama to northwestern South America.	**Natural History:** Summer Tanagers feed on a variety of woodland insects and larva, but they also eat some berries and fruits. One of their primary food items, however, is bees and wasps, a fact that makes them an attractive species to have around the rural homestead. Immature males resemble females their first summer. By the following spring they begin transformation into the bright red plumage of the adult male. During this transformation they are one of the most colorful birds in Kentucky woodlands (see inset photo above). Winters from southern Mexico to northern South America.

Class—**Aves** (birds)

Order—**Passeriformes** (songbirds)

Family—**Sturnidae** (mynas)	Family—**Passeridae** (weaver finches)
European Starling *Sturnis vulgaris*	**House Sparrow** *Passer domesticus*

Presumed range in Kentucky

Presumed range in Kentucky

Size: 8.75 inches.

Size: 6.25 inches.

Abundance: Very common.

Abundance: Very common.

Migratory Status: A non-migratory year-round resident throughout the state.

Migratory Status: Non-migratory, the House Sparrow is year-round resident of Kentucky.

Variation: Breeding plumage iridescent dark purple, non-breeding has white speckles. Immatures are drab brown.

Variation: Males have distinctive gray crown with black face mask. Females are a plain drab brown. See photos.

Habitat: Urban and suburban areas as well as farms and ranches. Starlings are closely tied to human activity and are rarely seen in true wilderness. By contrast, they can be quite common in large cities and small towns.

Habitat: The House Sparrow's name comes from its affinity for human habitations. These are mostly urban birds and when they do occur in rural areas it is always near farms and homesteads.

Breeding: Nest is made of grass, leaves, etc., stuffed into a cavity. Often uses cracks or holes in man-made structures. Also old woodpecker holes. Clutch size is typically five eggs.

Breeding: House Sparrows build bulky nests of grass, feathers, paper strips, etc., placed in hollows or crevices of barns, outbuildings, or even occupied homes. Five to six eggs on average.

Natural History: The Starling is one of the most familiar birds in America, but ironically it is a non-native species. All the Starlings in America are descendant from a handful of birds released in New York City in the 1890s. Contrary to popular belief, the Starling is not related to the blackbirds. Instead they belong to the same family as the old world mynas. These birds have enjoyed remarkable success since being introduced to North America and they are now found throughout the continent. They represent a real threat to many of our native species, especially those that nest in cavities. In winter they often join grackles and blackbirds in large mixed flocks that can become a messy nuisance in urban and suburban areas.

Natural History: A European immigrant, the House Sparrow was released into the United States about 150 years ago. They have spread across the continent and they are now perhaps the most familiar bird species in America. They roost communally in dense vegetation. Roosting sites are often in yards or foundation plantings next to houses. They are common scavengers around outdoor restaurants and fast-food parking lots. They are often considered to be a nuisance bird, but their tame demeanor endears them to many. Despite being extremely common in urban areas, they are quite rare in wilderness. These highly successful birds may nest up to four times in a season.

Class—**Aves** (birds)		
Order—**Passeriformes** (songbirds)		
Family—**Emberizidae** (sparrows)		

Swamp Sparrow *Melospiza georgiana*	**Song Sparrow** *Melospiza melodia*	**Lincoln's Sparrow** *Melospiza lincolnii*

Presumed range in Kentucky	Presumed range in Kentucky	Presumed range in Kentucky
Size: 5.75 inches.	**Size:** 5.5 inches.	**Size:** 5.5 inches.
Abundance: Fairly common.	**Abundance:** Common.	**Abundance:** Uncommon in Kentucky.
Migratory Status: Swamp Sparrows are seen in Kentucky only during the winter. They summer in Canada, New England, and the Great Lakes region.	**Migratory Status:** Year-round in most of Kentucky. Rare in the Coastal Plain of Kentucky except in winter, when they are fairly common.	**Migratory Status:** Spring and fall migrant. Exact routes of migration through Kentucky poorly known. Winters from the southwest U.S. to Central America.
Variation: Breeding males are richer in color and show a decidedly reddish crown. Otherwise, the sexes are quite similar.	**Variation:** There are dozens of subspecies nationwide with light and dark color morphs. Most Kentucky birds resemble photo above.	**Variation:** There is no sexual dimorphism in this species. Seasonal and ontogenetic variation is also insignificant. All Kentucky specimens will be similar.
Habitat: Summers in wetlands. Swamps, marshes (including salt marsh), and wet meadows. More diverse habitats may be used in winter, including upland fields.	**Habitat:** Overgrown fields, dense underbrush, and rank weeds are the preferred habitat of the Song Sparrow throughout Kentucky. They are especially common in edge habitats.	**Habitat:** Summer habitat is boreal regions of Canada and northern Rockies where it occupies damp woodlands with dense brush such as willow. Spruce bogs and wetlands are favored.
Breeding: Nest is made of grasses and placed in cattails, grasses, or low bush. Three to six eggs, four on average.	**Breeding:** Nests are built low to the ground in weeds or shrubs. Four eggs is typical.	**Breeding:** Nests on the ground amid sedges or at the base of willow in boreal wetlands. Lays three to five eggs.
Natural History: Secretive and elusive, the Swamp Sparrow is less familiar to Kentuckians than most of its kin. They will visit feeders during the winter, but they are rarely a commonly seen bird in Kentucky. These birds are highly dependent upon wetlands for breeding, and they may be negatively impacted by loss of wetlands. At this time, however, populations appear stable. Although they can be quite common in summer habitats and in the bayous of of the deep south in winter, they do not flock and are nearly always seen singly. Often uses uplands in winter.	**Natural History:** Both the common and scientific names of the Song Sparrow are references to its distinct and melodic song. Primarily seed eaters, these sparrows migrate in response to heavy snow cover, and they are common at bird feeders throughout the southern United States each winter. Breeds in the eastern mountains of Kentucky but is seen in the Coastal Plain only in winter. Sharp-shinned and Cooper's Hawks are major predators of adults, and the young and eggs are vulnerable to a variety of snake predators. However, they remain a thriving species.	**Natural History:** Lincoln's Sparrows are more common west of the Mississippi and are somewhat rare in Kentucky. In addition it is shy and secretive and tends to stick to heavy cover. Add to this the fact that it is a transient species in Kentucky and sightings are uncommon. During migration they are believed to be fairly widespread across the state. When excited raises feathers on the back of the head giving it a "crested" look. Due to their secretive habits the biology of these sparrows is not well understood. Feeds on seeds and insects and will rarely visit feeders.

Class—**Aves** (birds)		
Order—**Passeriformes** (songbirds)		
Family—**Emberizidae** (sparrows)		
Chipping Sparrow *Spizella passerina*	**American Tree Sparrow** *Spizelloides arborea*	**Field Sparrow** *Spizella pusilla*

Presumed range in Kentucky 	Presumed range in Kentucky 	Presumed range in Kentucky 
Size: 5.5 inches.	**Size:** 6.25 inches.	**Size:** 5.75 inches.
Abundance: Common.	**Abundance:** Uncommon in Kentucky.	**Abundance:** Common.
Migratory Status: A summer resident that returns as early as March.	**Migratory Status:** A winter migrant that summers as far north as the Arctic.	**Migratory Status:** Year-round resident.
Variation: No sexual dimorphism, but winter plumage is much more subdued and head markings are greatly reduced.	**Variation:** Adults show no variation and the sexes are alike. Immatures have dusky streaks on the sides and breast.	**Variation:** Sexes alike. No seasonal plumage changes but immature birds have dark streaks on the breast.
Habitat: Edge areas and woods openings. Thrives in human altered habitats including farmsteads, suburban yards, and parks.	**Habitat:** In winter they use overgrown fields, edge areas, brushy patches with weeds and grasses. Summer habitat is open tundra and taiga.	**Habitat:** Open and semi-open areas with good cover in the form of weeds and taller grasses. Also shrubby, early regenerative woodland areas.
Breeding: Breeds earlier than most other Kentucky songbirds. Nests may be complete and eggs can being laid as early as mid-April in Kentucky.	**Breeding:** Nest is on the ground. Four to six eggs. These hardy sparrows will nest as far north as the Arctic Circle and well above the tree line.	**Breeding:** Nest is on the ground usually at the base of a clump of grass or in a low bush. Two broods per year is common. Two to five eggs.
Natural History: Most Chipping Sparrow move to the deep south in winter. But in mild winters they have been seen throughout the winter in the Coastal Plain of the westernmost tip of the state. Nesting has been recorded throughout the state, but they are more common in the central and eastern parts of the state in summer months. They adapt well to human disturbance of natural habitats and they are undoubtedly more common today than prior to settlement. The Chipping Sparrow feeds mostly on the seeds of grasses and forbs, and does most of its foraging on the ground. Insects are eaten during the breeding season and are fed to the young. They can be a common bird at feeders.	**Natural History:** The American Tree Sparrow is a northern species that is never seen in Kentucky except in winter. Even then it rarely gets farther south than the northern portions of the state. It almost never seen in the Coastal Plain of far western Kentucky except in the harshest of winters, when heavy snow cover in the northern regions pushes migrating flocks southward. Like most sparrows, seeds are the staple food in winter. Seeds are also eaten in summer months but insects are more important, especially when rearing young. Seeds of a wide variety of grasses and weeds are consumed, and this species is regularly seen at bird feeders in northern states.	**Natural History:** Another species that has adapted well to man-made changes in natural landscapes, the Field Sparrow is probably more numerous today than in historical times. Unlike many sparrows, however, the Field Sparrow is a "country" sparrow that prefers rural regions over towns and suburbs. Although they are seen year-round in Kentucky, some southerly movement occurs in northern populations and some of our winter birds may have summered farther to the north. Food is mostly grass seeds; insects are also eaten, especially during the breeding season. Very similar to the American Tree Sparrow, but has all pink bill instead of dark upper mandible.

Class—**Aves** (birds)

Order—**Passeriformes** (songbirds)

Family—**Emberizidae** (sparrows)

Vesper Sparrow *Pooecetes gramineus*	**Lark Sparrow** *Chondestes grammacus*	**Savannah Sparrow** *Passerculus sandwichensis*

Presumed range in Kentucky 	Presumed range in Kentucky 	Presumed range in Kentucky 
Size: 6.25 inches.	**Size:** 6.25 inches.	**Size:** 5.5 inches.
Abundance: Rare in Kentucky.	**Abundance:** Rare in Kentucky.	**Abundance:** Fairly common.
Migratory Status: Migratory and transient. Most sightings in Kentucky apparently occur in the spring (mid-March to mid-April).	**Migratory Status:** Summer migrant that may occasionally breed sporadically in the state. Winters in the southwestern United States and Mexico.	**Migratory Status:** Winter resident in western Kentucky, rare summer resident in the Bluegrass Region, and a migrant throughout much of the rest of the state.
Variation: No sexual differences. Immatures are similar but drabber in color.	**Variation:** No sexual variation. Immatures have streaks on breast.	**Variation:** Highly variable with as many as 28 subspecies.
Habitat: This is a bird of open country. Its natural habitats are grasslands and today it also uses agricultural fields. Prefers dry areas.	**Habitat:** The Lark Sparrow is restricted to open habitats and is most common in dry grasslands of the southwest. Barrens and pastures are used in Kentucky.	**Habitat:** Pastures, grasslands, mowed areas in vacant lots, and cultivated fields are used in Kentucky. Elsewhere salt marsh, tundra, and bogs are habitats.
Breeding: Nest is on the ground in open fields, sometimes concealed by grass tussock. Three to five eggs.	**Breeding:** Nest is usually on the ground but may be in a low bush. Three to six eggs is typical.	**Breeding:** Nests on the ground beneath overhanging vegetation. Four to five eggs is typical. Nesting is rare in Kentucky.
Natural History: The Vesper Sparrow is more common in the western region of North America, but they have nested (historically) in the Bluegrass Region of the state. They are declining in the eastern portions of their range which includes much of the Midwest and Great Lakes region. They winter across the southern U.S. and southward to northern Central America. There is little data on the routes of their migration, but as they may be found directly north of Kentucky in summer and directly south in winter, it is presumed that they may be seen throughout the state during migration periods.	**Natural History:** A western species that ranges into Kentucky very rarely and sporadically. In Kentucky they occur mostly to the west of the Appalachian Plateau, which represents the easternmost distribution for the species. Males are reported to perform a courtship "dance" that resembles that of a turkey's strutting behavior. The Lark Sparrow's facial pattern of vivid black and white stripes with chestnut cheek patch is distinctive. As with most sparrows, seeds are the primary food in winter. During warmer months both seeds and insects are eaten. Grasshoppers are reported to be a major food item.	**Natural History:** Most Savannah Sparrows seen in Kentucky are seen during migration. However, in the Eastern Gulf Coastal Plain of the state this species is fairly common in winter. This is one of the most widespread sparrow species in America. Between breeding range, winter range, and migration routes the Savannah Sparrow may be seen anywhere on the continent. Feeds on arthropods in summer and seeds in winter. The name comes from the Georgia town of Savannah (where the first specimen was described) rather than from the habitat type. Loss of grassland habitat is a threat.

Class—**Aves** (birds)		
Order—**Passeriformes** (songbirds)		
Family—**Emberizidae** (sparrows)		
Henslow's Sparrow *Ammodramus henslowii*	**Grasshopper Sparrow** *Ammodramus savannarum*	**Le Conte's Sparrow** *Ammodramus leconteii*
 Presumed range in Kentucky	 Presumed range in Kentucky	 Presumed range in Kentucky
Size: 5 inches.	**Size:** 5 inches.	**Size:** 4.75 inches.
Abundance: Uncommon.	**Abundance:** Fairly common.	**Abundance:** Very rare.
Migratory Status: A rare summer resident of Kentucky that winters in the lower coastal plain of the southeast U.S.	**Migratory Status:** Spring/fall migrant with a few summer residents; winters from the southeastern U.S. to Mexico.	**Migratory Status:** Seen in Kentucky in during migration in spring and fall and rarely in winter. Summers in Canada.
Variation: No variation among adults.	**Variation:** No variation among adults.	**Variation:** None among adults.
Habitat: Undisturbed, overgrown grassy / weedy fields in open areas. Unmowed hayfields and reclaimed strip mines are used in Kentucky.	**Habitat:** A grassland species, the Grasshopper Sparrow likes short and midgrass prairie. In Kentucky it uses heavily grazed pastures and hayfields.	**Habitat:** Wet meadows, damp hayfields, and marshy areas as well as grassy, upland fields. Summer habitat is prairie regions of Canada.
Breeding: Nest is on the ground in thick grass and well concealed. Two to five eggs are laid in May. Double-broods are known.	**Breeding:** Nest is on the ground and well hidden beneath overhanging grass. Two broods per summer is usual with four to five eggs per clutch.	**Breeding:** Four to five eggs are laid in a nest woven from grass and placed in a clump of grass. Nests widely across south central Canada and Great Lakes region.
Natural History: Henslow's Sparrow is nowhere a common species and in Kentucky its scarcity and secretive nature make it one of the least familiar birds in the state. This is a species in decline throughout its range. Not surprising since the tallgrass prairies that once provided ample nesting habitat are all but gone. Insects, especially grasshoppers and crickets, are important food items in the summer. In winter eats mostly seeds, especially small grass seeds. Snakes are reported to be a major predator on nests, along with a variety of carnivorous mammals. Breeds across much of northern Kentucky and presumably can be seen as a migrant throughout the state.	**Natural History:** In many ways similar to the preceding species, but much more common. Its name is derived from the sound of its song, which mimics the buzzing sound made by some types of orthopteran insects. Throughout its range (which includes most of the U.S. east of the Rocky Mountains) it is a rather inconspicuous bird. Though unfamiliar to most Kentuckians, in the high plains region of the north-central U.S. it is commonly seen (and heard). Feeds entirely on the ground. Food is mostly grasshoppers and other insects in summer. In winter eats both insects and seeds, especially tiny grass seeds. Most range maps show the entire state within Grasshopper Sparrow's summer range.	**Natural History:** This is a small and secretive sparrow that eludes attempts to study it closely. Little is known about many aspects of its biology. For instance only a small number of nests have ever been found. Usually remains hidden from view in dense grasses, and when flushed flies only a short distance before diving back into cover. Food items listed include small grass seeds and arthropods. There is even less information available regarding the habits of birds that winter in Kentucky. Most migrate west of the Mississippi River and sightings of this sparrow in Kentucky are usually in the western end of the state.

Class—**Aves** (birds)		
Order—**Passeriformes** (songbirds)		
Family—**Emberizidae** (sparrows)		
White-throated Sparrow *Zonotrichia albicollis*	**White-crowned Sparrow** *Zonotrichia leucophrys*	**Dark-eyed Junco** *Junco hyemalis*

Presumed range in Kentucky	Presumed range in Kentucky	Presumed range in Kentucky
Size: 6.75 inches.	**Size:** 7 inches.	**Size:** 6 inches.
Abundance: Common.	**Abundance:** Fairly common.	**Abundance:** Common.
Migratory Status: A fall/winter to early spring bird in Kentucky (October to April). Summers in Canada and the Great Lakes region. Migrates at night.	**Migratory Status:** Winter resident. Summers as far north as the Arctic Circle. May be seen in Kentucky from October through April.	**Migratory Status:** Winter resident (November to March); most summer in Canada. Year-round in Kentucky in the higher elevations of the Appalachians.
Variation: Two adult morphs. One has bright white eye stripe, other has tan. Immatures have striped breasts.	**Variation:** First year birds have chestnut and beige head stripe as opposed to black and white (see photos). Sexes alike.	**Variation:** Highly variable. Most birds seen in Kentucky are the typical "Slate-colored" morph shown above.
Habitat: Brushy thickets, fence rows, weedy fields, edges areas, and regenerative woodlands. Both in upland and lowland areas.	**Habitat:** In Kentucky they may be seen in any area where there are weeds, grasses, and brush. Woodland edges and overgrown fence rows are best.	**Habitat:** Occupies a wide variety of habitats in winter, but is most fond of semi-open areas or woods openings. Summer habitat is boreal forests.
Breeding: Nest is on the ground in open areas, forest edges, etc. Four eggs is typical. As many as seven recorded.	**Breeding:** Breeds in boreal regions, tundra, and mountain meadows. Nest is in a low bush with about four eggs.	**Breeding:** Nesting in Kentucky has been recorded only on Black Mountain, Kentucky's highest mountain.
Natural History: This is one of Kentucky's most common sparrows during winter. In early spring just before flying north to summer breeding grounds, the White-throated Sparrow serenades the fields and woodlands with its distinctive whistling song. As these birds are ground foragers, snow cover is one of the most important conditions that influence migratory patterns. Feeds mostly on insects in summer and switches to seeds in winter. When feeding uses both feet with a backward thrusting motion to clear away leaf litter. They are well represented at bird feeders throughout the state in winter.	**Natural History:** Similar in many respects to the White-throated Sparrow to which it is closely related. Ranges farther west (all the way to the Pacific). The White-crowned Sparrow produces multiple broods (as many as four per season in some western populations). Most will have at least two broods annually. Some summer well into the Arctic Tundra and make annual migrations of over 4,000 miles up and down the continent. Eats insects and seeds in summer, mostly seeds in winter. Forages on the ground near cover. Less common than the White-throated Sparrow, but still a familiar bird at winter feeders.	**Natural History:** Juncos are a familiar winter bird at feeders throughout Kentucky. They arrive with the colder weather fronts and are often associated with snowstorms. In fact a common nickname in Kentucky is "Snowbird." They arrive in most of Kentucky in November and most are gone by mid-March. Those that summer in the southern United States do so only at the highest elevations in the Appalachian Mountains (above 3,500 feet). The combined summer, winter, and migratory ranges of the Dark-eyed Junco includes nearly all of the North American continent except peninsula Florida.

Class—**Aves** (birds)

Order—**Passeriformes** (songbirds)

Family—**Emberizidae** (sparrows)

Eastern Towhee *Pipilo erythrophthalmus*	**Fox Sparrow** *Passerella iliaca*	**Lapland Longspur** *Calcarius lapponicus*

Presumed range in Kentucky	Presumed range in Kentucky	Presumed range in Kentucky
Size: 8 inches.	**Size:** 7 inches.	**Size:** 6.25 inches.
Abundance: Fairly common.	**Abundance:** Uncommon.	**Abundance:** Uncommon in Kentucky.
Migratory Status: A year-round resident throughout the state. They are most commonly seen in winter when they are attracted to feeders.	**Migratory Status:** This is a winter-only species in Kentucky. They breed and spend the summer in the far north and in the northern Rockies.	**Migratory Status:** A winter migrant from the far north that is usually seen in Kentucky only during exceptionally harsh winter weather.
Variation: Sexually dimorphic. Males are black on back, head, and wings whereas females are reddish brown. No seasonal variation.	**Variation:** This is a highly variable species and includes reddish, grayish, and sooty brown morphs. Kentucky birds are usually like the photo above.	**Variation:** Seasonal and sexual plumage differences. Birds seen in Kentucky are always in winter plumage (see above). Winter females are less vivid.
Habitat: Succesional woodlands, overgrown fields / fence rows, edges of stream courses and woodlots where honeysuckle, briers, weeds, and saplings are predominate.	**Habitat:** The Fox Sparrow is a lover of dense cover and thickets, thick weeds and shrubs bordering woodlands or thickets. A mixture of brier, saplings, weeds, regenerating timberlands, etc.	**Habitat:** Winter migrants in Kentucky use very open areas with nearly bare ground. Large acreage harvested crop fields of are the primary habitat for flocks wintering in Kentucky.
Breeding: Two broods per year are common in Kentucky. Four to five eggs per clutch. Nest is usually in a dense bush.	**Breeding:** Nests are low to the ground or even on the ground. Does not nest in Kentucky. Usually four eggs.	**Breeding:** Nests on the ground in Arctic Tundra. Eggs (three to seven) are not laid until early June.
Natural History: Our largest member of the sparrow family. Sometimes called "Rufous-sided Towhee." Its "tow-wheee" song is a familiar sound beginning as early as March. The widespread range of the Eastern Towhee corresponds closely to the Eastern Temperate Forest ecoregion, but they normally do not occur in dense populations. Most bird feeders in rural Kentucky will have a pair for the winter, but rarely more than two pairs. The similar Spotted Towhee (*P. maculatus*) replaces the Eastern Towhee in the western half of America.	**Natural History:** The Fox Sparrow is widespread across the North American continent, summering in the far north (Canada, Alaska, and the northern Rockies) and wintering across much of the southern United States. Several distinct subspecies are recognized. They feed on a variety of insects and other arthropods in summer and subsist mainly on seeds in winter. They can be an occasional to regular visitor at bird feeders in Kentucky during winter, especially during periods of snowy weather. Unlike many other sparrows, the Fox Sparrow is never seen in large flocks.	**Natural History:** This hardy sparrow breeds and summers in Arctic Tundra and is circumpolar in its distribution. It is very common on its breeding grounds where it is sometimes the only songbird present. In winter they move far to the south, but are not very abundant east of the Mississippi River. Changes wrought on the landscape by modern agriculture have made for more hospitable habitat for this species in Kentucky. On breeding grounds they eat dipterous insects (flies, mosquitoes) and seeds. Winter diet is mostly seeds and waste grain.

Class—**Aves** (birds)

Order—**Passeriformes** (songbirds)

Family—**Cardinalidae** (grosbeaks)

Dickcissel *Spiza americana*	**Northern Cardinal** *Cardinalis cardinalis*	**Rose-breasted Grosbeak** *Pheucticus ludovicianus*

Presumed range in Kentucky 	Presumed range in Kentucky 	Presumed range in Kentucky 
Size: 6.25 inches.	**Size:** 8.75 inches.	**Size:** 8 inches.
Abundance: Uncommon in Kentucky.	**Abundance:** Very common.	**Abundance:** Fairly common.
Migratory Status: Summer resident (May to September) that winters from southern Mexico to northern South America.	**Migratory Status:** A non-migratory species, the Northern Cardinal is a year-round resident of Kentucky.	**Migratory Status:** Spring and fall migrant the passes through Kentucky in April/May and September/October.
Variation: Males are slightly larger. Females similar to males but are duller and lack the black "bib" of the male.	**Variation:** Pronounced sexual dimorphism. Male bright red, female buff-tan with reddish wings, crest, and tail.	**Variation:** Sexually dimorphic. Female drab brown, males striking black and white with rose-colored breast.
Habitat: Fallow lands with weeds, saplings, and grasses. Weedy fields in open areas are the preferred habitat.	**Habitat:** From undisturbed natural areas to suburbs, the Northern Cardinal favors edge areas with shrubs and brush.	**Habitat:** A forest species primarily, but enjoys edge areas and regenerative woodlands with thick shrubby cover.
Breeding: Breeds sporadically across the western half of Kentucky.	**Breeding:** Nest is usually in a thick shrub or bush. About four eggs on average.	**Breeding:** Three to five eggs are laid in a nest of twigs , grass, and plant fibers.
Natural History: The bulk of the Dickcissel's summer range is in the central Great Plains. Its presence in Kentucky today is likely a result of range expansion into suitable habitats created by deforestation and subsequent conversion of woodlands to cropland and pasture. Outside their core breeding range they are distributed sporadically and they are also known to wander well outside their core range. Flocks numbering in the thousands have been recorded during migration. Eats seeds almost exclusively during migration and on winter range. During breeding is more omnivorous, consuming insects and seeds. An open country bird, the Dickcissel avoids the heavily forested mountains of eastern Kentucky.	**Natural History:** Conspicuous and highly recognizable, the Northern Cardinal enjoys the distinction of being the state bird for a total of seven states (including Kentucky). They are also a popular mascot for sports teams. They are mainly seed and berry / fruit eaters, but they will eat insects and feed insects to the young. They are common birds at feeders throughout their range, especially during winter. In the last century they have expanded their range farther to the north into the Great Lakes region and New England. Today they are seen throughout much of the United States east of the Rockies. The southern extent of their range is northern Central America. They are commonly known by the nickname "Redbird."	**Natural History:** Most Rose-breasted Grosbeaks seen in Kentucky are passage migrants. A few individuals will stay in northern and eastern Kentucky throughout the summer. Breeding has been noted on Kentucky's highest mountain, Black Mountain. Most will nest well to the north of Kentucky and pass through again in the fall en route to wintering habitats in Central and South America. Food in summer is about 50 / 50 insects and plant material such as seeds, fruits, flowers, and buds. During migration they are readily attracted to bird feeders where sunflower seeds are a favorite food. Bird watchers throughout the state enthusiastically await the return of migrant songbirds each spring, and the Rose-breasted Grosbeak is a favorite.

Class—**Aves** (birds)

Order—**Passeriformes** (songbirds)

Family—**Cardinalidae** (grosbeaks)		Family—**Fringillidae** (finches)

Blue Grosbeak
Passerina caerulea

Presumed range in Kentucky

Size: 6 inches.

Abundance: Fairly common.

Migratory Status: Summer resident that winters in southern Mexico and Central America.

Variation: Females are uniformly brown with a blueish wash that is apparent only on close examination. Juvenile males resemble females.

Habitat: On summer range the Blue Grosbeak enjoys overgrown fields dominated by forbs and saplings. Also uses fencerows, thickets, brambles, etc.

Breeding: Nest is a tightly woven cup placed in a low bush or tangle of vines, brush. About four eggs. Double brooding is known in the southern part of range.

Natural History: Although the Blue Grosbeak can probably be found throughout the Bluegrass State in spring and summer, it is most common in the western half of the state. It is least common in the higher mountains and more densely forested regions of the southeastern edge of Kentucky. During summer they feed mostly on crickets, grasshoppers and other insects, but eat mostly seeds in the early spring and fall. They often will visit bird feeders at these times. These birds are more common in the eastern United States today than they were in historic times and they seem to be expanding their range.

Indigo Bunting
Passerina cyanea

Presumed range in Kentucky

Size: 5.5 inches.

Abundance: Very common.

Migratory Status: A summer resident that arrives in Kentucky in mid to late April and leaves in early fall.

Variation: Pronounced sexual dimorphism (see photos above). Immature males resemble females but with varying amounts of blue mottling.

Habitat: Edge areas, fence rows, rural roadsides with substantial brushy / weedy cover, and overgrown fields or early successional woodlands.

Breeding: Two broods are common. Lays two to four eggs in a nest of woven grasses that is usually placed in thick cover only a few feet above the ground.

Natural History: Indigo Buntings are common in Kentucky. Probably more so today than in historical times when forests dominated the state's habitats. The neon blue color of the male makes it one of the most striking of North American birds. These birds are found throughout the eastern U.S. in summer, generally ranging from the short grass plains eastward to the Atlantic and as far north as southern Canada. Their annual migration may encompass up to 2,500 miles and many make the long flight across the Gulf of Mexico. Seeds and berries are the primary food with insects eaten during the breeding season.

Pine Siskin
Spinus pinus

Presumed range in Kentucky

Size: 5 inches.

Abundance: Uncommon.

Migratory Status: Pine Siskins are northern birds that often winter as far south as Kentucky.

Variation: Males have a yellowish wash, while females and juveniles are heavily streaked with brown. See photos above.

Habitat: Pine Siskins prefer coniferous woodlands but in winter they are often seen in mixed or even pure hardwood forests.

Breeding: Nest is woven of grasses, twigs, rootlets, etc., and lined with mosses or fur. Three to four eggs is typical. May nest in loose colonies.

Natural History: The Pine Siskin is a coniferous forest species, though it is also found in mixed deciduous/coniferous woodlands and in pure deciduous woods during winter irruptions. Mostly a bird of the far north and the Rocky Mountains, they sometimes range as far south as the gulf coast in winter. In Kentucky they are least common in the Coastal Plain where they may be seen only once every few years. Feeds on seeds of coniferous trees, grass seeds, and weed seeds and will regularly visit feeders in winter where thistle seeds are favored. Insects are also eaten during breeding.

Class—**Aves** (birds)

Order—**Passeriformes** (songbirds)

Family—**Fringillidae** (finches)

Goldfinch *Spinus tristis*	**Purple Finch** *Haemorhous purpureus*	**House Finch** *Haemorhous mexicanus*

Presumed range in Kentucky	Presumed range in Kentucky	Presumed range in Kentucky
Size: 5 inches.	**Size:** 6 inches.	**Size:** 6 inches.
Abundance: Common.	**Abundance:** Uncommon.	**Abundance:** Common.
Migratory Status: Year-round resident throughout Kentucky.	**Migratory Status:** A winter-only resident of Kentucky, breeds far to the north.	**Migratory Status:** A non-migratory, year-round resident in Kentucky.
Variation: Exhibits sexual and seasonal plumage variations. See above. Female resembles winter male.	**Variation:** Significant plumage differences between the sexes. See photos above.	**Variation:** Plumage differences between males and females make sexes easily recognizable. See photos above.
Habitat: Edge areas and successional habitats, fence rows, overgrown fields, and floodplains in open and semi-open areas.	**Habitat:** Summer habitat is moist coniferous forests. In winter they are seen in almost all habitats across the eastern half of the United States.	**Habitat:** As implied by the name, House Finches in Kentucky are usually associated with human habitation. Found both in cities and rural areas.
Breeding: Four to six uniformly white eggs are laid. Nest is a tightly woven cup of grasses usually wrapped around a triad of upright branches.	**Breeding:** Nest of twigs, roots, and grasses is built in a fork on the outer portion of a branch of a conifer. Three to six six eggs per clutch. Two broods per year.	**Breeding:** Typical woven nest of grasses is usually placed in a dense evergreen shrub, cedar, or conifer tree. Three to five eggs are reported from nests in Kentucky.
Natural History: This well-known species is widespread across North America. The transition of the male Goldfinch into its strikingly yellow breeding plumage in spring is a profound example of what is known as a prealternate (or springtime) molt. The Goldfinch is a common visitor to bird feeders and is especially attracted to thistle seeds. Unlike many other species that eat seeds in winter and insects in summer, the Goldfinch is mainly a seed eater. This species is apparently immune to parasitism by the Brown-headed Cowbird as young cowbirds cannot develop on a diet that contains no insects.	**Natural History:** The Purple Finch seems to be a declining species in the eastern United States. Competition with the House Finch may be to blame. Although at least a few Purple Finches are seen in Kentucky every winter, they may be move well south all the way to the Gulf Coast in years of poor cone production. Seeds are the major food item, including seeds of trees (elm, maples, ash) and seeds of fruits. Buds are also eaten. Insects are also consumed. As with most other seed eaters, the Purple Finch will frequent bird feeders in winter. Easily confused with the House Finch, but is larger headed and has a heavier bill.	**Natural History:** House Finches have extended their range into the eastern United States over the last few decades. Originally native to the southwestern United States, the first House Finches appeared in Kentucky in the 1970s. Today they are found throughout the United States including all of Kentucky. Primarily a seed eater, these birds can be very common at urban feeders. Weed seeds, fruit, buds, and flowers are also reported to be eaten. Birds seen at feeders sometimes exhibit signs of a disease that causes swelling of the eyes with occasional blindness or death. Similar to and easily confused with the less common Purple Finch.

Class—**Aves** (birds)

Order—**Apodiformes** (swifts & hummingbirds)		Order—**Coraciiformes** (kingfishers)
Family—**Apodidae** (swifts)	Family—**Trochilidae** (hummingbirds)	Family—**Alcedinidae** (kingfisher)
Chimney Swift *Chaetura pelagica*	**Ruby-throated Hummingbird** *Archilochus colubris*	**Belted Kingfisher** *Megaceryle alcyon*
 	 	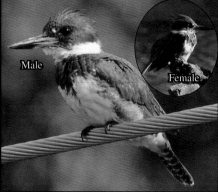 

Size: 5.5 inches.

Abundance: Fairly common.

Migratory Status: Summer resident that winters in South America.

Variation: No sexual dimorphism. Immatures slightly lighter.

Habitat: Mainly seen in open and semi-open country and in urban/suburban areas.

Breeding: Nest is a flimsy cup plastered to the inside of a chimney. Two to five eggs are laid.

Natural History: This is a species that has benefited from human population expansion. Historically, the Chimney Swift nested mainly in hollow trees. These birds require a vertical surface within a sheltered place for nesting. When people began to build houses and large structures like schools, churches, and factories equipped with chimneys, their populations exploded. Today they are perhaps less common than a few decades ago when most dwellings and other buildings had chimneys. Some nesting in natural hollows still occurs. Swifts have long, narrow, pointed wings that allow for extreme maneuverability and these birds feed entirely on the wing. Small flying insects are their prey. During migration they are sometimes seen in large flocks that can contain over 1,000 birds.

Size: 3.75 inches.

Abundance: Common.

Migratory Status: A summer resident that winters mostly in Central America.

Variation: Female lacks ruby throat patch. See photos above.

Habitat: Woodlands. Both deciduous and mixed forests are utilized. Edge areas and open fields are used for feeding.

Breeding: Nest is a tiny cup of fine plant fibers and lichens glued together with spiderwebs. Two eggs is typical.

Natural History: The tiny hummingbirds are ounce for ounce one of the world's greatest travelers. Many fly across the Gulf of Mexico each year during migration! Considering that they weigh barely more than 0.1 of an ounce that is a remarkable feat of endurance. The range of the Ruby-throated Hummingbird includes all of the Eastern Deciduous Forest Level 1 Ecoregion, as well as portions of the Boreal Forest and Great Plains ecoregions. Nectar is the major food item for hummingbirds and they show a preference for red, tubular flowers. They possess a highly specialized beak and tongue for reaching nectar deep within flowers. They will also eat some small, flying insects caught on the wing, and are known to pluck tiny invertebrates from foliage or small spiders from their webs.

Size: 13 inches.

Abundance: Uncommon.

Migratory Status: Year-round resident. Some may move south during winter.

Variation: Female has a rust colored band across belly (see inset above).

Habitat: Kingfishers require water and in Kentucky they haunt creeks, rivers, lakes, swamps, and farm ponds.

Breeding: Kingfishers nest in burrows they excavate into vertical banks of dirt or sand that are at least eight feet high.

Natural History: The Belted Kingfisher is one of the most widely distributed birds in North America. In fact they range throughout the continent from Alaska and northern Canada south to Panama. In Kentucky they are most common in the lowlands of the Mississippi Alluvial Plain. Although widespread they are widely dispersed. The presence of suitable nesting habitat in the form of vertical earthen cliffs may be a limiting factor in their abundance. Human activities such as digging of quarries and road cuts through hills and mountains may have helped this species in modern times by providing the requisite vertical banks for nest sites. Small fish are the primary food item. They are known for diving headfirst into the water from a perch or while hovering to catch fish near the surface.

Class—**Aves** (birds)

Order—**Piciformes** (woodpeckers)

Family—**Picidae** (woodpeckers)

Pileated Woodpecker *Dryocopus pileatus*	**Northern Flicker** *Colaptes auratus*	**Red-headed Woodpecker** *Melanerpes erythrocephalus*

Presumed range in Kentucky 	Presumed range in Kentucky 	Presumed range in Kentucky 
Size: 16.5 inches.	**Size:** 12.5 inches.	**Size:** 9.25 inches.
Abundance: Uncommon.	**Abundance:** Fairly common.	**Abundance:** Uncommon.
Migratory Status: Year-round resident.	**Migratory Status:** Year-round resident.	**Migratory Status:** Year-round resident.
Variation: Male has a red cheek patch.	**Variation:** Male has black "mustache."	**Variation:** No sexual variation.
Habitat: A forest species, the Pileated Woodpecker prefers mature woodlands. It is also seen in semi-open areas where large tracts of woods occur nearby. Floodplain forests are a favorite habitat.	**Habitat:** Semi-open areas and open lands with at least a few large trees. Farmlands, older urban neighborhoods, and parks are also used. Least common in dense, mature woodlands.	**Habitat:** Savanna-like habitats with widely spaced, large trees are the preferred habitat of the Red-headed Woodpecker. They seem to show a preference for areas near rivers.
Breeding: Nest is a hollow cavity excavated into the trunk of a tree (usually a dead tree, but sometimes living). Nests are usually fairly high up. Four eggs.	**Breeding:** Nest is usually excavated in a fairly large diameter dead tree. Also known to use natural hollows. Averages six to eight eggs.	**Breeding:** Nest hole is usually in a dead tree but it is also fond of using utility poles. Five eggs is typical and some may produce two broods per summer.
Natural History: By far Kentucky's largest woodpecker, Pileated Woodpeckers play an important role in the mature forest ecosytem. Their large nest cavities are utilized as a refuge by many other woodland species including small owls, Wood Ducks, bluebirds, and squirrels. In the boreal forests of Canada the Pine Marten is reported to use their holes. Using their powerful, chisel-like beaks to break apart dead snags and logs they also help accelerate decomposition of large dead trees. In addition to mast and fruit such as wild cherries, they eat insects, mainly carpenter ants and beetle larva. In Kentucky this species is most common in the heavily forested Appalachian Plateau and in the Mississippi Alluvial Plain in the western tip of the state.	**Natural History:** In addition to feeding on insects (mainly ants) usually caught on the ground, the Flicker also eats berries and in winter, grains (including corn). Two distinct subspecies of Northern Flicker occur in North America. The "Yellow-shafted Flicker" is native to Kentucky and the rest of the eastern U.S. In the Rocky Mountain west the "Red-shafted Flicker" occurs. The two are distinguished by the dominant color on the underneath side of the wing, which is visible only in flight. As with Kentucky's other large woodpecker (Pileated), the Northern Flicker is regarded as a "keystone" species that is important to other species that use its excavations for shelter and nesting. Thus recent declines in the population of this species is cause for concern.	**Natural History:** Once regarded as very common, this handsome woodpecker has declined significantly in the last century. It eats large amounts of acorns and other mast, especially in fall and winter, and may move about in fall and winter in search of areas with good mast crops. Insects are regularly eaten in warmer months and some may be caught on the wing, but they also commonly forage on the ground. In Kentucky this woodpecker is much more common in the western end of the state and is uncommon in much of the heavily forested Appalachian Plateau in the east. They can also be fairly common in the Great Plains states. The Red-headed Woodpecker was apparently well known to many native Americans, and was a war symbol of the Cherokee.

Class—**Aves** (birds)		
Order—**Piciformes** (woodpeckers)		
Family—**Picidae** (woodpeckers)		

Red-bellied Woodpecker *Melanerpes carolinus*	**Downy Woodpecker** *Picoides pubescens*	**Hairy Woodpecker** *Picoides pubescens*

Presumed range in Kentucky	Presumed range in Kentucky	Presumed range in Kentucky
Size: 9.75 inches.	**Size:** 6.75 inches.	**Size:** 9.25 inches.
Abundance: Common.	**Abundance:** Very common.	**Abundance:** Fairly common.
Migratory Status: Year-round resident.	**Migratory Status:** Year-round resident.	**Migratory Status:** Year-round resident.
Variation: Female has gray crown.	**Variation:** Male has red spot on nape.	**Variation:** Male has red spot on nape.
Habitat: A woodland species that inhabits all forest types in the eastern U.S. Semi-open and open woods are favored.	**Habitat:** Occupies a wide variety of habitats throughout the state. From wilderness to farms and urban areas.	**Habitat:** A forest species that likes woodlands with larger, more mature trees. Also in parks and neighborhoods.
Breeding: Nests in holes excavated by the adults. Four to five eggs are laid in mid-April to early June.	**Breeding:** Nest is usually excavated in a dead limb. Eggs range from three to as many as eight. Eggs hatch in 12 days.	**Breeding:** Nest hole may be in dead snags or living trees with heart rot. Four eggs is typical.
Natural History: Feeds on all types of tree dwelling arthropods as well as seeds, nuts, fruits, and berries. In Kentucky they are most common in the western half of of the state and least common in the Appalachian Plateau. These woodpeckers are known to take over the nest holes of the endangered Red-cockaded Woodpecker where their ranges overlap in the southern United States. Conversely, the introduced Starling sometimes takes over the nest hole of the Red-bellied Woodpecker. Due to its fairly large size and its tendency to be quite vocal year-round, the Red-bellied Woodpecker is a fairly conspicuous bird in both rural and urban areas in much of Kentucky. Because both males and females have a significant amount of red on the head they are often misidentified as the much rarer Red-headed Woodpecker.	**Natural History:** Ranging across all of North America except the far north and the desert southwest, the Downy is one of the most widespread woodpeckers in America and is the most common woodpecker in Kentucky. These appealing little woodpeckers are well known and frequent visitors to bird feeders where they eat suet and seeds. Arthropods are the most important food item making up as much as 75 percent of the diet. Fruit and sap is also eaten. Like other woodpeckers, the Downy's nest holes in dead limbs and trunks may be utilized by a wide array of other species as a home and shelter. Many small cavity nesting birds may use old woodpecker holes, and mice, lizards, snakes, treefrogs, spiders, and insects can often be found using their abandoned nests. Very similar to the Hairy Woodpecker but smaller and with a thinner beak.	**Natural History:** The range of the Hairy Woodpecker closely coincides with that of the smaller Downy Woodpecker. Both species can be found from Alaska to southern Florida. The two are often confused but the Hairy is a much larger bird and has a heavier, longer bill. Like the Downy, this woodpecker excavates nest holes that may be used by a variety of other species, making it an important species in forest ecosystems. A wide variety of insects and other arthropods are eaten along with seeds and fruits. This species can be seen at feeders throughout Kentucky, often in the company of the smaller Downy Woodpecker. When both are seen together, size differences become more apparent. The Hairy Woodpecker varies somewhat geographically in both size and coloration. Specimens shown above are typical for Kentucky.

Class—**Aves** (birds)

Order—**Piciformes** (woodpeckers)	Order—**Cuculiformes** (cuckoos, anis, roadrunner)	
Family—**Picidae** (woodpeckers)	Family—**Cuculidae** (cuckoos)	

Yellow-bellied Sapsucker *Sphyrapicus varius*	Black-billed Cuckoo *Coccyzus erythropthalmus*	Yellow-billed Cuckoo *Coccyzus americanus*
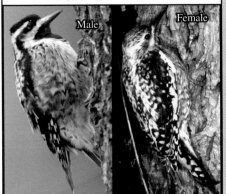		
Presumed range in Kentucky	Presumed range in Kentucky	Presumed range in Kentucky
Size: 8.5 inches.	**Size:** 12 inches.	**Size:** 12 inches.
Abundance: Uncommon.	**Abundance:** Uncommon.	**Abundance:** Fairly common.
Migratory Status: A winter (September to April) resident that summers in the northern U.S. and Canada.	**Migratory Status:** Spring and fall migrant throughout the state and summer resident in the eastern half of Kentucky.	**Migratory Status:** A summer resident that winters in South America. Seen in Kentucky from May through September.
Variation: Male has red throat.	**Variation:** No sexual variation.	**Variation:** No sexual variation.
Habitat: In winter this woodpecker occupies a wide variety of woodland habitats.	**Habitat:** Successional areas, thickets, and mature woodlands with some open areas.	**Habitat:** Open woodlands, edge areas, regenerative woodlands near open fields, overgrown fence rows, etc.
Breeding: Nest is an excavated hole in dead tree or a living tree with heart rot. Clutch size ranges from two to seven eggs.	**Breeding:** Breeds sparingly in the eastern portion of Kentucky and well to the north. Clutch size averages two to four eggs.	**Breeding:** Breeds from early June through the summer. Nest is flimsy and placed in thick vegetation. Two to four eggs.
Natural History: The Yellow-bellied Sapsucker is unique among Kentucky birds in that it creates feeding opportunities by drilling small holes into the bark of trees. These holes, called "sap wells," fill with sap, which the sapsucker then drinks. Sapsuckers regularly visit the "sap wells," to maintain them and defend them from other sapsuckers. Many other bird species benefit from the sapsuckers' activities, especially the Ruby-throated Hummingbird, which will also drink sap from the woodpeckers' holes. The sap also attracts insects, which in turn feed many species of insectivorous birds. In addition, the nest holes excavated by the sapsucker may be used other birds, flying squirrels, etc. Though widespread across Kentucky in winter months, they are not common anywhere in the state.	**Natural History:** Although once common, the Black-billed Cuckoo has declined in abundance over the past several decades. Widespread use of pesticides may be to blame. Caterpillars are a primary food and pesticide-depleted caterpillar numbers results in a scarce food source for the birds. Ironically, large flocks of these handsome birds once acted as a natural control of caterpillars, and historical observers reported seeing flocks of Black-billed Cuckoos descend on a tree full of caterpillars and eat every caterpillar on the tree! Today it is rare to see more than one of these birds at a time. Cicadas are another important insect food, and in years of cicada outbreaks cuckoos (and many other bird species) will produce larger clutches and successfully rear more young.	**Natural History:** The Yellow-billed Cuckoo is one of the latest arriving of Kentucky's neotropical migrant songbirds. In Kentucky they often go by the name "Raincrow" and folklore states that they call right before a rain. Although much more common than the Black-billed, Yellow-billed Cuckoos are not abundant birds today. Like our other cuckoo, their numbers have diminished significantly in modern times. Caterpillars are an important food and widespread pesticide use is likely the major contributing factor in their decline. These are secretive birds that are heard more often than seen. Their call is quite distinctive and is heard most frequently during the "dog days" of mid to late summer. The young of this species develop rapidly and may leave the nest within 17 days of hatching.

Class—**Aves** (birds)
Order—**Columbiformes** (doves)
Family—**Columbidae** (doves)

Rock Pigeon *Columba livia*	**Mourning Dove** *Zenaida macroura*	**Eurasian Collared-Dove** *Zenaida decaocto*

 Presumed range in Kentucky	 Presumed range in Kentucky	 Presumed range in Kentucky
Size: 13 inches.	**Size:** 12 inches.	**Size:** 13 inches.
Abundance: Very common.	**Abundance:** Very common.	**Abundance:** Rare but increasing.
Migratory Status: Year-round resident.	**Migratory Status:** Year-round resident.	**Migratory Status:** Year-round resident.
Variation: Highly variable.	**Variation:** No variation among adults.	**Variation:** No variation among adults.
Habitat: Farms and ranches in rural areas and parks and downtown streets in urban environments.	**Habitat:** Agricultural areas and open lands with short grass or areas of bare ground. Open to semi-open areas.	**Habitat:** Open and semi-open lands. Agricultural areas and small towns are favored over wilderness.
Breeding: Nests on man-made ledges and beneath overhangs in cities. Bridges and barns are used in rural areas. Multiple nesting with two eggs per clutch.	**Breeding:** Builds a flimsy nest of small sticks in sapling or low branch usually from 6 to 15 feet above ground. Two eggs is usual with multiple broods per year.	**Breeding:** Usually nests in trees or bushes near human habitation. Lays two eggs per clu tch but can nest several times per year.
Natural History: Although the Rock Pigeon is about the same overall length as the Mourning Dove and Collard Dove, the pigeon is a much stockier, heavier bird that weighs over twice as much as the Mourning Dove. Despite the fact that this familiar bird ranges from coast to coast across North America, the Rock Pigeon is not a native species. It was introduced into North America by the earliest European settlers in the 1600s. Pigeons followed the first settlers into the west (including Kentucky), colonizing towns and settlements and living in close proximity to rural farms and livestock. Today they are one of the most familiar urban birds in America and are also common around farms and ranches. Young pigeons known as "squab" are eaten in many places throughout the world.	**Natural History:** Although these birds are found year-round in Kentucky their numbers swell each fall with migrants from farther to the north. Mourning Doves are regarded as a game species throughout much of the southern United States, including Kentucky. The U.S. Fish and Wildlife Service estimates that as many as 20 million are killed each fall during America's dove season. While that seems an appallingly high number, the Mourning Dove is actually one of the most numerous bird species in America and the total population is estimated at around 350 million birds! Seeds are the chief food item. They will eat everything from the tiniest grass seeds to every type of seed crop produced by man, including corn, wheat, sorghum, millet, and sunflower as well as peanuts and soybeans.	**Natural History:** Originally native to Eurasia, the Collared-Dove has colonized much of the southern United States since its release in the Bahamas in the 1970s. Today they are found mostly in the western half of Kentucky but may soon colonize the entire state. In food habits and other aspects of its biology the Collard-Dove is similar to the Mourning Dove. Young Collard-Doves disperse widely and this species continues to increase across North America. Cold weather does not seem to be a limiting factor but food availability may limit range expansion. How far this species will extend its range in North America is still unknown. As with all other members of the Columbidae family, young birds are feed a semi-liquid "crop milk" regurgitated from the adults crop.

Class—**Aves** (birds)

Order—**Galliformes** (chicken-like birds)

Family—**Phasianidae** (grouse)

Family—**Odontophoridae** (quail)

Ruffed Grouse *Bonasa umbellus*	**Wild Turkey** *Meleagris gallopavo*	**Bobwhite** *Colinus virginianus*
		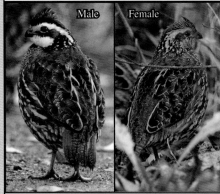

 Presumed range in Kentucky

 Presumed range in Kentucky

Size: 17.5 inches.

Abundance: Uncommon.

Migratory Status: Year-round resident.

Variation: Two color morphs. Red and Gray. Red morph occurs in Kentucky. Male has larger "ruff" on neck.

Habitat: Forests. Mainly successional forests, forest clearings, and disturbed woodlands.

Breeding: Nest is on the ground in woodland. Usually placed near the base of a tree, stump or beneath downed tree. Nine to 14 eggs.

Natural History: Mainly a bird of the northern forests, the Ruffed Grouse ranges southward in the Appalachian chain as far as northern Georgia. In Kentucky they are restricted mainly to the eastern half of the state, though they once probably occurred statewide. Re-introduction into some areas of western Kentucky has had only limited success. The name comes from the "ruff" of feathers around the neck which are erected by the males during courtship displays. At this time the male also produces a deep, resonate sound similar to that produced by blowing across the top of a soda bottle. Known as "drumming," the sound carries quite a distance in the spring forest. This species has declined extensively in since the settlement of Kentucky.

Size: Female 37 inches, male 46 inches.

Abundance: Fairly common.

Migratory Status: Year-round resident.

Variation: Females are smaller, duller, have less red on head and neck and lack "beard."

Habitat: Inhabits all major habitats in the state except for urban areas. Most common in mixture of woods and farms.

Breeding: Nests on the ground in thick cover such as thickets, honeysuckle, multiflora rose, or tall grasses. Lays up to 14 eggs.

Natural History: The courtship of the male Wild Turkey includes a "strutting" display that involves spreading the tail feathers, drooping the wings and producing a low frequency "drumming" sound. When attempting to attract females in the spring breeding season males become quite vocal and regularly emit a loud "gobble" that can be heard for a mile. The saga of the disappearance and resurgence of the Wild Turkey in America is one of wildlife management's greatest success stories. In pioneer days turkeys were found throughout Kentucky but by the early 1900s they had nearly disappeared. Re-stocking efforts by the KDF-WR agency aided by sportsmen groups has been highly successful and Wild Turkeys are now found throughout Kentucky.

Size: 10 inches.

Abundance: Fairly common.

Migratory Status: Year-round resident.

Variation: Male has white eye stripe and throat patch, trimmed in black. Female has tan on face and throat.

Habitat: Small woodlands, edge areas and overgrown fields bordering agricultural land are the favorite habitats.

Breeding: Ground nester. Clutch size averages about 15 eggs but nest failure due to predation is high. Multiple nestings are common.

Natural History: Bobwhite Quail have always been an important game bird throughout the southern United States. In recent decades, however, the species has experienced significant population declines, especially in the northern portions of its range (including Kentucky). Modern agricultural practices that have eliminated fence rows and created expansive crop fields are the main factor contributing to the decline of the Bobwhite in Kentucky. Throughout the fall and winter Bobwhites stick together in family groups known as a "covey." In spring adults pair off for breeding with the resultant offspring and their parents producing the next fall's covey. By late winter predation and human hunting reduces covey size and several surviving groups may band together until spring.

Class—**Aves** (birds)

Order—**Caprimulgiformes**

Family—**Caprimulgidae** (nightjars)

Order—**Strigiformes** (owls)

Family—**Tytonidae** (barn owl)

Common Nighthawk *Chordeiles minor*	genus—*Antrostomus* (poor-wills) **Whip-poor-will / Chuck-will's-widow** *A. vociferus / A. carolinensis*	**Barn Owl** *Tyto alba*

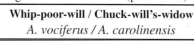
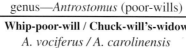

Presumed range in Kentucky

Presumed range in Kentucky
(light gray)Whip-poor-will only
(dark gray) both species

Presumed range in Kentucky

Size: 9.5 inches.

Abundance: Fairly common.

Migratory Status: Summer resident that winters in South America as far south as Brazil and Paraguay.

Variation: Sexes are very similar but males have a white tail band.

Habitat: Open and semi-open areas. Can be common around cities and towns but also in rural areas.

Breeding: No nest is constructed and two eggs are laid on bare gravel. Most nests are on flat, gravel covered rooftops.

Natural History: These birds sometimes go by the nickname "Bullbat." They are most common in urban areas but they are also seen in open and semi-open rural areas. Like our other nightjars the Common Nighthawk feeds on the wing, but unlike the others this bird is active both at night and at dawn and dusk, or sometimes on cloudy days. Around towns and cities they chase airborne insects attracted to streetlights at night. This is one of the great travelers of the bird world and one of the later migrants to arrive in Kentucky in spring and one of the earliest to leave in fall. They often migrate in large flocks. Although they may be seen migrating throughout the state, most summer residents stay to the west of the Appalachian Plateau.

Size: 9.75 inches and 12 inches.

Abundance: Both are uncommon.

Migratory Status: Late spring through summer residents that winter in Florida, the Caribbean, and Central America.

Variation: No variation within either species. Chuck-will's-widow is darkest.

Habitat: Forest edge, power-line cuts through wooded areas and xeric woods. Both species favor thickets.

Breeding: Nests on the ground amid leaf litter. No nest is built and the eggs (usually two) are laid on the ground.

Natural History: Few animals exhibit a more cryptic color and pattern than these two species. When resting on the forest floor during the day they are nearly invisible. Whip-poor-will is smaller and is grayer. The two are easily differentiated by the their songs, usually described as *whip-prrr-weel* for the Whip-poor-will and as *chuk-wills wee-dow* for the Chuck-will's-widow. Both calls are usually repeated rapidly and at times incessantly. Equiped with a very large mouths for feeding on moths and other large flying insects, they are strictly nocturnal and catch most of their food in mid-air. These birds are much more frequently heard than see but when discovered they may be surprisingly tame and approachable, especially when roosting during the day.

Size: 16 inches.

Abundance: Uncommon.

Migratory Status: Northern populations may migrate in winter but this is a year-round resident of Kentucky.

Variation: Very little variation. Females are usually slighter darker below.

Habitat: Prefers open and semi-open habitats. Probably more common around farms and small towns.

Breeding: Nested in hollow in trees or in caves historically. Now uses old buildings or barns. As many as 11 eggs.

Natural History: The Barn Owl is one of the most widespread owl species in the world, being found throughout most of North America south of Canada, all of Central and South America, most of Europe and sub-saharan Africa, parts of southern Asia and all of Australia. In spite of its wide range they are usually not common anywhere. Small rodents are the primary prey, especially mice and voles. When feeding a large brood of young a pair of Barn Owls may catch over two dozen mice in a single night. Like other owls their hearing is so acute they can catch mice unseen beneath leaves by homing in rustling sounds. Ironically, man's attempts to control rodents with poisoned baits may be in part responsible for the demise of rodent eating species like the Barn Owl.

Class—**Aves** (birds)

Order—**Strigiformes** (owls)

Family—**Strigidae** (typical owls)

Barred Owl *Strix varia*	**Great Horned Owl** *Bubo virginianus*	**Eastern Screech Owl** *Megascops asio*
	 Young	 Gray Morph
 Presumed range in Kentucky	 Presumed range in Kentucky	 Presumed range in Kentucky
Size: 21 inches.	**Size:** 23 inches.	**Size:** 8.5 inches.
Abundance: Common.	**Abundance:** Fairly common.	**Abundance:** Common.
Migratory Status: Year-round.	**Migratory Status:** Year-round resident.	**Migratory Status:** Year-round resident.
Variation: No sexual variation. Three subspecies are known in America with a fourth in central Mexico, only one (Northern Barred Owl, *S. v. varia*) occurs in Kentucky.	**Variation:** Males are slightly smaller and have a larger white patch on throat. There are 10 subspecies in North America. The Eastern Great Horned Owl (*B. v. virginianus*) is found in Kentucky.	**Variation:** Two distinct color morphs occur in Kentucky. Gray phase (inset) is more common in the eastern mountainous areas with the red phase occurring throughout the rest of the state.
Habitat: Woodlands primarily. Especially common in bottomlands, swampy areas, and riparian corridors.	**Habitat:** Woodlands, semi-open and open habitats are all utilized, but most common in upland woods.	**Habitat:** All types of habitats within the state may be used, including suburban areas and in the vicinity of farms.
Breeding: Nest is usually in tree cavities but known to nest tree crotches or old hawk nests. Usually two (rarely three or four) eggs are laid.	**Breeding:** One of the earliest nesting birds in Kentucky, Horned Owls may be sitting on eggs by late January. Nest is often an old hawk nest. Two eggs is usual.	**Breeding:** Nest is in tree hollows and old woodpecker holes. Four to six eggs are laid in April or May and the young owls are usually fledged by mid-June.
Natural History: In Kentucky this owl is most common in the lowlands in the western end of the state. The eight noted call of the Barred Owl is described as "Hoo-hoo-hoo-hoo, hoo-hoo-hooaahh." In addition the species is capable of a wide array of hoots, screeches, and coarse whistles. Small vertebrates are the main prey, especially rodents like voles, mice, and flying squirrels. Birds, lizards, small snakes, and amphibians are also eaten. In the eastern United States the range of the Barred Owl closely coincides with that of the Red-shouldered Hawk and the two predators are often regarded as ecological counterparts occupying the same niche but at different times of the day.	**Natural History:** This widespread species occurs throughout the Americas from Alaska to southern South America. In the U.S. specimens from the western portions of the country are much paler than those seen in Kentucky. In Kentucky Red Cedars and other evergreen trees are a favorite roosting site. The Great Horned Owl is the ecological counterpart of the Red-tailed Hawk, hunting much the same prey in the same regions, with the hawk hunting by day and the owl at night. These powerful predators eat a wide variety of small animals. Rabbits are a favorite food item. Also known to eat larger mammals like muskrats, groundhogs, and even skunks or rarely, domestic cats!	**Natural History:** The eerie call of the Screech Owl is often described as "haunting and tremulous." Despite being at times vocal birds, these small owls often go unnoticed. They may even live in suburban yards and small towns, especially if older, large trees with hollow limbs and trunks are present. They feed on insects such as crickets and grasshoppers and on a wide variety of small vertebrate prey including mice, voles, and songbirds that are plucked from their roosts at night. These wide-ranging birds are found throughout the eastern United States as far west as the Rocky Mountains, where they are replaced by the very similar Western Screech Owl.

Class—**Aves** (birds)

Order—**Strigiformes** (owls)

Family—**Strigidae** (typical owls)

Short-eared Owl *Asio flammeus*	**Long-eared Owl** *Asio otus*	**Northern Saw-whet Owl** *Aegolius acadicus*

Presumed range in Kentucky 	Presumed range in Kentucky 	Presumed range in Kentucky 
Size: 15 inches.	**Size:** 15 inches.	**Size:** 8 inches.
Abundance: Rare in Kentucky.	**Abundance:** Very rare in Kentucky.	**Abundance:** Rare in Kentucky.
Migratory Status: Mostly a wintertime resident or winter migrant, but some breeding has been recorded in KY.	**Migratory Status:** A wintertime only resident, or a winter migrant.	**Migratory Status:** Most records for this species in Kentucky are in November and early December.
Variation: Females tend to be slightly darker.	**Variation:** Female is darker with more rusty facial disk, and is slightly larger.	**Variation:** Immature has buff belly, dark facial disk with white eyebrow.
Habitat: These are open country birds and the primary habitat is prairie, marsh, and tundra. In forested regions they haunt fields, pastures, meadows, etc.	**Habitat:** Prefers open and semi-open woodlands and riparian habitats in open regions. Breeds and summers in boreal regions and mountains.	**Habitat:** Spruce-fir-pine dominated forests in the north and in the Rocky Mountain west. Also the higher elevations of the Appalachian Mountains.
Breeding: Nest is on the ground. A slight depression is scraped out by the owl and lined with grasses. Five or six eggs is typical.	**Breeding:** Usually nests in trees in abandoned stick nests built by hawks, crows, or other large bird species. Five or six eggs is typical.	**Breeding:** Uses old woodpecker holes almost exclusively for nesting. Five to six eggs is typical with a survival rate to fledging of about 50 percent.
Natural History: In Kentucky the Short-eared Owl is most likely to be seen in open regions during winter, but a few have nested in the state in large areas of reclaimed strip mines. The food is mostly small rodents. Voles are the most significant item in their diet. Rodent prey is located mostly by sound while flying low and slow over open, grassy fields. Most hunting is done at night or dusk and dawn, but these owls are more diurnal than most and may hunt during the day. The erectile feathers on the face that form the "ears" are not usually visible unless the owl is agitated or defensive. This species appears to be in decline in much of America.	**Natural History:** Although this rare owl could possibly be seen anywhere in the state, most sightings in Kentucky are in northern and western Kentucky. The name comes from the well developed feather tufts on the head which are erected when resting. These "ear tufts" are folded against the head and not visible on owls in flight. Long-eared Owls during winter can sometimes be seen in small flocks that roost in close proximity to each other. These birds are quite rare in Kentucky and they are regarded as an endangered species in the state. Food is almost exclusively small mammals, mostly voles and mice of the *Peromyscus* genus.	**Natural History:** Small mammals (mice, voles, and shrews) make up the bulk of this little owl's diet. Mice of the genus *Peromyscus* make up as much as 75 percent of the food consumed. Insects are oddly not listed as a major food item. Small and secretive, the Saw-whet Owl roosts in thick evergreens and is typically silent except during the breeding season. Thus these birds are difficult to observe in the wild. Within its range in the Rockies and Appalachians, seasonal migration is mostly vertical, with the owls moving to lower elevations in winter. These are rare birds in KY and in many areas of the state they may not be observed at all.

Class—**Aves** (birds)

Order—**Falconiformes** (raptors)

Family—**Accipitridae** (hawks, eagles, kites)

Red-tailed Hawk—*Buteo jamiacensis*

Typical Adult

Light Morph

Dark Morph

Typical Juvenile

Presumed range in Kentucky

Size: 19 inches.

Abundance: Very common in the western two-thirds of the state. Fairly common to common in the eastern mountains.

Migratory Status: Year-round resident. Numbers are supplemented in winter with migrants from farther north.

Variation: Highly variable. Can vary from nearly solid dark brown to very pale (almost white). Most adult Kentucky birds are like the typical specimen pictured above. Light and dark morphs are mostly winter migrants in Kentucky. Females are about 20 percent larger than males. Juveniles have brownish tails with dark crossbars. Some experts recognize as many as 16 subspecies throughout North America.

Habitat: Found in virtually all habitats within the state. Likes open and semi-open areas and is least common in continuous forest, although they do occur there.

Breeding: In Kentucky the large stick nest is built high in trees. Nest is usually situated in place that is remote from human activities. Lays two to four eggs. Young fledge at six weeks.

Natural History: This is the most common and widespread large *Buteo* hawk in America. Their range includes all of North America south of the Arctic and much of the Caribbean and Central America. The Red-tailed Hawk is generally regarded as the daytime counterpart of the Great Horned Owl, hunting by day many of the same species in the same habitats utilized by the owl at night. "Red-tails" prey mostly on rodents (mice, voles, and ground squirrels). Much larger prey like rabbits may also be taken on occasion. In some areas ground dwelling birds like pheasants and quail are taken, and they have been known to attack large flocks of blackbirds. In summer they also take large snakes such as the Pine Snake (*Pituophis*) and the Woodland Rat Snakes (*Pantherophis*). Large examples of these snakes (which are strong constrictors) have been known to turn the tables and end up killing a hungry hawk. During winter these large hawks sometimes resort to eating carrion and can sometimes be seen feeding on road kills. In Kentucky (and in much of the south), the Red-tailed Hawk is often known by the nickname "Chicken Hawk" in the mistaken belief that they prey on chickens. Although they may certainly catch a few chickens occasionally, their main food is rats, mice, and other rodents, making them an overall useful species to man. Their habit of perching conspicuously in dead trees, snags, and power poles along highways makes them one of the more easily observed of Kentucky's hawk species. Historically, the Red-tailed Hawk and other raptors were regarded as varmints and for many decades they were shot on sight by uninformed individuals. By the 1950s many birds of prey were becoming scarce in America. Since the passage of the Migratory Bird Treaty Act in the early 1970s providing federal protection to all of America's raptor species, they have become quite common.

Class—**Aves** (birds)

Order—**Falconiformes** (raptors)

Family—**Accipitridae** (hawks, eagles, kites)

Broad-winged Hawk *Buteo platypterus*	**Rough-legged Hawk** *Buteo lagopus*	**Red-shouldered Hawk** *Buteo lineatus*

Presumed range in Kentucky 	Presumed range in Kentucky	Presumed range in Kentucky 
Size: 16 inches.	**Size:** 21 inches.	**Size:** 17 inches.
Abundance: Fairly common.	**Abundance:** Uncommon in Kentucky.	**Abundance:** Fairly common.
Migratory Status: Summer resident.	**Migratory Status:** Winter only.	**Migratory Status:** Year-round resident.
Variation: First year plumage is mottled brown (similar to juvenile Red-shouldered Hawk on this page).	**Variation:** Two distinct color morphs, a dark (nearly black phase) and a lighter morph with paler head and shoulders.	**Variation:** No variation in Kentucky. Four subspecies occur. Ours is the Eastern race (*B. l. lineatus*). Female larger.
Habitat: Favors large tracts of unbroken deciduous woodlands in upland areas. More common in Kentucky in the eastern mountains.	**Habitat:** This is a northern species that summers as far north as the Arctic. Favors tundra in summer and farmlands and prairies in winter.	**Habitat:** Woodlands of all kinds, but especially likes woods bordering swamps or rivers, or along wooded creek-sides. Less common in uplands.
Breeding: Stick nest is in a tree crotch, usually in deep woods. Lays two to three eggs on average.	**Breeding:** Nests well to north in Arctic or subarctic regions of tundra and tiaga. Clutch size (three to seven) is prey dependent.	**Breeding:** Bulky stick nest is in the fork of a tree about 20–40 feet high and often near water. Two to four eggs in April.
Natural History: A decidedly woodland raptor whose range closely mimics the Eastern Temperate Forests ecoregion. In Kentucky this species is more common in the eastern mountainous regions, which are more heavily forested. Additionally, this species tends to avoid lowlands, which are more common in the western end of the state. Less conspicuous than most hawks except during the migration when they band together in large flocks known as "kettles." Extremely large flocks that may contain 200 birds are usually seen during fall migrations. Hunts by scanning for prey from a perch. Food includes insects, but consists mostly of small vertebrates like rodents as well as a large amount of reptile and amphibian prey, including lizards and small snakes.	**Natural History:** The Rough-legged Hawk is an arctic species that moves south in winter, sometimes as far south as Kentucky. Their migrations are sporadic depending upon weather, snow cover, and prey availability, but in most winters at least a few can be seen in northern Kentucky. They prey primarily on small mammals and lemmings are an important food on the breeding grounds. During years of high lemming populations more eggs will be laid and more young fledged. In winter they take mice, voles, and shrews mostly. Hunts by soaring and hovering over open country. While these are fairly large hawks, they have relatively small feet and small beaks and are thus unable to take the larger prey taken by hawks like the Red-tailed Hawk.	**Natural History:** The Red-shouldered Hawk is the daytime counterpart of the Barred Owl, and the two species often occur in the same territory. These are vocal birds. Their call, described as "kee-ah, kee-ah, kee-ah" is rapidly repeated about a dozen times. They can be fairly tame if unmolested and their raucous calling will not go unnoticed when the nest is nearby. They feed on a wide variety of small vertebrates but mostly eat reptiles and amphibians. The range of the Red-shouldered Hawk coincides closely with the level 1 ecoregion known as the Eastern Temperate Forest. However, a disjunct population (subspecies *elegans*) is found on the west coast of North America in the Mediterranean California Ecoregion. Populations in Kentucky are stable.

Class—**Aves** (birds)

Order—**Falconiformes** (raptors)

Family—**Accipitridae** (hawks, eagles, kites)

Golden Eagle	Bald Eagle	Osprey
Aquila chrysaetos	*Haliaeetus leucocephalus*	*Pandion haliaetus*

Presumed range in Kentucky

Size: 30 inches.

Abundance: Very rare in Kentucky.

Migratory Status: Winter migrant. November through February.

Variation: Sexes are alike in appearance but female is about 20 percent larger. Juvenile birds have white in tail.

Habitat: Rugged mountains, deserts, and open plains.

Breeding: A large stick nest up to six feet across is usually built on the face of a steep cliff. Usually lays two eggs.

Natural History: Although they are slightly smaller than the Bald Eagle, Golden Eagles are probably the most fearsome hunting bird in America. Ground squirrels and other small mammals make up to bulk of their prey, with larger species like jackrabbits and the young of wild sheep, goats, and pronghorn also being taken. They are sometimes persecuted by sheep ranchers in the western U.S., who blame them for killing young lambs in the spring. Indigenous to the entire northern hemisphere, in America the Golden Eagle is found mostly in the west. Like many large raptors they are capable of significant seasonal movements. Although very rare east of the Great Plains, they may sometimes show up in Kentucky, especially during winter months.

Presumed range in Kentucky

Size: 31 inches.

Abundance: Uncommon.

Migratory Status: Both a year-round resident and winter migrant.

Variation: May not acquire the characteristic white head and tail until their fourth annual molt at five years of age.

Habitat: In Kentucky Bald Eagles are associated with large rivers and lakes.

Breeding: Extremely bulky stick nest is re-used and gets larger each year. Usually only two eggs per clutch.

Natural History: One of the great conservation success stories, Bald Eagles were highly endangered just a few decades ago. Strigent protection, banning of the pesticide DDT, and a widespread education campaign has lead to a remarkable recovery. They first returned to Kentucky as a breeding species in the mid-1980s when one successful nest was recorded in far western Kentucky. By 2016 there were 151. Feeds largely on fish and carrion but also a capable hunter. Some Bald Eagles specialize in hunting migratory waterfowl in winter, picking off birds wounded by hunters. Bald Eagles wander widely in the winter and may be seen virtually anywhere in the state, but they are nowhere numerous. Adopted as the national emblem of the United States by congress in 1782.

Presumed range in Kentucky

Size: 30 inches.

Abundance: Fairly common.

Migratory Status: Spring through fall resident that winters in the southern U.S.

Variation: No variation in plumage of adults and immatures. Females are slightly larger than males.

Habitat: Typically seen in the vicinity of Kentucky's large lakes and rivers.

Breeding: Bulky stick nest is often built on man-made structures like bridges and power line towers. Two to four eggs.

Natural History: Subsists mainly on fish. Hunting tactics consist of a steep dive that ends with the Osprey plunging feet first into the water, allowing them to catch fish up to three feet below the surface. Most fish caught in freshwater are non-game species, thus they have little to no impact on sport fisheries. Like the Bald Eagle, Osprey populations in the mid-United States plummeted dramatically in the first half of the 20th century. The same types of conservation efforts that restored the Bald Eagle (including re-introduction programs), have brought Osprey numbers back to respectable levels. Most major rivers and lakes in the western portion of Kentucky now boast healthy populations of nesting Ospreys and they continue to increase across the state.

Class—**Aves** (birds)

Order—**Falconiformes** (raptors)

Family—**Accipitridae** (hawks, eagles, kites)

Northern Harrier *Circus cyaneus*	**Mississippi Kite** *Ictinea mississippiensis*	**Cooper's Hawk** *Accipiter cooperii*

 Presumed range in Kentucky	 Presumed range in Kentucky	 Presumed range in Kentucky
Size: 18 inches.	**Size:** 14 inches.	**Size:** 14–19 inches.
Abundance: Fairly common.	**Abundance:** Uncommon.	**Abundance:** Common.
Migratory Status: Though known to rarely breed in the state, most Northern Harriers in KY are winter residents.	**Migratory Status:** A spring and summer resident that winters in South America.	**Migratory Status:** A year-round resident, but some winter birds may be migrants that nested farther to the north.
Variation: Females are mottled brown above and below. Males are gray-brown above and pale gray below.	**Variation:** Juveniles are streaked with brown on the breast. Adults very similar but males have lighter gray heads.	**Variation:** First year birds are brown with streaked breast. Females are about 30 percent larger than males.
Habitat: Open country. Pastures, marshes, agricultural fields and grasslands.	**Habitat:** In Kentucky the Mississippi Kite mostly frequents the low-lying regions in the western end of the state.	**Habitat:** Woodlands, regenerative areas, and edge habitats are favored. Can also be seen in tree-lined urban yards.
Breeding: Nests on the ground in thick grass. Builds a nest of grasses and weed stems. Lays four to six eggs.	**Breeding:** Builds a stick nest high up in a large tree. Nesting in Kentucky is rare but increasing. Lays two eggs.	**Breeding:** Stick nest is built high in tree and eggs are laid in April or May. Clutch size averages four to six.
Natural History: The range of the Northern Harrier is circumpolar and includes Europe and northern Asia as well as North America. Unlike most diurnal raptors that hunt entirely by sight, the Northern Harrier mimics the technique used by owls and hunts largely by sound. A special "parabola" of feathers surround the face and directs sound waves to the ears. It hunts by flying low to the ground with a slow, buoyant flight that resembles a giant butterfly. Food is mostly small mammals and birds but reptiles and amphibians are also listed as food items. Roosting and nesting on the ground and hunting as much by sound as by sight, the Northern Harrier is unique among America's diurnal raptors.	**Natural History:** With its small beak and feet the Mississippi Kite appears somewhat delicate looking compared to other raptors. In flight they are one of the most graceful. The several species that make up the raptor group known as kites are mainly tropical birds. The Mississippi Kite is the most northerly ranging of the kites, and can be seen as far north as southern Illinois in summer months. Long distance migrants, they arrive in western Kentucky by early May and leave for South America by mid-September. These are gregarious birds and in some parts of their range it is not uncommon to see several nests in close proximity or see groups of birds soaring together. They feed on insects and small vertebrates.	**Natural History:** Feeds almost exclusively on birds and is known to haunt backyard bird feeders. These hawks are a major predator to the Bobwhite, an important game species that is in decline throughout most of its range. Cooper's Hawks are fierce hunters that will fearlessly attack birds as large or larger than themselves, including grouse, waterfowl, and domestic chickens. Although quite widespread and fairly common, they are not as observable as the *Buteo* hawks. Cooper's Hawks tend to stay in wooded areas and thickets with heavier cover than their bulkier cousins. These birds are fast fliers and capable of great maneuverability, an adaptation to hunting in forest and thickets.

Class—**Aves** (birds)

Order—**Falconiformes** (raptors)

Family—**Accipitridae** (hawks, eagles, kites)	Family—**Cathartidae** (vultures)	
Sharp-shinned Hawk *Accipiter striatus*	**Turkey Vulture** *Cathartes aura*	**Black Vulture** *Coragyps atratus*

Presumed range in Kentucky | Presumed range in Kentucky | Presumed range in Kentucky

Size: 9–13 inches.

Size: 26 inches.

Size: 25 inches.

Abundance: Fairly common.

Abundance: Common.

Abundance: Common.

Migratory Status: Some stay year-round but most move north in summer.

Migratory Status: A year-round resident in Kentucky. A few may migrate.

Migratory Status: Year-round resident, but some birds go south in harsh winters.

Variation: Ontogenetic plumage variation (see photos). Females are as much as twice the size of males.

Variation: Essentially no variation. Skin on face is pinkish gray on immature birds, bright pink on adult.

Variation: No variation among adults. Older birds have lighter gray heads with more wrinkles on skin than immatures.

Habitat: Forests and thickets. Found in both rural and urban areas where vegetative cover is present.

Habitat: Seen in all habitats but least common in the heavily forested southeastern tip of the state.

Habitat: Found in a wide variety of habitats. Least common in the eastern mountains, common in western KY.

Breeding: Pine trees are a favored locale for placing the nest. Lays as many as eight eggs, with five to six being the average.

Breeding: Nests on cliff faces, in large tree hollows, or on the ground in hollow logs. Almost always lays two eggs.

Breeding: No nest is built and the two eggs are laid on a bare surface. The nest site is often in a derelict building.

Natural History: A relentless hunter of small songbirds, the Sharp-shinned Hawk is sometimes seen raiding backyard bird feeders. These small raptors are capable of rapid, twisting flight while pursuing their small songbird prey through woodlands and thickets. In Kentucky they are more common during migration period when birds that summer farther north move southward. Although some birds are breeding residents in the state, most nest far to north, some as far north as Alaska and the Yukon Territory. The Sharp-shinned Hawk is a widely distributed species that ranges across all of North America south of the arctic region and southward all the way to southern Central America.

Natural History: The absence of feathers on the head and neck of vultures is an adaptation for feeding on carrion. Vultures may stick the head deep inside a rotting carcass and feathers would become matted with filth. The bare skin on the neck and face on the other hand is constantly exposed to the sterilizing effects of sunlight. Turkey Vultures are one of the few birds with a well developed sense of smell, and food is often located by detecting the odor of rotting flesh. Sight is also important and they are quick to notice a fresh carcass on a roadway. Newly mowed fields and other disturbed areas within their range are closely scanned for small animal victims. Highly social, they roost communally, sometimes with Black Vultures.

Natural History: Kentucky's vultures are named for the color of the skin on the face. Turkey Vultures have reddish skin (like a turkey); the Black Vulture has dark gray or black facial skin. Black Vultures also have shorter tails and lesser wingspan, giving them a much "stubbier" look than the Turkey Vulture. Vultures were once regarded as a threat to livestock by spreading disease. In fact, the powerful digestive juices of the gut of vultures destroys bacteria. Both the Turkey Vulture and the Black Vulture have the unappealing habit of defecating on the legs and feet as a way of disinfecting the feet (which can become quite nasty and the birds feed on rotted carcasses). Black Vultures rely on their keen eyesight to locate food.

Class—**Aves** (birds)

Order—**Falconiformes** (raptors)

Family—**Falconidae** (falcons)

American Kestrel *Falco sparverius*	Merlin *Falco columbarius*	Peregrine Falcon *Falco peregrinus*
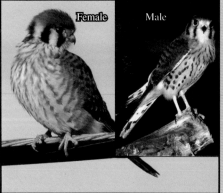		
Presumed range in Kentucky 	Presumed range in Kentucky 	Presumed range in Kentucky 
Size: 10 inches.	**Size:** 11 inches.	**Size:** 17 inches.
Abundance: Fairly common.	**Abundance:** Very rare in Kentucky.	**Abundance:** Rare in Kentucky.
Migratory Status: A year-round resident that breeds in Kentucky. Winter migrants increase the population in winter.	**Migratory Status:** A rarely seen migrant. Passes through in spring and fall, mostly in the western end of the state.	**Migratory Status:** A few nest and live year round in parts of the state, but most birds seen in Kentucky are migrants.
Variation: Sexually dimorphic. Male has gray wings, female brown.	**Variation:** Male has blue-gray back, female and immatures have brown back.	**Variation:** Juvenile birds have dark-streaks on the breast rather than bars.
Habitat: Throughout Kentucky the Kestrel is seen in open country. Least common in the mountains of the east.	**Habitat:** Habitat is open regions. Mostly seen in Kentucky along the Mississippi and Ohio River valleys.	**Habitat:** Requires cliffs in remote wilderness areas but has adapted to living among skyscrapers in many cities.
Breeding: Usually nests in tree cavities or old woodpecker holes within trees situated in open fields. May also nest in man-made structures. Four to five eggs.	**Breeding:** Breeds far to the north in Canada, Alaska, and parts of the north-central Rockies and plains. Uses old crow or hawk nests as well as cliffs.	**Breeding:** Nests on ledges of cliff faces and on man-made structures like sky-scrapers and bridges. Four eggs is typical, sometimes up to six.
Natural History: While the Kestrel is a fairly common bird in open regions throughout Kentucky, there has been some decline in populations in the eastern United States in recent years. Sometimes called "Sparrow Hawk," the Kestrel is widespread throughout North and Central America and as many as 17 subspecies are recognized. They are often seen perched on power lines and poles along roadways in rural farmlands throughout the state, but they are uncommon in the heavily forested mountains of eastern Kentucky. Insects are the major food in summer (especially grasshoppers). In winter they eat small mammals and rarely, small birds. Hunts both from a perch and by hovering over open fields.	**Natural History:** The Merlin is seen in Kentucky only during migration (or an occasional wandering individual). These small falcons are only slightly larger than the Kestrel and they are easily confused with that species. The facial markings of the Merlin are less distinct than the Kestrels. Summering far to the north of Kentucky and wintering along both coastlines, their migration routes are mostly to the west of Kentucky or east along the Atlantic coast. Like most falcons, however, these birds are prone to wander widely. Although they may occur almost anywhere in Kentucky they are quite rare in the state, and most sightings in Kentucky are east of the Appalachian mountains. Food is mostly small birds.	**Natural History:** Falcons are fast flying birds and the Peregrine is among the fastest. Hunts pigeons, waterfowl, grouse, etc. Hunting technique usually involves soaring high above and diving in on birds in flight, or diving toward resting birds and panicking them into flight. Once airborne, no other bird can match the Peregrine's speed. Diving Peregrines may reach speeds approaching 200 mph, making them perhaps the fastest animal on earth. In Kentucky this species currently breeds only on bridges over the Ohio River near Louisville and on cliffs along the Kentucky River. However, the name "peregrine" means "wanderer," and these birds may be seen almost anywhere in the state, albeit quite rarely.

Class—**Aves** (birds)

Order—**Ciconiiformes** (wading birds)

Family—**Ardeidae** (herons)

Great Blue Heron *Ardea herodias*	**Great Egret** *Ardea alba*	**Snowy Egret** *Egretta thula*

Presumed range in Kentucky 	Presumed range in Kentucky 	Presumed range in Kentucky 
Size: 47 inches.	**Size:** 39 inches.	**Size:** 24 inches.
Abundance: Common.	**Abundance:** Fairly common.	**Abundance:** Uncommon in Kentucky.
Migratory Status: Both year-round residents and migrants can be seen throughout Kentucky.	**Migratory Status:** Spring through fall resident that breeds sporadically along the large rivers and lakes of western KY.	**Migratory Status:** A warm weather resident only (April to September). Winters well to the south of Kentucky.
Variation: Juveniles are duskier.	**Variation:** Breeders acquire plumes.	**Variation:** Breeders acquire plumes.
Habitat: Along rivers and streams, swamps, marshes, ponds, and wet meadows and floodplains.	**Habitat:** Along major streams, lakes, swamps, and marshes. Also low lying areas subject to flooding.	**Habitat:** Along major streams, lakes, swamps, and marshes. Also low lying areas subject to flooding.
Breeding: Nests in colonies. Most nesting in Kentucky is in the western third of the state. Nest is a platform of sticks in tree or bush above water. Three to four eggs is typical.	**Breeding:** Most nesting occurs farther south although a few nests have been recorded in Kentucky. Nest is a platform of sticks in tree or bush above water. Nests in colonies. Lays three to four eggs.	**Breeding:** Nests mostly well to the south of Kentucky. Will nest in colonies with other heron species. Nest is made of sticks and twigs. Three to five eggs is average.
Natural History: The largest heron in North America, the Great Blue Heron will eat almost anything it can swallow. Fish and frogs are major foods, but it also eats snakes, salamanders, small mammals, and even small turtles. Birds are sometimes eaten, including other, smaller heron species. All food items are swallowed whole. Large prey is killed by stabbing repeatedly with the beak or by bashing against a hard object. Smaller prey is often swallowed alive. Will hunt both day and night and reportedly has good night vision. Great Blue Herons are found throughout most of the United States and much of Canada, including riparian habitats in desert regions. A solid white subspecies is found in parts of southern Florida.	**Natural History:** This heron species (along with the Snowy Egret and several other herons) was nearly hunted to extinction during the last half of the 19th century. The long, wispy feathers (known as "plumes") were once used to adorn the hats of fashionable ladies. The plumes are most pronounced during the breeding season. Thus the catastrophic impact of the plume hunters was magnified as hunters killed birds at their nesting colonies. Efforts to save this and other plume bird species lead to some of Americas earliest laws to protect wildlife. Today this species is still a symbol of conservation efforts and is the logo of the National Audubon Society. It is sometimes known by the name Common Egret.	**Natural History:** As with several other heron species, the Snowy Egret during breeding season sports long "plume" feathers on the back. As with other plume bird species the Snowy Egret was nearly wiped out by the feather trade of the late 1800s. Today the species has recovered to healthy numbers but remains under threat due to its dependence upon coastal wetlands. This species feeds on smaller prey such as worms, insects, crustaceans, amphibians, and small fish. It is an active feeder that often chases prey through the shallows rather than using the stealth method employed by its larger cousins. It also often feeds by swishing its feet in the mud to disturb benthic organisms. Told from the Great Egret by its black bill.

Class—**Aves** (birds)		
Order—**Ciconiiformes** (wading birds)		
Family—**Ardeidae** (herons)		

Little Blue Heron *Egretta caerulea*	**Cattle Egret** *Bulbulcus ibis*	**Green Heron** *Butorides virescens*

Presumed range in Kentucky 	Presumed range in Kentucky 	Presumed range in Kentucky 
Size: 24 inches.	**Size:** 19 inches.	**Size:** 19 inches.
Abundance: Rare in Kentucky.	**Abundance:** Rare in Kentucky.	**Abundance:** Common.
Migratory Status: Found in Kentucky from late spring through early fall.	**Migratory Status:** A summer resident that retreats to the deep south in winter.	**Migratory Status:** A summer resident that breeds widely across the state.
Variation: First year birds have white plumage (see inset photo).	**Variation:** Orange on crown and throat more pronounced during breeding.	**Variation:** Juvenile birds are browner above and have streaked throat.
Habitat: Wetlands. In Kentucky seen mostly along the major rivers and wetlands in the western part of the state.	**Habitat:** Unlike other herons, these birds are usually seen in open pastures and fields in association with cattle.	**Habitat:** Usually seen in the vicinity of wetlands or rivers and streams. Also common around lakes and small ponds.
Breeding: Builds a stick nest platform in bushes and low trees in wetlands. Lays three to five eggs.	**Breeding:** Stick nest built in trees or bushes. Nests in large colonies. Three to four eggs is average.	**Breeding:** Usually nests singly rather than in colonies. Nest is a stick platform in a tree fork. Lays three to five eggs.
Natural History: Even within the heart of its range along the lower coastal plains of the southeastern U.S., the Little Blue Heron is generally less common that other heron species. In Kentucky it is a rather rare bird. In addition, the dark plumage of adults and its rather secretive nature make it one of the least observable of Kentucky herons. Like most herons, it is an opportunistic feeder that eats almost anything it can swallow. Food is mostly frogs, fish, crustaceans, and insects. It is a daytime hunter that hunts by stalking slowly through wetland habitats. The transitional plumage of the juvenile Little Blue Heron is unique, and produces for a brief time a white bird with blue splotches. Blue increases throughout the molt ending in a solid blue adult.	**Natural History:** The Cattle Egret is one of our most interesting bird species. Originally native to Africa, Cattle Egrets began an inexplicable range expansion in the early 1800s. They first migrated across the Atlantic to South America and then appeared in North America around 1950. The first sighting in Kentucky was in 1960. The species continues to expand its range and is today a fairly common summer resident in western Kentucky. Their name is derived from their habit of associating with cattle herds in pastures. Before expanding their range out of Africa they associated with herds of Cape buffalo, hippopotamus, and wild ungulates. They feed mostly on insects that are disturbed by the large grazers they follow through pastures and grasslands.	**Natural History:** In Kentucky, the Green Heron often goes by the name "Shypoke." This is one of Kentucky's most familiar herons and its range encompasses all of the eastern United States as well as the west coast. It also ranges southward throughout Central America. When flushed it nearly always emits a loud "squawking" alarm call. Feeds mostly in shallow water and often feeds from a perch on a floating log or a limb just above the water's surface. Hunts by stealth and may remain frozen for long periods as it watches and waits for prey. Fish is its primary food item with small frogs probably being the next most common prey. Amazingly, this species has been reported to catch insects and worms to use as bait for luring in fish.

Class—**Aves** (birds)

Order—**Ciconiiformes** (wading birds)

Family—**Ardeidae** (herons)

Yellow-crowned Night Heron *Nyctanassa violacea*	**Black-crowned Night Heron** *Nycticorax nycticorax*	**Least Bittern** *Ixobrychus exilis*

Presumed range in Kentucky 	Presumed range in Kentucky 	Presumed range in Kentucky 

Size: 25 inches.	**Size:** 25 inches.	**Size:** 13 inches.
Abundance: Uncommon.	**Abundance:** Rare in Kentucky.	**Abundance:** Rare in Kentucky.
Migratory Status: Returns to Kentucky in April, winters along the gulf coast, Florida, Mexico, and Central America.	**Migratory Status:** Spring through fall resident that winters in the southernmost U.S., Mexico, and Central America.	**Migratory Status:** A summer resident that winters in the southern U.S., Mexico, and Central America.
Variation: Juveniles are heavily streaked with brown and white.	**Variation:** Juvenile birds are heavily streaked with brown (see inset).	**Variation:** Male has black cap and black back. See both sexes above.
Habitat: Swamps and marshes. Favors heavier cover than many herons.	**Habitat:** Wetlands, river valleys, and in the vicinity of large impoundments.	**Habitat:** Favors marshes with dense growths of tall grasses and sedges.
Breeding: Most breeding in Kentucky is in the Coastal Plain or Ohio River Valley. Flimsy stick nest is fairly high in tree, usually over water. Three to five eggs.	**Breeding:** Nests in colonies that are usually situated over swamps or on an island. Colonies may contain hundreds of birds, with three or four eggs per nest.	**Breeding:** Nest is a well concealed platform built amid dense growth of cattails or other sedges/grasses. Up to six eggs are laid.
Natural History: These birds are often active at night, hence the name "night heron." Food is mostly crustaceans. Crabs are important foods in coastal regions, while crayfish are eaten in fresh-water areas. A classic ambush predator, the Yellow-crowned Night Heron does most foraging from a stationary position, sitting like a statue and waiting for prey to wander into striking range. They will also stalk slowly and methodically with slow, deliberate movements that are largely undetectable to prey. Diet may be supplemented with fish and invertebrates, but this heron is mainly a crustacean specialist. Has recovered nicely from low numbers decades ago and now seems to be expanding its range farther to the north.	**Natural History:** Although the Black-crowned Night Heron may be locally common near breeding colonies, it is a rarely seen bird in Kentucky. Surprisingly, this is a widespread species that is found not only in much of the United States, but in fact throughout most of the world. They can be found on every continent except Australia and Antarctica. As its name implies this species is often active at night. The food is primarily fish. However, the list of known foods is quite long and includes, insects, leeches, earthworms, crustaceans, gastropods, amphibians, snakes, small turtles, small mammals, and even birds! A secretive bird that prefers to feed in shallow water along the margins of weedy ponds, marshes, and swamps.	**Natural History:** This smallest of American herons is also a secretive bird that often stays hidden in dense marsh grasses and sedges. When alarmed they point their bill skyward and freeze, mimicking the vertical vegetation of their habitat. These small herons move with ease through thick stands of marsh vegetation. When flushed they fly only a short distance just above the vegetation before dropping back down. Despite their seemingly weak flying abilities, they migrate great distances from wintering areas to summer breeding grounds that may be as far north as northern Minnesota. They have very long toes for grasping stems of grass and sedge. Feeds on small fish, insects, crayfish, and amphibians.

Class—**Aves** (birds)

Order—**Ciconiiformes** (wading birds)	Order—**Gruiformes** (rails, cranes)	
Family—**Ardeidae** (herons)	Family—**Rallidae** (rails)	
American Bittern *Botaurus lentiginosus*	**King Rail** *Rallus elegans*	**Sora** *Porzana carolina*

Presumed range in Kentucky 	Presumed range in Kentucky 	Presumed range in Kentucky 
Size: 26 inches.	**Size:** 16 inches.	**Size:** 9 inches.
Abundance: Uncommon in Kentucky.	**Abundance:** Very rare in Kentucky.	**Abundance:** Uncommon in Kentucky.
Migratory Status: Migrates through Kentucky in spring and fall.	**Migratory Status:** Transient spring and fall migrant and rare summer resident.	**Migratory Status:** A spring and fall migrant throughout Kentucky.
Variation: None. Sexes alike.	**Variation:** None. Sexes alike.	**Variation:** Juvenile lacks black face.
Habitat: Marshes of the plains and boreal forests in summer, coastal marshlands in winter.	**Habitat:** Marshes. Found mostly along southeastern coasts but a few move into inland wetlands in summer.	**Habitat:** Primarily a marsh dweller. On migration may visit ponds or wet meadows.
Breeding: Nest is in dense emergent vegetation of the marsh and is well hidden. Three to five eggs is typical.	**Breeding:** Builds a loosely woven cup from marsh vegetation. Nesting has been recorded in far western Kentucky.	**Breeding:** Builds a nest platform of aquatic vegetation a few inches above water level. Lays 8 to 11 eggs.
Natural History: The biology of this species is not well known. Presumably they may be seen anywhere in Kentucky during migration, but they are probably most likely to be seen along the major rivers of the state. Few Kentuckians will ever see one, as they are usually quite secretive. Hunts by stealth and may remain motionless for long periods of time. The eyes of this heron are situated with a downward slant, better facilitating the bird's ability to see into the water. When startled they will throw the head back and point the beak straight up. The streaked brown pattern of the neck and breast is remarkably cryptic amid the vertical stalks of marsh grasses and sedges. Like most herons, an opportunistic feeder. Eats fish, amphibians, crayfish, small mammals, and some insects.	**Natural History:** Rails are well adapted to life in the marsh. They move with ease through thick grasses and rarely fly except when migrating. They can run quite fast through the grass and rarely offer more than a glimpse. They can also swim and dive beneath the surface, using the wings to swim underwater. Despite the fact that rails are listed as a game bird by most state wildlife agencies, almost no one hunts them, due probably to their scarcity and secretiveness. They feed mostly on aquatic insects and their larva, spiders, and other invertebrates. Some plant material is also eaten. The **Virginia Rail** (*R. limicola)* is similar rail species that is a transient migrant in Kentucky. It may be seen throughout much of KY and is more common. It is very similar to the King Rail but smaller (9.5 inches).	**Natural History:** The Sora is one of the more observable of America's rails. Still, it is fairly secretive, especially during fall migration. They are usually observable on both breeding and wintering grounds, but catching a glimpse of this species as it moves through Kentucky is difficult. They are vocal birds, however, and their whinnying call can be heard for a long distance. They feed on a variety of aquatic invertebrates and also eat seeds of aquatic plants, particularly wild rice. Another small rail species, the **Yellow Rail** (*Coturnicops noveboracensis*), also migrates through parts of Kentucky. But that species is so scarce and secretive that even serious bird watchers may go their entire lives and never see it! Even within its core winter range on the Gulf Coast the Yellow Rail is almost impossible to see.

Class—**Aves** (birds)

Order—**Gruiformes** (rails, cranes)

Family—**Rallidae** (rails)

Family—**Gruidae** (cranes)

American Coot *Fulica americana*	**Common Gallinule** *Gallinula chloropus*	**Sandhill Crane** *Grus canadensis*

Juvenile

Presumed range in Kentucky

Presumed range in Kentucky

Presumed range in Kentucky

Size: 15 inches.

Abundance: Fairly common.

Migratory Status: Winter resident in western Kentucky. Mostly migrant elsewhere in the state.

Variation: Sexes alike. Juvenile paler gray with yellowish beak.

Habitat: Rivers, lakes, large ponds, and wetlands in Kentucky.

Breeding: Breeds to the north and to the west of Kentucky. Nest is a platform built amid emergent vegetation. About six eggs are laid.

Natural History: The American Coot is a common sight on Kentucky's major impoundments throughout the winter. They are especially evident in the western half of the state. They are considered a game species, but rarely hunted as most waterfowl hunters regard them as a "trash" species. They sometimes go by the nickname "Mud Hen." Although the feet are not webbed as with ducks and geese, their long toes are equipped with lateral lobes that flare out when swimming and create an ample surface for pushing against the water. Thus they are good swimmers. They feed both on land (on grasses) and in the water (aquatic plants, algae, and aquatic invertebrates). Small fish and small amphibians are also taken.

Size: 14 inches.

Abundance: Rare in Kentucky.

Migratory Status: Summer resident and spring / fall migrant. Usually arrives in the state by mid-April.

Variation: Sexes alike. Juvenile is paler gray without red bill and forehead.

Habitat: Wetlands and lake shores with abundant vegetation.

Breeding: Nest is a platform of vegetation slightly above the waterline and usually well concealed. Will lay as many as 10 eggs.

Natural History: Sometimes known as the Common Moorhen, but that name is properly reserved for a very similar bird that lives in Europe. Although these birds may be seen in suitable habitat throughout much the state, they are rare Kentucky. Farther south in places like Louisiana and Florida they can be quite common. Feeds largely on seeds of aquatic plants but also eats animal matter including most predominately snails and insects. Although similar to the American Coot in size and appearance, the Common Gallinule is rarely seen in the open and prefers to stay close to heavy cover. However, they are sometimes quite tame and approachable, especially within the heart of their range in Florida and the lower Coastal Plain.

Size: 42 inches.

Abundance: Uncommon in Kentucky.

Migratory Status: Spring and fall migrant through the western two thirds of the state.

Variation: Juveniles are splotched with large amounts of rusty brown.

Habitat: Open lands, farm fields, mudflats, and shallow water areas.

Breeding: Cranes that migrate through Kentucky breed well to the north, as far as the Arctic. Typically lays two eggs on a platform nest built of vegetation.

Natural History: Standing over three feet tall, the Sandhill Crane is one of the largest birds seen in Kentucky. Populations were seriously depleted by the beginning of the 20th century, but the species has recovered dramatically in the last few decades. The largest populations are seen west of the Mississippi River and number tens of thousands. Eastern populations have been slower to recover but are now reasonably healthy. Several states including Kentucky treat them as a game species and have regulated hunting seasons. Some conservationists question the wisdom of hunting seasons on this species. Their habit of concentrating large flocks in small geographic areas render them vulnerable to natural disasters like tornadoes.

Class—**Aves** (birds)

Order—**Charadriiformes** (shorebirds)

Family—**Charadriidae** (plovers)

Killdeer *Charadrius vociferus*	Semipalmated Plover *Charadrius semipalmatus*	Piping Plover *Charadrius melodus*

Presumed range in Kentucky	Presumed range in Kentucky	Presumed range in Kentucky
Size: 10.5 inches.	**Size:** 7.25 inches.	**Size:** 7.5 inches.
Abundance: Common.	**Abundance:** Uncommon in Kentucky.	**Abundance:** Very rare in Kentucky.
Migratory Status: Year-round resident.	**Migratory Status:** Spring/fall migrant.	**Migratory Status:** Fall migrant.
Variation: None. Sexes are alike and there is no significant seasonal or ontogenetic plumage variations.	**Variation:** See photos above. Both winter and summer plumages may be seen in Kentucky.	**Variation:** Seasonal plumage variations (see above). Sexes are alike but winter plumage is paler.
Habitat: Open lands. Mudflats, agricultural fields, lake shores, sandbars, and even gravel parking lots. Found in both rural and urban areas.	**Habitat:** Winter habitat is along coastlines from southern North America southward to southern South America. Summer habitat is open tundra.	**Habitat:** Winters along America's southern coastlines from North Carolina to Mexico. Breeds in the Great Plains and northeastern U.S. coastal region.
Breeding: Lays four eggs directly on the ground. Nest is often in gravelly or sandy situations in wide-open spaces.	**Breeding:** Nests on the ground, usually near water. Nesting grounds are in northern Canada and Alaska. Four eggs.	**Breeding:** Nest is a simple scrape in gravel or sand. Dunes and sand/gravel bars are often used. Three or four eggs typical.
Natural History: Although the Killdeer is found state-wide, they are much more common in the western two-thirds of the state where open habitats are more widespread. This is a species that has likely benefited significantly from human alterations of natural habitats. The creation of open spaces where there was once grassland or forest has resulted in a habitat boom the Killdeer. They are found all over North America south of the Arctic Circle. They were once hunted for food and their populations suffered a serious decline in the days of "market hunting." They feed on the ground and earthworms are a major food source along with grasshoppers, beetles, and snails. A few seeds are also consumed.	**Natural History:** Most Semipalmated Plovers migrate along the coasts of North America, but a few travel overland and they are occasionally seen in Kentucky. Most sightings will likely be west of the Appalachian Mountains, as they tend to avoid areas of deep forest in favor of open spaces. The food of the Semipalmated Plover is mostly invertebrate animals plucked from the mud. They hunt these "benthic" organisms along the edges of marshes, lakes, seashores, etc. Aquatic food items include insect larva, polychaete worms, crustaceans, and small bivalves. On dry land these plovers will eat spiders, flies, and beetles. In Kentucky these birds are most often observed during fall migration on exposed mudflats of large lakes.	**Natural History:** These little plovers are regarded as threatened species in Kentucky and and they are quite rare within the state. Cornell Laboratory of Ornithology reports that fewer than 6,000 specimens were found in a 2001 nationwide survey. Rare sightings of migrant specimens occur in Kentucky from July through early October. Food items listed are as would be expected for seashore and inland mudflat dwelling species; i.e. small marine invertebrates and their eggs, insects and small crustaceans and mollusks. Continued development of beaches along America's coastline is a major threat to coastal nesting populations as well as to some populations that will winter along America's coasts.

Class—**Aves** (birds)

Order—**Charadriiformes** (shorebirds)

Family—**Charadriidae** (plovers)

Black-bellied Plover	**Golden Plover**
Pluvialis squatarola	*Pluvialis dominica*

Presumed range in Kentucky

Presumed range in Kentucky

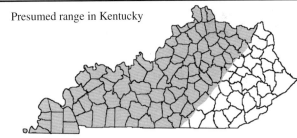

Size: 11.5 inches.

Abundance: Uncommon in Kentucky.

Migratory Status: Spring and fall migrant in Kentucky.

Variation: Seasonal plumage variations (see above). Most birds seen in Kentucky will be in summer plumage.

Habitat: Beaches are the preferred winter habitat. Inland migrants will use shorelines, mudflats, and bare fields.

Breeding: Nest is a shallow cup scraped into the Arctic Tundra and lined with lichens. Four eggs are laid.

Natural History: Black-bellied Plovers occur in both the new and old worlds and in fact they are one of the most widespread shorebirds in the world. They occur throughout much of the old world as well as most of the western hemisphere. North American birds winter along both coastlines from just south of Canada to South America, including the Caribbean. Summers are spent within the Arctic Circle of Alaska and Canada. During migration they are seen mostly along America's coastlines and in the Great Plains region, but a few will pass through Kentucky. Unlike many shorebirds, the Black-bellied Plover exhibits nocturnal tendencies and will often feed at night. Food items are marine worms and small clams and mussels plucked from the mud at low tide. On the breeding grounds in the far north they will eat insects, small freshwater crustaceans, and berries. Climate change may be a threat if tundra nesting habitat undergoes transformation.

Size: 10.5 inches.

Abundance: Uncommon in Kentucky.

Migratory Status: Spring and fall migrant in Kentucky.

Variation: Sexes similar with seasonal plumage variations (see above). Both plumages can be seen in Kentucky.

Habitat: Beaches are the preferred winter habitat. Inland migrants will use shorelines, mudflats, and bare fields.

Breeding: Nest is a scrape on tundra soil. Four eggs are laid and young are highly precocial, able to walk immediately.

Natural History: Like the similar Black-bellied Plover, the American Golden Plover is a long-distance traveler that nests in the Arctic and spends its winters in southeastern South America. Its epic migrations sometimes include extensive flights over vast expanses of open ocean. Many migrate through inland regions and they are known for their propensity to appear almost anywhere during migrations. Food items include some plant material (berries, seeds, foliage) as well as a wide variety of invertebrate prey. Like many shorebirds the American Golden Plover was hunted relentlessly during the days "market hunting" throughout the 1800s. Tens to perhaps hundreds of thousands were killed annually. Today they are still legally hunted hunted in some South American countries. Habitat loss remains an ever present threat and some scientists have expressed concern about potential changes on tundra breeding grounds due to climate change.

Class—**Aves** (birds)

Order—**Charadriiformes** (shorebirds)

Family—**Scolopacidae** (sandpipers)

Sanderling *Calidris alba*	**Pectoral Sandpiper** *Calidris melanotus*	**Dunlin** *Calidris alpina*

Sanderling	Pectoral Sandpiper	Dunlin
Presumed range in Kentucky	Presumed range in Kentucky	Presumed range in Kentucky
Size: 8 inches.	**Size:** 8.5 inches.	**Size:** 8.5 inches.
Abundance: Uncommon in Kentucky.	**Abundance:** Fairly common.	**Abundance:** Uncommon in Kentucky.
Migratory Status: Transient seasonal migrant throughout western two-thirds of state.	**Migratory Status:** A seasonal migrant that is much more common farther west.	**Migratory Status:** Transient seasonal migrant seen mostly in west Kentucky.
Variation: Significant seasonal variation (see photos above).	**Variation:** Male breeding plumage is darker brown and more vivid.	**Variation:** Significant seasonal plumage changes (see photos above).
Habitat: Shorelines. In winter lives on the beach. During migration frequents lake shores and river bars.	**Habitat:** Migrants use wet meadows, flooded fields, marshes, and lake or pond shorelines.	**Habitat:** During migration uses rice fields, flooded agricultural fields, and seasonally flooded lowland pastures.
Breeding: Nests on the Arctic Tundra on bare ground. Lays four eggs.	**Breeding:** Nests on the ground in the Arctic Coastal Plain. Four eggs.	**Breeding:** Another high Arctic breeder. Lays four eggs on ground in open tundra.
Natural History: Unlike most members of the sandpiper family, which are more likely to be found on mudflats, the Sanderling is commonly found on seashores. Except during migration or when breeding, these birds inhabit sandy beaches throughout the Americas. Any person who has been to the seashore has probably been amused by watching this species running back and forth in front of the waves. On beaches feeds by running just in front of oncoming wave and chasing right behind receding wave, picking up tiny marine crustaceans, bivalves, and polycheates. On the breeding ground it will eat both terrestrial and aquatic invertebrates and insects. Most Sanderlings migrate along the coastlines of America or through the Great Plains. A few will be seen in Kentucky, however, especially in the west.	**Natural History:** Breeding males of this species perform displays in which they erect the feathers of the breast, droop the wings, raise the tail feathers, and emit "hooting" sounds. They are the only member of the sandpiper family that vocalizes in this manner. They also perform flight displays above the heads of grounded females. These birds are remarkable travelers that breed in the high Arctic and winter in the Pampas region of southern South America. Some individuals will cross the Arctic Ocean to breed in Siberia, then migrate back to South America, a round-trip journey of over 18,000 miles each year! The food is mostly small mud-dwelling invertebrates. In Kentucky this species is most likely to be seen during spring migration in flooded crop fields in the Mississippi Alluvial Plain.	**Natural History:** The Dunlin winters along both coasts of North America where it haunts estuaries and inter-tidal regions. In southern Louisiana and gulf coastal Texas it often uses rice fields in winter. Various clams, insects, worms, and amphipods are picked from the mud or plucked from vegetation with its moderately long, probing bill. Like other shorebird species it is usually seen in flocks, sometimes numbering in the thousands or even tens of thousands. In the early 1800s market hunters killed these birds in enormous numbers. Using cannon-like shotguns known as "punt guns" that were loaded with bird shot, a single blast could kill scores of shorebirds in a closely packed flock. Today's threats include pesticides and other contaminants and loss of wintering habitat.

Class—**Aves** (birds)

Order—**Charadriiformes** (shorebirds)

Family—**Scolopacidae** (sandpipers)

The "Peep" Sandpipers
Genus—*Calidris* (five species in Kentucky, three pictured below)

Least Sandpiper *Calidris minutilla*	White-rumped Sandpiper *Calidris fuscicollis*	Semipalmated Sandpiper *Calidris pusilla*

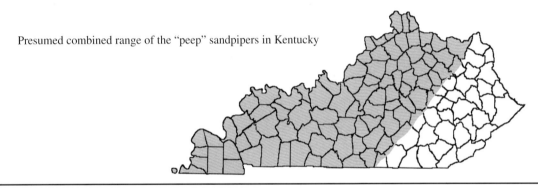

Presumed combined range of the "peep" sandpipers in Kentucky

Size: 6 to 8 inches.

Abundance: Some species like the Least Sandpiper and Semipalmated Sandpiper are commonly seen in Kentucky during migration. The White-rumped and Bairds are fairly common in the state, while the Western Sandpiper is uncommon in Kentucky.

Migratory Status: All five species are transient spring and fall migrants in Kentucky. Most of these birds that pass through Kentucky will use the Mississippi Flyway. They are least likely to be seen in the Appalachian highlands in the eastern portion of the state, but occasional strays can be seen almost anywhere the state, especially the Least and Semipalmated Sandpipers. Some species take different routes in spring than in fall, and in at least one species (Baird's Sandpiper), adults sometimes take different routes from those taken by juveniles.

Variation: All five of these species exhibit seasonal plumage changes. All are comparably paler in winter than in summer.

Habitat: The name "Mudpiper" would be a more appropriate name for these birds as they favor mudflats and flooded fields over sandy beaches. All can be seen along the coastlines but many migrate through the interior of North America.

Breeding: All "peep" sandpipers nest on the ground in the barren Arctic Tundra. Four eggs is typical.

Natural History: These five species are all similar in their natural history and are confusingly alike in appearance. While serious birders and professional ornithologists take pride in being able to correctly identify any species, most casual observers are satisfied with calling these homogeneous birds simply "peeps." Food habits and feeding methods are also similar in these sandpipers, with mud dwelling benthic invertebrates making up the bulk of the diet in winter and during migration. Aquatic insect larva and some terrestrial insects are eaten on the breeding grounds. The hordes of mosquitoes for which the Arctic Tundra is famous in summer make up a high protein smorgasboard for both the adult birds and the newly hatched young. All the sandpipers are known for their epic migrations. Some species travel nonstop for a thousand miles or more over open ocean. Flights lasting as long as five days have been reported. Quite a feat of endurance for birds that can weigh as little as 0.75 to 1.5 ounces! Above are shown three of the more common species observed during migrations through Kentucky. The two additional species that may also be seen in Kentucky are: **Baird's Sandpiper** (*C. bairdi*) and the **Western Sandpiper** (*C. mauri*). Recent population declines have been reported for the Least Sandpiper and the Semipalmated Sandpiper. By contrast, the Western Sandpiper is one of the most abundant shorebirds in America with a population estimate of 3.5 million birds.

Class—**Aves** (birds)

Order—**Charadriiformes** (shorebirds)

Family—**Scolopacidae** (sandpipers)

Stilt Sandpiper *Calidris himantopus*	**Buff-breasted Sandpiper** *Calidris subruficollis*	**Upland Sandpiper** *Bartramia longicauda*

Presumed range in Kentucky 	Presumed range in Kentucky 	Presumed range in Kentucky 
Size: 8.5 inches.	**Size:** 7.5 inches.	**Size:** 12 inches.
Abundance: Uncommon in Kentucky.	**Abundance:** Rare in Kentucky.	**Abundance:** Very rare in Kentucky.
Migratory Status: Transient spring and fall migrant.	**Migratory Status:** A rarely seen migrant in late summer and early fall.	**Migratory Status:** Rare transient migrant. Seen mostly during spring.
Variation: Winter birds are much paler, more grayish.	**Variation:** Sexes alike. Juvenile birds are similar but paler on breast.	**Variation:** Fall and juvenile plumages slightly paler than breeding adults.
Habitat: Ponds, marshes, flooded fields, and lake shorelines.	**Habitat:** Likes short grass fields. Prairies, pastures, golf courses, etc.	**Habitat:** An obligate of grasslands and prairies. Migrants use pastures and fields.
Breeding: Nests in lowland areas near the Arctic Ocean. Lays four eggs.	**Breeding:** Nest is a shallow scrape on the tundra. Lays three to four eggs.	**Breeding:** Nest is a shallow scrape on the ground lined with grass. Four eggs.
Natural History: The Stilt Sandpiper gets its name from its long legs. The long legs are an adaptation that allow it to feed in deeper water than most other *Calidris* sandpipers. Its body shape and habit of feeding in deeper water rather than on mudflats is unusual for its genus and mimics the yellowlegs sandpipers (genus *Tringa*, next page). The migratory routes for this sandpiper are mainly west of the Mississippi River, but wanderers have be seen in many areas of Kentucky on rare occasions. They nest along the northernmost coast of North America and will spend the winter in the interior of the South American continent. As with many other sandpiper species, the Stilt Sandpiper shows a remarkable fidelity to the nest site. After migrating thousands of miles from South America they often return to the same exact spot on the arctic coastline to lay their eggs.	**Natural History:** Males perform breeding displays that consist of spreading wings and leaping and fluttering. These displays usually occur in a confined area (known as a Lek). They are one of the few sandpipers that exhibit this behavior. These birds are great travelers. They winter in the Pampas region of southern South America and fly to the shores of the Arctic Ocean for breeding in the spring. Most transit through the U.S. in the Great Plains region, but in fall a few will move southward through the eastern half of the country. Their tame behavior and unusual tendancy to return to a wounded flock member made them easy targets for market hunting in the late 1800s. This, coupled with the destruction of the native American prairies, devastated this species and they have never fully recovered. Current attempts to protect them are complicated by the scope of their range.	**Natural History:** The bulk of the Upland Sandpiper's summer range is in the northern Great Plains. A few summer very sparsely east of the Mississippi River but even these birds occupy territories that are well to the north of Kentucky. Unlike most other members of the sandpiper family, the Upland Sandpiper avoids coastal areas in favor of prairies and grasslands well into the interior of the continent. Historically, these birds were much more numerous. Market hunting in the late 19th century saw countless numbers of dead Upland Sandpipers shipped by rail from their nesting grounds on the northern plains to markets in the east. At the same time they were being hunted mercilessly on their winter habitats in the Pampas of South America. Even more devastating to their populations was the conversion of the native American prairie to cropland. Amazingly, the species survives.

Class—**Aves** (birds)		
Order—**Charadriiformes** (shorebirds)		
Family—**Scolopacidae** (sandpipers)		

Greater Yellowlegs *Tringa melanoleuca*	**Lesser Yellowlegs** *Tringa flavipes*	**Solitary Sandpiper** *Tringa solitaria*

Presumed range in Kentucky	Presumed range in Kentucky	Presumed range in Kentucky
Size: 14 inches.	**Size:** 10.5 inches.	**Size:** 8.5 inches.

Abundance: Both species are seen during migration periods, mostly in the western-most portion of the state. The Lesser is probably more common in Kentucky.	**Abundance:** Uncommon in most of state. Fairly common in west Kentucky.
Migratory Status: Both species are transient spring and fall migrants.	**Migratory Status:** Spring/fall migrant.
Variation: Speckled appearance is less prominent on winter adults and juveniles of both species.	**Variation:** Summer plumage has more distinct white spotting on the back.
Habitat: Both species are seen in a wide variety of wetland habitats during migration. In Kentucky both species are most common in the Mississippi Alluvial Plain.	**Habitat:** Pond margins, lake shores, and along creeks and rivers.
Breeding: Greater breeds in northern bogs, Lesser in drier, more upland habitats. Both species nest on the ground and three to four eggs is the typical clutch size for both.	**Breeding:** Nests in trees and uses old songbird nests. Three to five eggs, usually four.

Natural History: These two related species are frequently seen together. When seen together they are easily recognized by size. When not found in mixed flocks they are best identified by the shape of the bill. The Greater Yellowlegs's bill is longer and ever so slightly upturned at the tip. The Greater Yellowlegs is the less social of the two, and although it is seen in small flocks it can also be seen singly. Both species were once heavily hunted and during the days of market hunting both species experienced steep population declines. Hunting still occurs in some areas of their migratory range, especially in the Caribbean. Both spend the summer in the boreal regions of Canada and Alaska and winter from the Gulf Coast of the southeastern United States southward into South America. Food items for the Greater include both aquatic and terrestrial invertebrates as well as some small aquatic vertebrates like small frogs or fish. Lesser Yellowlegs's food items are mainly invertebrates, both aquatic and terrestrial, but some small fish are also eaten. Both feed mostly by wading in shallows, but the Lesser is a more active feeder, wading rapidly and picking food from both the surface and the water column. It will also feed in this manner in terrestrial habitats such as grassy shorelines or meadow areas. Greater Yellowlegs feeds both diurnally and at night, when it employs a sweeping motion of the bill back and forth through the water, apparently catching food by feel. The major threat to both species today is probably loss of habitat, both on wintering grounds in South America (loss of wetlands) and on summer range in North America, i.e., logging in boreal forests (Greater), and loss of wetlands in Alaska (Lesser).

Natural History: As implied by their name, the Solitary Sandpipers are nearly always seen alone during migration. In this respect they differ markedly from most other members of their family. They also differ in their nesting habits, as they are the only North American member of the *Scolopacidae* family that nests in trees. When feeding it wades in shallows and plucks its food from the surface or beneath the water. Rarely probes the mud with its bill. Food is mostly invertebrates, both aquatic and terrestrial. Insects make up the bulk of the terrestrial foods. They also take aquatic insects and their larva, small crustaceans, snails, and some vertebrate prey such as small minnows or tadpoles. Due to their solitary habits and the fact that they breed in trees in remote boreal forests, little is known about their population status, but it appears to be stable.

Class—**Aves** (birds)		
Order—**Charadriiformes** (shorebirds)		
Family—**Scolopacidae** (sandpipers)		

Spotted Sandpiper *Actitis macularia*	**Wilson's Phalarope** *Phalaropus tricolor*	**Short-billed Dowitcher** *Limnodromus griseus*

Presumed range in Kentucky 	Presumed range in Kentucky 	Presumed range in Kentucky 
Size: 7.5 inches.	**Size:** 9.5 inches.	**Size:** 11 inches.
Abundance: Fairly common.	**Abundance:** Rare in Kentucky.	**Abundance:** Fairly common.
Migratory Status: Mostly a migrant, but a few may summer in the state.	**Migratory Status:** Mostly a spring/fall migrant, may be rarely seen in summer.	**Migratory Status:** Spring and late summer / early fall migrant.
Variation: Winter birds lack the spots on the breast and are grayer on the back. Most Spotted Sandpipers seen in Kentucky will be in summer plumage.	**Variation:** Sexual, seasonal, and ontogenetic variations. Non-breeding birds are gray above and all white beneath. Juveniles are mottled brown above.	**Variation:** Breeding birds are rich brown. Winter birds uniformly gray with whitish belly. Sexes are alike (see photos above).
Habitat: In migration uses edges of ponds, lake shores, stream courses, and river bars.	**Habitat:** Uses marshes on breeding range, shallow water habitats along lake shores, ponds, etc., in migration.	**Habitat:** In inland migrations dowitchers use mudflats and lake shores. Many migrate along the coasts.
Breeding: Nests on the ground in grassy situations. Lays two to four eggs. Nesting has been recorded in Kentucky.	**Breeding:** Breeds on inland marshes and wetlands in the west-central U.S. and Canada. Always lays four eggs.	**Breeding:** Breeds in bog and muskeg habitats of northern Canada and Alaska. Both species lay four eggs.
Natural History: Unlike most sandpipers that exhibit strong flocking tendencies, the Spotted Sandpiper is always seen singly or in very small groups. This is one of the most widespread sandpipers in America and one of the few that nests in the lower forty-eight. The distinctly spotted breast along with a habit of constantly bobbing up and down makes the Spotted Sandpiper one of the most recognizable members of the Scolopacidae family. Feeds on a wide variety of aquatic and terrestrial invertebrates, especially dipteran (fly) larva. Also eats significant quantities of mayflies, crickets, grasshoppers, caterpillars, beetles, and mollusks, crustaceans, and worms.	**Natural History:** Phalaropes are known for the unique role reversal of the sexes. In these birds the female is the most vividly colored while the male has drab plumage. Even more unusual, it is the male that incubates the eggs in the nest. These birds are salt lake specialists and during migration they congregate in large flocks around alkaline and highly saline lakes of the interior of North America. The winter habitat is similar saline lakes in the Andes Mountains of South America. Birds seen in Kentucky are rare wanderers. The slightly smaller (8 inch) **Red-necked Phalarope** (*P. lobatus*) is a related species that can also be seen in Kentucky on rare occasions.	**Natural History:** The nearly identical **Long-billed Dowitcher** (*Limnodromus scolopaceus,* not shown) may also be seen in Kentucky during spring and fall migrations. Distinguishing between the two in the field is difficult even for experts. The Long-billed is slightly larger at 11.5 inches. It migrates earlier in the spring and later in the fall than the Short-billed. It also is more likely to be seen in inland habitats. Like many shorebirds both species of dowitcher were heavily hunted during the days of market hunting. At that time, it was not known that the two similar dowitchers constituted two distinct species. The existence of two species was not finally confirmed until 1950.

Class—**Aves** (birds)

Order—**Charadriiformes** (shorebirds)

Family—**Scolopacidae** (sandpipers)

Woodcock *Scolopax minor*	**Wilson's Snipe** *Gallinago delicata*	**Ruddy Turnstone** *Arenaria interpres*

Presumed range in Kentucky	Presumed range in Kentucky	Presumed range in Kentucky

Size: 11 inches.

Size: 10.5 inches.

Size: 9.5 inches.

Abundance: Fairly common.

Abundance: Fairly common.

Abundance: Uncommon in Kentucky.

Migratory Status: Year-round resident. Winter migrants increase population.

Migratory Status: Can be seen in Kentucky from late August through May.

Migratory Status: Spring and fall migrant, seen in KY mostly in August and September.

Variation: No plumage variations. Females are significantly larger.

Variation: None.

Variation: Seasonal plumage variations. Breeding plumage shown above.

Habitat: Swamps, regenerative woodlands, thickets, and weedy fields in bottomlands or uplands with moist soils.

Habitat: Mudflats, flooded grassy fields, marshes, river bars, water-filled ditches, temporary pools, and grassy pond banks.

Habitat: Winters on sandy beaches along both coasts. May use lake shores, mudflats, or river banks during inland migrations.

Breeding: Nest is on the ground and not concealed. Lays four eggs as early as late February.

Breeding: Nests far to the north of Kentucky in wetlands where it lays four eggs on a hummock in marsh or bog.

Breeding: Breeds in the Arctic Tundra and coastlines from Siberia and Alaska across Canada to Greenland.

Natural History: The Woodcock is unique among Kentucky sandpipers in that it is strictly an inland species. It is also the only member of its family that breeds widely throughout the state. Woodcocks are known for their elaborate courtship flights that consist of an upward twisting corkscrew accompanied by a twittering call. The long beak is used to probe moist soils for invertebrates. Among its unique features are a flexible upper bill that aids in extracting the favorite food, earthworms, and eyes that are situated far back on the head, allowing for backward vision while feeding. One of the most remarkably cryptic of the sandpipers, Woodcocks are nearly impossible to detect when motionless on the forest floor.

Natural History: As with other members of the sandpiper family, the beak of the Wilson's Snipe contains sensory pits near the tip which helps to locate invertebrate prey hidden in the mud. It also shares the Woodcock's rearward positioned eyes for watching behind and above while feeding. This is another highly camouflaged species that is nearly invisible when immobile. It is one of the most common and widespread members of the sandpiper family that often relies on its cryptic coloration when approached. Sitting quietly until nearly trod upon it will burst from the grass with a twisting, erratic flight while emitting a raspy call. Like the Woodcock the Wilson's Snipe is regarded as a game bird, but few people hunt them.

Natural History: Most Ruddy Turnstones travel up and down America's coastlines during migration, but a few migrate through inland regions of the continent, and few appear in Kentucky occasionally. This is one of the most northerly ranging birds in America, traveling to the northernmost extreme of the continent to breed each summer. Its name comes from its habit of using its beak to overturn pebbles and stones on beaches in search of small invertebrate prey. It also feeds on ocean carrion found on beaches. On the breeding grounds the primary food source is mosquitoes and other dipteran insects. The unusual genus (*Arenaria*) contains only two species and their position in the phylogeny of the shorebirds is unclear.

Class—**Aves** (birds)

Order—**Charadriiformes** (shorebirds)

Family—**Scolopacidae** (sandpipers)	Family—**Recurvirostridae** (avocets, stilts)	
Willet *Catoptrophorus semipalmatus*	**American Avocet** *Recurvirostra americana*	**Black-necked Stilt** *Himantopus mexicanus*

Presumed range in Kentucky

Presumed range in Kentucky

Presumed range in Kentucky

Size: 15 inches.	**Size:** 18 inches.	**Size:** 14 inches.
Abundance: Rare in Kentucky.	**Abundance:** Rare in Kentucky.	**Abundance:** Very rare in Kentucky.
Migratory Status: Migrant. Seen in Kentucky in spring and again in late summer to early fall.	**Migratory Status:** Migrant. Most sightings in Kentucky are during fall migration.	**Migratory Status:** Mostly migrant. Most sightings in Kentucky are in April and May and again in July and August.
Variation: Winter plumage (not seen in Kentucky) lacks brown speckling.	**Variation:** Breeding birds have bright rusty-orange head and neck.	**Variation:** Sexes alike. Juvenile birds are dark brown above rather than black.
Habitat: In migration uses pond banks, mudflats, lake shores, riverbanks, and flooded fields.	**Habitat:** Marshes, shallow lakes, and wetlands. Especially fond of saline wetlands and alkaline lakes of the west.	**Habitat:** Marshes and flooded fields, especially flooded pastures or grassy roadside ditches filled with rainwater.
Breeding: Lays four eggs in nest on the ground.	**Breeding:** Nests on the ground in a shallow scrape lined with grass. Four eggs.	**Breeding:** Nests in or adjacent to wetlands in clumps of vegetation. Four eggs.

Natural History: The Willet is a true "shorebird" that is quite familiar to those who frequent America's seashores. Both coasts of America are home to Willets during the winter, and some will nest in coastal marshes. Others fly into the interior of North America and nest as far north as the central Canadian prairie. It is these migrants that can sometimes be seen in Kentucky. Crustaceans, mollusks, insects, small fish, and polychaete worms are listed as food items. Feeds both day and night. In the 1800s they were hunted for food and for their eggs, which were also eaten, resulting in a significant decrease in populations. Today these are fairly common shorebirds whose population appears stable at an estimate of about a quarter of a million birds. They are known to live at least ten years.

Natural History: Few will be lucky enough to see the American Avocet in Kentucky, but those who do will not easily forget it. With its dramatic coloration, long legs, and long upturned bill it is one of the most striking birds in America. Feeds by sweeping its upturned bill back forth through the water. Feeds mostly on small aquatic insects (especially midges) and eats both adult insects and their aquatic larva. They also feed on brine shrimp and brine flies in saline wetlands and akaline lakes. Along the coastal marshes where they spend the winter amphipods and marine worms are important foods. Their breeding habitat is in the prairies and inter-mountain basins of the western United States, where they utilize marshes and wetlands. These habitats have been greatly reduced in recent times.

Natural History: Common names for birds are usually descriptive, none more so than this species with its black neck and long, stilt-like legs. With their exceptionally long legs, Black-necked Stilts can feed in fairly deep waters. Their food is mostly aquatic invertebrates, but a few small fishes are also taken. They winter along southern coastlines of North America and in Mexico and Central America, where many are residents that will breed on these wintering grounds. But some move inland to breed and summer on marshlands in the western United States. Some breeding by this species has been recorded in the Mississipppi Alluvial Plain of extreme western Kentucky, but most specimens seen in the state are migrants that are merely passing through.

Class—**Aves** (birds)		
Order—**Charadriiformes** (shorebirds)		
Family—**Laridae** (gulls, terns)		
Ring-billed Gull *Larus delawarensis*	**Herring Gull** *Larus argentatus*	**Bonaparte's Gull** *Chroicocephalus philadelphia*

Presumed range in Kentucky 	Presumed range in Kentucky 	Presumed range in Kentucky
Size: 17.5 inches.	**Size:** 25 inches.	**Size:** 13.5 inches.
Abundance: Common.	**Abundance:** Uncommon in Kentucky.	**Abundance:** Uncommon.
Migratory Status: Mainly a winter resident, but a few may be seen nearly year-round in the state.	**Migratory Status:** Primarily a winter resident in Kentucky. A few may be seen in spring or late summer and early fall.	**Migratory Status:** Winter resident in westernmost Kentucky. Winter migrant elsewhere in the state.
Variation: Juveniles are brownish gray and have greenish legs and bill.	**Variation:** First year juveniles are brownish, second year birds are grayer.	**Variation:** Summer plumage has all-black head (not usually seen in KY).
Habitat: Primarily in the vicinity of lakes and rivers, but also in rural crop fields and in urban areas.	**Habitat:** In Kentucky these birds stick close to the major rivers and lakes. They are most common in western KY.	**Habitat:** Frequents large rivers and larger lakes when in Kentucky. Summers in Canada.
Breeding: Nests in inland areas well to the north and west of Kentucky. Nest is on the ground on sandbars or rocky beaches. Lays two to four eggs.	**Breeding:** Nest is on the ground in a bowl-shaped scrape lined with vegetation. Two or three eggs are laid. Does not nest in Kentucky.	**Breeding:** The only gull that nests in trees, using conifers bordering remote lakes in Canada and Alaska. Typically lays three eggs.
Natural History: The Ring-billed Gull is one of the most common and widespread gull species in America. Most population estimates put their number in the millions, and they may be increasing. This is the gull commonly seen around inland lakes in summer and along coastal beaches in winter. They are also seen in urban parking lots or hanging around fast-food restaurants ready to swoop in and grab a dropped french fry. They are common in garbage dumps and may be seen foraging with starlings and other urban birds around dumpsters. These are highly gregarious birds that travel in flocks and nest in colonies. Food is almost anything, from carrion to insects, fish, rodents, earthworms, and human refuse.	**Natural History:** Like the smaller Ring-billed Gull, the Herring Gull is an opportunistic feeder that will eat almost anything, including human garbage. Like other gull species, they are gregarious and they often nest in large colonies. Only about 50 percent of the young gulls hatched each year reach adulthood, but the species seems to be thriving. Their numbers were drastically reduced during the 1800s but they have recovered completely and may be more numerous now than in historic times. The presence of man-made garbage dumps that serve as a smorgasbord for these birds may explain their recent population expansion. They are widespread in their distribution and are common on both of America's coastlines.	**Natural History:** Many people tend to lump all gull species together and refer to them all as "seagulls." Most species, however, including the Bonaparte's Gull, are often inland birds during the breeding season. Like other gulls, many Bonaparte's Gulls will spend the winter along America's coastlines and sometimes far out to sea. Small to moderately large flocks can be seen on inland rivers and lakes in western Kentucky throughout the winter. One of our smaller gulls, they feed mostly on small fish such as shad and shiners, but like other gulls they are highly opportunistic feeders and will eat a wide variety of insects and other invertebrates. Unlike other gull species, however, they are not typically seen around towns or dumps.

Class—**Aves** (birds)

Order—**Charadriiformes** (shorebirds)

Family—**Laridae** (gulls, terns)

Franklin's Gull *Leucophaeus pipixcan*	**Laughing Gull** *Leucophaeus atricilla*	**Forster's Tern** *Sterna forsteri*
	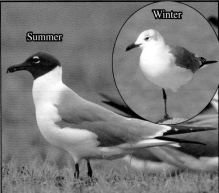	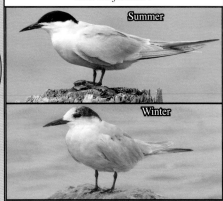
 Presumed range in Kentucky	 Presumed range in Kentucky	 Presumed range in Kentucky
Size: 14.5 inches.	**Size:** 16.5 inches.	**Size:** 14 inches.
Abundance: Rare in Kentucky.	**Abundance:** Rare in Kentucky.	**Abundance:** Uncommon in Kentucky.
Migratory Status: Migrant. Most migrate through the Great Plains but a few wanderers may be seen in KY in the fall.	**Migratory Status:** Migrant. Wandering individuals are occasionally seen the state, especially in western Kentucky.	**Migratory Status:** Migrant. Seen in Kentucky in both spring and fall. Some may stay into early winter (December).
Variation: Specimen shown above is an adult in breeding plumage. In winter and juvenile birds the black hood is replaced by a gray head with a white forehead and the bill is solid black.	**Variation:** Summer plumage is shown above. Winter adults lack black hood and instead have gray heads with white forehead and a black bill. First year juveniles are brown.	**Variation:** Exhibits both seasonal and age-related plumage variations. Juveniles resemble winter adults (see photos above) but juveniles have more of a brownish coloration on the back.
Habitat: Migrants use lakes, rivers, marshes, flooded fields, and pastures.	**Habitat:** These are primarily coastal birds that sometimes wander inland.	**Habitat:** Marshes. Both fresh and salt. Also beaches and coastlines.
Breeding: Breeds in marshes in the great plains of Canada and north central U.S. Nest is on floating mats of vegetation amid marshland. Lays two to four eggs.	**Breeding:** Nests in colonies along the Atlantic and Gulf coasts. Nests are built on the ground in salt marshes or islands. Three eggs is typical.	**Breeding:** Breeds both along the Gulf Coast and on inland marshes in the center of the continent. One to four eggs in nest of matted vegetation within marsh.
Natural History: Adults in breeding plumage have a faint pinkish blush on the breast and belly feathers. A few of these breeding birds may pass through Kentucky in spring and early summer, but most Franklin's Gulls seen in Kentucky appear during southward migration in the fall. As with other gull species, the Franklin's Gull matures slowly and it takes three years to achieve the mature adult plumage shown in the photo above. Like other gulls the Franklin's is an opportunistic feeder that will eat both plant and animal matter. Most foods are invertebrates (insects, worms, crustaceans, etc.). The bulk of this bird's range is west of the Mississippi.	**Natural History:** Although they are only rarely seen in Kentucky, they are quite common and familiar along the Atlantic and Gulf coasts, and they are commonly seen in a variety of habitats as much as 60 miles inland. Following breeding, some birds may follow major river systems well into the continent and a few make it as far inland as Kentucky. Most Laughing Gulls seen in Kentucky appear in the spring or fall, but they may rarely be seen almost anytime of the year. It takes three years for the Laughing Gull to obtain the characteristic black hood worn in summer plumage, but these are apparently long-lived birds with a longevity record of 19 years.	**Natural History:** This is probably the most common tern species seen in Kentucky. Here they usually frequent the state's major river systems and their associated large impoundments. They are sometimes seen in the company of gulls and other tern species, especially in winter along coastlines where gulls and terns are both extremely common. These medium-size terns feed almost exclusively on small fish that are captured by diving from above. When "fishing" they fly back and forth over water with the bill pointed downward and plunge headlong into the water. They are graceful fliers that sometimes hover when schools of fish are located.

Class—**Aves** (birds)

Order—**Charadriiformes** (shorebirds)

Family—**Laridae** (gulls, terns)

Common Tern *Sterna hirundo*	**Caspian Tern** *Hydroprogne caspia*	**Least Tern** *Sternula antillarum*

Presumed range in Kentucky 	Presumed range in Kentucky 	Presumed range in Kentucky 
Size: 15 inches.	**Size:** 21 inches.	**Size:** 9 inches.
Abundance: Rare in Kentucky.	**Abundance:** Uncommon in Kentucky.	**Abundance:** Uncommon in Kentucky.
Migratory Status: Migrant. Seen in Kentucky mostly in the fall, but a few may also be seen in the spring.	**Migratory Status:** Migrant. Wanders into Kentucky in spring, late summer, and early fall.	**Migratory Status:** Summer resident that nests on sandbars and islands of major rivers in western Kentucky.
Variation: First year juveniles and winter birds have white foreheads and all-black bill. White on forehead reduced on second year juvenile in summer colors.	**Variation:** In winter birds the black cap becomes mottled with white. Juveniles are similar to winter adults. Sexes are alike.	**Variation:** No variation among adults in Kentucky. Birds that nest in Kentucky are a distinct subspecies of Least Tern that are inland nesters.
Habitat: Migrating birds usually associate with major rivers and large lakes. Islands and beaches are frequently used.	**Habitat:** Mainly coastal birds in winter, they use rivers, large lakes and marshes in migration.	**Habitat:** Kentucky Least Terns follow the major river systems in the western end of the state.
Breeding: Nests mostly in Canada and along the Atlantic coastline. Lays two or three eggs in nest on ground. Some birds will produce two broods per year.	**Breeding:** North American populations nest both on coasts and large bodies of water in the interior of the continent, including the Great Lakes. One to three eggs.	**Breeding:** Least Terns that breed in Kentucky use river bars on the Mississippi River. Nest is a scrape in sand or gravel. One to four eggs.
Natural History: The Common Tern is well known to conservationists. They are symbolic of the fight to save many of America's bird species from wanton slaughter. From the early European settlement of North America to the late 1800s, unregulated over-hunting of America's wildlife nearly wiped out many species. Millions of herons, egrets, waterfowl, and shorebirds were killed for food and for the millinery trade. At the same time America's large mammal species also suffered dramatic population declines. Today many wildlife species, including terns, have recovered dramatically, but tern populations are still below historical numbers.	**Natural History:** The worlds largest tern and also the most widespread. Found all over the world, the Caspian Tern breeds on every continent except Antarctica. Feeds almost entirely on fish. Feeds by hovering and diving. When diving often submerges completely. Food is mostly fish. This is the only large tern regularly seen inland. They are found along the southern coastlines as well and in winter stay along the coasts. They are also seen inland in winter throughout the Florida peninsula. They are seen in Kentucky from April through October, but their occurance in the state is rather rare. These large terns are known to live up to 26 years.	**Natural History:** The race of Least Tern that nests in Kentucky is regarded as endangered. Flooding has always been a perennial threat, as high water can flood nests located just inches above the waterline. Newer threats are modern dams along the Mississippi and Ohio rivers that have raised river levels for barge traffic but have inundated much of their nesting habitat on natural river sandbars. Least Terns winter along southeastern coastlines and some as far south as the Caribbean and Central America. In the 1800s these birds were killed and skinned to adorn womens hats. Coastal development is a major threat to the species today.

Class—**Aves** (birds)

Order—**Charadriiformes** (shorebirds)	Order—**Pelecaniformes** (pelicans)	Order—**Suliformes** (tropical sea birds)
Family—**Laridae** (gulls, terns)	Family—**Pelecanidae**	Family—**Phalacrocoracidae** (cormorants)

Black Tern *Chlidonias niger*	**White Pelican** *Pelecanus erythrorhynchos*	**Double-crested Cormorant** *Phalacrocorax auritus*

Presumed range in Kentucky 	Presumed range in Kentucky 	Presumed range in Kentucky 

Size: 9.75 inches.

Size: 62 inches.

Size: 33 inches.

Abundance: Uncommon in Kentucky.

Abundance: Uncommon in Kentucky.

Abundance: Fairly common.

Migratory Status: Migrant. Seen in Kentucky mostly late summer and early fall. A few will pass through in May.

Migratory Status: Mostly a spring to fall migrant. Occasionally a winter resident on large lakes in western Kentucky.

Migratory Status: Cormorants can be seen nearly year-round in western Kentucky. Mostly migrant elsewhere.

Variation: In winter and in juvenile birds the dramatic black color of the breast and belly is replaced by white.

Variation: Juvenile birds are duskier and have a dusky gray bill. Breeding birds develop a projection on the bill.

Variation: Juveniles are much browner and have whitish throat and breast. Breeding plumage has white crest.

Habitat: Breeding habitat is shallow, freshwater marshes in the north central United States and Canada.

Habitat: In Kentucky restricted to larger lakes and rivers. Elsewhere commonly uses large marshlands and coastlines.

Habitat: Lakes, rivers, estuaries, and swamplands. In Kentucky usually seen around the state's larger impoundments.

Breeding: Nest is built upon floating vegetation or muskrat platforms. Two or three eggs is typical.

Breeding: Nests in colonies in protected areas (often islands on large lakes). Lays two eggs, but often only one survives.

Breeding: Colony nester. Nests are built of sticks and floating debris. Lays two to four eggs. Formerly nested in KY.

Natural History: Winters along coastlines from Central America to northern South America. There is a European subspecies that winters in Africa. Like most terns these birds are highly social and usually seen in flocks. Unlike other terns, however, they feed heavily on insects, especially in summer. This is the only tern seen in Kentucky that has a dark breast and belly. In early spring they are mottled with black and white as they transition from winter to summer plumage (see inset above). Although the number of Black Terns today is estimated to be in the hundreds of thousands, this figure is paltry compared to the size of the population that existed before modern agricultural practices destroyed much of their breeding habitat.

Natural History: Although wandering flocks of White Pelicans may suddenly appear on almost any large body of water in Kentucky, they are regularly seen only in the western tip of the state. Unlike their cousin the Brown Pelican, which feeds by plunging into the water, White Pelicans feed in a more placid manner. Flocks of feeding White Pelicans corral fish by swimming in a coordinated group and dipping the head beneath the surface in perfect unison. The appearance of a feeding flock is that of a perfectly choreographed ballet. Competition between baby White Pelicans in the nest is fierce, and the stronger nestling often kills its sibling. Thus, usually only one of the two young survive.

Natural History: Cormorants are rarely seen far from water. They are thoroughly aquatic birds that have webbed feet and frequently submerge and swim underwater in search of fish. Their exclusive diet of fish and their uncanny aquatic abilities have caused these birds to come into conflict with man. Occurring in large flocks, they will concentrate in areas where food is most readily available. Under natural conditions they catch a wide variety of fish species and thus do not impact significantly upon fisheries. However, around fish farms or hatcheries they can become quite a nuisance. In some regions they have come under attack from commercial and sport fisherman, who blame cormorants for reduced catches.

Class—**Aves** (birds)

Order—**Gaviiformes** (loons)	Order—**Podicipediformes** (grebes)	
Family—**Gaviidea**	Family—**Podicipedidae**	
Common Loon *Gavia immer*	**Pied-billed Grebe** *Podilymbus podiceps*	**Horned Grebe** *Podiceps auritus*

<table>
<tr>
<td>

</td>
<td>

</td>
<td>

</td>
</tr>
<tr>
<td>Presumed range in Kentucky</td>
<td>Presumed range in Kentucky</td>
<td>Presumed range in Kentucky</td>
</tr>
</table>

Size: 32 inches.	**Size:** 13 inches.	**Size:** 14 inches.
Abundance: Uncommon in Kentucky.	**Abundance:** Fairly common.	**Abundance:** Uncommon in Kentucky.
Migratory Status: Migrant. Has been seen in Kentucky every month of the year, but mostly seen in spring and fall.	**Migratory Status:** May be seen year-round, but is most numerous in spring, fall, and winter months.	**Migratory Status:** Winter mostly, but they may be seen in Kentucky from October through April.
Variation: Sexes are alike but exhibits significant seasonal plumage changes.	**Variation:** Winter birds are grayer and lack the prominent dark ring on bill.	**Variation:** Winter plumage (shown) is usually seen in Kentucky.
Habitat: Highly aquatic. In inland areas the Common Loon lives on lakes. They may also be seen along both coasts in winter.	**Habitat:** Completely aquatic, the Pied-billed Grebe uses everything from large lakes to small farm ponds. Also open water areas of swamps and marshes.	**Habitat:** In Kentucky this species uses the larger lakes as well as large marshes with open water. They are not usually seen on small ponds.
Breeding: Nests on small islands in northern lakes. Usually lays two eggs.	**Breeding:** Nests on floating platform among emergent vegetation. Four to eight eggs.	**Breeding:** Nests on floating platform among emergent vegetation. Five to seven eggs.

Natural History: On lakes and marshes in the far north the call of the Common Loon echoes through the wilderness. The sound is so distinctive and unique that it has inspired many poetic depictions. "Haunting," "ethereal," and "lonely" are words that are often used in conjunction with describing its yodeling cry that can carry for a great distance. They call both day and night on the breeding grounds in the northern half of the continent, but they are rarely heard calling on their winter range. Remarkable swimmers, they dive beneath the surface and propel themselves through the water with their powerful webbed feet. Fish caught in this manner are the main food item. Adult loons are sometimes seen swimming with babies perched on their back.

Natural History: A night-time migrator, this little grebe evades potential threats by submerging, and they sometimes swim with just the head sticking out the water. They feed on a wide variety of small fish and other aquatic vertebrates as well as crustaceans and insects. This is the most widespread and common grebe in North America, they are most common during summer in the "Prairie Pothole" habitats of the west-central U.S. and Canada. In winter they move as far south as Central America. They can be seen all winter across the southern half of the U.S., but tend to concentrate along the Gulf Coast in winter. Most breed in more northerly regions of the continent, but there are a few records of Pied-billed Grebes breeding in Kentucky.

Natural History: As is the case with other grebes (and loons), their adaptations for an aquatic lifestyle include the legs being positioned far back on the body. The legs can also be flared outward to a remarkable degree to facilitate underwater swimming maneuvers. As a result of this adaptation, these birds are very clumsy on land and walk with difficulty. Breeding on marshes and lakes in the northernmost portions of the continent, these birds are a transient migrant in much of Kentucky. However, some may be winter residents in the western tip of the state. Breeding birds (not usually seen in Kentucky) are handsomely marked with chestnut neck and flanks and golden brown head stripe that flares out to form "horns." Food is small fish, crustaceans, insects, etc.

Class—**Aves** (birds)

Order—**Anseriformes** (waterfowl)

Family—**Anatidae** (ducks, geese, swans)

Mallard *Anas platyrhynchos*	**Black Duck** *Anas rubripes*	**Northern Pintail** *Anas acuta*

Presumed range in Kentucky	Presumed range in Kentucky	Presumed range in Kentucky
Size: 23 inches.	**Size:** 23 inches.	**Size:** Male 25 inches, female 21.
Abundance: Very common.	**Abundance:** Uncommon.	**Abundance:** Uncommon.
Migratory Status: Both a year-round breeding resident and a winter migrant.	**Migratory Status:** Winter migrant and occasional winter resident.	**Migratory Status:** Winter resident in Coastal Plain, migrant elsewhere in KY.
Variation: Pronounced sexual plumage variation (see photos above).	**Variation:** Sexes are very similar; females have a darker bill than males.	**Variation:** Profound sexual dimorphism (see photos above). Male larger.
Habitat: Found in aquatic situations everywhere, from deserts to tundra to southern swamplands, ponds, lakes, etc.	**Habitat:** Fond of estuaries and coastal marshes. Inland will use other aquatic habitats (lake, marshes, swamps, etc.).	**Habitat:** Open country. In Kentucky uses large flooded bottomland fields and marshes along river valleys.
Breeding: Nests on the ground in close proximity to water. Lays up to 13 eggs and will re-nest if nest is destroyed.	**Breeding:** For breeding favors coastal marshes and beaver ponds and bogs in boreal forests. Lays up to 14 eggs.	**Breeding:** Breeds in marshes, potholes, and tundra in the northern and western portions of the continent. Three to 12 eggs.
Natural History: By far the most familiar duck in America. The Mallard has been widely domesticated but it is also the most common wild duck in the United States. Many parks and public lakes around the country have semi-wild populations that are non-migratory. Highly adaptable, this is the most successful duck species in America, perhaps in the world. It is the source of all breeds of domestic duck except the Muscovey and they are thus an important food source for humans. They are also a highly regarded game bird and they are hunted throughout North America. They range throughout the northern half of the globe and their range in the western hemisphere closely coincides with the North American continent. Semi-tame Mallards are one of the few ducks that breed in Kentucky.	**Natural History:** The Black Duck is very similar to the Mallard in size, shape, and voice, and the two species are known to hybridize. In appearance and other traits, however, they are quite different. This is one of the few puddle ducks that does not range throughout the continent, being restricted to the eastern half of America. Like many of America's duck species, the Black Duck has been impacted negatively by human related changes to the landscape and environment in America. Drainage of wetlands, urbanization along northeastern coastlines, and deforestation have hit this species harder than most other ducks and the population has declined significantly in the last half-century. Interbreeding with the more adaptable Mallard may also be a threat to this uniquely American duck.	**Natural History:** Northern Pintail populations are in decline. Modern agricultural practices on the Great Plains of the U.S. and Canada are the greatest threat. They are also highly susceptible to droughts in the prairie regions, which limit breeding habitat. Food is mostly plant material but some aquatic invertebrates are also eaten. On wintering grounds waste grain from farming operations has become an important food source. In recent decades the species has benefited from a number of conservation efforts by state and federal agencies as well as private organizations, most notably Ducks Unlimited, an organization funded by duck hunters. Conservation efforts that have recently benefited the species are reduced hunter harvest and changing agricultural practices in the prairie pothole region.

Class—**Aves** (birds)

Order—**Anseriformes** (waterfowl)

Family—**Anatidae** (ducks, geese, swans)

Gadwall *Anas strepera*	**American Wigeon** *Anas americana*	**Green-winged Teal** *Anas crecca*

Gadwall
Anas strepera

American Wigeon
Anas americana

Green-winged Teal
Anas crecca

Presumed range in Kentucky

Presumed range in Kentucky

Presumed range in Kentucky

Size: 20 inches.

Size: 19 inches.

Size: 14 inches.

Abundance: Fairly common.

Abundance: Fairly common.

Abundance: Fairly common.

Migratory Status: Winter resident.

Migratory Status: Winter migrant.

Migratory Status: Winter resident.

Variation: Significant sexual dimorphism (see photos above).

Variation: Significant sexual variation. See photos above.

Variation: Significant sexual variation. See photos above.

Habitat: Marshes and potholes of the Great Plains in summer. Uses all aquatic habitats in winter.

Habitat: Winter range includes all types of aquatic habitats in the state (swamps, marshes, lakes, ponds, etc.).

Habitat: Winter range includes all types of aquatic habitats in the state (swamps, marshes, lakes, ponds, etc.).

Breeding: Nests among thick vegetation near water, often on islands in marshes or lakes. Lays 7 to 12 eggs.

Breeding: Nests near shallow freshwater wetlands and potholes mostly in the North American prairie. Three to 12 eggs.

Breeding: Nest is in dense vegetation in wetland habitats of the far north. Six to nine eggs are laid as early as May.

Natural History: Gadwalls breed and summer largely in the Great Plains region. In winter they are seen all across the southern half of America, with the greatest numbers wintering along the western Gulf Coast coastal plain. Populations of this duck can fluctuate significantly depending upon water levels in the prairies of Canada and the north-central U.S. Droughts and poor agricultural practices that eliminate habitat can cause populations to plummet. Conversely, good rainfall and good wildlife conservation practices by farmers have shown to be a real boon to this and many other duck species that depend on the marshes and potholes on the Great Plains for nesting habitat. Adult Gadwalls feed mostly on plant material. Ducklings rely heavily upon high protein invertebrates for growth and development.

Natural History: The American Wigeon also goes by the name "Baldpate," a reference to the white crown of the male. This duck has a very similar old world counter-part, the Eurasian Wigeon, which ranges throughout much of Europe and Asia. American birds feed mostly on plant material, but females when breeding opt for a higher protein diet of invertebrates. One of the more northerly ranging members of the "puddle duck" group, some individuals will summer as far north as the Arctic Coastal Plain of Alaska. These ducks may be seen in Kentucky from October through April, but peak numbers occur in mid-winter. Most merely pass through the state during north-south migrations, but a few may reside in Kentucky throughout the winter. As with other puddle ducks, this species is susceptible to population declines during droughts.

Natural History: This is the smallest of America's "puddle ducks," and also one of the more common. They range throughout the northern hemisphere, with a distinct subspecies being found in Eurasia. They are fast and agile fliers and flocks of Green-winged Teal move back and forth across the southern half of the continent all winter in response to weather patterns. Populations of this duck appear stable and may even be increasing. About 90 percent of the population breeds in Canada and Alaska where they favor river deltas and boreal wetlands over the typical "pothole" habitats used by many puddle ducks. Their remote nesting habitats are largely undisturbed by man, which may account in part for this species' abundance. As with many species, the increasing daylight hours of spring triggers migration and breeding instincts.

Class—**Aves** (birds)

Order—**Anseriformes** (waterfowl)

Family—**Anatidae** (ducks, geese, swans)

Blue-winged Teal *Anas discors*	**Shoveler** *Anas clypeata*	**Wood Duck** *Aix sponsa*
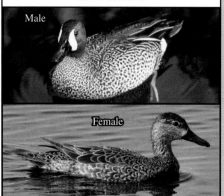 	 	 
Presumed range in Kentucky	Presumed range in Kentucky	Presumed range in Kentucky
Size: 15.5 inches.	**Size:** 19 inches.	**Size:** 18.5 inches.
Abundance: Fairly common.	**Abundance:** Fairly common.	**Abundance:** Common.
Migratory Status: Mainly a transient migrant in spring and fall. In mild winters some may linger in the Coastal Plain of western Kentucky. They have nested sporadically in the Interior Low Plateau in the south-central part of the state.	**Migratory Status:** The Shoveler is mainly a transient fall/winter/spring migrant in much of Kentucky. However, they may often be a winter resident in the the western end of the state, particularly in the lowlands of the Gulf Coastal Plain.	**Migratory Status:** Year-round resident. Local populations are supplemented by winter migrants and some resident birds may move farther south in harsh winters, but the species can be seen year-round in the state and regularly breeds here.
Variation: Significant sexual dimorphism (see photos above).	**Variation:** Significant sexual dimorphism (see photos above).	**Variation:** Significant sexual dimorphism (see photos above).
Habitat: Marshes, beaver ponds, bays, and other shallow water habitats.	**Habitat:** Prefers shallow habitats. Swamps, marshes, flooded fields, bays.	**Habitat:** Beaver ponds, swamps, flooded woodlands, and farm ponds.
Breeding: Nest is concealed in dense vegetation near water but above high waterline. Lays 6 to 12 eggs.	**Breeding:** Breeds in northern and western United States (including Alaska) and in Canada. Averages 10 to 12 eggs.	**Breeding:** Nests in tree hollows and takes readily to artificial nest boxes. Lays about 8 to 12 eggs typically.
Natural History: The food of this species is mostly plant material including algae and aquatic greenery. Many seeds and grains are also eaten, especially in winter when they converge on rice fields and other flooded agricultural areas in America's lower coastal plain. Breeding females will consume large amounts of invertebrates during the breeding season. These ducks are early fall migrators and one of the last to migrate back north in the spring. Many will winter as far south as South America, but substantial numbers can be seen along the lower coastal plain of North America all winter. Most breed and spend the summer on the central prairies of the U.S. and Canada.	**Natural History:** The Shoveler's name is derived from the unique shape of its bill, which is a highly effective sieve for straining tiny organisms from water. They are often observed swimming along with the bill held under water or skimming the surface. Like several of America's duck species, the Shoveler is Holarctic in distribution and it breeds in Europe and Asia as well as North America. Eurasian birds winter southward to North Africa and the Pacific region. All ground-nesting birds are vulnerable to mammalian predators and the Shoveler is no exception. Red Foxes and Mink are significant predators on the nesting females, while skunks are a major threat to the eggs.	**Natural History:** Male Wood Ducks are one of the most brilliantly colored birds in America. The bulk of the Wood Duck population in America occurs in the forested eastern half of the country. Populations plummeted during the latter half of the 19th century as America's forests were felled and swamplands drained. Populations began to recover by the 1950s and today the species is thriving. Wood Ducks are widely hunted and make up a significant number of ducks killed by hunters annually. Although they are a small duck, they are considered by many as highly palatable. This is the only totally wild duck species that is a regular and widespread breeder in Kentucky.

Class—**Aves** (birds)		
Order—**Anseriformes** (waterfowl)		
Family—**Anatidae** (ducks, geese, swans)		

Lesser Scaup *Athya affinis*	**Ring-necked Duck** *Athya collaris*	**Redhead** *Athya americana*
 	 	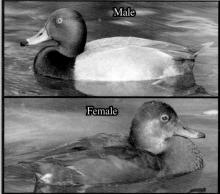 
Presumed range in Kentucky	Presumed range in Kentucky	Presumed range in Kentucky
Size: 16.5 inches.	**Size:** 17 inches.	**Size:** 19 inches.
Abundance: Fairly common.	**Abundance:** Fairly common.	**Abundance:** Uncommon.
Migratory Status: Winter resident in western Kentucky. Winter migrant elsewhere in the state.	**Migratory Status:** Winter resident in west KY and on the Ohio River north to Louisville. Winter migrant elsewhere.	**Migratory Status:** May be seen in Kentucky from October through April, but is most common in winter.
Variation: Sexually dimorphic. See photos above.	**Variation:** Pronounced sexual dimorphism. See photos above.	**Variation:** Pronounced sexual dimorphism. See photos above.
Habitat: Likes larger bodies of water and deeper water than many other ducks. Regularly uses large lakes and rivers in the state as well as flooded river bottoms.	**Habitat:** Open water habitats including shallow bays and flooded river bottoms. Also uses open marshes and large rivers and lakes, where it tends to use mostly shallow-water areas.	**Habitat:** Primarily a marshland species that alternates between prairie potholes and gulf coastal marshes. In migration they will use a variety of wetland habitats, especially the bays of large lakes.
Breeding: Eight to 10 eggs is typical. Nests in west-central U.S., Canada, and in Alaska.	**Breeding:** Nests in subarctic regions of Canada and the northern Rockies in the United States. Lays 6 to 14 eggs.	**Breeding:** Breeds almost entirely in the "prairie pothole" region. Females often lay their eggs in other ducks' nests.
Natural History: These ducks are the most widespread and common of the "diving ducks." Diving ducks are capable of diving deeper and prefer deeper waters than the "puddle ducks." They are also more clumsy on land and need a running start on the water to get airborne. They thus favor larger lakes and rivers over small ponds and swamplands. A slightly larger version of the Lesser Scaup, known as the **Greater Scaup** (*Athya marila*) can also be seen in Kentucky in winter. Both species like open water. The Greater Scaup tends to favor coastal areas and salt or brackish marshes, but it does migrate through much of the eastern U.S., including Kentucky.	**Natural History:** Closely related to and very similar in appearance to the scaups, the Ring-necked Duck should be called the Ring-billed duck. Although there is a brownish ring around the neck of the male, it is only visible when the bird is in the hand. The broad white ring near the tip of the bill and the narrow white ring at the base of the bill are both readily discernible on birds in the field. Unlike its relatives the scaups, which will feed on crustaceans, insects, and other aquatic invertebrates, the diet of the Ring-necked Duck is mostly vegetarian. Ring-billed Ducks also favor small lakes, ponds, and swamps over large rivers and lakes.	**Natural History:** An entirely North American species, the Redhead is mostly a vegetarian and feeds heavily on tubers and aquatic vegetation. Most Redheads congregate in winter on the western gulf coast of Louisiana, Texas, and northwest Mexico. In fact, hundreds of thousands will concentrate in this region each winter. Here they feed mostly on the roots of shoalgrass. They will also eat some animal matter, mostly aquatic invertebrates. Redheads are easily decoyed and during the days of the market hunting their populations suffered dramatic declines. Recovery in the last few decades has been significant and in a good year the population may reach a million birds.

Class—**Aves** (birds)

Order—**Anseriformes** (waterfowl)

Family—**Anatidae** (ducks, geese, swans)

Canvasback *Athya valisineria*	**Bufflehead** *Bucephala albeola*	**Common Goldeneye** *Bucephala clangula*

Presumed range in Kentucky	Presumed range in Kentucky	Presumed range in Kentucky
Size: 21 inches.	**Size:** 13.5 inches.	**Size:** 18.5 inches.
Abundance: Uncommon.	**Abundance:** Fairly common.	**Abundance:** Uncommon.
Migratory Status: Seen in Kentucky from November through March.	**Migratory Status:** Can be seen in Kentucky from November through March.	**Migratory Status:** Winter. Seen in Kentucky November through March.
Variation: Strong sexual variation. See photos above.	**Variation:** Significant sexual variation. See photos above.	**Variation:** Significant sexual variation. See photos above. Juvenile like female.
Habitat: The primary breeding habitat for this species is known as "Aspen Parkland" habitat, which is found mostly in Canada. Winters mostly in marshes and bays along both coasts.	**Habitat:** Most winter in salt water habitats on the coast but a few overwinter on inland lakes and rivers in Kentucky. In summer they use boreal forests and parklands in Canada.	**Habitat:** In winter this species uses large lakes and rivers in Kentucky. They are also fairly common in winter in coastal regions. In summer they are a bird of the boreal forests.
Breeding: The large nest is built from grasses and hidden vegetation. Clutch size averages around seven or eight.	**Breeding:** Cavity nester. Nest is often an old woodpecker hole. Clutch size ranges from a few to over a dozen eggs.	**Breeding:** Cavity nester that will use artificial nest boxes. May nest over a mile from water; 7 to 12 eggs.
Natural History: One of the most adept of the diving ducks, Canvasbacks have been known to dive to a depth of 30 feet. Feeds mostly on plant material including roots and rhizomes, but will also eat mud-dwelling invertebrates. This is strictly a North American species and is one of the least common duck species in America. They are vulnerable to droughts, habitat loss (mostly from agriculture), and water pollution that can impact the abundance of aquatic food plants. The Canvasback population is closely monitored by the U.S. Fish and Wildlife Service and in years of low numbers hunting of this species may be banned. Even in years when hunting is allowed, the bag limits are typically very low (one per day).	**Natural History:** America's smallest of the diving ducks, the Bufflehead is one of the few duck species that will remain with the same mate year after year. Breeding pairs usually return to the same pond or marsh to breed each year as well. With the exception of some seeds, these ducks are mostly carnivorous, feeding on aquatic insects, crustaceans, and mollusks. Unlike the puddle ducks, which often feed on the surface, the Bufflehead finds all its food by diving. Although they are often seen on deep-water lakes in Kentucky, they feed in the shallows along the banks or in the backs of bays. Although rarely seen in large flocks, this is one of the few duck species that has actually increased in numbers in the last few decades.	**Natural History:** As with other diving ducks the Common Goldeneye is an excellent swimmer that feeds by diving beneath the surface. They propel through the water using only the feet, with the wings held tight against the body. They are mostly carnivorous but they do eat some plant material in the form of tubers and seeds. Aquatic invertebrates are the main food and include (in order of importance) crustaceans, insects, and mollusks. Fish constitute only a small portion of the diet. Male Common Goldeneyes engage in a complex courtship display to attract females or reinforce the pair bond. These ducks are Holarctic in distribution, breeding in boreal forests throughout the northern hemisphere.

Class—**Aves** (birds)
Order—**Anseriformes** (waterfowl)
Family—**Anatidae** (ducks, geese, swans)

Ruddy Duck *Oxyura jamaicensis*	**Long-tailed Duck** *Clangula hyemalis*	**Black Scoter / Surf Scoter** *Melanitta fusca / Melanitta perspicillata*
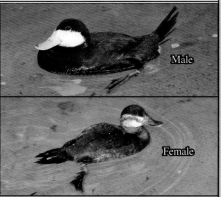		
Presumed range in Kentucky	Presumed range in Kentucky	Presumed range in Kentucky
Size: 15 inches.	**Size:** 16.5 to 21 inches.	**Size:** 21 inches.
Abundance: Uncommon in Kentucky.	**Abundance:** Very rare in Kentucky.	**Abundance:** Very rare in Kentucky.
Migratory Status: May be seen in Kentucky from October through April.	**Migratory Status:** May be seen in Kentucky from November through March.	**Migratory Status:** Winter. Seen in Kentucky November through March.
Variation: Significant sexual variation. See photos above.	**Variation:** Males have very long tails and are more strikingly colored.	**Variation:** Significant variation. Females and juveniles are brownish.
Habitat: Marshes, ponds, lakes, and to a lesser extent rivers. This is a true "Prairie Pothole" species and nearly 90 percent of nesting occurs in the prairie pothole habitats in the northern plains.	**Habitat:** Summer habitat is arctic wetlands and seashores and deep-water lakes. Winter habitat mostly coastal marine environments, but also large freshwater lakes, especially the Great Lakes.	**Habitat:** In fall and winter Scoters may rarely use large lakes and rivers in Kentucky. They can be fairly common in winter in coastal regions. In summer they are a bird of the boreal forests.
Breeding: Nest is usually built in cattails or other aquatic vegetation. Seven or eight eggs is average.	**Breeding:** Nests in the Arctic on islands and peninsulas of freshwater lakes or in wetland tundra. Six to eight eggs.	**Breeding:** Nests near shallow inland lakes in the far north, often well into the Arctic Circle. Seven to 12 eggs.
Natural History: Ruddy Ducks are primarily western birds that range generally from the Great Plains to the west coast. Winter range includes most of the western U.S. and a few individuals are regularly seen in the western half of the Kentucky in winter. Although they may rarely appear on impoundments in the Appalachian region, these ducks are more commonly seen in Kentucky farther to the west or sometimes along the Ohio River. The larva of aquatic insects of the order Diptera (flies, mosquitos, midges) are reported to be a primary food of these ducks. Although they are small ducks, their eggs are quite large and are in fact the largest eggs (relative to body size) of any North American duck.	**Natural History:** Also known as "Old-squaw," these are primarily northern ducks that often wander far south in winter. Although they have been recorded in a variety of localities around the state, in Kentucky they are most likely to be seen on the Ohio River in northernmost Kentucky. These little ducks are great divers, and can dive to depths over 150 feet to reach marine invertebrate foods consisting mostly of benthic crustaceans. Also eat insects and their larva and to a lesser extent fish and fish eggs. There is some evidence that populations on the west coast are in decline. Status of eastern populations unknown but believed stable. Often roosts in large "rafts" well offshore along coastlines or in large inland lakes.	**Natural History:** There are a total of three Scoter species in North America and all three have been seen in Kentucky during winter months. They sometimes are seen on the Ohio River or other major rivers and impoundments in Kentucky during winter. But they usually associate with coastal waters and they are often collectively referred to as "Sea Ducks." They will summer inland in the far north of northern Canada and Alaska. Waterfowl of all species are well known for wandering widely and sometimes appearing in areas far from their normal habitats. In addition to the two species shown above the **White-winged Scoter** (*M. fusca*) can also rarely be seen in the state, though it is probably the rarest in Kentucky.

Class—**Aves** (birds)

Order—**Anseriformes** (waterfowl)

Family—**Anatidae** (ducks, geese, swans)

Common Merganser *Mergus merganser*	Red-breasted Merganser *Mergus serrator*	Hooded Merganser *Lophodytes cucullatus*

Presumed range in Kentucky	Presumed range in Kentucky	Presumed range in Kentucky
Size: 25 inches.	**Size:** 23 inches.	**Size:** 18 inches.
Abundance: Uncommon in Kentucky.	**Abundance:** Uncommon in Kentucky.	**Abundance:** Fairly common.
Migratory Status: Fall and winter migrant.	**Migratory Status:** Fall, winter, and spring migrant.	**Migratory Status:** Mostly a fall and winter resident. Has bred in Kentucky.
Variation: Exhibits pronounced sexual dimorphism in breeding plumage with males having dark greenish head and white breast. Winter plumage (seen in Kentucky) is similar in both sexes.	**Variation:** Significant plumage variations between the sexes during the breeding season. Also exhibits seasonal variation with winter males (and juveniles) resembling females.	**Variation:** Shows strong sexual dimorphism. Males are strikingly marked, having black heads with white "hood" and black wings and back. Females are more subdued (see above).
Habitat: In winter uses large lakes and rivers and larger reservoirs.	**Habitat:** Uses larger lakes and rivers when migrating through Kentucky.	**Habitat:** In winter uses swamps, shallow bays of lakes, and river floodplains.
Breeding: Nests in tree cavities or sometimes in root crevices on the ground; 10 or 12 eggs is average.	**Breeding:** Nests on the ground. Nest is well hidden beneath overhanging vegetation or in cavities. Five to 24 eggs.	**Breeding:** Cavity nester. Most nest in Great Lakes region, but nesting has occurred in KY. Lays 12 eggs maximum.
Natural History: Most Common Mergansers seen in Kentucky will be in non-breeding plumage (shown above). A bird of northern climates and cold waters, the Common Merganser spends the summer on lakes in the boreal forests of Canada, Alaska, and in the cold water streams of the Rocky Mountains. They are also found throughout Eurasia. Fish is the primary food for this species. Their bill is serrated for holding slippery prey and they are excellent divers and underwater swimmers. They are excellent fishermen and can dive to a depth of tens of yards and have been known to stay submerged up to two minutes. They use their bill to probe in mud or gravel for aquatic insects, mollusks, crustaceans, and worms.	**Natural History:** During winter these birds show a preference for coastal regions where they use estuaries and salt water bays and salt / brackish water marshes. Like its larger relative the Common Merganser, the Red-breasted has a Holarctic distribution and is found in Europe and Asia as well as North America. In summer this species ranges even farther north than its larger cousin, being found as far north as the Arctic Ocean and southern Greenland. Food is mostly small fish that are grasped with the serrated bill. Also eats aquatic invertebrates and amphibians. Feeds both in shallow water and in deep water up to at least 25 feet deep. Flocks may feed cooperatively, with all the birds diving together to corral schools of minnows.	**Natural History:** Unlike our other two merganser ducks, both of which are Holarctic in distribution, the Hooded Merganser is strictly a North American duck. Another odd distributional trait is the fact that these birds are rare in the Great Plains region, where many North American duck species are most common. They have a more diverse diet than the larger mergansers, feeding less on fish and more on aquatic invertebrates that are located by means of well developed underwater vision capability. Winter waterfowl surveys indicate that over 50 percent of the population winters in the Mississippi flyway. Most birds winter to the south of Kentucky, but this species can be seen regularly throughout the winter in western Kentucky.

Class—**Aves** (birds)		
Order—**Anseriformes** (waterfowl)		
Family—**Anatidae** (ducks, geese & swans)		

Snow Goose *Chen caerulescens*	**Canada Goose** *Branta canadensis*	**Greater White-fronted Goose** *Anser albifrons*

 Presumed range in Kentucky	 Presumed range in Kentucky	 Presumed range in Kentucky
Size: 30 inches.	**Size:** 36 to 45 inches.	**Size:** 28 inches.
Abundance: Fairly common.	**Abundance:** Very common.	**Abundance:** Uncommon.
Migratory Status: Winter migrant.	**Migratory Status:** Year-round resident.	**Migratory Status:** Winter migrant.
Variation: Two distinct color phases occur. Juveniles are uniformly gray.	**Variation:** No variation. Sexes and juveniles are all alike.	**Variation:** Juveniles lack black spots on belly. Sexes are alike.
Habitat: In Kentucky these geese are mostly seen in western Kentucky where they use very large agricultural fields, especially along the Mississippi River.	**Habitat:** In Kentucky the habitat includes all types of aquatic situations, from urban parks to remote and inaccessible marshes, swamps, or beaver ponds.	**Habitat:** When migrating through Kentucky they will use large agricultural fields for feeding and roost on open water or bays in large lakes.
Breeding: Nests only in the high Arctic Tundra of Canada and Alaska.	**Breeding:** Nests above the waterline but near water. Four to eight eggs is typical.	**Breeding:** Breeds in the Arctic Coastal Plain. Average clutch size is four or five.
Natural History: Snow Goose populations have exploded in the last few decades, probably as a result of having so much habitat and food available throughout migration routes and on wintering grounds. The grain fields of the midwestern and southern U.S. provide a more than adequate food source. Mid-continent populations are expanding their migration routes eastward from their historical range west of the Mississippi River. Today they can be found every winter in the Coastal Plain of west Kentucky and are sometimes seen as far east as northern and central Kentucky. Snow Geese often occur in huge flocks that number hundreds or even thousands of birds. They are an important game species in places. The **Ross's Goose** is a is a smaller version of the Snow Goose that may rarely be seen in extreme western Kentucky.	**Natural History:** This is the most recognized wild goose in America, due in large part to the fact that tame and semi-tame populations are found in parks and on rivers, ponds, and lakes in both urban and rural regions. Resident Canada Geese are numerous in Kentucky, but their numbers are swelled dramatically during winter, as birds from farther north visit the state for either a brief stopover or a months-long stay. The characteristic "V formation" of Canada Geese in flight is a familiar sight and their musical, honking call is to many a symbol of wild America. They are heavily hunted throughout America both for sport and for food. Tens of thousands are killed in Kentucky by hunters each year. They are long-lived birds and have been known to survive over 40 years. A small race called the **Cackling Goose** is the size of a Mallard.	**Natural History:** Although they may migrate throughout the much of state west of the Appalachian Plateau, White-fronted Geese are usually found in the western end of Kentucky. While they are circumpolar in distribution, they are not as common in North America as the Canada Goose or Snow Goose. Most of the North American populations of these geese use the Mississippi and Central Flyways, but a smaller population occurs in the Pacific Flyway. Oddly, they are rarely seen in the Atlantic Flyway. Mississippi Flyway birds that pass through western Kentucky will usually winter along the Gulf Coast from Louisiana and Texas to northeastern Mexico. During migration small flocks may be seen traveling with larger flocks of Canada or Snow Geese, but they tend to segregate themselves when resting or feeding.

Class—**Aves** (birds)
Order—**Anseriformes** (waterfowl)
Family—**Anatidae** (ducks, geese, swans)

Mute Swan *Cygnus olor*	**Tundra Swan** *Cygnus columbianus*

Presumed range in Kentucky	Presumed range in Kentucky
Size: 56 inches.	**Size:** 53 inches.
Abundance: Uncommon.	**Abundance:** Very rare in Kentucky.
Migratory Status: Year-round resident.	**Migratory Status:** Winter migrant.
Variation: Some juveniles are brownish for the first year.	**Variation:** Juveniles are "dingy" white with orange bill.
Habitat: Ponds, lakes, marshes, and swamps in both urban and rural areas.	**Habitat:** Large lakes and large, open agricultural fields are used in migration.
Breeding: Nest is large platform of grasses. Near water but above flood-plain. About six eggs per clutch.	**Breeding:** Breeds on the tundra of the Arctic Coastal Plain. Three to five eggs are laid.
Natural History: The Mute Swan is a Eurasian species that is common in parks, zoos, farms, and private preserves all across America. Many have become feral or semi-feral and the species seems to be increasing in the wild in America. The impact of this exotic species on native wildlife populations is unknown, but some state wildlife agencies regard them as a nuisance animal. Many state wildlife agencies have active removal programs. In other states they are protected. These large waterfowl are primarily vegetarians, but they will eat small amounts of animal matter. When threatened Mute Swans arch the wings over the back and pull the long neck back between the wings in a display known as "busking." They are graceful and elegant in flight or on the water, but rather clumsy on land due to the fact that the legs are located so far back on the body.	**Natural History:** Although the Tundra Swan is America's most common swan species, these large swans are rare in Kentucky. But they do pass through the state during migration occasionally. Most winter along the Atlantic coast from the Chesapeake Bay south to North Carolina and on the Pacific Coast from Washington to central California. In winter they use coastal estuaries and will fly inland to forage on waste grain in agricultural fields. Young swans stay with the parents throughout the first year until returning to their arctic breeding grounds the following spring. Prior to the passage of the first migratory bird protection legislation in 1918, these birds had become quite rare. Today their numbers have recovered substantially and a few states now allow a limited harvest during waterfowl season. No hunting of Tundra Swans is allowed in Kentucky.

CHAPTER 5
THE TURTLES OF KENTUCKY

Table 7.
The Orders and Families of Kentucky Turtles.

Class—**Chelonia** (turtles)

Order—**Cryptodira** (straightneck turtles)

Family	**Chelydridae** (snapping turtles)
Family	**Kinosternidae** (mud and musk turtles)
Family	**Emydidae** (sliders and box turtles)
Family	**Trionychidae** (softshell turtles)

Class—**Chelonia** (turtles)
Order—**Cryptodira** (straightneck turtles)
Family—**Chelydridae** (snapping turtles)

Common Snapping Turtle	**Alligator Snapping Turtle**
Chelydra serpentina	*Macrochelys temminckii*

Presumed range in Kentucky 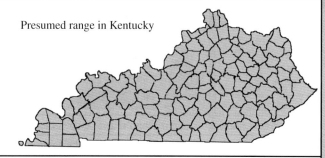	Presumed range in Kentucky 
Size: Maximum length 20 inches. Record weight 86 pounds.	**Size:** Maximum length 31 inches. Record weight 251 pounds.
Variation: No variation occurs in Kentucky specimens. Specimens found on the Florida peninsula differ slightly.	**Variation:** No variation in Kentucky. Males attain a larger size than females and all the really large specimens are males.
Abundance: Very common.	**Abundance:** Very rare in Kentucky.
Habitat: Found in virtually every aquatic environment in the state. Ponds, lakes, rivers, creeks, swamps, and marshes.	**Habitat:** Large rivers and their impoundments. Also oxbow lakes and small tributaries near their confluence with rivers.
Breeding: Eggs are deposited in underground chambers excavated by the female turtle. A typical clutch contains 25 to 50 eggs. Hatchlings are about the size of a quarter.	**Breeding:** Adult females leave the water to lay up to 50 eggs in an underground chamber dug by the turtle. The leathery shelled eggs hatch in three or four months.
Natural History: These common turtles can be found in any aquatic habitat in the state, including tiny farm ponds or tributaries narrow enough for a person to step across. They even can exist in waters that are heavily polluted with sewage. They will feed on some plant material but are mainly carnivorous and will eat virtually anything they can swallow. Fish, frogs, tadpoles, small mammals, baby ducks, crayfish, and carrion are all listed as food items. Hatchlings turtles often must travel long distances to find a home in a pond or creek, and adults occasionally embark on long overland treks, presumably in search of a more productive habitat after depleting the food source in a small pond or creek. These long hikes overland usually occur in the spring. The ferociousness of a captured snapping turtle is legendary and their sharp, powerful jaws can inflict a serious wound. When cornered on land they will turn to face an enemy and extend the long neck in a lunging strike that is lightning fast and so energetic that it may cause the entire turtle to move forward several inches. By contrast when under water they almost never bite.	**Natural History:** Alligator Snapping Turtles are the most completely aquatic of any American Turtle. In fact, they never leave the water except for egg laying excursions by the female. Unlike most aquatic turtles, they do not bask and rarely show more than the tip of the snout when coming up to breathe. They spend most of their time "bottom walking" or lying in ambush in the muck or mud. They possess a specialized structure on the tongue that resembles a worm and can be wriggled to effectively lure fish into striking distance. They also eat other turtles, carrion, crayfish, and in fact probably any type of animal matter that can be swallowed. Mussels are reportedly an important food item, the hard shell being no match for the powerful jaws of these huge turtles. The longevity of this turtle in the wild is unknown, but some specimens have been in captivity for over 70 years, suggesting a long life span. These interesting and unique animals have declined significantly throughout their range. In Kentucky the Alligator Snapping Turtle is now regarded as a threatened species.

Class—**Chelonia** (turtles)
Order—**Cryptodira** (straightneck turtles)
Family—**Kinosternidae** (mud, musk turtles)

Common Musk Turtle *Sternotherus odoratus*	**Common Mud Turtle** *Kinosternon subrubrum*

 Presumed range in Kentucky	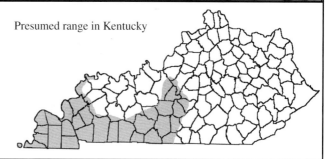 Presumed range in Kentucky

Size: About 4 inches in length as an adult.	**Size:** Adults range from 4 to 4.75 inches in length.
Abundance: Fairly common.	**Abundance:** Fairly common.
Variation: In some regions females are larger than males, but there is no variation in Kentucky specimens.	**Variation:** There are three subspecies. Two are found in Kentucky but there is very little difference between subspecies.
Habitat: Primarily a stream dweller, but can be found in a variety of aquatic habitats including swamps, oxbows, lakes, etc. They reach their highest densities in waters with abundant aquatic vegetation.	**Habitat:** Found in all aquatic habitats withing its range, but prefers shallow water areas with abundant aquatic vegetation. They are turtles of the lower elevations and are most common in Kentucky in the Gulf Coastal Plain.
Breeding: Female lays two to five eggs under leaf litter or sometimes merely on top of the ground. Eggs hatch into tiny turtles that are barely an inch in length.	**Breeding:** Reaches breeding age at about five to seven years old. Breeds in the spring. Females dig a hole and deposit an average of two to four eggs, sometimes as many as eight.
Natural History: Nocturnal and crepuscular and completely aquatic in habits. Unlike most aquatic turtles in Kentucky, the Musk Turtle rarely basks, but when it does it may climb several feet up into branches that overhang the water. When disturbed while basking these turtles will launch themselves clumsily into the safety of the water. Since they seldom leave the water, the carapace is often covered with a thick growth of algae. Their name comes from the presence of musk-producing glands that emit an unpleasant odor when the turtles are handled. This musk also accounts for their other common name, "Stinkpot." The Common Musk Turtle is widespread throughout the eastern U.S., being found from the Gulf Coast north to the Great Lakes, but they are absent from most of the higher elevations of the Appalachian Plateau. They are an omnivorous species that feeds on a variety of aquatic plant and animal matter. Like many turtle species, the Eastern Musk Turtle is a long-lived species and one captive zoo specimen lived for 55 years.	**Natural History:** There are two subspecies native to Kentucky. They are the Eastern Mud Turtle (*K. s. subrubrum*, pictured above) and the Mississippi Mud Turtle (*K.s. hippocrepis*). The latter is found only within a narrow strip of land known as the Mississippi Alluvial Plain, which borders the Mississippi River in westernmost Kentucky. Although they are very aquatic turtles, they sometimes embark on overland treks, presumably to find new habitats or seek a mate. These are the only aquatic turtles in Kentucky that have a double hinged plastron, a characteristic that is rare in North American turtles. Their diet is omnivorous. A variety of aquatic plants are eaten and animal foods include crustaceans, aquatic insects, mollusks, amphibians, and carrion. Locates food by "bottom walking" when in water, but may also feed on land near the water's edge. They can remain under water for up to 20 minutes. These small turtles have been known to live up to 40 years and perhaps can survive even longer.

Class—**Chelonia** (turtles)

Order—**Cryptodira** (straightneck turtles)

Family—**Emydidae** (water, box turtles)

Red-eared Slider *Trachemys scripta*	**Eastern River Cooter** *Pseudemys concinna*	**Painted Turtles** *Chrysemys picta*
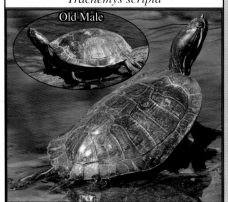		
Presumed range in Kentucky	Presumed range in Kentucky	Presumed range in Kentucky
Size: Average 6 to 8 inches.	**Size:** 10 to 12 inches.	**Size:** 4 to 6 inches.
Abundance: Very common.	**Abundance:** Fairly common.	**Abundance:** Common.
Variation: Males are smaller than females and have longer claws on the front feet. Hatchlings have a yellowish carapace boldly marked with green and black lines or circular patterns.	**Variation:** Males are smaller than females and have long, needle-like claws on the front feet. Some experts recognize several subspecies, but there is little geographic variation in Kentucky.	**Variation:** Two subspecies in Kentucky. The **Midland Painted Turtle** (subspecies *marginata;* top photo above) and the **Southern Painted Turtle** (subspecies *dorsalis*; bottom photo above).
Habitat: Most common in large bodies of water but can be found in any aquatic habitat in the state except for very small streams.	**Habitat:** Primarily a turtle of large rivers and lakes, but they can also be common in swamps and oxbows that are adjacent to larger streams.	**Habitat:** Avoids fast flowing streams in favor of still or slow-moving waters. Common in swamps, marshes, ponds, and lakes throughout its range.
Breeding: Females leave the safety of the water and crawl hundreds of yards to upland areas to deposit their eggs in an underground nest chamber dug with the hind legs. Large females may lay 20 eggs, younger females lay fewer.	**Breeding:** Lays about 20 eggs in an underground chamber dug with the females hind legs. Egg deposition is in late spring or early summer with the eggs hatching in August or September. Babies are slightly larger than a quarter.	**Breeding:** Females lay 10–15 eggs within a flask shaped underground nest chamber dug with the turtle's hind legs. Egg laying occurs from late May to early July. Eggs hatch in about 10 weeks. Hatchlings are the size of a quarter.
Natural History: Highly aquatic but sometimes seen far from water. Omnivorous. Eats a variety of water plants as well as mollusks, minnows, dead fish, aquatic insects, crustaceans, etc. Young are more carnivorous, while mature turtles will consume more plants. Old specimens tend to darken with age and very old specimens can be nearly all black (see inset). These are hardy turtles that will emerge from the mud to bask on logs on warm, sunny days throughout the winter. There are three subspecies of slider turtles in America, one of which, the **Red-eared Slider** (subspecies *elegans*), is found in Kentucky.	**Natural History:** The largest member of the *Emydidae* family in Kentucky. They primarily eat aquatic plants, including large quantities of algae. Some animal matter is consumed usually in the form of aquatic invertebrates or fish, especially so with younger turtles that need a higher protein diet. In habits they are strictly diurnal. Like many other aquatic turtles, they spend the winter buried in the mud at the bottom of a body of water. Their metabolic processes slowed significantly by cold temperatures, they absorb oxygen throught the lining of the cloaca. These large turtles are often utilized as food by humans.	**Natural History:** On the range map above, the range of the Southern Painted Turtle appears as the darker gray area. Light gray indicates the range of the Midland Painted Turtle. The Painted Turtles are among the most common and widespread of the Emydidae turtles in America. Like other members of their family they spend a great deal of time basking on floating logs and they are quick to slide into the water if approached too closely. These are omnivorous turtles that eat a very wide array of plant and animal foods as well as carrion. Some experts regard the two subspecies as two distinct species.

Class—**Chelonia** (turtles)

Order—**Cryptodira** (straightneck turtles)

Family—**Emydidae** (water, box turtles)

Common Map Turtle *Graptemys geographica*	**False Map Turtle** *Graptemys pseudogeographica*	**Ouachita Map Turtle** *Graptemys ouachitensis*
 Female		 Male (Top), Female (Bottom)
Presumed range in Kentucky 	Presumed range in Kentucky	Presumed range in Kentucky 
Size: Up to 11 inches.	**Size:** Between 6 and 10 inches.	**Size:** From 5 to 10 inches.
Abundance: Uncommon.	**Abundance:** Uncommon.	**Abundance:** Fairly common.
Variation: In mature adults, females are larger and have larger heads. Hatchlings are miniature replicas of the adult but more vivid in color and pattern.	**Variation:** Two subspecies are recognized, the False Map Turtle (subspecies *geographica*) and the Mississippi Map Turtle (subspecies *kohnii*).	**Variation:** Males are smaller than females and have longer front claws. Young resemble adults but have prominent markings on the plastron.
Habitat: Primarily found in larger rivers and lakes, but also found in smaller tributaries near their confluence with larger streams.	**Habitat:** These turtles show a preference for large, slow flowing rivers and their associated impoundments, oxbows, and swamps.	**Habitat:** Primarily lives in rivers and river impoundments. They can also be found in the oxbows and swamps associated with major rivers.
Breeding: Breeds in early spring and eggs are laid in June. Most egg laying occurs in the morning. The average clutch size is about 10 eggs.	**Breeding:** Lays an average of 8 to 10 eggs in late may through June. Eggs hatch in about 10 weeks. Two clutches per year are sometimes produced.	**Breeding:** Breeds in spring and fall. Eggs are laid in early summer and average about 10 per clutch. May lay two clutches per year.
Natural History: Diurnal and crepuscular in activity. These turtles are fond of basking on logs but are very wary and will disappear into the water if approached. Food items include crustaceans, fish, insects, and aquatic plants. They also eat mollusks and the thick, crushing surface of the jaws suggests that small mussels may be an important element in the diet. The Common Map Turtle is one of the more widely distributed of the map turtles and can be found from the Great Lakes southward into Arkansas and Alabama. They also range widely through middle Kentucky between the Appalachian Plateau and the Coastal Plain, but the exact range in the state is unclear. They have a life span in the wild of at least 20 years.	**Natural History:** When not feeding or breeding these turtles spend most of their time basking. They are quite wary and will dive into the water at the slightest disturbance. They eat mainly insects but also eat other aquatic invertebrates and will scavenge on dead fish. They eat less plant material than other aquatic turtles. The longevity record for this species is 35 years. With the exception of the three map turtle species shown on this page, this genus of turtles are mostly animals of America's Lower Gulf Coastal Plain. It is here that they reach their greatest diversity and some have very small geographic ranges. The range of some species in the Gulf Coast region is restricted to a single small river drainage.	**Natural History:** Food includes insects, dead fish, aquatic invertebrates, and plant material, especially algae. The carapace (top shell) of this species has a rough, serrated appearance that is more pronounced in younger turtles. They are good climbers and will bask on steep trunks or limbs overhanging water. This turtle's name is derived from the Ouachita Mountains of Arkansas, where the first specimen described to science was found. This species is widespread west of the Mississippi River and possibly more widespread in Kentucky than indicated on the range map above. The map above is at best an approximation, as the exact range of this species in the state is not fully known.

Class—**Chelonia** (turtles)
Order—**Cryptodira** (straightneck turtles)
Family—**Emydidae** (water, box turtles)

Eastern Box Turtle
Terrapene carolina

Female Laying Eggs

Presumed range in Kentucky

Size: Averages 4 to 6 inches in length. The record length is just under 8 inches.

Abundance: Very common.

Variation: There are four subspecies of this common land turtle. Only the eastern race occurs in Kentucky. They are a highly variable subspecies. In fact, no two specimens look exactly alike (see photos above). The color and pattern on each specimen is as individual as a fingerprint. Sexes can be differentiated by examination of the bottom part of the shell (plastron). Males have a concave plastron and females a flat plastron. In adult turtles, males tend to be slightly larger than females.

Habitat: Occupies a wide variety of habitats from open fields and pastures to deep woods. Can be found in both upland areas and lowlands, but is most common in damp woods, edge areas near creeks and streams, and wooded bottom lands.

Breeding: Breeding takes place in late April and May with egg deposition in late June or early July. Up to six eggs may be laid but two or three is more common. Young hatch in late fall and some may overwinter in their underground nest chamber before emerging the following spring. Newly hatched baby Box Turtles do not possess the hinged plastron and are thus unable to tightly close themselves within their shell.

Natural History: These familiar turtles often go by the name "Terrapin." They are primarily diurnal and are most active in the morning and the late afternoon. They sometimes burrow into the mud during hot weather, and overwinter by burrowing themselves into loose soil or deep leaf litter. The hibernation burrow is quite shallow, only a few inches deep. Studies have shown that they are tolerant of some freezing, a trait that enables survival of such a shallow hibernator. Still, hibernation is a significant source of mortality among adults. Their diet is omnivorous and they consume berries, fruits, and mushrooms as well as a wide variety of insect prey and other invertebrates. Earthworms and snails are a favorite animal food and blackberries and mulberries are among the favorite plant foods. Box Turtles are known for their longevity and reports of their living up to a century are common but difficult to verify. Some researchers report a life span of 80 years, while others say 30 to 40 years is probably the average in the wild. When threatened they will retract the head and feet into the shell, which can then close tightly by means of hinges on the front and back of the plastron. The muscles that close the shell are remarkably strong and efforts to pry open the shell of a frightened Box Turtle are futile. They are tough little turtles that can sometimes survive serious injury such as the shell being cracked open by a glancing blow from an automobile tire. Turtles with badly deformed but completely healed shells are sometimes found. In regions where wildfires are common many are seen with shells that are completely scarred by fire. There is some concern among conservationists that commercial collecting of these turtles for foreign markets may be threat to their long-term survival. Habitat degradation is a much more imminent threat, and automobiles take a fearful toll on these endearing animals on highways throughout their range each summer.

Class—**Chelonia** (turtles)
Order—**Cryptodira** (straightneck turtles)
Family—**Trionychidae** (softshell turtles)

Smooth Softshell Turtle *Apalone mutica*	Spiny Softshell Turtle *Apalone spinifera*

Presumed range in Kentucky 	Presumed range in Kentucky 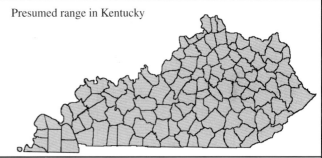
Size: 12 to 14 inches.	**Size:** Maximum of 18 inches.
Abundance: Uncommon in Kentucky.	**Abundance:** Fairly common.
Variation: No significant variation in Kentucky. There are two other Smooth Softshell species found in parts of the southeast. Females are significantly larger than males.	**Variation:** No subspecific variation among Kentucky specimens, but there are a total of five subspecies in America. Adult females can be twice the size of males.
Habitat: Essentially an inhabitant of streams, both large rivers and small creeks. Flowing water is a requirement for this species, but it is found in large river impoundments.	**Habitat:** Occurs in both large and small steams and in impoundments. May also be found in farm ponds in some areas. Shows a preference for habitats with sandy substrates.
Breeding: Eggs are laid in excavated chambers on exposed sandbars or sandy stream banks in late spring or early summer. About a dozen eggs is typical.	**Breeding:** A dozen or more eggs are laid between May and August (most in June or July). Nests are often on sandbars of creeks or rivers.
Natural History: The Smooth Softshell is found mostly in flowing streams with fine gravel or sand bottoms. They are capable of great speed in the water and will actively forage for fish and other small aquatic animals. They are also ambush predators that burrow into the soft substrate of streams and extend their long necks with blinding speed to grab passing fish. Insects are also an important food item, along with various small aquatic animals and some plant material such as seeds and berries. Because of their permeable skin and requirement of clear streams and rivers these turtles may be under significant threat from water pollution. Damming of major rivers can also impede their natural movements and dispersal. All species of softshell turtles have elongated, snorkel-like snouts that they will use to breathe when buried in sand or mud at the water's edge.	**Natural History:** Crayfish, fish, and insects are the primary food items, but dead fish and other carrion can be an important food item, especially in lakes where fishing is common. Spiny Softshells are active from April to October in Kentucky. They hunt both by ambush and by active pursuit. When immobile they can remain under water for several hours. Because of the soft, permeable shells and skin, softshells are more susceptible to dehydration than other turtle species and thus they seldom stray far from water. These turtles are harvested as food in many parts of their range, and much of this harvest is to date unregulated. Some believe this practice may pose a long-term threat to the species. Like all softshell turtles the Spiny has a long and flexible neck, which makes handling these turtles without being bitten difficult. Wild adults may bite savagely if handled.

THE REPTILES
OF KENTUCKY

PART 1: LIZARDS

CHAPTER 6
THE REPTILES OF KENTUCKY

Table 8.
The Orders and Families of Kentucky Reptiles.

Class—**Reptilia** (reptiles)
Order—**Squamata** (lizards, snakes)
Suborder—**Lacertilia** (lizards)

Family	**Phrynosomatidae** (spiny lizards)
Family	**Teiidae** (whiptail lizards)
Family	**Anguidae** (glass lizards)
Family	**Scincidae** (skinks)

Suborder—**Serpentes** (snakes)

Family	**Colubridae** (harmless egg laying snakes)
Family	**Dipsadidae** (small rear-fanged snakes)
Family	**Xenodontidae** (large rear-fanged snakes)
Family	**Natricidae** (harmless live-bearing snakes)
Family	**Crotalidae** (pit vipers)

Class—**Reptilia** (reptiles)

Order—**Squamata** (snakes, lizards)

Suborder—**Lacertilia** (lizards)

Family—**Phrynosomatidae**	Family—**Teiidae** (whiptails)	Family—**Anguidae** (glass lizards)
Eastern Spiny Lizard *Sceloporus undulatus*	**Six-lined Racerunner** *Aspidoscelis sexlineatus*	**Slender Glass Lizard** *Ophisaurus attenuatus*

Presumed range in Kentucky	Presumed range in Kentucky	Presumed range in Kentucky

Size: Maximum of 7.25 inches.

Abundance: Very common.

Variation: Males have bright blue patches on each side of the belly. There are no variants in Kentucky, but several subspecies occur in the western U.S.

Habitat: Dry, upland woods. Found in both pure deciduous woods and in pine dominated woodlands.

Breeding: Egg layer. Deposits 6 to 15 eggs in rotted logs, stumps, etc. Two clutches per year are common.

Natural History: A woodland species, the Eastern Fence Lizard spends much of its time on tree trunks and fallen logs. Its color and pattern perfectly matches the bark of most trees within its range. This is one of the most common lizards in Kentucky. They are quite arboreal in habits and will regularly climb trees to great heights. Feeds on insects, spiders, etc. Both sexes are often seen perched on rocks, logs, or stumps in wooded areas. Breeding males are especially conspicuous as they attempt to attract females by sitting atop rocks or stumps and methodically raising and lowering their body to show off the bright blue patches on the undersides. This is the only representative of its family in eastern North America.

Size: From 6 to 10 inches.

Abundance: Uncommon.

Variation: Males and subadults are a bit more vividly colored than mature females. An additional subspecies is found west of the Mississippi River.

Habitat: Habitat requirements are sandy or gravelly soils in dry upland areas with prolonged exposure to the sun.

Breeding: Breeds in April or May. Six or eight eggs are laid in and underground nest chamber in sandy soil.

Natural History: The Teiidae lizards are a common and diverse family in the southwestern United States, but they are represented in the east by this single species. The Teiidae lizards are famous among biologists because in some species there are no males and reproduction is accomplished by parthenogenesis (the development of unfertilized eggs into embryos). These speedy lizards are aptly named as they can reach a speed of up to 20 mph. They are active at higher temperatures than many reptiles and they will spend the first few minutes of the day basking in the sun to raise their body temperature. At night they retreat to an underground burrow dug into loose soil. Food is insects and other invertebrates.

Size: 2–3 feet. Record 43 inches.

Abundance: Rare in Kentucky.

Variation: Males (inset) have light and dark speckling. Juveniles resemble females but longitudinal stripes are more vivid on younger lizards.

Habitat: Dry soils with an open canopy seem to be important factors in this lizard's habitat. Woods, fields, and edge.

Breeding: Females lay as single clutch of eggs in late June or early July. Average clutch size is about 10 eggs.

Natural History: These lizards are often confused with snakes due to their lack of limbs. They are easily recognized as lizards, however, by the presence of ear openings and eyelids. When grasped these lizards will thrash about wildly and break off their tail. The tail is quite long, making up about two-thirds of their total length. The apparent fragility of these lizards and the shiny appearance of their skin has led to the common name "glass lizard." The highly specialized escape mechanism of breaking off the tail is shared with many other lizard species, as is the rare ability to regenerate a new tail. Regenerated tails never attain the original length. Like other Kentucky lizards they prey on small invertebrates.

Class—**Reptilia** (reptiles)

Order—**Squamata** (snakes, lizards)

Suborder—**Lacertilia** (lizards)

Family—**Scincidae** (skinks)

Ground Skink *Scincella lateralis*	**Coal Skink** *Plestiodon anthracinus*	**Broad-headed Skink** *Plestiodon laticeps*

 Presumed range in Kentucky	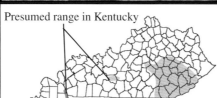 Presumed range in Kentucky	 Presumed range in Kentucky

Ground Skink	Coal Skink	Broad-headed Skink
Size: 3 to 5 inches.	**Size:** 5 to 7 inches.	**Size:** Average 8 inches. Maximum 13.
Abundance: Common.	**Abundance:** Rare.	**Abundance:** Fairly common.
Variation: Color may vary from reddish brown to golden brown or chocolate brown. Color has a metallic quality. Some have small dark flecks on the back.	**Variation:** There are two subspecies (Northern and Southern) and the northern subpecies is found in Kentucky. Young and juveniles are darker on the back and may have blue or black tails.	**Variation:** Young have blue tails and yellow stripes and resemble Five-lined Skinks. In adults females have faded, indistinct lines and males are uniformly brown with bright red cheeks.
Habitat: Dry upland woods and pine woodlands. Micro-habitat consists of leaf litter and detritus on the forest floor.	**Habitat:** Coal Skinks inhabit the forest floor in damp woodlands. They are frequently found near creeks.	**Habitat:** Mesic woodlands, wetland areas, and also dry upland woods with moist micro-habitat.
Breeding: Small clutches of three to five eggs is typical. May lay two clutches per year. Unlike other Kentucky skinks, the female Ground Skink does not remain with the eggs until hatching.	**Breeding:** From 6 to 12 eggs are laid under rocks, logs, or other sheltering structures. Females will remain with and guard the eggs until hatching. Babies are less than two inches in length.	**Breeding:** Females will vigorously defend their eggs that are usually laid on the ground in a hollowed out depression beneath sheltering log or inside a hollow stump.
Natural History: These tiny ground dwellers dive quickly beneath leaf litter when approached and they are easily overlooked. Often, their presence is revealed by the rustling sound made as they forage through the dry leaves. Despite being rarely observed, they can be quite common in many areas. Foods are tiny insects and other small invertebrates living among the leaf litter on the forest floor. They also go by the name "Little Brown Skink." They are widespread throughout the southeastern half of America and are most common in the deep south. They are the smallest lizard found in Kentucky.	**Natural History:** Termites, ant larva and pupae, and earthworms are listed as known food items. Probably feeds on a wide variety of small insects and other tiny invertebrates encountered on among leaf litter on the forest floor. As with all lizards found in Kentucky, they are diurnal. They shelter at night beneath logs, stones, or loose bark on dead snags, stumps, etc. The range of the Coal Skinks is discontinuous in Kentucky. There appears to be three widely separated populations within the state. Map above shows two smaller populations in the vicinity of Mammoth Cave and in the Eastern Highland Rim.	**Natural History:** These very large skinks are quite arboreal and often den in tree hollows many feet above the ground. These arboreal dens are used only during summer and hibernation takes place underground. In much of the southeast they are known as "Scorpion Lizards" and some believe the myth that they are dangerously venomous. Although they will bite if handled, they are totally harmless to humans. This is Kentucky's largest lizard species and the largest individuals can barely exceed a foot in length. Insects are the main food but they will also eat small mammals such as baby mice.

Class—**Reptilia** (reptiles)
Order—**Squamata** (snakes, lizards)
Suborder—**Lacertilia** (lizards)
Family—**Scincidae** (skinks)

Five-lined Skink *Plestiodon fasciatus*	Southeastern Five-lined Skink *Plestiodon inexpectatus*
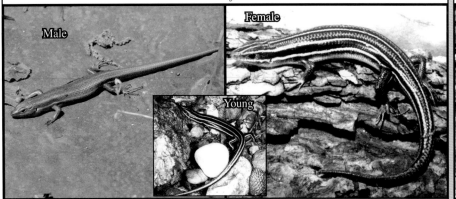	
Presumed range in Kentucky	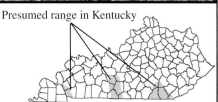Presumed range in Kentucky
Size: Average 4 to 6 inches. Maximum of about 8 inches.	**Size:** Averages about 5 inches.
Abundance: Very common. The most common skink in Kentucky.	**Abundance:** Rare in Kentucky.
Variation: Young are the most brightly colored with distinct pale yellow stripes and bright blue tails. Adult females resemble the young but with age become faded with indistinct stripes less blue in the tail. Adult males are plain brown above with reddish cheek patches that become very vivid during the breeding season.	**Variation:** Young are more vividly colored than adults. Adults resemble young but pattern is less vivid on males and older females.
Habitat: Most common in damp woodlands but also found in swamps and in drier upland areas. The presence of rocks and logs is important for micro-habitat, serving as hiding and denning locations. Patches of sunlit areas for basking is also important.	**Habitat:** In Kentucky this species occurs most frequently in wooded uplands. Prefers pine or mixed woods over pure deciduous forests.
Breeding: Eggs (6 to 12) are laid in May or early June in rotted logs, stumps, sawdust, mulch or other moisture retaining material. Females may remain with eggs until they hatch in late July or early August.	**Breeding:** Reproduction is similar to that of the Five-lined Skink. 3 to 10 eggs are laid.
Natural History: The young of this species are strikingly colored with bright blue tails and they sometimes are mistaken by laypersons as being another species going by the name "Blue-tailed Skink." These common and well-known lizards are fond of sunning on decks, porches, sidewalks, and patios of homes in rural areas. They can often be found in suburban environments as well, particularly older neighborhoods with abundant large trees and shrubbery. They feed on a wide variety of insects, spiders, and arthropods and they are a useful species in controlling invertebrate pests around the home. Unfortunately they are highly vulnerable to pesticides and are easily killed by exterminators who commonly spray around the foundation of houses. These lizards do a much safer job of controlling insects and spiders around the outside of the home and exterminators should be encouraged to avoid spraying outside foundations, landscapes, and yards. Like the male Broad-headed Skink, male Five-lined Skinks develop bright red cheek patches during the breeding season. And, like their larger cousin they are sometimes regarded and venomous and referred to as "Scorpion Lizards." In truth there are no venomous lizards found in the southeastern United States. The only venomous lizard in the United States is the Gila Monster of the desert southwest region of America.	**Natural History:** The species' scientific name *"inexpectatus"* is an acknowledgment of the fact that until a few decades ago these lizards had remained undiscovered by biologists. They are so similar in appearance, habitat, and distribution to the Five-lined Skink that they managed to go unnoticed until relatively recent times. They tolerate drier situations than most other skinks. The bulk of their range is in the southeastern U.S. where sandy, well drained soils predominate. Their distribution in Kentucky is rather spotty and disjunct (see range map above). They tend to retain the juvenile pattern into adulthood much more than our other two "five-lined" species (Broad-headed and Five-lined).

THE REPTILES OF KENTUCKY

PART 2: SNAKES

Class—**Reptilia** (reptile		
Order—**Squamata** (snakes, lizards)		
Suborder—**Serpentes** (snakes)		
Family—**Colubridae** (harmless egg layers)		

Racer—*Coluber constrictor*		**Scarlet Snake** *Cemophora coccinea*
Southern Black Racer C. c. priapus	**Northern Black Racer** C. c. constrictor	

Presumed range in Kentucky

Northern Black Racer (light gray)

Southern Black Racer (dark gray)

Presumed range in Kentucky

Size: Average about 4 feet. Maximum 6 feet.	**Size:** 24 to 30 inches.
Abundance: Very common.	**Abundance:** Very rare in Kentucky.
Variation: Nine subspecies of *Coluber constrictor* are found across North America. Two occur in Kentucky, the Northern and Southern Black Racers. Differences between the two are very slight. As a rule the southern race has more white on the chin and throat. Young racers have a pattern of distinctive saddles (see inset photo).	**Variation:** Two subspecies. The Northern Scarlet Snake (subspecies *copei*) occurs in Kentucky with no variation within the subspecies.
Habitat: Black Racers are habitat generalists that may be found in virtually any habitat within the state. They favor dry upland woods and overgrown fields and like many predators they are most common in edge areas where two habitats meet.	**Habitat:** Very little is known about this rare species in Kentucky. It seems to prefer woodlands with sandy soils.
Breeding: Females lay about a dozen (from 5 to 20) eggs in rotted logs, humus, or frequently in sawdust piles around old sawmills. Eggs are laid in early summer and hatch in about two months. Like most egg layers, the Black Racer reproduces annually (some live-bearing snakes breed only every other year).	**Breeding:** Probably breeds in early spring. Lays from two to nine eggs in late June or early July. Eggs hatch in late August or early September.
Natural History: Racers are alert, active snakes that relentlessly prowl in search of almost any type of animal prey that can be swallowed. They will eat insects, amphibians, lizards, other snakes (including the young of venomous species), nestling birds, eggs, and small mammals. They are also adept at catching fish trapped in drying pools of streams and swamps. Unlike many snake species, the Racer is a diurnal animal and may be active even during the heat of the day in mid-summer. They are apparently intelligent, curious snakes that will follow livestock and other large animals in hopes of capturing insects and other prey that may be disturbed by the larger animals passing. This is probably how they gained the reputation as aggressive snakes that will chase a human. Their name is appropriate as they are probably the fastest snake in Kentucky and one of fastest in America. Quite speedy for a snake, they can reach a blazing 12 to 15 mph. Due to their catholic feeding habits and ability to adapt to a wide variety of habitats, the racers are among the most successful snakes in America. When threatened these snakes can use their speed to literally disappear into thick cover. When hard pressed out in the open they will climb into bushes or shrubs to escape. If captured they will bite vigorously.	**Natural History:** Although recorded from a few widely scattered localities throughout the state, recorded sightings are few and it appears to be a very rare animal in Kentucky. It is a nocturnal, secretive species that spends much time below ground or beneath bark and logs. Feeds mostly on the eggs of other reptiles, but is also known to eat small snakes and young lizards. Very little is known about this snake in Kentucky and any sightings should be reported to the herpetology professor at a nearby university or to the non-game division of the Department of Fish and Wildlife Resources to john.macgreor@ky.gov.

Class—**Reptilia** (reptiles)
Order—**Squamata** (snakes & lizards)
Suborder—**Serpentes** (snakes)
Family—**Colubridae** (harmless egg layers)

Common Kingsnake—*Lampropeltis getulus*		Prairie Kingsnake *Lampropeltis calligaster*
Speckled Kingsnake (formerly subspecies—*L. g. holbrookii*)	**Black Kingsnake** (formerly subspecies—*L. g. nigra*)	

Presumed range in Kentucky

Speckled Kingsnake (light gray)

Black Kingsnake (dark gray)

Presumed range in Kentucky

Size: Average about 4 feet. Maximum 74 inches.

Size: Average 3.5 feet. Record 58 in.

Abundance: Both subspecies are fairly common within their respective ranges.

Abundance: Fairly common.

Variation: Two forms of Common Kingsnakes occur in Kentucky. These two vary in the amount of white or cream colored spots on the body. Specimens from farther west have more light spotting, with individuals from the Mississippi Alluvial Plain typically having a spot on every dorsal scale (Speckled Kingsnake). Black Kingsnakes have fewer spots and older snakes from farther to the east may be nearly solid black. Young specimens always have easily discernible light spots.

Variation: Two color phases occur in Kentucky—a dark morph and a spotted morph (see photos above). Young specimens resemble the spotted morph. Dark morph specimens are usually older adults.

Habitat: Mature woodlands, successional areas, weedy fields, and edge habitats in uplands, bottom lands, swamps, and marshes. Nearly all habitats in the state are utilized except areas where large amounts of land has been converted to row crops. They are absent as well from intensively urbanized regions.

Habitat: Prefers open fields overgrown with weeds, brush, and briers, but can also be found in woodlands and woodland edges.

Breeding: An annual breeder that lays 8–12 eggs in early summer. Eggs are laid in moisture retaining medium, often inside rotted stumps or logs. Eggs hatch in about 60 days. Young Black Kingsnakes have a chain-like pattern of white spots.

Breeding: Females produce about a dozen eggs that are laid in an underground nest chamber in early summer.

Natural History: Common Kingsnakes are best known for their habit of killing and eating other snakes, including venomous species. These powerful constrictors are immune to the venom of pit vipers and will kill and eat any snake that is small enough to be swallowed whole. They also eat rodents, birds, lizards, and baby turtles. They are mainly terrestrial in habits but have been found inside of standing dead trees several feet off the ground. They may be active both day and night but are mostly crepuscular and during hotter months tend to become more nocturnal. This species is a favorite captive pet of many reptile enthusiasts in America. After some time in captivity they will become quite tame and rarely bite. When they do bite, however, they do so with very strong jaws! They are common in many areas of the state but like many other snakes they can be quite secretive. Some herpetologists regard all the Common Kingsnakes in Kentucky as Black Kingsnakes (*Lampropeltis nigra*). These experts disregard the concept of subspecies in Common Kingsnakes and relegate the Speckled Kingsnakes (*Lampropeltis holbrookii*) to regions west of the Mississippi River.

Natural History: Three subspecies are found in the southern United States but only one of those occurs in Kentucky (the Prairie Kingsnake—*L. c. calligaster*). This is a subterranean species that is only rarely seen above ground, usually in early spring. It feeds mostly on small mammals that it hunts in their underground burrows. They also eat bird eggs and nestlings, but they are a threat only to those that nest on or near the ground. Despite the fact that this is a fairly common snake in the western half of Kentucky, they are rarely observed due to their burrowing habits.

Class—**Reptilia** (reptiles)

Order—**Squamata** (snakes & lizards)

Suborder—**Serpentes** (snakes)

Family—**Colubridae** (harmless egg layers)

Milk Snake—*Lampropeltis triangulum*		Scarlet Kingsnake *Lampropeltis elapsoides*
Eastern Milk Snake (formerly subspecies—*L. t. triangulum*)	**Red Milk Snake** (formerly subspecies—*L. t. syspila*)	

Presumed range in Kentucky

Red Milksnake (light gray)

Eastern Milksnake (dark gray)

Presumed range in Kentucky

Size: The record for the Eastern Milk is 52 inches. Red Milk record is 42 inches.

Size: Average 18–20 inches, up to 2 feet.

Abundance: The Eastern Milk Snake can be fairly common in some areas. Red Milk Snakes are rather uncommon in Kentucky.

Abundance: Rare in Kentucky.

Variation: Milk Snakes are one of the most wide-ranging and diverse snake species in America. Experts once recognized as many as eight subspecies in the U.S., and several more south of the Mexican border. The two pictures above show typical examples of Kentucky's two forms. Some intermediate forms between the Eastern and Red Milk Snakes can be expected to be seen where their ranges meet.

Variation: There is apparently little variation in this species in Kentucky. In fact, the species is remarkably uniform in appearance throughout its range, which includes most of the southeast.

Habitat: Eastern Milk Snakes are fond of the mountains and heavily wooded areas. Like the rat snakes (next page), Eastern Milk Snakes often enter barns and outbuilding in search of mice. Red Milk Snakes can be found in both dry woodlands and in wetland areas. Both are drawn to fallen logs and dead snags with loose bark as a micro-habitat.

Habitat: In the deep south this species prefers flatwoods and wet woodlands where it lives beneath the bark of dead snags. In Kentucky it appears to be species of upland woods.

Breeding: Both forms are egg layers. Eggs are deposited in rotten logs, stumps, or beneath a flat rock. Eastern Milk lays from 6 to 24 eggs. Red Milks lay few eggs (from two or three up to about a dozen).

Breeding: Clutch size is small. Rarely more than six eggs, often fewer. Probably breeds in the spring.

Natural History: The name comes from the habit these snakes have of entering stock barns in search of mice. Early settlers erroneously thought the snakes were there to suckle from the milk cow (that every pioneer family kept on the farm). These snakes eat many lizards and will also consume other, smaller snakes. Reptile eggs may also be eaten along with amphibians and small mammals like mice. Like the Common Kingsnakes, the Milk Snakes enjoy a resistance to snake venom and baby copperheads, cottonmouths, or rattlesnakes may be eaten by large adults. Young snakes feed mostly on skinks. Additionally, eggs and nestlings of ground-nesting birds may be a food item on occasion. Both races of Milk Snake found in Kentucky are primarily nocturnal snakes that usually remain hidden during daylight hours beneath rocks, logs, and other woodland debris. They are thus not as readily observed as many other snakes in Kentucky. A recent evaluation of the Milk Snake complex by herpetologists regards both the above snakes as Eastern Milk Snakes and disregards subspecies status for the forms found in Kentucky.

Natural History: This is a rare snake in Kentucky and there is not much known about the natural history of this species within the state. They are fairly common in some regions of the lower coastal plain of the deep south and most natural history studies on this species are conducted there. Their favorite micro-habitat in northern Florida and in the lower Gulf Coastal Plain is beneath the bark of standing dead pine trees within wet woodlands. Lizards are the primary prey in the wild but captive specimens will often eat small mice.

Class—**Reptilia** (reptiles)
Order—**Squamata** (snakes & lizards)
Suborder—**Serpentes** (snakes)
Family—**Colubridae** (harmless egg layers)

Midland Rat Snake *Pantherophis spiloides*	**Corn Snake** *Pantherophis guttata*

 Presumed range in Kentucky	Presumed range in Kentucky 

Size: Average 5 to 6 feet as adults. Maximum 8 feet 4 inches. | **Size:** Average 4 feet. Record 6 feet.

Abundance: Very common. | **Abundance:** Rare in Kentucky.

Variation: These snakes exhibit some variation in the dorsal pattern of adults. Most show a blotched pattern on the back, but in some individuals this pattern is obscured by an overall dark coloration. The color between the dorsal blotches also varies. It may be cream or yellowish, brownish, or varying shades of gray. Specimens from the southeastern edge of the state are typically solid black as adults. Some experts consider this species to belong to a differnent genus, classifying it in the genus *Scotophis*. Young are light gray with charcoal blotches. | **Variation:** Kentucky Corn Snakes will vary slightly in the amount of red and in the brightness of their colors. The color between the blotches ranges from reddish to grayish. Young Corn Snakes are similar to adults but the dorsal blotches are darker and more vivid.

Habitat: Found in virtually all habitats within the state, from the highest mountains in the east to the lowlands of the west. They are least common in areas of intensive agriculture or urbanized areas, but they can persist in urban regions if there is some cover and large trees. | **Habitat:** In Kentucky this snake is found in woodlands, overgrown fields, and edge habitats where woods and fields meet.

Breeding: An egg layer that breeds in the spring and lays up to 20 (average about a dozen) eggs. Eggs are laid in old woodpecker holes or hollow limbs above ground or on the ground in rotted stumps, beneath logs, or any sheltered place where some form of humus is present to prevent dessication. Breeds annually. Eggs are laid in early summer and hatch in late summer or early fall. | **Breeding:** Breeds annually in spring and may lay over two dozen eggs (averages less). Eggs are laid in sheltered place with adequate moisture to prevent dessication. Eggs hatch in late summer.

Natural History: This is the most arboreal snake species in Kentucky and adults spend a great deal of time in trees. They often choose a regular den site in old woodpecker holes or hollows of trees and may be seen sunning with the forepart of the body emerged from a hole. Excellent climbers, they can ascend straight up a tree trunk using only the bark to gain a purchase with their belly scales. They will climb to great heights in search of bird nests. In addition to baby birds and eggs they will also eat rodents, squirrels, and other small mammals up to the size of a rabbit. They are also quite fond of barns and derelict buildings as a habitat. In Kentucky these large snakes are well known to rural dwellers and they often go by the nickname "Chicken Snake," a reference to their historical habit of raiding henhouses for eggs and chicks. They are also call "Cowsuckers" in some parts of the state. This name comes from the erroneous belief rural people once had that they would enter barns to suck milk from cows. In fact, they enter barns to hunt rodents. | **Natural History:** The Corn Snake is a southern snake that ranges northward into a few areas of Kentucky. The two populations of this species that occur in Kentucky are many miles apart and are considered to be "relict populations" left over from a time when the species was more widespread in the state. Corn Snakes are good climbers and regularly ascend into trees in search of bird nests. They also eat mice and lizards and young specimens may eat some invertebrates.

Class—**Reptilia** (reptiles)		
Order—**Squamata** (snakes, lizards)		
Suborder—**Serpentes** (snakes)		
Family—**Colubridae** (harmless egg laying snakes)		

Rough Green Snake *Opheodrys aestivus*	Northern Pine Snake *Pituophis melanoleucus*	Southeastern Crowned Snake *Tantilla coronata*

Presumed range in Kentucky	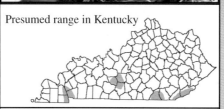Presumed range in Kentucky	Presumed range in Kentucky
Size: Average 2–3 feet. Max 45 inches.	**Size:** 4 to 6 feet. Maximum 7.5 feet.	**Size:** 8 to 10 inches. Maximum 13.
Abundance: Fairly common.	**Abundance:** Rare. Threatened in KY.	**Abundance:** Uncommon in Kentucky.
Variation: None.	**Variation:** No variation in Kentucky.	**Variation:** No significant variation.
Habitat: Open fields, pastures, and edges of woods and fields. Often common in wetlands where there are low bushes and shrubs overhanging water.	**Habitat:** Dry uplands, especially where there are sandy soils. Open deciduous woodlands, overgrown fields, and pastures.	**Habitat:** May be found in a variety of habitats but most common in woodland situations. Micro-habitat is leaf litter and beneath rocks or logs.
Breeding: Three to 12 eggs are laid in late spring or early summer. The babies are slender, miniature replicas of the adult.	**Breeding:** Female Pine Snakes create an underground nest chamber for laying an average of a dozen eggs.	**Breeding:** From two to five eggs are laid beneath leaf litter in mid-summer. Hatchlings are only about three inches long.
Natural History: Rough Green Snakes live in dense bushes and shrubs where their bright green color renders them invisible. Arthropods of many varieties are their prey. Food includes spiders, caterpillars, crickets, and grasshoppers to name a few of their favorites. These snakes are sometimes called "grass snakes" in reference to their bright green coloration. In Kentucky there is a widespread belief that they have become extremely rare and endangered. In fact their populations are probably fairly stable, although they are certainly vulnerable to habitat destruction wrought by modern agricultural practices. The widespread use of chemical insecticides poses another likely threat to these and all other insect eating vertebrates. Anecdotal evidence suggests they are still widespread.	**Natural History:** In spite of the fact that theses are large snakes they are rarely seen due to their habit of staying in rodent burrows below the ground. When they do emerge their large size and light color makes them very conspicuous, which often leads to their death at the hands of humans. They hunt rodents and other burrowing mammals in their subsurface tunnels. They will also consume the eggs and nestlings of ground-nesting birds. When cornered they will put on an impressive display by hissing loudly and striking savagely. Regarded as threatened in Kentucky they occur in four widely disjunct populations in the state (see range map above). They are associated mostly with pine savannas to the south and east of Kentucky, but even within their core range they are an uncommon species.	**Natural History:** These tiniest of Kentucky's serpents are no bigger around than a matchstick. Their name comes from the black colored "crown" on the top of the head. These are secretive snakes that spend most of their time hiding beneath leaf litter, rocks, bark, or logs. They feed on tiny insect larva, termites, and other miniature invertebrates. Although they may be found in upland woods, their tiny size renders them vulnerable to dessication and they thus seek mesic conditions as a micro-habitat. The range in Kentucky is discontinuous and the species is absent from much of the area shown on the map above. The protected woodlands of Mammoth Cave National Park and Land Between the Lakes National Forest are where this snake is most likely to be encountered in Kentucky.

Class—**Reptilia** (reptiles)

Order—**Squamata** (snakes, lizards)

Suborder—**Serpentes** (snakes)

Family—**Dipsadidae** (harmless rear-fanged snakes)

Ringneck Snake *Diadophis punctatus*	**Wormsnake** *Carphophis amoenus*
 Mississippi Ringneck	 Midwest Worm Snake
 Presumed range in Kentucky — Northern Ringneck (dark gray); Mississippi Ringneck (light gray)	 Presumed range in Kentucky — Eastern Worm Snake Wormsnake (dark gray); Midwest Wormsnake (light gray)

Size: Average about 14 inches. Maximum 2 feet.

Size: 8 to 11 inches.

Abundance: Very common.

Abundance: Common.

Variation: A highly variable species with 12 subspecies nationwide, two of which are found in Kentucky. They are the Northern Ringneck Snake and the Mississippi Ringneck Snake (pictured above). The northern race lacks the black spots on the belly seen on the specimen pictured above.

Variation: There are two subspecies of this snake, the Eastern and Midwest Wormsnake, both found in Kentucky. The characters that separate the two relate to a pair of scales on the snout, so for all practical purposes they are the same in appearance. Pictured above is the subspecies *helenea*, the Midwest Wormsnake.

Habitat: A woodland species that lives in rotted logs, stumps, and beneath rocks and leaf litter on the forest floor.

Habitat: Found in a variety of habitats, but mostly in woodlands. Like other small terrestrial snakes its micro-habitat is beneath the leaf litter, logs, rocks, etc.

Breeding: Lays up to a dozen eggs, usually fewer in rotted logs or other moisture retaining places. Young are about five inches long at hatching.

Breeding: From 1 to 12 eggs are laid in late June or July and hatch in two or three months. Hatchlings are only about three inches in length.

Natural History: Ringneck snakes are both widespread and common in Kentucky. In fact this is one of the most abundant snake species in the state. They are often uncovered by humans beneath boards, stones, leaves, or other debris. The distinctive yellow or cream-colored collar around the neck readily identifies them, and even those unfamiliar with reptiles have no trouble recognizing this species. They feed mostly on soft-bodied insects and other invertebrates. Earthworms are a favorite food. When threatened they will often hold aloft the tightly curled up tip of the underside of their bright yellow tail to distract a predator. This defense mechanism is probably designed to direct an attacker's attention away from the vulnerable head to the less vulnerable tail. Despite having enlarged grooved teeth in the rear of the jaw for envenoming small prey, they are harmless to man.

Natural History: A confirmed burrower that lives under leaf litter, logs, rocks, and even man-made debris such as old boards, discarded shingles, etc. Feeds almost exclusively on earthworms, but some experts list tiny soft-bodied invertebrates such as insect larva or termites as food. The aptly named wormsnakes do in fact resemble earthworms. Their tiny, conical head and smooth glossy scales help to facilitate burrowing through tiny tunnels created by earthworms, termites, or insect larva. These snakes are often turned up in backyards by people gardening, raking leaves, or doing other types of yard work. Like the Ringneck snakes, wormsnakes possess tiny grooved teeth in the rear of the jaw that serve to introduce a mild venom into the bodies of prey. These tiny teeth are too small to penetrate human skin and these snakes are thus completely harmless to man.

Class—**Reptilia** (reptiles)
Order—**Squamata** (snakes, lizards)
Suborder—**Serpentes** (snakes)
Family—**Dipsadidae** (harmless rear-fanged snakes)

Eastern Hognose Snake *Heterodon platyrhinos*	**Mud Snake** *Farancia abacura*

Black Morph

Yellow and Black Morph "Hooding"

Feigning Death

Orange and Black Morph

Presumed range in Kentucky

Eggs in Floating Log

Presumed range in Kentucky

Size: Averages about 2.5 feet. Maximum 45 inches.

Size: Average 3–4 feet. Maximum 6 feet.

Abundance: Fairly common to uncommon in Kentucky.

Abundance: Uncommon.

Variation: Highly variable (see photos above). Individuals range from solid black to uniform olive green. Others may be variously spotted or blotched with dark saddles on a yellowish or orange background. Often one color morph will be dominant in a given area. The young always exhibit a spotted pattern.

Variation: There are two subspecies of Mud Snake. Only one (*reinwardtii*) occurs in Kentucky and there is no variation among Kentucky specimens.

Habitat: Hognose Snakes are most common in habitats with sandy soils that facilitate easy burrowing. They tend to be more common in sandy creek bottoms and river valleys. They prefer areas with moist soils but can also be found in upland woods and fields.

Habitat: This is a snake of swamps, marshes, and wetland areas. In Kentucky they are found mostly in the coastal plain of westernmost Kentucky.

Breeding: Hognose Snakes breed in early spring and lay up to two dozen eggs. Nests are probably in an underground chamber in sandy soil. Young snakes are about eight inches in length and always have a spotted pattern. Babies are grayish brown with well defined dark gray or black blotches.

Breeding: Lays very large clutches of eggs (the record is over 100). Eggs are place in hollows of floating logs or stumps above the waterline.

Natural History: The Eastern Hognose Snake is famous for the elaborate performance it puts on when threatened. First, they will spread the neck like a cobra (hence the nickname "Spreading Adder"), and with the mouth wide open they will strike repeatedly. They always intentionally miss with the strike and never bite even when picked up and handled. The initial "cobra display" is always accompanied by loud hissing. When their complicated bluff fails to deter the threat they will roll onto their backs, stick out their tongue and give a convincing impression of being dead. Their primary food is frogs and toads. They possess enlarged teeth in the back of the upper jaw that are used to puncture the bodies of toads that have gulped air and inflated themselves in an attempt to become too large to be swallowed. The saliva of these snakes is mildly toxic, but is not considered to be a threat to humans. The food of these snake is almost entirely toads and frogs, making them one of the more specialized feeders among Kentucky snakes. Salamanders are reported to have been found in the stomachs of a few individuals as well. Anecdotal evidence suggests they may be declining. Their habit of feeding on toads and frogs almost exclusively may make them vulnerable to insecticides, as frog and toads are primarily insect eaters and poisoning through secondary ingestion is a possibility.

Natural History: Few people who are not actively seeking this species will ever see one. Living among the tangled mass of vegetation and plant roots in the muck of swamps and marshes, they prey primarily on several species of aquatic salamanders along with frogs and fish. The tail of this snake terminates in a stiff, sharp spine that is erroneously believed to be able to sting. Some also believe these snakes to be the mythical "hoop snake," that according to legend can take its tail into its mouth forming a hoop and then roll down hills. This fable also sometimes includes the myth that the spine on the tail is used as a deadly stinger.

Class—**Reptilia** (reptiles)

Order—**Squamata** (snakes, lizards)

Suborder—**Serpentes** (snakes)

Family—**Natricidae** (harmless live-bearing snakes)

Mississippi Green Water Snake *Nerodia cyclopion*	**Southern Water Snake** *Nerodia fasciata*	**Diamondback Water Snake** *Nerodia rhombifer*

Presumed range in Kentucky	Presumed range in Kentucky	Presumed range in Kentucky
Size: 3 to 3.5 feet. Record 50 inches.	**Size:** About 2 feet. Record 45 inches.	**Size:** Average 4 ft. Record 64 inches.
Abundance: Rare. Endangered in KY.	**Abundance:** Rare. Endangered in KY.	**Abundance:** Fairly common.
Variation: Little variation exists in this snake in Kentucky. Young specimens tend to be lighter in color.	**Variation:** None in Kentucky. There are two other subspecies found farther to the south.	**Variation:** The dorsal pattern is more evident on young snakes and freshly molted specimens. Females are larger.
Habitat: These snakes are totally aquatic and inhabit large bodies of water—large lakes, oxbows, rivers, and the mouths of larger creeks. In Kentucky they occur only in the Mississippi Alluvial Plain.	**Habitat:** Southern Water Snakes live in swamps, marshes. sloughs, lakes, and flooded ditches in the far western end of Kentucky. They are most common near the Mississippi River, but they do invade creeks a bit farther east.	**Habitat:** Diamondback Water Snakes frequent most aquatic habitats within their range except for small ponds and smaller streams. They show a definite preference for large swamps and marshes, lakes, and reservoirs.
Breeding: The 15 to 20 young are born in late summer and are about six to eight inches long at birth.	**Breeding:** Breeds in early spring and gives birth in late summer to one or two dozen young.	**Breeding:** Produces very large litters of up to 30 or 40 babies in late summer. Babies are 8 to 10 inches long.
Natural History: Primarily nocturnal in habits. In the spring it may be seen sunning by day atop drift, beaver lodges, or branches overhanging water. Green Water Snakes feed mainly on fish but they may also eat frogs and salamanders. This is a rare snake in Kentucky and they are seen in the state only in the Mississippi Alluvial Plain. They are much more piscivorous than most other water snakes and show a definite preference for large bodies of water. Unlike many other water snakes that sometimes wander far overland, the Mississippi Green rarely ventures far from water.	**Natural History:** The race of Southern Water Snake found in Kentucky is the Broad-banded Water Snake (subspecies *confluens*), pictured above. This snake and its sibling subspecies (Banded Water Snake and Florida Water Snake) are all denizens of the deep south, hence the common name "Southern Water Snake" for the species. This species approaches its northernmost limits in western Kentucky where it is represented by the Broad-banded subspecies shown above. Feeds mostly on frogs, but also eats salamanders, fish, and crayfish. It is active both day and night but becomes nocturnal in hot weather.	**Natural History:** The water snakes have a reputation among herpetologists for their pugnacious attitudes and none is more deserving of that reputation than the Diamondback Water Snake. When captured they will thrash wildly and bite savagely and repeatedly. The bite, though harmless, can be painful. These snakes attain an impressive size and can be very heavy bodied. A large female may have a girth the size of a man's wrist. Like all water snakes they are mainly nocturnal during hot summer months. But in the early spring they can be very obvious as they bask on logs, beaver lodges, stumps, and branches.

Class—**Reptilia** (reptiles)
Order—**Squamata** (snakes, lizards)
Suborder—**Serpentes** (snakes)
Family—**Natricidae** (harmless live-bearing snakes)
Plain-bellied Water Snake—*Nerodia erythrogaster*

Yellow-bellied Water Snake (formerly subspecies—*N. e. flavigaster*)	Copperbelly Water Snake (formerly subspecies—*N. e. neglecta*)

Juvenile

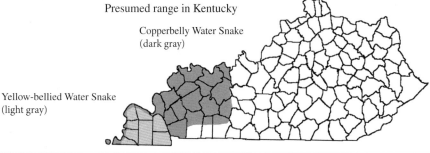

Presumed range in Kentucky

Copperbelly Water Snake (dark gray)

Yellow-bellied Water Snake (light gray)

Size: Average about 4 feet. Yellow-bellied can reach 5 feet in length. Copperbelly is slightly smaller.

Abundance: The Yellow-bellied is common. The Copperbelly is uncommon and is a subspecies of concern in Kentucky.

Variation: There are a total of four color morphs of Plain-bellied Water Snakes in America and until recently they were all considered to be distinct subspecies. The two shown above range into Kentucky. Where the range of the two subspecies meet intergradation is common. They young of both subspecies are markedly different from the adults and have a distinct banded pattern (see middle photo above). Females are larger.

Habitat: Although all subspecies of this snake are primarily aquatic, they are less tied to water than any of their kin and they will often wander far from permanent water. They are found in creeks, rivers, lakes, ponds, and wetlands throughout their range. They may also occur in seasonal marshes and wet meadows and they may be found in dry habitats on occasions.

Breeding: These are among the more prolific of the water snakes and large females will produce litters numbering over 40 babies. Breeding takes place in early spring and birthing occurs in late summer.

Natural History: These snakes feed primarily on aquatic and semi-aquatic vertebrates such as frogs, toads, salamanders, and fish. They are active both day and night in the spring but are more nocturnal or crepuscular during hot weather. Like many other water snakes, they are fierce fighters if caught and will bite and smear the attacker with foul-smelling feces and a pungent musk. As with most water snake species the female grows considerably larger than the male. They will wander far from water and may even be seen in the driest of habitats atop wooded ridges at higher elevations not usually associated with water snakes. In Kentucky the Yellow-bellied is found mostly in the Coastal Plain and it may be quite common many lowland areas. The Copperbelly, on the other hand, is an uncommon animal that may be in decline in much of its range. The range of the Copperbelly in Kentucky coincides closely with the Shawnee Hills physiographic province, which is also known as "Kentucky's Western Coal Field." Strip mining within the range of the Copperbelly is widespread and may have contributed to this snake's decline. Ironically, reclamation of strip mine lands along with old "strip pits" that have filled with water are now providing valuable habitat for the re-population of this snake in many areas. Today most experts now lump all four subspecies of the Plain-bellied Water Snake into one highly variable species. Other herpetologists who are proponents of the subspecies concept regard the four morphological types to be separate subspecies. In the end, it boils down to whether one is a "splitter" or a "grouper." This author is a splitter that favors the subspecies concept.

Class—**Reptilia** (reptiles)	
Order—**Squamata** (snakes, lizards)	
Suborder—**Serpentes** (snakes)	
Family—**Natricidae** (harmless live-bearing snakes)	

Northern Water Snake—*Nerodia sipedon*		Queen Snake *Regina septemvittata*
Northern Water Snake N. s. sipedon	**Midland Water Snake** N. s. pleuralis	

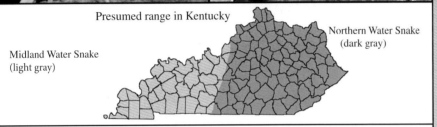

Presumed range in Kentucky

Northern Water Snake (dark gray)

Midland Water Snake (light gray)

Presumed range in Kentucky

Size: Average about 3.5 feet. Record is 59 inches (Midland Water Snake).

Size: Average 2 feet. Maximum 3 feet.

Abundance: Both subspecies are very common within their respective ranges.

Abundance: Fairly common.

Variation: There are four subspecies nationwide and two can be found in Kentucky. Both vary somewhat in color, ranging from brown, tan, reddish brown, or gray-brown. They will always exhibit a pattern of darker bands across the back that contrasts with the lighter color between the bands. In the Northern Water Snake the light spaces between the bands are much narrower than in the Midland Water Snake.

Variation: There are no subspecies of the Queen Snake and there is very little variation among specimens in Kentucky. Young snakes are miniature replicas of the adult.

Habitat: These snakes are aquatic animals but they do sometimes wander away from water in search of a mate or as a result of natural dispersal. They are very fond of small farm ponds or small streams as habitat, but they can also be found in large lakes and in swamps and marshes.

Habitat: Found mostly in limestone creeks in the central portion of the state. They will also occupy lakes in the central region of the state.

Breeding: Females may mate with several males in the spring. Birthing occurs in late summer to early fall. Live-born young can number two or three dozen, but the largest females may produce nearly 100 babies. Young females may have as few as six or eight.

Breeding: The Queen Snake is a live-bearer that will produce up to a dozen young per litter, a relatively small number for an aquatic snake.

Natural History: Northern Water Snakes adapt well to man-made environments like large lake impoundments where they can thrive in the rip-rap of dams and levees. Frogs and fish are the two favorite food items for these snakes. Around man-made impoundments they can become very numerous near boat docks and fishing areas where they scavenge on dead or dying fish and fish heads left behind by fishermen. Like most other water snake species, they are fond of basking in the sun atop debris and limbs overhanging water. As with other water snakes they are commonly confused with the venomous Cottonmouth, even in areas of the state where the Cottonmouth does not occur. Their dorsal pattern of dark brownish bands on a lighter brown background also causes them to be mistaken for another venomous species, the Copperhead. But Copperheads are terrestrial snakes that only rarely enter water. Thus snakes seen in the water are almost invariably not Copperheads, but Northern/Midland Water Snakes.

Natural History: The Queen Snake is a specialized feeder that preys almost exclusively on recently molted, soft-bodied crayfish. In one study, over 95 percent of stomach contents examined contained crayfish (Branson & Baker, 1974). As a result their distribution is limited to areas where this common crustacean is abundant. They are often found hiding beneath flat stones in creeks throughout their range. Like other water snakes they may be seen basking from limbs and branches overhanging water.

Class—**Reptilia** (reptiles)

Order—**Squamata** (snakes, lizards)

Suborder—**Serpentes** (snakes)

Family—**Natricidae** (harmless live-bearing snakes)

Western Ribbon Snake *Thamnophis proximus*	**Eastern Ribbon Snake** *Thamnophis sauritus*	**Eastern Garter Snake** *Thamnophis sirtalis*

Presumed range in Kentucky 	Presumed range in Kentucky 	Presumed range in Kentucky 
Size: 20 to 30 inches, record 39.	**Size:** 18 to 28 inches, record 38.	**Size:** Average 2 feet. Max 51 inches.
Abundance: Rare. Threatened in KY.	**Abundance:** Uncommon.	**Abundance:** Very common.
Variation: There are four subspecies total. Only the race shown above (the Western Ribbon Snake, *T. p. proximus*) is found in Kentucky. The color of the stripes may vary from greenish to bluish, yellow, or orange.	**Variation:** A total of three subspecies are found in the eastern United States. The Eastern Ribbon Snake, *T. s. sauritus* (shown above), is the only variation seen in Kentucky. The color of the light stripes may vary from yellow to orange.	**Variation:** There are nine subspecies of this widespread snake in the United States. The eastern subspecies, *T. s. sirtalis*, is the only one in Kentucky. Somewhat variable. Some have stripes reduced and more prominent spots.
Habitat: Lives in semi-aquatic habitats, i.e. wet meadows, swamps, marshes, and edges of streams and lakes. Also damp, weedy fields in bottoms.	**Habitat:** Occupies aquatic and semi-aquatic habitats from swamps and marshes to streams, stream edges, and mesic bottomland woodlands.	**Habitat:** A habitat generalist that favors pastures, fields, and rural yards. Can be seen almost anywhere, including vacant lots in urban areas.
Breeding: Live bearing. Gives birth to between 10 and 20 young. Births usually occur in August.	**Breeding:** Ten to 20 young is typical. Birthing occurs in late summer following breeding in the early spring.	**Breeding:** Garter Snakes are live-bearers that give birth to enormous litters of up to 60 babies.
Natural History: Frogs, toads, fish, and lizards are listed as some to this snake's prey. During certain times of the year tadpoles and the recently transformed young of frogs and toads are a primary food item. During periods of drought these snakes will gorge on small fishes trapped in drying pools. Insects and earthworms are also important in the diet. The range of the Western Ribbon Snake lies mostly west of the Mississippi River and this snake is found in Kentucky mainly in the narrow strip of land bordering the Mississippi River (the Mississippi Alluvial Plain).	**Natural History:** Eastern Ribbon Snakes are both diurnal and nocturnal in habits. They often climb into low shrubs and vines. They are alert snakes that hunt by both smell and with their excellent eyesight that is attuned to quick movements of fleeing prey. Food items include insects, frogs, minnows, crayfish, and tadpoles. Although these snakes are nearly always found near water, they tend to live near the edges of wetlands rather than within them. In many ways the ribbon snakes occupy a niche that is halfway between an aquatic and a terrestrial species.	**Natural History:** Garter snakes are non-specialized feeders that will eat insects, earthworms, frogs, toads, salamanders, fish, and rarely small mammals such as baby mice or voles. Their name is derived from their resemblance to the old fashioned "garters" that were used to hold up men's socks. The name has been widely familiarized to "Garden Snake" in many places—still appropriate as they are often encountered in people's gardens. They are a ubiquitous species that may be found in both wilderness or urban regions. They are most common in edge habitats.

Class—**Reptilia** (reptiles)		
Order—**Squamata** (snakes, lizards)		
Suborder—**Serpentes** (snakes)		
Family—**Natricidae** (harmless live-bearing snakes)		
Kirtland's Snake *Clonophis kirtlandii*	**Redbelly Snake** *Storeria occipitomaculata*	**Brown Snake** *Storeria dekayi*

 Presumed range in Kentucky	 Presumed range in Kentucky	 Presumed range in Kentucky
Size: Record length is 24 inches.	**Size:** 10 to 12 inches, record 16.	**Size:** Average 12 inches, record 19.
Abundance: Rare. Threatened in KY.	**Abundance:** Uncommon.	**Abundance:** Common.
Variation: No significant variation and no subspecies. In fact, most specimens are remarkably similar.	**Variation:** Three subspecies. One occurs in Kentucky (the Northern Redbelly Snake—*S. o. occipitomaculata*).	**Variation:** This species varys little, most Kentucky specimens will closely resemble the specimen above.
Habitat: Usually associates with moist environments both in woodlands and open areas. Also inhabits swamps and marshes.	**Habitat:** Mostly found in wooded areas, in both lowland and uplands. They can also be found in fields around the edges of woods.	**Habitat:** Woodlands, grassy fields, and wetlands. May sometimes be found even in urban areas, especially vacant lots littered with old boards or scrap tin.
Breeding: Live-bearer. Litters may be as small as three or four or as many as 10 or 15. Young are born in late summer to early fall.	**Breeding:** Live-bearer. Litters number from 5 to 15. Newborn babies are only about three inches in length an no bigger around than a matchstick.	**Breeding:** Gives birth to 5 to 20 young (rarely more, as many as 40). Baby snakes are about three inches long with the girth of a toothpick.
Natural History: The Kirtland's Snake is an enigmatic species in Kentucky. It is found in four small, widely dispersed areas in the state. It apparently is at least as common in urban areas as it is in more natural habitats within its Kentucky range. Earthworms and slugs are listed as its primary prey. It is mostly a nocturnal hunter and hides by day beneath boards, stones, or other structures. When threatened these snakes will flatten the body to such an extreme as to create a ribbon-like appearance. A disjunct population was recently discovered in Terrapin Creek Nature Preserve in southern Graves County.	**Natural History:** Redbelly Snakes usually remain hidden by day beneath rocks, logs, etc., and emerge at night to hunt insects and small soft-bodied invertebrates such as earthworms, slugs, beetle larva, isopods, etc. These snakes sometimes exhibit a peculiar behavior when threatened. If voiding of feces and musk fails to discourage a handler, they will curl their upper lip in an strange expression of apparent ferocity. It is a purely fallacious display, however, as their tiny teeth could never penetrate human skin. Although these little snakes are widespread across much of Kentucky, they are less common than many other small snake species.	**Natural History:** This diminutive snake is often found in vacant lots of large cities and towns, where it hides beneath boards, trash, even small pieces of cardboard. It feeds primarily on earthworms and slugs, but also reportedly eats insects, amphibians eggs, and tiny fishes. Brown Snakes are known to hibernate communally, an odd behavior for a tiny snake that should have no trouble finding adequate crevices in which to spend the colder months. These snakes are sometimes called "Dekay's Snake," in honor of an early American naturalist. These little snakes make interesting pets and will readily eat earthworms in captivity.

Class—**Reptilia** (reptiles)
Order—**Squamata** (snakes, lizards)
Suborder—**Serpentes** (snakes)
Family—**Natricidae** (harmless live-bearing snakes)
Smooth Earth Snake—*Virginia valeriae*

Western Smooth Earth Snake *V. v. elegans*	Eastern Smooth Earth Snake *V. v. valeriae*

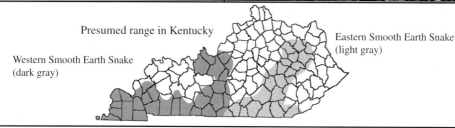

Presumed range in Kentucky

Western Smooth Earth Snake (dark gray)

Eastern Smooth Earth Snake (light gray)

Size: Usually around 10 inches in length. The record is 15 inches.

Abundance: Both subspecies are fairly common snakes.

Variation: There are three subspecies nationwide and two are found in Kentucky. The differences between the two are very slight. The eastern race has 15 scale rows at midbody verses 17 scale rows for the western race. The overall color of both may vary slightly from brown to grayish or reddish brown.

Habitat: Smooth Earth Snakes are basically a forest species but they can also be found in open fields near forests and around forest edges. Though they live mostly in upland habitats, their micro-habitat is moist soils beneath leaf litter, logs, stones, etc.

Breeding: These snakes are live bearers that give birth to from 4 to 12 young. The young snakes resemble the adults and measure about 3 to 3.5 inches in length. They are about the girth of a pencil lead and may at first be mistaken for an earthworm. Like all live-bearing snakes, Earth Snakes are "ovoviviparous." The term refers to the fact that although young are born fully developed (rather than hatching from an egg), the developing young inside the mother's body are nurished by a yolk rather than directly from the mother's body via a placenta (as is common in mammals).

Natural History: The Smooth Earth Snakes are tiny, docile snakes that could not manage to bite a human even if they were so inclined, which they are not. They have tiny heads, even for their size, and thus their food consists of small invertebrates—insects, snails, and mostly, earthworms. These are secretive little serpents that sometimes emerge to prowl about on the surface after summer rains. Otherwise they are easily overlooked except by herpetologists who know where to find them beneath logs, stones, or amid accumulated humus on the forest floor. As with other small snakes that burrow beneath detritus on the floor of woodlands, these little snakes are occasionally turned up by rural residents as they rake mulch from flower beds in the spring. They are often active above ground in early fall following periods of heavy rainfall. Brian Miller (*The Reptiles of Tennessee*, 2012) reports that these snakes will sometimes play dead when captured, a unique behavior that is common with the Eastern Hognose Snake but rather rare in other snake species.

Class—**Reptilia** (reptiles)	
Order—**Squamata** (snakes, lizards)	
Suborder—**Serpentes** (snakes)	
Family—**Crotalidae** (pit vipers)	

Eastern Copperhead—*Agkistrodon contortrix*		Northern Cottonmouth *Agkistrodon piscivorus*
Southern Morph (formerly subspecies—*A. c. contortrix*)	**Northern Morph** (formerly subspecies— *A. c. mokasen*)	

Young

Presumed range in Kentucky

Northern Copperhead (dark gray)

Southern Copperhead (light gray)

Presumed range in Kentucky

Size: Average 2.5 to 3 feet. The record is 58 inches.

Size: Average 3 feet. Record 62 inches.

Abundance: Can be fairly common in suitable habitat, especially in the mountains.

Abundance: Fairly common.

Variation: Kentucky specimens can be quite variable in color but always exhibit the same pattern of dark bands on a lighter background. The background color is some shade of brown, tan, orange, or grayish with darker brown or gray-brown hourglass shaped crossbands across the back. Most specimens from the Coastal Plain of Kentucky resemble the photo above on the left. The specimen on the right is typical of snakes from the Appalachian Plateau region. Until recently the two color morphs were regarded as distinct subspecies called Southern and Northern Copperheads. Some experts still consider that to be the case. Baby copperheads are identical to the adults but have a bright yellow tail tip that is wriggled to lure prey.

Variation: Adults vary from uniform brown to nearly black. Freshly molted specimens often show a pattern of dark bands on an olive or grayish background. Young have a strongly banded pattern and resemble their cousin the Copperhead. Like the Copperhead young Cottonmouths have a bright yellow tail tip used to lure prey.

Habitat: Copperheads are primarily woodland animals, but they do wander into overgrown fields and thickets where rodent prey is abundant. Edge areas and small woodland openings choked with briers, saplings, and weeds are prime habitat. They will inhabit both upland and lowland regions, but avoid permanently wet areas such as swamps and marshes.

Habitat: Wetlands primarily. A highly aquatic species, the Cottonmouth inhabits mostly swamps and marshes, but they can also be found at times in creeks, lakes, or ponds.

Breeding: Breeds in spring or in the fall. From 4 to 12 young are born in late August through September. The resources required to produce a litter by a live-bearing snake are considerable and can be quite stressful on the female. Thus many Copperheads likely produce litters only ever other year.

Breeding: Produces 3 to 12 babies in late August or early September. Unlike the Copperhead, female Cottonmouths may reproduce annually.

Natural History: Like most pit vipers Copperheads are primarily nocturnal, especially during hotter months. In early spring and fall they may be seen abroad during the day. Young snakes eat some invertebrates and small vertebrates such as young frogs, lizards, and small snakes. Larger snakes prey on small mammals (mice and voles), and the young of ground-nesting birds. Insects are also taken, especially cicadas and during years when the Periodic Cicada emerges by the millions they will stuff themselves with these high protein, high fat insects. In areas of undisturbed habitat these can be common snakes but they are secretive and discreet. They account for more snakebites than any other venomous snake in Kentucky.

Natural History: The name "Cottonmouth" is derived from the habit these snakes have of gaping open the mouth when threatened. The inside of the mouth is white, hence the name. Cottonmouths attain a large size and have powerful venom that is capable of killing a human. Frogs, fish, salamanders, and small mammals are prey.

Class—**Reptilia** (reptiles)
Order—**Squamata** (snakes, lizards)
Suborder—**Serpentes** (snakes)
Family—**Crotalidae** (pit vipers)

Timber Rattlesnake *Crotalus horridus*	Pygmy Rattlesnake *Sistrurus miliarius*

Presumed range in Kentucky (Timber Rattlesnake)

Presumed range in Kentucky (Pygmy Rattlesnake)

Timber Rattlesnake	Pygmy Rattlesnake
Size: Averages about 4 feet. Record length is 6 feet 2 inches.	**Size:** About 18 inches. Max 25 inches.
Abundance: Uncommon to rare.	**Abundance:** Very rare. Threatened.
Variation: Timber Rattlesnakes can be highly variable (see photos above). Yellow and brown "light morphs," along with very dark (nearly black) morphs, occur in the southeastern portions of the state. Typical color morphs appear elsewhere in KY.	**Variation:** There are three subspecies but only one (the Carolina Pygmy, subspecies *miliarius*) occurs in Kentucky.
Habitat: As their name implies Timber Rattlesnakes are forest animals. Within their woodland habitats they are most common in upland areas with rocky outcrops and talus slopes. They inhabit both mature forests and second growth woodlands, as well as forest edges. In some areas they may occur in bottomland woods as well, but usually only when the lowland areas are in proximity to ridges and uplands.	**Habitat:** In Kentucky this snake is found only in wooded habitats in the Land Between the Lakes National Forest and along the Kentucky Lake shoreline in eastern Calloway County.
Breeding: Timber Rattlesnakes in Kentucky typically breed in August and the females delay implantation of embryos until the following spring. The young snakes are then born in late summer or early fall, about a year after breeding. Females will produce young only every other year. Average litter is 6 to 12.	**Breeding:** Breeds in the fall with young being born the following summer in July or August. The tiny babies can coil on a coin the size of a nickel.
Natural History: This is one of the largest rattlesnake species in America and their bite is quite capable of killing a human. Fortunately they are peace-loving animals that only strike as a last resort. Timber Rattlesnake populations are declining in many areas of their range, including in Kentucky. Though they are still present in healthy numbers in some mountainous areas in the eastern part of the state, they are less numerous than in earlier times and are now rare or extirpated in much of their former range. Today they are absent from vast areas of their former range shown on the map above. As a result, the Kentucky Department of Fish and Wildlife Resources now protects them against wanton exploitation and slaughter. These large snakes feed mostly on mammals, with squirrels and chipmunks being a favorite food. They are known to lie in ambush beside fallen logs that are frequently traveled by ground-foraging chipmunks and squirrels. Almost any type of small mammal can be food and many types of mice and voles are eaten. Nestlings of ground-dwelling birds can also be prey. Mice are probably the main food for the young and a even a newborn Timber Rattlesnake is large enough to swallow a young mouse. This is Kentucky's most dangerous venomous snake.	**Natural History:** These tiny rattlesnakes are both secretive and cryptic and are thus easily overlooked. Though they can be found in dry, upland woods they show a preference for areas near water, i.e. swamps, marshes, and especially near springs and seeps. Food items include frogs, lizards, and mice as well as some invertebrates. Their tiny rattle is audible for a distance of only a few feet. They are quick to strike if molested and although they possess virulent venom, their small venom glands do not hold enough volume to kill a healthy adult human. This is one of the rarest snake species in Kentucky.

CHAPTER 7
THE AMPHIBIANS OF KENTUCKY

Table 9.
The Orders and Families of Kentucky Amphibians.

Class—**Amphibia** (amphibians)

Order—**Anura** (frogs, toads)

Family	**Ranidae** (true frogs)
Family	**Hylidae** (treefrogs)
Family	**Scaphiopodidae** (spadefoots)
Family	**Microhylidae** (narrowmouth toads)
Family	**Bufonidae** (true toads)

Order—**Caudata** (salamanders)

Family	**Ambysotmatidae** (mole salamanders)
Family	**Salamandridae** (newts)
Family	**Plethodontidae** (lungless salamanders)
Family	**Proteida** (mudpuppies)
Family	**Cryptobranchidae** (hellbenders)
Family	**Amphiumidae** (amphiumas)
Family	**Sirenidae** (sirens)

THE AMPHIBIANS OF KENTUCKY

PART 1: FROGS AND TOADS

Class—**Amphibia** (amphibians)

Order—**Anura** (frogs, toads)

Family—**Ranidae** (true frogs)

Green Frog—*Lithobates clamitans*		Bullfrog *Lithobates catesbeianus*
Bronze Morph (formerly subspecies—*L. c. clamitans*)	**Green Morph** (formerly subspecies—*L. c. melanotus*)	

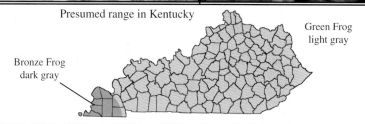
Presumed range in Kentucky
Green Frog light gray
Bronze Frog dark gray

Presumed range in Kentucky

Size: 2 to 4 inches.	**Size:** Averages 4 to 6 inches. Max 8.
Abundance: Both color morphs are very common within their respective ranges.	**Abundance:** Fairly common.
Variation: There are two color morphs and both can be found in Kentucky. The difference between the two is slight and usually relates to the color of the snout (see photos). Some experts regard the two morphs as different subspecies.	**Variation:** Females grow larger. Males (pictured) have a larger tympanum and a yellow throat (whitish in females).
Habitat: Found in virtually every aquatic habitat within the state, from small ponds and large lakes to streams and wetlands. Often found in uplands in temporary puddles on dirt roads and logging lanes or in the vicinity of springs or seeps. Less commonly can be found in wet meadows or damp woodlands.	**Habitat:** Ponds, lakes, and streams as well as swamps and marshes. May travel overland between ponds or wetland areas during rainy weather.
Breeding: Breeding can begin as early as May and continue until August. As with other frogs, eggs are fertilized externally by the male who clasps onto the females back and deposits sperm onto the eggs as they are extruded by the female. Up to 4,000 eggs may be deposited. Two clutches per year can occur. Eggs hatch in as little as a week and larva (tadpoles) metamorphose in two to three months. Young frogs may disperse up to a mile or more.	**Breeding:** Breeding and egg laying occurs from late spring through mid-summer. Several thousand eggs can be laid and two clutches per year is not uncommon. Tadpole metamorphosis does not occur until the following summer.
Natural History: A drive through a wetland on a rainy night in late summer when the tadpoles of *Lithobates clamitans* are emerging onto land will reveal astounding numbers of small frogs crossing the roadway as they disperse into new territories. Adult frogs feed on insects primarily but other arthropods including small crayfish are frequently eaten. Minnows and other small aquatic vertebrates are also potential prey. These frogs are easily confused with the much larger Bullfrog, but are distinguished by the presence of a fold of skin (known as a dorso-lateral fold) that runs along each side of the back. These frogs require smaller bodies of water than the larger Bullfrog and they can be found in almost any moist environment. Like other aquatic frogs they sometimes wander away from water on rainy nights to forage for insects in grassy areas. Despite the fact that this species is still very common, frogs in general are in a steep decline in North America. The much larger Bullfrog (next column) was extremely common in Kentucky just a few decades ago, but that species has experienced a decline in some populations. The filling of small stock ponds for row cropping and use of herbicides and pesticides may be the cause.	**Natural History:** These are the largest frogs in Kentucky (and in fact in the U.S). Their hind legs are considered to be a delicacy by many. They are regarded as a game animal and are hunted for food during the annual "frog season." In some places they are raised commercially for food and for research or teaching laboratories. They may venture far from water and will travel from pond to pond during rainy weather. Food is almost any animal small enough to be swallowed, including other frogs. There is even a record of a large Bullfrog eating a baby rattlesnake!

Class—**Amphibia** (amphibians)		
Order—**Anura** (frogs, toads)		
Family—**Ranidae** (true frogs)		

Wood Frog *Lithobates sylvatica*	**Northern Leopard Frog** *Lithobates pipiens*	**Southern Leopard Frog** *Lithobates sphenocephalus*

Presumed range in Kentucky	Presumed range in Kentucky	Presumed range in Kentucky
Size: About 3 inches.	**Size:** 3 to 4 inches.	**Size:** Average 3 inches. Max 5 inches.
Abundance: Fairly common.	**Abundance:** Uncommon in Kentucky.	**Abundance:** Common.
Variation: There is single, wide ranging species of Wood Frog found across the entire northern half of the continent. May vary from light tan to dark brown.	**Variation:** The color of the skin between the dark spots varies from greenish to brown or tan. Always has a spot on the snout.	**Variation:** Individuals vary from bright green to light tan (see photos above). Very similar to the preceding species but without a spot on the snout.
Habitat: This is a forest species that is most common in Kentucky in the Appalachian Mountains region. It prefers mesic woods near streams.	**Habitat:** Wet meadows, vegetated fields, wetland, and stream edges. This species wanders extensively into grassy fields in bottom lands.	**Habitat:** Found in virtually all aquatic habitats within its range. Like the Northern Leopard Frog they often wander into grassy fields far from water.
Breeding: Breeds in winter. This is the earliest breeding frog in Kentucky and they may breed as early as January. Eggs are laid in ephemeral pools and small fishless bodies of water.	**Breeding:** Breeding occurs in the early spring in ponds, marshes and swamps. Females will lay 2,000 to 5,000 eggs. Tadpoles grow from less than an inch to nearly four inches before transforming.	**Breeding:** Breeds mostly in April and May. Breeding localities are ponds, ditches, marshes, and swamps. Lays up to 5,000 eggs in several clumps. Young frogs emerge in mid-summer.
Natural History: Despite the fact that this is the most widespread frog species in America, there is but a single species that shows little variation. Wood Frogs from Canada and Alaska are identical to those found northern Alabama or northern Georgia. This is the most cold tolerant frog species in Kentucky and it ranges farther to the north than any of its kin. They can be frozen solid and recover without harm when thawed. Food is a variety of small invertebrates. Like many frogs, Wood Frogs migrate overland during periods of heavy rainfall. They can be commonly seen on roadways at night during the breeding season.	**Natural History:** Insects and spiders are the mainstay of this frog's diet. It is not uncommon for these frogs to be seen far from water during the summer months. But they retun to ponds and wetlands in the late fall to hibernate in the mud underwater. These are familiar animals to anyone who has dissected frogs in a biology class. In recent years their numbers in the wild have experienced an unexplained decline. In many regions specimens are being found with deformities to limbs. Some possible causes include chemical pollutants, acid rain, a pathogenic fungus that attacks frogs, or a combination of these and other, as yet unknown factors.	**Natural History:** Leopard frogs are frequently found some distance from permanent water sources in meadows and overgrown fields. They can even be seen in rural lawns on occasion, especially in late summer. Southern Leopard Frogs can be told from their northen cousin by the lack of a dark spot on the snout. They are easily discerned from the Pickerel Frog by their round rather than squarish spots; while the Northern Crayfish Frog is much stouter with a more rounded snout. A wide variety of insects, spiders, and other invertebrates are eaten. Like most frogs, they spend the winter in the mud at the bottom of a pond, creek, or other permanent water.

Class—**Amphibia** (amphibians)		
Order—**Anura** (frogs & toads)		
Family—**Ranidae** (true frogs)		
Plains Leopard Frog *Lithobates blairi*	**Pickerel Frog** *Lithobates palustris*	**Crayfish Frog** *Lithobates areolatus*

Presumed range in Kentucky	Presumed range in Kentucky	Presumed range in Kentucky
Size: To 3.75 inches, record 4.375.	**Size:** Average about 3 inches.	**Size:** Average 3–4 inches, record 4.5.
Abundance: Very rare in Kentucky.	**Abundance:** Uncommon.	**Abundance:** Rare in Kenucky.
Variation: Ground color (skin color between the spots) varies from tan to brown or greenish.	**Variation:** Ground color (skin color between the spots) varies from tan to brown.	**Variation:** Ground color between the spots varies from light gray to brown or tan.
Habitat: Mainly a prairie species. In Kentucky occupies lowlands in the Mississippi Alluvial Plain.	**Habitat:** Prefers spring-fed streams and clear, cool waters in woodland areas. May also occur in fields near streams.	**Habitat:** Floodplains, bottomland fields, and other low-lying areas with mesic substrates supporting crayfish.
Breeding: Nothing is known about breeding in Kentucky. Elsewhere breeds from late winter through spring. Lays up to 6,500 eggs.	**Breeding:** Breeds in ponds, ditches, or permanent streams. Lays 2,000 to 4,000 eggs. Tadpoles transform in about three months.	**Breeding:** An early breeder. In Kentucky most breeding occurs during periods of heavy rainfall in March. Up to 7,000 eggs may be laid.
Natural History: This is probably the rarest frog in Kentucky and was only recently discovered in the state by John MacGregor of the Kentucky Department of Fish and Wildlife Resources. So far the species is known only from a very small area in the Mississippi Alluvial Plain in southwestern Fulton County. The bulk of this frog's range is far to the west and north in the Great Plains region. There it can be a common species. Food is mostly insects and other invertebrates. In Kansas this species has been reported to sometimes emerge from hibernation during warm spells in mid-winter. In the lowlands of Fulton County it could possibly be seen any month of the year if weather conditions are favorable. Sightings should be reported to john.macgregor@ky.gov.	**Natural History:** Pickerel Frogs are distinguished from Leopard Frogs by their square rather than round spots. These frogs secrete a toxin from the skin that protects them from many predators and is strong enough to kill other frogs placed with them in a small container. Among the predators that are able to eat them, however, is another frog species, the Bullfrog. Northern populations of Pickerel Frogs (including those in Kentucky) show a preference for clean water and an intolerance for pollution. In this respect the Pickerel Frog may be an indicator species that can provide an early warning regarding environmental threats like water pollution. Sadly for Kentuckians, populations of this frog (and in fact frogs in general) may be declining in the state.	**Natural History:** This frog's name is derived from their habit of utilizing crayfish burrows as a home. They are quite secretive and are rarely observed except during the breeding season when they will travel overland in search of suitable breeding ponds or pools in wetland areas. Crayfish, other amphibians, small reptiles, and of course insects are food items. This species appears to be in decline in Kentucky. Modern agricultural practices such as tiling of wetland meadows to remove water and thus enable row cropping, along with the filling of small isolated ponds, is possibly the cause of this decline. Remaining populations in Kentucky appear to be fragmented and isolated from each other, which is never a good thing for the survival of a species.

Class—**Amphibia** (amphibians)

Order—**Anura** (frogs, toads)

Family—**Hylidae** (treefrogs)

Barking Treefrog *Hyla gratiosa*	**Green Treefrog** *Hyla cinerea*	**Bird-voiced Treefrog** *Hyla avivoca*
 Presumed range in Kentucky	 Presumed range in Kentucky	 Presumed range in Kentucky
Size: Record size of 2.75 inches.	**Size:** Record size 2.5 inches.	**Size:** Maximum of 2 inches.
Abundance: Rare. Threatened in KY.	**Abundance:** Uncommon.	**Abundance:** Uncommon in Kentucky.
Variation: Can change its color from green to brown. Sometimes has dark spots and small bright yellow flecks.	**Variation:** Varies in the amount of yellow spots on the back. May have several or none at all.	**Variation:** Changes color from solid gray with a lichen pattern to gray with a bright green back.
Habitat: Woodlands in the vicinity of wetlands suitable for breeding seems to be the habitat requirement for this frog.	**Habitat:** Green Treefrogs are lowland animals that are found in swamps and marshes mostly.	**Habitat:** Wetlands. Found mainly in swamps and marshes or in their immediate vicinity.
Breeding: Shallow, fishless ponds are the preferred breeding sites for this species. Breeds from late spring through the summer.	**Breeding:** Breeds in early to mid-summer. Lays up to 1,500 eggs in shallow waters of swamps or marshes. Multiple clutches may be produced in a summer.	**Breeding:** Breeds in spring or summer in shallow, vegetated waters of swamps and marshes. Metamorphosis of tadpoles occurs in about four weeks.
Natural History: This is the largest native treefrog in America. They are both arboreal and terrestrial in habits. Unspotted specimens such as the one shown above closely resemble Green Treefrogs (*H. cinerea*), but the Barking Treefrog has a much stockier appearance and a granular skin rather than smooth. Their name comes from the fact that large breeding congregations when calling produce a sound that from a distance resembles the sound of dogs barking. The presence of this mostly southern species in Kentucky is somewhat puzzling, and the Kentucky population is disjunct from any of the contiguous populations that are found throughout the deep south. Modern agricultural practices that convert wetland areas to cropland may be a major threat.	**Natural History:** Similar to the Barking Treefrog but has smooth skin and a much slimmer appearance overall. One of this frog's favorite daytime perches are the stems of cattails and sedges where its deep green color renders it almost invisible. Its primary prey consists of caterpillers, spiders, grasshoppers, and other insects. Green Treefrogs are primarily nocturnal in habits but they are sometimes seen during the day, especially during rainy weather. As with most other treefrogs of the genus *Hyla,* this is another mainly southern species. Its range extends northward through western Kentucky and into southern Illinois where the Gulf Coastal Plain Province reaches its northernmost extension. A disjunct population occurs in lowlands in Henderson County.	**Natural History:** These handsome little treefrogs are easily confused with the frogs of the Gray Treefrog complex (see next page). Bird-voiced Treefrogs have a greenish wash on the inner thighs as opposed to the orange or yellow inner thigh seen on the Gray Treefrogs. These are mainly southern animals that reach the northernmost limits of their range in the upper Coastal Plain region. Their name comes from the sound of the male's breeding call, which resembles the whistling song of a bird. This species survival is dependant upon wetlands. Thus the range of these frogs in Kentucky is restricted to the western end of the state where lower elevations and the presence of wetland habitats mimic habitat conditions common farther to the south.

Class—**Amphibia** (amphibians)

Order—**Anura** (frogs, toads)

Family—**Hylidae** (treefrogs)

Cope's Gray Treefrog & Gray Treefrog *Hyla chrysoscelis & Hyla versicolor*	Eastern Cricket Frog *Acris crepitans*

Gray Phases   Green Phase

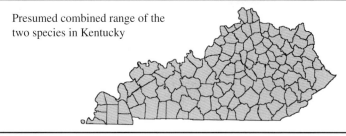

Presumed combined range of the two species in Kentucky

Presumed range in Kentucky

Size: Averages about 2 inches. Maximum of just under 2.5 inches.

Size: Tiny, usually less than 1 inch.

Abundance: Cope's Gray Treefrog is common. Gray Treefrog is rare in Kentucky.

Abundance: Very common.

Variation: There are actually two identical species in the Gray Treefrog complex. They can only be reliably differentiated by the sound of their call or by laboratory examination of the number of cell chromosones. Of the two species, the Cope's Treefrog (*Hyla chrysoscelis*), is widespread in Kentucky. Both species have the ability to change color from gray to green. Additionally, the shade of gray can range from a dark sooty gray to a light smoky gray (see photos above).

Variation: Highly variable. Most commonly some shade of brown to reddish brown or tan. May also be gray green like the specimen above. Many will have bright green markings on the back with dark stripes on the back and side.

Habitat: Habitat is chiefly woodlands. These treefrogs are more adapted to dry uplands than most members of their genus and they can be found far from water in dry upland woods.

Habitat: Shorelines of ponds, along creeks, temporary pools, marshes, swamps, wet meadows, and uplands.

Breeding: Breeds from late spring through summer in small bodies of water ranging from small ponds to roadside ditches. Up to 2,000 eggs are laid.

Breeding: Breeds from spring through late summer. Up to 400 eggs per clutch.

Natural History: These highly arboreal treefrogs are rarely seen on the ground and they often climb high into treetops to forage for insects. They are mainly nocturnal but they may be active by day on cloudy or rainy days or in cooler weather. They shelter by day in small hollows in tree trunks or limbs and have been known to take up residence in small bird nest boxes such as a wren box or bluebird box. They will also live in the rain gutters of house roofs. They can sometimes be seen sitting in the opening of their hiding place with the head and front feet exposed. They possess remarkable camouflage abilities and the gray, lichen-like pattern of their skin will perfectly match the bark of the tree they occupy. They can produce a natural antifreeze in the blood that allows them to hibernate in tree hollows above the ground, or in leaf litter on the forest floor. Most members of the genus *Hyla* are southern animals, but these frogs range far into the northern states and even into parts of southern Canada. Food items are small insects and arthropods. The identical species known as the Gray Treefrog (*Hyla versicolor*) occurs sympatrically with *H. chrysoscelis* in Kentucky in two small populations, one in the vicinity of Louisville and the other in extreme northeastern Kentucky. Recent observations suggest that in western Kentucky increasing populations of Green Treefrogs may be out-competing Cope's Gray Treefrogs (author's anecdotal observation).

Natural History: These tiny frogs are most commonly seen along the receding shorelines of ponds and lakes in late summer or early fall. When startled by a passing human they will often jump into the water and then immediately swim back to shore. This may be an "out of the frying pan into the fire" behavior intended to keep them from the jaws of hungry fish. They are often seen far from water in fields and woodlands, but are always more common in wetland habitats and permanently damp areas. Their name comes from their call, which resembles that of a cricket, but is more accurately described as sounding like two small stones being rapidly clicked together.

Class—**Amphibia** (amphibians)

Order—**Anura** (frogs, toads)

Family—**Hylidae** (treefrogs)

Upland Chorus Frogs	**Mountain Chorus Frog**	**Spring Peeper**
Pseudacris feriarum / Pseudacris triseriata	*Pseudacris brachyphona*	*Pseudacris crucifer*

Presumed range in Kentucky *P. feriarum*—light gray *P. triseriata*—dark gray 	Presumed range in Kentucky 	Presumed range in Kentucky 
Size: 0.75 to 1.25 inches.	**Size:** Average 1 inch. Record 1.5.	**Size:** About 1 inch.
Abundance: Common.	**Abundance:** Fairly common.	**Abundance:** Common.
Variation: Variable. Ground color varies from brown to grayish. Dorsal pattern can be stripes or spots.	**Variation:** Varies from brown to olive green. Dorsal pattern also varies from prominent to very vague or absent.	**Variation:** Ground color varies. Usually tan or brown. Sometimes grayish or reddish.
Habitat: Low wet fields, bottomland woods, swamps, marshes, ponds, or bogs. Also found in uplands that are in close proximity to bottomlands, creeks, or other permanent water.	**Habitat:** Mountain forests in the central and southern Appalachians. An upland adapted species that associates with mesic micro-habitats. Can be found far from water.	**Habitat:** Woodlands and thickets, usually near water. Most common in lowlands (swamps, marshes, etc.), but also found in upland areas adjacent to creek bottoms or wetlands.
Breeding: Very early breeders that may begin breeding as early as February. Breeding is in ephemeral pools in flooded fields, roadside ditches, etc.	**Breeding:** Breeds early (February and March). Utilizes woodland ponds, ephemeral pools, and even water-filled ruts in old logging roads.	**Breeding:** Spring Peepers begin breeding activity as early as late winter and continue into early spring. Several hundred eggs are laid in shallow water.
Natural History: At the first signs of spring these frogs appear and gather in large numbers to breed. Breeding may be interrupted several times by cold snaps and freezing weather. The name comes from their "chorus" of breeding calls that carries over quite a long distance. Standing water in flooded bottomlands and shallow, water-filled depressions in croplands are favorite breeding sites for this frog. Though amazingly common during the brief breeding season, most of the rest of the year they seem to disappear. There are two nearly identical Chorus Frog species in Kentucky (see range map above). Some experts regard them as a single species with two subspecies.	**Natural History:** This tiny frog is a mountain forest adapted species that can be found at high elevations. They are a shy species that is rarely observed except during the breeding season. The rest of the year they are scattered throughout the forest and are easily overlooked amid leaf litter and woodland debris. Mountain Chorus Frogs range throughout the central and southern Appalachians from Pennsylvania to northern Alabama and extreme northeast Mississippi. Despite their wide range the biology of this secretive little frog is not well understood. Mountain Chorus Frogs are true to their name and are only found in upland regions, whereas other chorus frogs will frequent lowlands.	**Natural History:** Another dimunitive frog that is heard more often than seen. The name comes from the sound made when breeding frogs are calling. The call is a rapidly repeated "peep, peep, peep." Despite being members of the treefrog family they live mostly on the ground. The species name "*crucifer*" is Latin for "cross bearer" and refers to the X-shaped mark that is always present on this frog's back. These little frogs, along with their cousins the Chorus Frogs, are a true harbinger of spring throughout much of the eastern United States. They may breed in the same flooded field pools with Chorus Frogs or even in the same pool. Feeds on tiny insects and arthropods.

Class—**Amphibia** (amphibians)	
Order—**Anura** (frogs, toads)	
Family—**Scaphiopodidae** (spadefoots)	Family—**Microhylidae** (narrowmouth toads)
Eastern Spadefoot *Scaphiopus holbrookii*	**Eastern Narrowmouth Toad** *Gastrophryne carolinensis*

Presumed range in Kentucky 	Presumed range in Kentucky 
Size: 2 to 3 inches.	**Size:** Average about an 1 inch.
Abundance: Uncommon in Kentucky.	**Abundance:** Uncommon in Kentucky.
Variation: Ground color varies from brown or olive through gray to black.	**Variation:** Ground color varies from grayish to dark brown.
Habitat: The main habitat requirement is loose, sandy soil that facilitates easy burrowing. Lives in both upland and lowland woods and meadows.	**Habitat:** Can be found both in dry upland and in more mesic bottomlands. Primarily a woodland animal.
Breeding: Breeds explosively during periods of heavy rainfall from late spring throughout the summer. Up to 5,000 eggs hatch within a few days.	**Breeding:** From 500 to 800 eggs are laid in late spring or summer. Development of both the eggs and the tadpoles is very rapid. Eggs hatch in two days and tadpoles transform in two to four weeks.
Natural History: The name "Spadefoot" come from a sickle-shaped horny structure on the hind feet that is used for digging into the ground. They spend much of their lives in burrows only a few inches deep and emerge only on rainy nights. During dry weather they may spend weeks in the burrow without feeding. They secrete a toxic substance that is highly irritant to mucous membranes, thus making these anurans unpalatable to many potential predators. Touching the face or other sensitive skin after handling a Spadefoot will result in an uncomfortable burning sensation. Although widespread and quite common farther to the south, in Kentucky the Spadefoot is sporadically distributed and may be absent from many areas shown on the range map above.	**Natural History:** Narrowmouth Toads are confirmed burrowers that are occasionally found hiding beneath flat rocks, boards, etc. Their call is a nasal "baaaa" and sounds like the cry of a young lamb. Ants and termites are recorded as prey and it is likely that other diminutive insects and other arthropods are eaten. The tiny mouth on this frog precludes eating anything larger than the average termite. Despite their name they are not true toads but are the sole representatives in the eastern United States of a specialized family of anurans known as Microhylidae. Microhylidae frogs are much more common in more tropical regions. Their are over 300 species in the family and they can be found on every major continent except Europe and Antarctica.

Class—**Amphibia** (amphibians)
Order—**Anura** (frogs, toads)
Family—**Bufonidae** (true toads)

American Toad *Bufo americanus*		Fowler's Toad *Bufo fowleri*
Dwarf American Toad—*B. a. charlesmithi*	**American Toad**—*Bufo a. americanus*	

Presumed range in Kentucky

American Toad (light gray)

Dwarf American Toad (dark gray)

Presumed range in Kentucky

Size: 2 to 4 inches. Of the two, the American Toad attains a much larger size.

Size: Average of 2 to 3 inches.

Abundance: Common.

Abundance: Very common.

Variation: There are two subspecies of *Bufo americanus* and both are found in Kentucky. The exact line of separation between the two races is unclear, but generally speaking the Dwarf American Toad occurs in the western third of Kentucky.

Variation: Varies in color from dark brown to reddish brown, tan, or grayish brown.

Habitat: Virtually anywhere. Inhabits dry uplands and moist lowlands from remote wilderness to urban lawns. Like most other toads the American Toad likes loose soils that facilitate easy burrowing. In the state of Kentucky the Dwarf form seems to be the less common of the two subspecies.

Habitat: All habitats within the state, including urban and suburban yards. Shows a preference for sandy, loose soils in bottomlands.

Breeding: Breeds as early as March in Kentucky. Eggs are laid in long strings of clear gelationous material. Breeding sites are small ponds, water-filled ditches, or temporary pools in seasonally flooded lowlands. Eggs hatch in about one week into tiny black tadpoles that metamorph into quarter-inch toadlets in mid-summer.

Breeding: Breeding is in May in shallow ponds, ditches, creeks, flooded fields, etc. From 5,000 to 10,000 eggs are laid.

Natural History: American Toads eat a wide variety of insects and other small arthropods. They are adept burrowers and like other toads possess hardened spade-like structures on the hind feet that are used for digging. These toads can be told from the similar and sympatrically occurring Fowler's Toad by the their larger warts and the fact that the dark spots on the back never have more than two warts per spot. The similar Fowler's Toad may have up to six warts per dark spot. Although they are sometimes active by day, these toads are primarily nocturnal in habits. They usually spend the day at least partially buried in loose soil or beneath leaf litter or other debris. When attacked by a predator they will inflate their bodies by gulping air. This behavior sometimes works if the predator is an animal like a snake that must swallow its food whole. The common Eastern Garter Snake along with the Eastern Hognose Snake are two of their major predators.

Natural History: The natural history of the Fowler's Toad is similar to that of the American Toad. Fowler's Toads breed later in the spring and young toadlets do not emerge from the tadpole stage until late summer. Like many toads (and many treefrogs) the Fowler's Toad secretes a toxic substance from the skin when threatened. While this toxin can cause irritation to sensitive areas and membranes, the old wives' tale that toads cause warts is a fallacy.

THE AMPHIBIANS OF KENTUCKY

PART 2: SALAMANDERS

Class—**Amphibia** (amphibians)

Order—**Caudata** (salamanders)

Family—**Ambystomatidae** (mole salamanders)

Tiger Salamander *Ambystoma tigrinum*	**Spotted Salamander** *Ambystoma maculatum*

Presumed range in Kentucky	Presumed range in Kentucky 
Size: Averages about 8 inches. Maximum length is around 14 inches.	**Size:** Average 6 inches. Maximum 9.
Abundance: Uncommon to fairly common.	**Abundance:** Common.
Variation: A good deal of variation occurs in this species. The light markings can appear as irregular spots, blotches, or stripes. The color of the light pigments can vary as well and may be yellow, orange, or greenish. They are easily confused with the Spotted Salamander, but that species has spots that are more rounded.	**Variation:** The polka-dot spots on the Spotted Salamander may be yellow or orange. The number of spots varies widely, and a few may lack spots.
Habitat: Woodlands and fields, in both upland an lowland areas. This species seems more common on the Interior Low Plateau Province and the Coastal Plain in regions that once had a mosaic of grasslands.	**Habitat:** Primarily woodland areas, but also found in overgrown fields and edges bordering agricultural lands.
Breeding: Breeds in small, fishless bodies of water like stock ponds, vernal pools, and "borrow pits." Breeding occurs in mid-winter with a few hundred to several thousand eggs produced by the female. Males meet females in breeding ponds and fertilize the eggs as they are laid, much like a fish. Eggs are encased in a ball of jelly-like material and hatch in about a month.	**Breeding:** Breeds during periods of heavy rainfall in late winter. Eggs are deposited in large gelatinous masses in ponds or wetland pools. Larva transform in two to four months.
Natural History: The large size of the Tiger Salamander allows it to feed on much larger prey than most salamander species. Although invertebrates such as earthworms and insect larva are the major foods, small vertebrates may also eaten and captive specimens will eat baby mice. The apparent decline of this salamander in Kentucky may be traced to the draining and filling of small ponds and wetlands and the destruction of vernal pools by modern agricultural practices. Many amphibians in our state require small bodies of water that do not hold significant numbers of aquatic predators such as predaceous fish that will eat amphibian larva. Amphibians are also vulnerable to toxins released into the environment by farming operations where both insecticides and herbicides are widely used. In fact, the amphibians are in decline throughout the globe and many scientists regard their diminishing populations as an environmental alarm call. Despite their large size, Tiger Salamanders are rarely seen except during the late winter breeding season when they make their nocturnal overland treks to breeding ponds. At this time they sometimes stumble into basement stairwells, old cisterns, etc., and become trapped.	**Natural History:** Primarily subterranean in habits. Lives in underground burrows and beneath rocks, logs, or leaf litter on the forest floor. During periods of hot dry weather retreats deeper underground or stays in the vicinity of perennially wet areas. Feeds on a wide variety of insects and invertebrates as well as a few small vertebrates. This is the most common member of the "mole salamander" group in Kentucky. In the late winter breeding season they are easily observed on rural roads at night during rainy weather as they make the migration to breeding ponds.

Class—**Amphibia** (amphibians)

Order—**Caudata** (salamanders)

Family—**Ambystomatidae** (mole salamanders)

Small-mouthed Salamander *Ambystoma texanum*	**Streamside Salamander** *Ambystoma barbouri*	**Jefferson Salamander** *Ambystoma jeffersonianum*

Size: 4 to 5 inches as an adult.	**Size:** 4 to 5 inches as adult.	**Size:** Up to 8 inches.
Abundance: Fairly common.	**Abundance:** Fairly common.	**Abundance:** Fairly common.
Variation: Varies in color from uniform dark gray to blue-gray with varying amounts of silver or light gray flecking.	**Variation:** Varies in color from uniform dark gray to light gray or blue gray. The amount of silver or whitish flecking also varies, and may be absent.	**Variation:** There is some variation in the amount of light blue spots that are present. Older adults tend to lose their spots and become darker.
Habitat: Found in a variety of habitats from woodlands to grassy meadows. Most common in lowlands and stream bottoms but also in upland areas.	**Habitat:** Found mostly in woodlands within close proximity to streams. Thus creek bottoms and river valleys are more frequently inhabited.	**Habitat:** An upland forest species mostly. This is primarily a northern species that reaches the southernmost limits of its range in Kentucky.
Breeding: Breeds in late winter or very early spring. May lay up to several hundred eggs in large clumps. Ponds, wetland pools, or flooded roadside ditches may be used for egg deposition. Larva transform into adults in about six to eight weeks, sooner in warmer weather.	**Breeding:** Breeds in limestone bottomed streams in late fall to early winter. This is the only *Ambystoma* salamander that breeds strictly in streams. It also lays fewer eggs than others and its eggs are deposited singly rather than in large clumps.	**Breeding:** Breeding occurs in late winter or early spring, with eggs being deposited in woodland ponds. As with all *Ambystoma* salamanders, the eggs hatch into larva that spend up to a year as thoroughly aquatic, gilled salamanders before transforming into adults.
Natural History: Like other members of its genus the Smallmouth Salamander spends most of its time in underground burrows or beneath rocks, logs, or leaf litter. They will emerge on rainy nights to forage above ground. Feeds on a wide variety of soft-bodied invertebrate prey such as earthworms, slugs, and grubs. The Smallmouth Salamander is very similar in appearance to the Streamside Salamander and the best clue to identification between the two species is to refer to their respective range maps.	**Natural History:** In most respects other than breeding habits the natural history of the Streamside Salamander is similar to that of the very similar looking Smallmouth Salamander. The two species are very difficult to distinguish based on appearance alone. In fact, they were once regarded as being members of the same species. Soft-bodied invertebrates are probably the main food item for the adults and the larva are known to eat small crustaceans (isopods, etc.), as well as worms and other benthic organisms.	**Natural History:** Much of this species' range is to the north of Kentucky in Ohio, West Virginia, Pennsylvania, and New York. In Kentucky they occur in the central portion of the state from northernmost Kentucky almost to the Tennessee line. They are most common in the northern portions of the state where limestone substrate dominates. Like all terrestrial salamanders in Kentucky, this is mainly a fossorial species. They will surface at night or on rainy, heavily overcast days with dim light and forage on the forest floor.

Class—**Amphibia** (amphibians)

Order—**Caudata** (salamanders)

Family—**Ambystomatidae** (mole salamanders) | Family—**Salamandridae** (newts)

Marbled Salamander *Ambystoma opacum*	**Mole Salamander** *Ambystoma talpoideum*	**Eastern Newt** *Notophthalmus viridescens*
 Presumed range in Kentucky	 Presumed range in Kentucky 	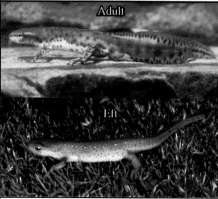 Presumed range in Kentucky — Red-spotted Newt (light gray); Central Newt (dark gray)
Size: 3 to 4 inches.	**Size:** Maximum of 5 inches.	**Size:** Adults to 5 inches. Efts 3 inches.
Abundance: Fairly common.	**Abundance:** Uncommon in Kentucky.	**Abundance:** Common.
Variation: Sexually dimorphic. Light colors are grayish or silver in the female and whiter in the male.	**Variation:** Some are uniformly dark gray. Others have a significant amount of light gray flecking on the sides.	**Variation:** Two subspecies in Kentucky. Significant ontogenetic variation (see Natural History section below).
Habitat: Most fond of bottomlands (especially during breeding) but also common in upland woods.	**Habitat:** Swamps, marshes, and bottomland woods prone to seasonal flooding. Less commonly in upland woods.	**Habitat:** Adults are found in ponds, swamps, or other permanent water. Eft stage is a terrestrial animal of woods.
Breeding: Breeds in the fall during rainy weather. Overland migration is common. Eggs are laid on land under rocks, logs, etc., in low-lying areas subject to flooding. Hatching is delayed until eggs are flooded by fall rains.	**Breeding:** Breeding occurs in late fall or early winter and overland treks to breeding areas are made. Eggs are laid in the waters of swamps and marshes. After a few months the gill-breathing larva develop into air-breathing adults.	**Breeding:** Breeds in spring. Males deposit packages of sperm that are taken up by the female into the cloaca where fertilization occurs internally; eggs are then laid. Hatchlings metamorph into efts in four to five months.
Natural History: This is one of the few salamanders to exhibit sexual dimorphism. The light markings are wider and whiter on the male and narrower and more silver or grayish on the female. Like other members of the "mole salamander" family, Marbled Salamanders are fossorial in habits. In fact, this species may be even more secretive than many of its kin. Thus, though they are fairly common they are not readily observed. They can reportedly produce a noxious secretion from the tail that may help to ward off some predators. Adults probably feed on most any small animal they can swallow. Larva have been known to eat the eggs of small frogs.	**Natural History:** This decidedly fossorial salamander is the namesake of the "mole salamander" family. This species is rarely seen above ground except during the breeding season when they will emerge on rainy nights and travel to areas of breeding congregations. They can sometimes be turned up beneath logs or other objects in low, perennially moist areas. These salamanders have a stout bodied appearance and a large head that distinguishes them from the similarly colored Small-mouthed Salamander and Streamside Salamander. When captured they will sometimes assume a defensive posture that consists of raising the body off the ground while lowering the head.	**Natural History:** Newts are unique among Kentucky salamanders in having an extra stage in their life cycle. Following hatching the young spend the summer as gill-breathing larva then undergo a transformation to an air-breathing semi-adult that lives on land. Newts in this terrestrial stage are call "efts." After one to three years the eft returns to the water and undergoes another metmorphosis into a totally aquatic adult. After returning to the water the coarse skin of the eft becomes smooth and the round tail flattens vertically to become fin-like. Their life span can be up to 15 years. Newts produce a neurotoxin in their skin that protects them from many predators.

Class—**Amphibia** (amphibians)

Order—**Caudata** (salamanders)

Family—**Plethodontidae** (lungless salamanders)

The Dusky Salamanders—genus *Desmognathus* (five species in Kentucky)

Spotted Dusky Salamander *Desmognathus conanti*	**Northern Dusky Salamander** *Desmognathus fuscus*	Presumed range of Spotted and Northern Dusky Salmanders in Kentucky
		Northern Dusky Salamander (light gray) Spotted DuskySalamander (dark gray) 
Allegheny Mt. Dusky Salamander *Desmognathus ochrophaeus*	**Seal Salamander** *Desmognathus monticola*	**Black Mountain Salamander** *Desmognathus welteri*
		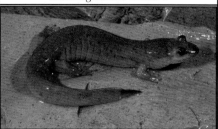
Presumed range in Kentucky 	Presumed range in Kentucky	Presumed range in Kentucky 

Size: Most average about 4–5 inches when fully grown. Spotted and Northern Dusky Salamanders are smaller (3–4 inches). Black Mountain Salamander is the largest and it can reach 6 inches, rarely nearly 7 inches.

Abundance: The Spotted and Northern Dusky Salamanders can be very common. Other species are common to fairly common within their respective ranges.

Variation: There are at least 19 species of *Desmognathus* salamanders found in the United States. All of the five species that are found in Kentucky can be quite variable. Some may change from light brown to very dark brown depending upon environmental conditions and the discernability of the dorsal patterns can also vary considerably. Distinguishing the individual species in this group of salamanders can be challenging for the average observer. Those who are interested in becoming familiar with the individual species in this group are advised to consult the list of amphibian references in the back of this book.

Habitat: Springs, seeps, and spring-fed creeks in wooded areas are the primary habitat for this group of salamanders. The Spotted Dusky can also be found in swampy areas and several may be found in damp woodlands in the vicinity of creeks and springs or seep areas.

Breeding: Breeding can occur in the spring or the fall. The eggs (average 15–30) are laid in clusters of individual eggs that are not contained in a gelatinous mass like the mole salamanders. Egg clusters are placed in very wet environments, sometimes in a stream or within a place that is bathed by spring waters. The eggs will hatch in six to eight weeks into an aquatic larva that metamorphoses into an adult in about a year. The larva of the large Black Mountain Salamander (*D. welteri)* may take up to two years to metamorphose into an adult.

Natural History: Dusky salamanders are a ubiquitous group of salamanders that are widespread and often common. They are well known to rural folk and many youngsters have amused themselves on a hot summer day by rolling stones and logs in mountain streams to try to catch these slippery and quick-moving salamanders. Mainly nocturnal, they will emerge from their daytime hiding places at night to forage and they can sometimes be located with aid of a flashlight. One species, the Seal Salamander, is especially conspicous at night as it perches on top of rocks within a stream with the forepart of the body raised. It resembles a tiny seal, thus the name. This group of salamanders are often collected by fishermen to use for bait and they are locally known as "spring lizards." They are frequently sold in bait stores in the Appalachian region. Although this practice probably has no significant impact on the more common species, accidental "by catch" of some rarer species may have an negative impact on those less common populations.

Class—**Amphibia** (amphibians)

Order—**Caudata** (salamanders)

Family—**Plethodontidae** (lungless salamanders)

Zigzag Salamanders *Plethodon dorsalis / Plethodon ventralis*	**Eastern Redback Salamander** *Plethodon cinereus*	**Ravine Salamander** *Plethodon richmondi*

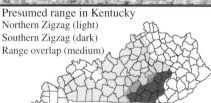Presumed range in Kentucky Northern Zigzag (light) Southern Zigzag (dark) Range overlap (medium)	Presumed range in Kentucky	Presumed range in Kentucky
Size: Average 3 to 4 inches.	**Size:** 3–4 inches. Maximum 5 inches.	**Size:** About 4 inches. Maximum 5.75.
Abundance: Fairly common.	**Abundance:** Uncommon in Kentucky.	**Abundance:** Common.
Variation: Both species vary somewhat in their ground color and in the intensity of the zigzag strip down the back. Some are uniformly gray above and lack the dorsal stripe altogether.	**Variation:** Considerable variation in the dorsal pattern. Some Redback Salamanders are not red on the back at all, but uniformly gray. This color morph is known as the "lead-backed phase."	**Variation:** Some variation in background color. The color of the widespread metallic-like flecking can vary somewhat from silverish to gold. The amount of this flecking can also vary.
Habitat: Both are forest species (mesic woodlands) and are most common in regions with a limestone substrate.	**Habitat:** Chiefly woodlands. This is another terrestrial but retiring species that hides beneath leaf litter, logs, etc.	**Habitat:** As its name implies this species prefers the steep slopes of deep, forested ravines in rugged terrain.
Breeding: Lays only a few eggs (as few as four or five). Eggs are deposited into an underground nest chamber.	**Breeding:** Female lays about 10 eggs on land and guards them until they hatch. Babies hatch fully formed.	**Breeding:** As with other *Plethodon* salamanders there is no larval stage and the young appear like miniature adults.
Natural History: The Northern Zigzag Salamander (*P. dorsalis*) and the Southern Zigzag Salamander (*P. ventralis*) were once regarded as single species with two subspecies. They were separated into two distinct species based on DNA analysis. For the layman identifying individual specimens is best accomplished by way of geography (see range map above). These are terrestrial salamanders that spend much of their life beneath leaf litter, logs, or other cover on the forest floor. They do emerge at night and forage for small invertebrate prey. They also capture worms and tiny insects beneath the leaf litter. Like all members of the *Plethodon* salamanders, young salamanders hatch fully formed.	**Natural History:** Most of this salamander's range is to the north and east of Kentucky, as far north as the Canadian provinces of Quebec, Nova Scotia, and New Brunswick. In the heart of its range this is not only the most common salamander species, but one of the most common vertebrate species. Ironically, in Kentucky this is an uncommon species and their range barely enters the area in northernmost region of the state. The Kentucky range of this salamander consists of a region that is highly urbanized and its natural habitats have been radically altered. Thus this is regarded as a species of concern in Kentucky. They are very similar to the Zigzag Salamanders and can be difficult to differentiate. Range is the best clue to identity.	**Natural History:** Of the several species of small, dark salamanders depicted in this book the Ravine Salamander is noteworthy because of its tiny legs and its predilection for living along the slopes of steep valleys and ravines. Like other diminutive woodland salamanders this species is easily overlooked hiding beneath rocks, logs, bark, and humus beneath our feet. Like many other small amphibians they disappear underground during hot, dry weather, remerging during rains or in cooler seasons. They are most active in the spring and fall and may be active during warm weather even in the dead of winter. Some experts now recognize two morphologically identical species that are differentiated by DNA analysis.

Class—**Amphibia** (amphibians)		
Order—**Caudata** (salamanders)		
Family—**Plethodontidae** (lungless salamanders)		
Slimy Salamanders		
Mississippi Slimy Salamander *Plethodon mississippi*	**Northern Slimy Salamander** *Plethodon glutinosus*	**Cumberland Plateau Salamander** *Plethodon kentucki*

Presumed range in Kentucky

Size: Mississipppi Slimy can reach 6 inches. Northern Slimy is larger with a maximum of 7.5 inches. Cumberland Slimy is intermediate in size reaching a maximum of about 6.75 inches. Most are between 4 and 5 inches as adults.

Abundance: All three species are common in suitable habitat. The Northern Slimy Salamander can be very common. Both the Cumberland Plateau and Mississippi Slimy are also common in suitable habitat, with the Mississippi Slimy being perhaps the least common species in Kentucky (although it can be a very common animal in the Land Between the Lakes area.).

Variation: All three species vary considerably in the amount of white spotting. Northern and Mississippi Slimys are often indistinguishable morphologically. Location is the most reliable way to distinguish those two. The Cumberland Plateau Salamander on average has fewer spots and the chin and throat are a lighter gray than the rest of the body.

Habitat: All three of these species are woodland animals. They inhabit both upland woods and the bottoms of ravines or valley and creek bottoms. As with all salamanders, some degree of moisture is imperative in their habitat requirements. But in much of their range they can be found in xeric woodlands on slopes and ridgetops where there is heavy shade and a thick cover of leaf litter to maintain semi-mesic conditions.

Breeding: These salamanders are terrestrial breeders and eggs are deposited in underground nest chambers. As many as 18 eggs are known for the Mississippi Slimy Salamander, a dozen for the Cumberland Plateau Salamander. Females of all three species remain with the eggs until they hatch. There is no larval stage in any of these salamanders and newly hatched specimens are fully formed replicas of the adults.

Natural History: Until the advent of DNA technology there was only one ubiquitous species of Slimy Salamander that ranged across most of the eastern United States. There are now over dozen individual species, nearly all of which are very similar in appearance and all of which show significant variation among local populations. The amount of white to brassy spots or flecks present on the sides and back can be a little or a lot on all species, and the overall body shape and size is also similar. With so much overlap in morphological characteristics it is nearly impossible to identify individual Slimy Salamanders outside the laboratory without knowing where they were found. Likewise, the most reliable clue to identity in the field is the geographic location of the specimen. In the case of the Cumberland Slimy (whose range overlaps that of the Northern Slimy) identification is best accomplished by noting the color of the chin and throat. On the Northern Slimy Salamander the chin and throat are the same color as the rest of the body (black), while on the Cumberland Plateau Salamander the throat and chin are lighter than the rest of the body (grayish). All species of slimy salamanders exude a thick, sticky mucus from the skin when handled. This material is difficult to wash off and once dried becomes black and crusty. Herpetologists capturing slimy salamanders sometimes wear the residue of salamander mucus on their hands for days before it finally wears off. The food of these woodland species is undoubtedly a wide variety of soft-bodied insects, insect larva, annelids, small crustaceans, and other tiny invertebrate life found among the leaf litter on the forest floor.

Class—**Amphibia** (amphibians)

Order—**Caudata** (salamanders)

Family—**Plethodontidae** (lungless salamanders)

Wehrle's Salamander *Plethodon wehrlei*	Green Salamander *Aneides aeneus*	Southern Two-lined Salamander *Eurycea cirrigera*

Presumed range in Kentucky 	Presumed range in Kentucky 	Presumed range in Kentucky 
Size: Maximum of 6.75 inches.	**Size:** Maximum about 5.5 inches.	**Size:** Max 4 inches, average about 2–3.
Abundance: Common within range.	**Abundance:** Generally uncommon.	**Abundance:** Fairly common.
Variation: Very little variation in Kentucky specimens.	**Variation:** Slight variation in the amount of lichen-like green markings.	**Variation:** Ground color varies slightly from bright yellow to dingy brownish.
Habitat: Damp upland forests in mountainous areas. Shows a preference for wooded, rocky slopes.	**Habitat:** Wet cliff faces and rocky outcrops with seeping water. Most common in areas of sandstone substrates.	**Habitat:** Streams, wetlands, and seeps. Mostly a lowland animal but also found in mesic upland environments.
Breeding: Little is known about breeding in this species. Presumably it is similar to other Plethodontidae salamanders (i.e. eggs laid on land, no larva).	**Breeding:** Lays its eggs in moist rock crevices. Up to 30 eggs are attached to the ceiling of a rock crevice. There is no larva and hatchlings resemble adults.	**Breeding:** Several dozen eggs are attached to the underside of rocks and brooks. Eggs hatch into aquatic larva that transform in one or two years.
Natural History: The species name (*wehrlei*) honors the naturalist who first discovered this salamander. Although this species is not widely distributed in the state, it is apparently common in the regions where it does occur. In Kentucky this salamander is restricted to the southeastern corner of the state where strip mining operations are common and may pose a threat. Like many other members of its family this is a terrestrial salamander that lives in mature forests on mountain slopes. As with other salamanders they can be very hard to find during hot, dry summer months as they will retreat into underground burrows beneath large rocks and boulders and aestivate. The members of the *Plethodon* genus of salamanders are often referred to by biologists as Woodland Salamanders, a reference to their preferred habitat.	**Natural History:** This is a salamander that is easily recognizable by its green, lichen-like markings on a black ground color. It is the only truly green salamander in Kentucky. This is a cliff-dwelling animal that lives in cracks and crevices of rock faces. Damp sandstone cliffs with seeping water are its primary habitat. The head and body are dorsoventrally flattened, an adaptation that enables it to squeeze its body through narrow cracks in the rocks. Some experts report that Green Salamanders have been found within crevices in the bark of trees. One well-known biologist from the University of Kentucky (the late Dr. Roger Barbour) suggested that the now extinct American Chestnut tree with its deeply furrowed bark may have once been an important habitat for the species. Few Kentuckians will ever see this secretive little salamander.	**Natural History:** The members of this genus (*Eurycea*) are often called "Brook Salamanders," in reference to their propensity to inhabit small, clear streams. Other habitats are also utilized and the Southern Two-lined Salamander is often found in swamps or bottomland woodlands in the vicinity of seeps. Springs and seeps that emerge from ridges and upland areas that border bottomlands and swamps are good places to find this small and secretive salamander. Brook Salamanders differ from their family relatives the Woodland Salamanders (genus *Plethodon*) in that they have a strong affinity to aquatic stream habitats as adults. They are also different in another important respect: Brook Salamanders must undergo an aquatic larval stage in their life cycle while Woodland Salamanders hatch into fully formed, tiny replicas of the adults.

Class—**Amphibia** (amphibians)

Order—**Caudata** (salamanders)

Family—**Plethodontidae** (lungless salamanders)

Long-tailed Salamander *Eurycea longicauda*	Three-lined Salamander *Eurycea guttolineata*	Cave Salamander *Eurycea lucifuga*

Presumed range in Kentucky 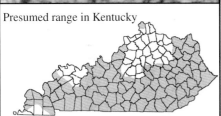	Presumed range in Kentucky 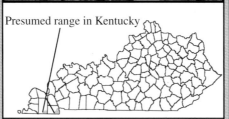	Presumed range in Kentucky 
Size: Record length 7.75 inches.	**Size:** Record 8 inches. Average 4 to 6.	**Size:** Record 7.125 inches.
Abundance: Fairly common.	**Abundance:** Uncommon in Kentucky.	**Abundance:** Fairly common.
Variation: Ground color varies from yellow to orange. Another subspecies occurs west of the Mississippi River. The Kentucky race is *E. l. longicauda*.	**Variation:** No significant variation. This species was once regarded as a subspecies of the Long-tailed Salamander.	**Variation:** Varies somewhat in the amount of dark spots on the dorsum. Ground color varies from bright red to reddish brown or orange.
Habitat: Spring runs, small clear creeks, in the vicinity of seeps, and near cave openings.	**Habitat:** A lowland species. Swamps, marshes, and wet bottomlands. Especially near springs or seeps.	**Habitat:** Although frequently found in caves, this salamander also lives in upland woods beneath rocks, logs, etc.
Breeding: Breeds in late winter or early spring. Eggs are deposited in streams and springs or often in caves. Larva metamorphose in about a year.	**Breeding:** Breeds from fall through late winter. Lays eggs in hidden areas in aquatic habitats like springs and seeps. Larva transform in a few months.	**Breeding:** Several dozen eggs are attached to the underneath side of rocks underwater in springs or waterways both inside and outside of caves.
Natural History: These salamanders can often be found beneath rocks within small clear streams. They also live in mesic woodland environments, usually in the vicinity of a permanent stream. Here they may be found hiding beneath or within rotted logs or stumps. On rainy nights they can be encountered on roads as they roam around in search of tiny invertebrate prey. Although they can reach an impressive length they are a slim-bodied animal and over half their length is tail. These are animals of the Appalachian Plateau and Interior Low Plateau provinces and they are replaced in the lowlands of the Coastal Plain by the very similar Three-lined Salamander. Autotomy (breaking off of the tail) is a common defense.	**Natural History:** Similar to the Three-lined Salamander and probably ecologically synonymous with that species within the Coastal Plain provinces. For all practical purposes the Three-lined Salamander might be regarded as a southern, lowland form of the Long-tailed salamander. In fact, until recently the two were considered to be two races of the same species. Morphologically the two are very similar in every respect except for the pattern of dark pigments in the skin. A lack of interbreeding between the two where their ranges meet supports their designation as two distinct species. This is a southern species that barely ranges into Kentucky in the southern portions of the Coastal Plain Province.	**Natural History:** The distribution of this species is restricted to regions with predominantly limestone substrates. They are thus absent from many areas of Kentucky, including all of the Coastal Plain. Adults of this species have prehensile tails and they are good climbers. They are sometimes seen clinging to the walls of caves. Despite their name these salamanders are not true troglodytes (cave dwellers). They inhabit mostly the twilight zone of caves as well as more typical terrestrial habitats in mesic upland woods. They can be found beneath rocks, logs, etc., and can be common near springs and seeps in upland areas. Like other salamanders on this page, the tail may break off if grasped.

Class—**Amphibia** (amphibians)

Order—**Caudata** (salamanders)

Family—**Plethodontidae** (lungless salamanders)

Spring Salamander *Gyrinophilus porphyriticus*	**Red Salamander** *Pseudotriton ruber*	**Mud Salamander** *Pseudotriton montanus*

 Presumed range in Kentucky	 Presumed range in Kentucky	 Presumed range in Kentucky
Size: Up to 9 inches.	**Size:** Average 4 to 6 inches. Max 7.125.	**Size:** Average 4 to 6 inches. Max 8.
Abundance: Fairly common.	**Abundance:** Common.	**Abundance:** Fairly common.
Variation: Dorsal ground color varies from pinkish or light red to reddish brown or purplish. Older individuals tend to be the darkest. Four subspecies.	**Variation:** Adults tend to darken with age, a condition known as "ontogenetic melanism." There are four subspecies in the southeastern U.S. One in KY.	**Variation:** There are four subspecies found across the eastern U.S. Only one, the Midland Mud Salamander (*P. m. diasticus*) is found in Kentucky.
Habitat: Springs, seeps, and spring-fed streams as well as caves. Also on the forest floor near water. Range includes the entire Appalachian Plateau.	**Habitat:** Found within and in the vicinity of springs and spring-fed brooks. Found both in the water and under moss, logs, etc., in the vicinity of water.	**Habitat:** Mud. Wet, mucky areas in close proximity to seeps and spring runs. Also found beneath leaf litter an accumulated detritus within streams.
Breeding: Eggs are laid in water (stream or spring) during summer and hatch in the fall. The aquatic larval stage can be exceedingly long, lasting on average four to five years. Rarely up to 10 years in cave dwelling populations.	**Breeding:** Several dozen eggs are laid in the water in spring fed streams during late summer/fall. Females will guard the eggs until they hatch in the winter. Totally aquatic larva can take 1.5 to 3 years to transform into adults.	**Breeding:** Eggs are laid in fall and winter in spring runs or bogs. About one to two dozen eggs are laid. Larva are less than 0.75 inch at hatching. They reach a up to 3 inches before transforming into adults after 1.5 to 2.5 years.
Natural History: This is one of the more diurnal salamander species, and adults have been observed prowling on the forest floor during daylight hours. In some areas of their range they are reportedly very common in cave habitats. These are large salamanders and they are fierce predators of a wide variety of small animal life, including other salamanders. There are four very similar subspecies, two of which range into Kentucky. They are the Northern Spring Salamander (*G. p. porphyriticus*) and the Kentucky Spring Salamander (*G. p. duryi*). Pictured above is the Kentucky Spring Salamander.	**Natural History:** Adult Red Salamanders will wander away from water and may be found in moist environments a good distance from springs or streams. Young adults are bright, fire-engine red with scattered black specks throughout the body. As they age they tend to become darker on the back and very old individuals may be uniformly dark gray or deep purple dorsally. These salamanders are easily observed on rural roads in the southern Appalachians on rainy nights in early spring. There are four subspecies. The northern subspecies (*P. r. ruber*) occurs in most of Kentucky. *P. r. viosca* may occur in the Coastal Plain.	**Natural History:** In both appearance and life history the Mud Salamanders are similar to the Red Salamanders. The easiest way to distinguish between the two is to note the size and concentration of the black spots. Mud Salamanders have larger, more widely spaced spots and the spots are more perfectly rounded, resulting in something akin to a polka-dot pattern. Most experts agree that Mud Salamanders are more closely tied to water than the similar Red Salamander. They are also are more secretive and less commonly seen than the more terrestrially oriented Red Salamander.

| Class—**Amphibia** (amphibians) |
| Order—**Caudata** (salamanders) |
| Family—**Plethodontidae** (lungless salamanders) |
| **Four-toed Salamander**—*Hemidactylium scutatum* |

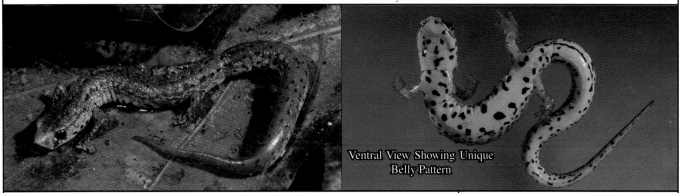

Ventral View Showing Unique Belly Pattern

Size: Average 2–3 inches. Record 4.

Abundance: Uncommon in most of Kentucky.

Variation: Dorsal ground color varies from light or dark brown to gray or orange. Most specimens have dark speckling on the dorsum but that can vary.

Habitat: Terrestrial but usually near woodland bogs, springs, and seeps, or small woodland ponds, or other mesic situations.

Presumed range in Kentucky

Breeding: Eggs are laid in winter at the edge of streams, ponds, etc. Females remain with the eggs until hatching in about four weeks. Aquatic larva stage is short, only two to three months.

Natural History: The name comes from the fact that they have only four toes on the hind foot (other terrestrial salamanders in Kentucky have five). There is also an obvious constriction at the base of the tail that is unique to this species. The most readily identifiable characteristic of this species, however, is its white belly with black spots. No other salamander in Kentucky is similarly colored and patterned. Like many amphibians this species is threatened by habitat destruction and may be declining in Kentucky. The disappearance of vernal pools, bogs, and streamside habitat to agriculture and development is probably the most significant threat. Although found in scattered, disjunct populations throughout the southeastern U.S., this salamander is mainly a northern species. Its range occupies a large swath of the northeastern U.S. as well as parts of upper Midwest. Its range in these northern regions is mostly contiguous. In Kentucky its range is disjunct.

| Family—**Proteidae** (muduppys, waterdogs) |
| **Mudpuppy** |
| *Necturus maculosus* |

Presumed range in Kentucky

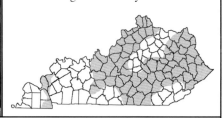

Size: Average 12 inches. Record 19.5 inches.

Abundance: Uncommon in most of Kentucky but can be locally common.

Variation: None in Kentucky or the Midwest. Another distinct species is found in the southern Ozarks and Quachita Mountains.

Breeding: Breeding and egg laying occurs in the fall. Female Mudpuppys hollow out a nest beneath a sunken log or rock where they will lay from a few score to over 100 eggs. The eggs are attached to the underside of a rock or log where the nest has been excavated. The female remains with eggs during incubation.

Natural History: Mudpuppys have extensive external gills that resemble downy feathers. Some think the gills are reminiscent of the ears of a dog, thus the name "Mudpuppy." These are totally aquatic salamanders that never lose the gills of the larva. This condition of permanent larval characteristics is known scientifically as "neotony" and is a phenomenon on that is not rare in salamanders of several species. Mudpuppys prey on fish eggs, insects, mollusks, small crustaceans, and annelids.

Class—**Amphibia** (amphibians)
Order—**Caudata** (salamanders)
Family—**Amphiumidae** (amphiumas)
Three-toed Amphiuma—*Amphiuma tridactylum*

 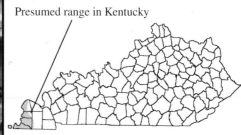

Presumed range in Kentucky

Size: Average about 2 to 3 feet. Record length is 42 inches, making this the longest salamander in Kentucky.

Abundance: Uncommon in Kentucky. More common in the deep south where wetland habitat is more predominant.

Variation: No variation. There is only a single species of this unique salamander with no subspecies.

Habitat: Swamps, oxbows, flooded roadside ditches, and ponds in low, swampy regions.

Breeding: Slithers onto land at night to lay eggs above the waterline. Fall rains inudate the eggs and stimulate development. There is a larval stage that has external gills.

Natural History: This is a large, eel-like salamander that is often mistaken for an eel. In fact, it often goes by the name "Congo Eel" in parts of the deep south (especially in Louisiana). Anglers occasionally catch them when fishing with worms. Close examination of these salamanders will reveal the presence of tiny, vestigial limbs, which of course are lacking on eels. Amphiumas are totally aquatic in habits but have lungs for breathing air and they can survive out of water as long as their is enough moisture to prevent dessication. During droughts they can aestivate in chambers hollowed out in the mud or within crayfish burrows. This species' range in Kentucky is limited to the Mississippi Alluvial Plain and the adjacent lowlands and creeks that drain directly into that region. They feed on earthworms, small fish, snails, insects, and crayfish. In Louisiana they often end up in crayfish traps where they will stuff themselves with those crustaceans. The legs of the Amphiuma are vestigial and so small that they are easily overlooked. There are three tiny toes on the legs, hence the name "Three-toed Amphiuma."

Family—**Sirenidae** (sirens)
Lesser Siren—*Siren intermedia*

 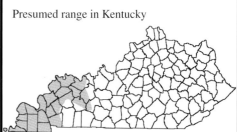

Presumed range in Kentucky

Size: Average 12 to 16 inches. Can reach a maximum length of up to 20 inches.

Abundance: Uncommon in Kentucky. More common farther to south in the lower coastal plain where swamps are common.

Variation: No variation in Kentucky. There are two subspecies. The Western subspecies (*nettingi*) is native to Kentucky.

Habitat: Wetlands. Swamps, marshes, oxbows, sloughs, slow-moving streams and low lying areas along stream courses.

Breeding: Lays several hundred eggs in a nest hollowed out in the mud. Probably breeds in late winter or early spring.

Natural History: Another completely aquatic salamander that breathes through external gills that are easily visible just in front of the forelimbs. Known food items include insects, crustaceans, mollusks, and worms, as well as some plant material such as algea. Capable of surviving drought periods by secreting slime that hardens into a cocoon-like structure, creating a sealed chamber in the mud. Like many wetland species the Lesser Siren has been negatively impacted by the conversion of wetlands to agricultural land. Both the Lesser Siren and the Amphiuma (above) are preyed upon by the Mud Snake (page 156), a snake species that specializes in feeding on aquatic salamanders. Sirens have elongated bodies with very small front legs and lack hind limbs completely. They are often mistaken for eels, but the feathery external gills of the sirens are diagnostic (eels are fish and have internal gills). This is one of the few salamanders that is capable of vocalization. They are reported to communicate with each other using clicking sounds, and when captured they sometimes emit a yelping sound.

Class—**Amphibia** (amphibians)
Order—**Caudata** (salamanders)
Family—**Cryptobranchidae** (giant salamanders)
Hellbender—*Cryptobranchus allegheniensis*

Size: Up to 30 inches in length and very heavy bodied.

Abundance: Rare. Populations throughout its range are in decline.

Variation: Some variation in ground color. Reddish, brown, tan, or chocolate. A very similar but distinct species occurs in the Ozarks region.

Habitat: Clear pure streams. Once found throughout the Appalachians and much of the Interior Plateau. Populations now restricted to remote, unpolluted streams. Large underwater rocks are used as a refuge.

Presumed range in Kentucky

Breeding: Fertilization is external and eggs are laid in a nest guarded by the male. Lays over 400 eggs.

Natural History: These huge, totally aquatic salamanders have deep folds and wrinkles in the skin. They have very large, dorsoventrally flattened heads and laterally flattened, fin-like tails. They are completely aquatic and feed on crustaceans, minnows, and invertebrates with crayfish reported as a primary prey. They require clean, unpolluted flowing waters and they are in decline throughout their range due to stream degradation, impoundments, and chemical pollutants. This is one of America's largest salamander species, but it is dwarfed by its larger relative from Japan. The world's largest salamander, the Pacific Giant Salamander, is native to pristine streams in the mountains of Japan, where it can reach five feet in length. The range map above may not be an accurate depiction of the Hellbender's range in the state today. Many streams throughout Kentucky lack their original water quality and can no longer support this bizarre and interesting creature.

CHAPTER 8
THE RIVERS AND STREAMS OF KENTUCKY

As a preface to the next chapter (Chapter 9: The Fishes of Kentucky), this short chapter is intended to provide a brief introduction into the waterways of Kentucky, which are home to the state's fish species. Many people are surprised to learn that the state of Kentucky boasts more miles of rivers and streams (over 89,000 miles) than any state other than Alaska.

With so many miles of waterways, it is not surprising that Kentucky is also home to more fish species than most other regions of the country. The number of native fish species that can be found in Kentucky waters numbers 248 (plus 19 introduced species), making the fishes the second most diverse group of vertebrates in the state. Kentucky's immediate neighbor to south, Tennessee, boasts over 300 fish species, the most of any state in the union. Both states owe their high variety of fishes to their geography. In Kentucky the Appalachian Plateau rises to an elevation of 4,139 feet on Big Black Mountain in the east, while the lowest elevation occurs on the opposite end of the state at 257 feet on the Mississippi River in Fulton County. This elevation variance coupled with ample rainfall has resulted in the state becoming highly dissected with drainages. Figure 14 below shows how completely the state of Kentucky is partitioned by waterways.

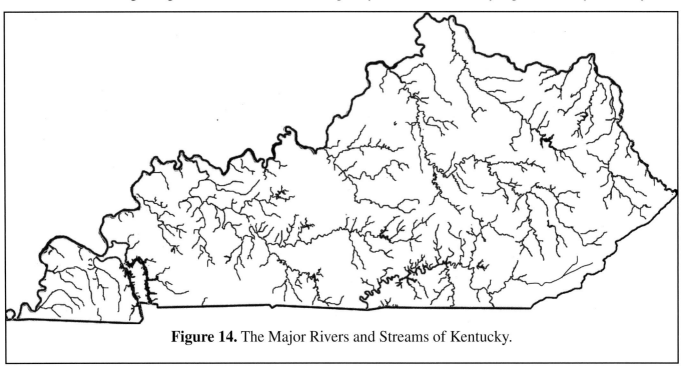

Figure 14. The Major Rivers and Streams of Kentucky.

Kentucky ranks third nationwide for number of fish species (267). In comparison with other nearby states, Kentucky is quite high in fish diversity. Our neighbor to the west, Missouri, has just under 200 fish species. Illinois has about the same number while Ohio has 176 and West Virginia 178. It is not just the many miles of rivers and streams that makes Kentucky's fish fauna so varied. Equally important (perhaps more so) are the different ecoregions and habitats within the state. The aquatic environments available to Kentucky fishes are quite variable. Clear, cool mountain streams with fast-moving water are present in the mountains and plateaus of the east; while warm, sluggish streams and quiet oxbows and swamps occur in the lowlands and plains in the western end of the state.

Counting the Ohio and the Mississippi, the state is drained by 11 major river systems. Kentucky's elevation variance is from east to west, but most of the rivers and streams of Kentucky ultimately turn northward and drain into the east-west flowing Ohio River. In fact *all* of the state's waterways except for a few smaller creeks in the Gulf Coastal Plain discharge into the Ohio. Figure 17 on page 191 shows the drainages of the state and what regions of the state are drained by each of the states 11 major river systems. Additional maps show the larger drainage systems of North American and where Kentucky fits within those drainages. Figure 15 on the next page shows the largest drainage system that affects Kentucky, the Mississippi River Basin. Figure 16 shows the next largest drainage system affecting Kentucky, the Ohio River Basin. The afore mentioned Figure 17 shows the 11 major river basins that affect Kentucky, and finally Figure 18 shows even smaller watershed regions within each of the state's 11 major river basins. Some appreciation of these drainage basins (or watersheds) can provide insight into the distribution of Kentucky's fish species. More importantly, conservation organizations can monitor these various watersheds for pollution and other factors that may impact upon the health of fish populations contained within them.

Although Kentucky still boasts an abundance of fish species, a few species no longer exist in the state, and a total of 58 more are now regarded as endangered, threatened, or species of concern. Like all other habitat types within the eastern United States, the waterways of Kentucky have been highly altered by man. There are 17 major impoundments on Kentucky's larger river systems, representing nearly 20 percent of the state's original stream courses. Countless smaller dams have inundated portions of many small creeks. Direct pollution from industry and coal mining is an important source of stream degradation in the state. But of equal importance is indirect contamination from agriculture. Agricultural related pollution and stream degradation can come in the form of chemical runoff or the destruction of vegetated buffer zones by farmers needing to maximize the production area of their land. Erosion and siltation from row cropping operations impact nearly every stream in the western two-thirds of the state. To a lesser extent, livestock operations statewide can also have negative impacts as cattle destroy creek banks and stir up silt from stream bottoms. Today at least 35 percent of the state's streams do not meet the state's water quality standards and over half of the state's waters are regarded as inadvisable for swimming.

Add to these problems the presence of over 3 million people and you have a significant threat to our fresh waters. All Kentuckians use prodigious amounts of water and collectively we produce many of tons of sewage and waste water, some of which in rural areas may wind up entering Kentucky's waterways. Today over two thirds of Kentucky's waterways are regarded as being at moderate to very high risk of habitat degradation.

Many of our rivers and streams no longer support the high diversity of fish and other aquatic species that once were abundant within their banks, and the future for many of Kentucky's fish species is, frankly, quite grim. If we regard this fact as a warning sign relating to the health of our aquatic ecosystems, and surely they are just that, then all Kentuckians should be acutely concerned about the future of our waterways. We often hear reasonable people argue against stringent protections of Kentucky's environment. But few things are more important than these protections. Humans can survive for a maximum of four minutes without air and maximum of four days without water. It follows then that our paramount priorities should be to insure that we all always have clean air to breathe and pure water to drink!

The next series of maps shown on the following two pages gives a good representation of how smaller streams and their watersheds are integrated into larger streams and larger watersheds. What also becomes apparent from these maps is that when it comes water, everything (and everyone) downstream is affected by the quality of the water and the overall environmental health of the waters upstream. The environmental quality of that tiny creek in your backyard or on your farm affects not only the life of organisms living within that stream, but also organisms within the larger streams into which it flows. And ultimately, the wildlife living in Louisiana's coastal marshes, the fishes living in the depths of the Gulf of Mexico, and the magnificent coral ecosystems of the great reefs of the Caribbean.

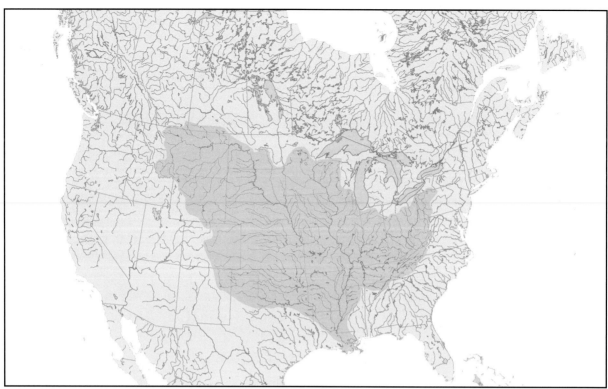

Figure 15.

The map above shows the major rivers and lakes of North America. The region drained by the Mississippi River Basin is shaded in gray. Note that this drainage basin includes the entire state of Kentucky.

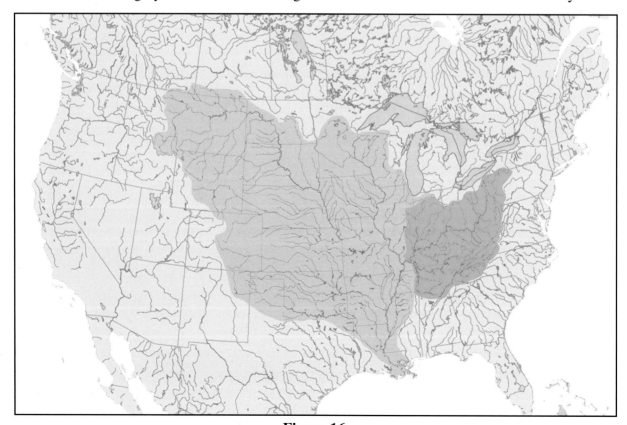

Figure 16.

The Mississippi River Basin can be divided into several smaller drainages. One of these smaller drainages is the Ohio River Basin. The area of the Mississippi River Basin drained by the Ohio River Basin is shown in orange. Note that the Ohio River drainage basin includes all but the western tip of Kentucky. The two maps shown above are derived from maps created by the Commission for Environmental Cooperation.

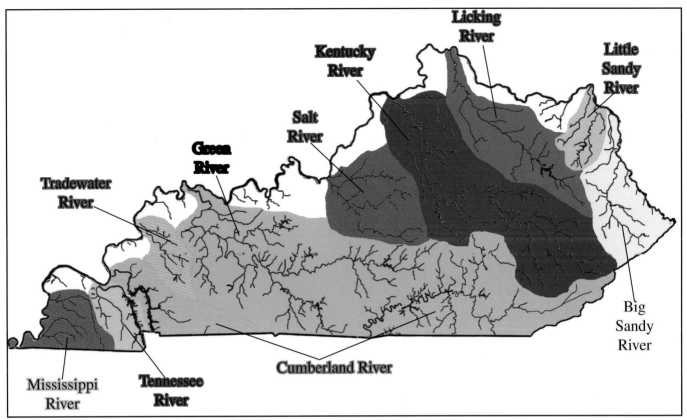

Figure 17.

The map above shows the 11 major river basin drainage systems in Kentucky. Note that except for the brown shaded area in the westernmost tip of the state (which drains directly into the Mississippi), all other streams in Kentucky flow to the Ohio River. White areas are regions drained directly into the Ohio River by small creeks. Both maps shown on this page are derived from originals created by the Division of Water, Kentucky Department of Environmental Protection.

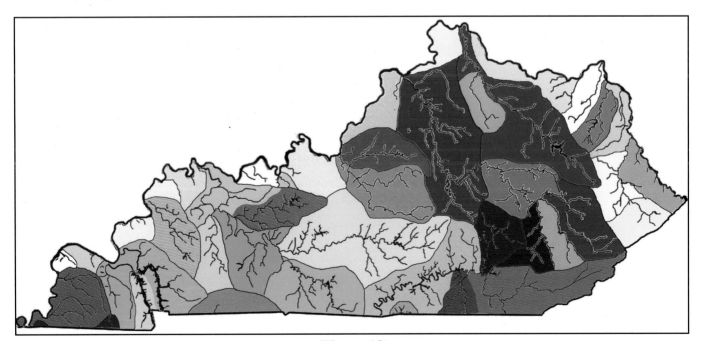

Figure 18.

Map above shows how the 11 major river basin drainages of Kentucky are further divided into smaller watersheds. Areas in white and off-white on the northern border are watersheds that drain directly into the Ohio.

CHAPTER 9
THE FISHES OF KENTUCKY

Table 10
The Orders and Families of Kentucky Fishes.

Class—**Actinopterygii** (ray-finned fishes)

Order—**Perciformes** (typical fishes)

Family	**Centrarchidae** (sunfishes)
Family	**Moronidae** (true basses)
Family	**Elassomatidae** (pygmy sunfishes)
Family	**Scianidae** (drums)
Family	**Percidae** (perches, darters)

Order—**Salmoniformes**

Family	**Esocidae** (pikes)
Family	**Umbridae** (mudminnows)
Family	**Salmonidae** (trouts)

Order—**Amiiformes** (bowfin)

Family	**Amiidae** (bowfin)

Order—**Gadiformes**

Family	**Gadidae** (codfish)

Order—**Clupeiformes** (sardines, herrings, shads)

Family	**Clupeidae** (herring, shad)

Order—Siluriformes (catfishes)

Family	**Ictaluridae** (American catfishes)

Order—**Acipenseriformes** (primitive fishes)

Family	**Acipenseridae** (sturgeons)
Family	**Polyodontidae** (paddlefish)

Order—**Lepisosteiformes** (gar)

Family	**Lepisosteidae** (gars)

Order—**Cypriniformes** (minnows, suckers)

Family	**Catostomidae** (suckers)
Family	**Cyprinidae** (minnows)

Order—**Cyprinodontiformes** (topminnows, livebearers)

Family	**Fundulidae** (topminnows)
Family	**Poeciliidae** (livebearers)

Order—**Atheriniformes**

Family	**Atherinidae** (silversides)

Order—**Osteoglossiformes** (bonytongues)

Family	**Hiodontidae** (mooneyes)

Order—**Anguilliformes** (eels)

Family	**Anguillidae** (freshwater eels)

Order—**Scorpaeniformes**

Family	**Cottidae** (sculpins)

Order—**Percopsiformes** (pirate perch, cavefish)

Family	**Aphredoderidae** (pirate perch)
Family	**Amblyopsidae** (cavefishes)
Family	**Percopsidae** (trout perch)

Class—**Actinopterygii** (bony fishes)		

Order—**Perciformes** (typical fishes)		

Family—**Centrarchidae** (sunfishes)		

Largemouth Bass *Micropterus salmoides*	**Smallmouth Bass** *Micropterus dolomieu*	**Spotted Bass** *Micropterus punctulatus*

 Presumed range in Kentucky	 Presumed range in Kentucky	 Presumed range in Kentucky
Size: May reach 38 inches and 22 lbs.	**Size:** Maximum of 12 lbs.	**Size:** Average adult is about 3 to 4 lbs.
Natural History: This is probably America's most popular freshwater game fish, pursued by anglers throughout the country. Found in virtually any large body of water in the state. Also in smaller streams and small farm ponds. Produced in captivity for stocking. Specimens in excess of 12 pounds are rare in Kentucky.	**Natural History:** Prefers clearer, cooler, more highly oxygenated waters than the Largemouth Bass. Crayfish are a preferred prey, especially for stream dwelling Smallmouth Bass. Like its cousin the Largemouth Bass, this is an important game species. It is renowned among sport fishermen for its tenacious fighting abilities when hooked.	**Natural History:** Intermediate between the two previous species in both the size of the mouth and in its habitat preferences. Primarily a fish of flowing waters but can tolerate warmer conditions than the Smallmouth. Avoids the still waters favored by the Largemouth. Tongue feels rough to the touch, smooth on the other two *Micropterus* bass.
Redeye Bass *Micropterus coosae*	**Spotted Sunfish** *Lepomis minuatus*	**Warmouth** *Lepomis gulosus*

 Presumed range in Kentucky	 Presumed range in Kentucky	 Presumed range in Kentucky
Size: Up to 14 inches and 2.25 lbs.	**Size:** Maximum of 8 inches.	**Size:** Up to 12 inches.
Natural History: Also called the "Coosa Bass." This small member of the Black Bass group (genus *Micropterus*) is a fish of mountain streams. It is native to the Appalachian regions of Georgia, Alabama, and southeastern Tennessee. It has been introduced the upper Cumberland River in Kentucky. The Kentucky record size is 1.21 lbs.	**Natural History:** The Spotted Sunfish is mostly a fish of the southern lowlands where it inhabits swamps and slow-moving streams. In Kentucky its range is restricted to the western end of the state. In Kentucky 80 percent of the original swampland habitat has been converted to agricultural land, thus this is now a threatened species in our state.	**Natural History:** A fish of lowland creeks and swamps, the Warmouth is most common in the western end of the state and is increasingly scarce farther to the east. Warmouths prefer waters with thick growths of aquatic plants. The name comes from a patch of teeth that are present on the tongue. Kentucky record size is 1 lb. 6 oz.

Class—**Actinopterygii** (bony fishes)

Order—**Perciformes** (typical fishes)

Family—**Centrarchidae** (sunfishes)

Redear Sunfish *Lepomis microlophus*	**Pumkinseed** *Lepomis gibbosus*	**Green Sunfish** *Lepomis cyanellus*

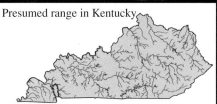
Presumed range in Kentucky

Presumed range in Kentucky

Presumed range in Kentucky

Size: Record 4 lbs 3 oz.

Size: Average about 5 inches.

Size: 6 to 8 inches, maximum 12.

Natural History: These fish also go by the name "Shellcracker," a reference to their habit of eating small freshwater mollusks such clams and snails. The natural distribution of this fish was originally the southeastern United States, including westernmost Kentucky. Today it has been widely introduced throughout most of the rest of the state.

Natural History: Found mainly in the northern United States and along the eastern seaboard. Inhabits still or slow-moving waters. Snails and bivalves are a major food source. In this sense the Pumpkinseed is similar to the Redear Sunfish. It also resembles the Redear Sunfish and could be considered the northern counterpart of that species.

Natural History: This is a fairly common fish throughout the state. It may be found in ponds and lakes, but its natural habitat is quiet pools or slow-moving streams. It is known to hybridize readily with other *Lepomis* sunfishes, especially the Bluegill. Tolerates warm, low oxygen, muddy waters better than most other sunfishes.

Bluegill *Lepomis macrochirus*	**Longear Sunfish** *Lepomis megalotis*	**Dollar Sunfish** *Lepomis marginatus*

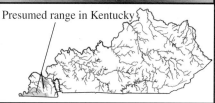

Presumed range in Kentucky

Presumed range in Kentucky

Presumed range in Kentucky

Size: Record of 4 lbs., 12 oz.

Size: Record 1 4 lbs., 12 oz.

Size: Maximum of about 5 inches.

Natural History: The Bluegill is Kentucky's best known sunfish. It is an important game fish throughout the state. They are regularly stocked in new impoundments and are found in virtually every significant body of water in Kentucky, including most farm ponds. Typical adult is about 10 inches and weighs about 13 ounces.

Natural History: Breeding male Longears are one of the most brilliantly colored of the sunfishes. Clear streams with gravelly or sandy substrates are the primary habitat, but they may also be found in impoundments. The name comes from the exceptionally long opercle flap. This species shows a considerable amount of geographic variation.

Natural History: Mostly a fish of the lower coastal plain, the Dollar Sunfish reaches in northernmost distribution in the western tip of Kentucky. It inhabits pristine waters in swamps and unpolluted streams in the Coastal Plain region of Kentucky. Unfortunately for this interesting little sunfish, pristine waters are increasingly rare in our state.

Class—**Actinopterygii** (bony fishes)

Order—**Perciformes** (typical fishes)

Family—**Centrarchidae** (sunfishes)

Redbreast Sunfish *Lepomis auritus*	**Bantam Sunfish** *Lepomis symmetricus*	**Orange-spotted Sunfish** *Lepomis humilis*

Presumed range in Kentucky

Size: Record 2 lbs.

Size: Maximum of 3.75 inches.

Size: Maximum of about 4 inches.

Natural History: The natural range of the Redbreast Sunfish is the Atlantic Slope from Maine to Florida. Today this species has been widely introduced into much of Kentucky. This is a popular game fish along the eastern seaboard where it is quite common.

Natural History: The smallest of Kentucky's *Lepomis* sunfishes, the Bantam Sunfish is an inhabitant of the lowlands of the Mississippi Valley and the Western Gulf Coastal Plain. Swamps with clean, clear water and ample aquatic vegetation are the favored habitats.

Natural History: Inhabits creeks and rivers where it favors quiet water pools with cover in the form of brush. When it occurs in lakes and impoundments it is found in shallow bays. Nests in gravel. Eats mainly small aquatic insect larva and small crustaceans.

Rock Bass *Ambloplites rupestris*	**Flier** *Centrarchus macropterus*	**White Croppie / Black Croppie** *Pomoxis annularis / Pomoxis nigromaculatus*

White Croppie

Presumed range in Kentucky

Presumed range in Kentucky (both species)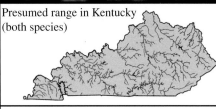

Size: Record size 3 lbs.

Size: Averages about 5 inches. Max 8.

Size: Max for White 5 lbs., Black 6 lbs.

Natural History: Also known as the "Goggle Eye," the Rock Bass is a fish of clear, cool waters. In Kentucky they are primarily a stream fish that is found in clear streams with good water quality throughout the state east of the Coastal Plain. The natural distribution is from the Great Lakes region south into northern Alabama, but it avoids the lowlands of the Coastal Plain.

Natural History: The Flier is a lowland species that is usually found in natural lakes, oxbows, swamps, or sluggish streams. Most often occurs in waters with mud bottom. In Kentucky this species is most common in the swamps of the Mississippi and lower Ohio River valleys. Draining and dredging of wetlands for agriculture has been a threat in Kentucky.

Natural History: The Black Croppie likes clearer waters than the White Croppie, though both are often found in the same waters. Popular game fishes, both species have been widely introduced across America. White Croppie is usually much lighter, but not always. Positive ID can be made by counting the stiff spines on the dorsal fin. White Croppie has only six, Black has seven or eight.

Class—**Actinopterygii** (bony fishes)

Order—**Perciformes** (typical fishes)

Family—**Moronidae** (true basses)

Yellow Bass *Morone mississippiensis*	**White Bass** *Morone chrysops*	**Striped Bass** *Morone saxatilis*

Presumed range in Kentucky	Presumed range in Kentucky	Presumed range in Kentucky

Size: Record 2 lbs., 4 oz.	**Size:** World record 5 lbs., 9 oz.	**Size:** World record 78.5 lbs.
Natural History: A clear-water fish, the Yellow Bass avoids muddy rivers and streams in favor of lakes, oxbows, and other still waters. Natural lakes with abundant vegetation are its main habitat but it has adapted well to man-made lakes. It is widespread in the Ohio river along the northern border of KY.	**Natural History:** These important game fish are famous for forcing schools of bait fish to the surface then attacking them in a feeding frenzy. Bait fish leaping from the water create a visible indicator of the presence of feeding bass. Savvy fishermen look for these eruptions of bait fish known as "jumps."	**Natural History:** Striped Bass were originally anadromous fish that lived in salt water but migrated into freshwater rivers to spawn. Now widely stocked in lakes by wildlife agencies, they have adapted to a freshwater existence. Hybrids between the Striped and the White Bass are known as "Rockfish."

Family—**Elassomatidae** (pygmy sunfishes)

Family—**Sciaenidae** (drums)

Banded Pygmy Sunfish *Elasoma zonatum*	**Freshwater Drum** *Aplodinotus grunniens*

Male / Female images	Freshwater Drum image

Presumed range in Kentucky	Presumed range in Kentucky

Size: Maximum 1.75 inches.	**Size:** Record size 54 lbs.
Natural History: These tiny, secretive fishes are unknown to most Kentuckians. They are widespread throughout the Coastal Plain from Texas to North Carolina where they live in swamps, oxbows, and slow-moving streams. In Kentucky they are restricted to the western end of the state. Here they are most common in the oxbows and swamps along the Mississippi River. They are actually quite common in Reelfoot Lake where it extends into Kentucky in soutwestern Hickman County. Unlike many larger fish species, the Banded Pygmy Sunfish exhibits sexual dimorphism (see photos above).	**Natural History:** This is the only member of the drum family that lives in fresh- water. Most are salt water fishes and several are important food and sport fishes. By contrast the Freshwater Drum is not highly regarded by sport anglers despite the fact that they obtain an impressive size.

Class—**Actinopterygii** (bony fishes)
Order—**Perciformes** (typical fishes)
Family—**Percidae** (perch, darters)

Yellow Perch *Perca flavescens*	Walleye *Sander vitreus*	Sauger *Sander canadensis*

Presumed range in Kentucky 	Presumed range in Kentucky	Presumed range in Kentucky 
Size: Record 4 pounds 3 ounces.	**Size:** World record is 25 pounds.	**Size:** Record 8 pounds 12 ounces.
Natural History: Native to the northern and eastern United States, Yellow Perch are relative newcomers to Kentucky. They began invading Kentucky waters in the 1980s and are now found in the Ohio, Mississippi, Cumberland, Tennessee, and Big Sandy rivers. They are a popular pan fish in the north.	**Natural History:** Walleye in Kentucky live in larger rivers and impoundments where deep water provides the cool temperatures these fish require. They are regarded as one of the most palatable of the game fishes, but they are much less common in Kentucky than in their core range farther to the north.	**Natural History:** Found throughout the Midwest and northward to Canada, the Sauger is a smaller relative of the Walleye that is more adapted to turbid waters. Hybridization between the Walleye and the Sauger results in a fish known as the "Saugeye," which can attain a much larger size than the Sauger.

The Sand Darters—genus *Ammocrypta* (2 species in Kentucky, 1 shown)

Eastern Sand Darter

Eastern Sand Darter *Ammocrypta pellucida*	Western Sand Darter *Ammocrypta clara*
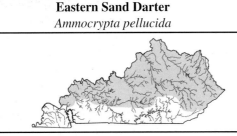	

Size: Eastern Sand Darter can reach 3.25 inches. Western is smaller at 2.75 inches.

Natural History: The aptly named Sand Darters are associated with sandy substrates of medium to large streams. When not swimming about in search of food or a mate they stay buried in the sand except for the top of head. Their translucent colored bodies render them effectively invisible under these conditions. Western Sand Darter is endangered. A third species known as the Crystal Darter is probably extirpated from Kentucky. These unsual little fish are virtually unknown to most Kentuckians.

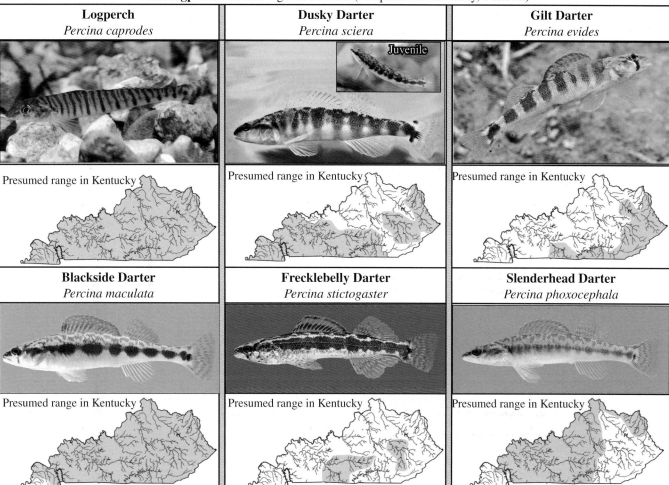

Class—**Actinopterygii** (bony fishes)

Order—**Perciformes** (typical fishes)

Family—**Percidae** (perch, darters)

The Logperch Darters—genus *Percina* (12 species in Kentucky, 6 shown)

Logperch	Dusky Darter	Gilt Darter
Percina caprodes	*Percina sciera*	*Percina evides*
Presumed range in Kentucky	Presumed range in Kentucky	Presumed range in Kentucky

Blackside Darter	Frecklebelly Darter	Slenderhead Darter
Percina maculata	*Percina stictogaster*	*Percina phoxocephala*
Presumed range in Kentucky	Presumed range in Kentucky	Presumed range in Kentucky

Size: Range in size from 6.5 inches (Logperch) to as small as 2.33 inches (Channel Darter). Most are between 3 to 4 inches.

Natural History: The darters of the genus *Percina* are represented by a total of 12 species in Kentucky and as many as 40 species ranging throughout much of the eastern United States. All *Percina* species occur east of the Rocky Mountains and most are found east of the Great Plains. The infamous Snail Darter, which was the subject of a great environmental controversy that arose over the construction of the Tellico Dam in Tennesse, is a member of this genus. Most of these fishes tend to inhabit the larger creeks (or even rivers), but some can be found in small (even tiny) creeks. A few species have adapted to lake life in reservoirs that have inudated their former riverine habitats, but all must return to streams to lay their eggs in flowing waters. Their habitats range from deep pools to shallow riffle areas, and all species spawn in the shallow gravel riffles of small or medium size creeks. The dependance upon clean, unaltered streams for breeding means these fishes face serious threats in Kentucky. Two species of *Percina* darters are endangered in the state (Longhead Darter—*P. macrocephala* and Olive Darter—*P. squamata*) and a third (Blotchside Logperch—*P. butoni*) is now possibly extirpated. Along with their smaller relatives the *Etheostoma* darters (next several pages) they are some of Kentucky's most interesting and colorful fishes. Both groups have become popular with aquarists, and in fact the darters have helped usher in a new style of fish keeping that focuses on native freshwater fishes of North America. Many aquarists, once introduced to the darters, will abandon the keeping of exotic tropical fishes for these beautiful "home grown" aquarium fishes. The diet of these fishes consists mostly of tiny aquatic insects and their larva, which makes keeping them in captivity quite challenging for the aquarist. For those interested in keeping these fascinating fish in captivity, the book *American Aquarium Fishes* from Texas A&M University Press is a handy reference. Longevity in the wild is probably no more than a few years. Generally the darters of this genus are larger than their relatives in the *Etheostoma* genus, which begin on the next page. The two groups can be told apart by the presence of a row of enlarged scales on the belly of the *Percina* group. Six representative examples of Kentucky's *Percina* are shown above. In addition to those species already discussed, there are four more *Percina* darters that are found in Kentucky. They are: Channel Darter (*P. copelandi*), Sharpnose Darter (*P. oxyrhyncha*), River Darter (*P. shumardi*), and Saddleback Darter (*P. vigil*). For more information regarding Kentucky's *Percina* Darters see the references section in the back of this book.

Class—**Actinopterygii** (bony fishes)

Order—**Perciformes** (typical fishes)

Family—**Percidae** (perch, darters)

The True Darters—genus *Etheostoma* (approximately 50 species in Kentucky, 34 shown here and on following pages)

Rainbow Darter *Etheostoma caeruleum*	**Johnny Darter** *Etheostoma nigrum*	**Bluegrass Darter** *Etheostoma jimmycarter*
Male / Female	Winter / Summer	Male / Female
Presumed range in Kentucky	Presumed range in Kentucky	Presumed range in Kentucky
Orangefin Darter *Etheostoma bellum*	**Firebelly Darter** *Etheostoma pyrrhogaster*	**Greenside Darter** *Etheostoma blennioides*
Breeding male	Breeding male	
Presumed range in Kentucky	Presumed range in Kentucky	Presumed range in Kentucky
Kentucky Snubnose Darter *Etheostoma rafinesquei*	**Bluebreast Darter** *Etheostoma camurum*	**Gulf Darter** *Etheostoma swaini*
Presumed range in Kentucky	Presumed range in Kentucky	Presumed range in Kentucky

Class—**Actinopterygii** (bony fishes)

Order—**Perciformes** (typical fishes)

Family—**Percidae** (perch, darters)

True Darters—genus *Etheostoma* (continued)

Spottail Darter *Etheostoma squamiceps*	**Cypress Darter** *Etheostoma proeliare*	**Slabrock Darter** *Etheostoma smithi*
Female	Male / Female	
Presumed range in Kentucky	Presumed range in Kentucky	Presumed range in Kentucky
Fantail Darter *Etheostoma flabellare*	**Speckled Darter** *Etheostoma stigmaeum*	**Relict Darter** *Etheostoma chienense*
Male / Female	Male / Female	
Presumed range in Kentucky	Presumed range in Kentucky	Presumed range in Kentucky
Ashy Darter *Etheostoma cinereum*	**Striped Darter** *Etheostoma virgatum*	**Orangethroat Darter** *Etheostoma spectabile*
Female		
Presumed range in Kentucky	Presumed range in Kentucky	Presumed range in Kentucky

Class—**Actinopterygii** (bony fishes)

Order—**Perciformes** (typical fishes)

Family—**Percidae** (perch, darters)

The True Darters—genus *Etheostoma* (continued)

Mud Darter *Etheostoma asprigene*	**Teardrop Darter** *Etheostoma barbouri*	**Bluntnose Darter** *Etheostoma chlorosoma*
Presumed range in Kentucky	Presumed range in Kentucky	Presumed range in Kentucky
Harlequin Darter *Etheostoma histrio*	**Cumberland Darter** *Etheostoma gore*	**Saffron Darter** *Etheostoma flavum*
Presumed range in Kentucky	Presumed range in Kentucky	Presumed range in Kentucky
Headwater Darter *Etheostoma lawrencei*	**Splendid Darter** *Etheostoma barrenense*	**Variegate Darter** *Etheostoma variatum*
Presumed range in Kentucky	Presumed range in Kentucky	Presumed range in Kentucky

Banded Darter—*Etheostoma zonale*

Presumed range in Kentucky

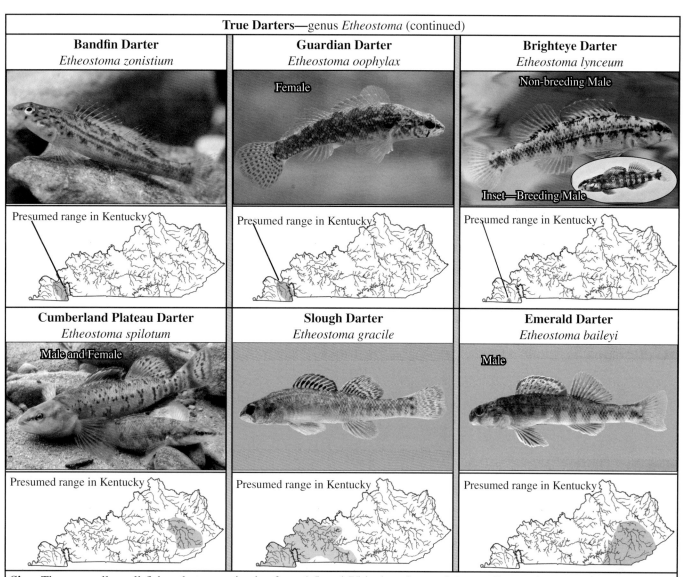

True Darters—genus *Etheostoma* (continued)

Bandfin Darter
Etheostoma zonistium

Presumed range in Kentucky

Guardian Darter
Etheostoma oophylax

Female

Presumed range in Kentucky

Brighteye Darter
Etheostoma lynceum

Non-breeding Male

Inset—Breeding Male

Presumed range in Kentucky

Cumberland Plateau Darter
Etheostoma spilotum

Male and Female

Presumed range in Kentucky

Slough Darter
Etheostoma gracile

Presumed range in Kentucky

Emerald Darter
Etheostoma baileyi

Male

Presumed range in Kentucky

Size: These are all small fishes that range in size from 1.5 to 4.75 inches. Some of the smaller species are among the world's smallest bony fishes. There is one species from Missouri that reaches a whopping 5.25 inches and a couple of Kentucky's true darters can exceed 4 inches (Greenside Darter and Variegated Darter); but most are between 2.25 to 3.25 inches as adults.

Natural History: With at least 148 species distributed across North America, the genus *Etheostoma* boasts more species than any other genus of freshwater fish in the United States. Among them are some of America's rarest fish and some of our most common. In coloration they range from a camouflaging mottled brown to remarkably colorful. In many species the breeding males rival the most colorful of tropical aquarium fishes. Most species are strongly sexually dimorphic, with the females being more subdued in color and sometimes outright drab. The stunning breeding color of the male is usually temporary and replaced by a much more faded appearance through the rest of the year following spring breeding. The females of these fishes are often so similar that even expert ichthyologists can have difficulty identifying them. New species have been recently described and there are most likely new species yet to be discovered. Unlike most fishes, they lack air bladders for flotation and they are mostly bottom dwellers that hug the sand and gravel bottoms of flowing streams. When startled they will move in quick, short dashes, hence the common name "darter." Kentucky may be home to as many as 50 species of *Etheostoma*. Collectively their habitats include probably every drainage within the state and they are found in waterways ranging from swamps to large rivers to small creeks. A few species have a very restrictive distribution, being confined to a single small creek or drainage. Many species require pristine water conditions and these little fish can be a barometer to help determine the quality of Kentucky's waterways. Like "the canary in the coal mine" they are often the first fishes to suffer from the effects of water pollution, siltation, and other forms of stream degradation. Several Kentucky species are regarded as threatened, endangered, or as species of concern. One species has been extirpated. The very small size of these fishes restricts their diet to micro-invertebrates such as small aquatic insects and their larva, tiny crustaceans and other very small aquatic life forms. A representative example of some of Kentucky's *Etheostoma* darters is shown on the previous four pages, but many others are not pictured. To see links to photographs of all of the darters in the state, visit the Kentucky Department of Fish and Wildlife Resources website and select the "Wildlife" tab from the drop-down menu. Then navigate to Wildlife Diversity / Species Information / Fish. Then click on either the common or scientific name.

Class—**Actinopterygii** (bony fishes)

Order—**Salmoniformes**

Family—**Esocidae** (pikes)

Chain Pickerel *Esox niger*	**Grass Pickerel** *Esox americanus*	**Muskellunge** *Esox masquinongy*

Presumed range in Kentucky	Presumed range in Kentucky	Presumed range in Kentucky
Size: Record size 9 pounds 6 ounces.	**Size:** Average 8 to 10 inches. Max. 14.	**Size:** Record size 70 pounds.
Natural History: The Chain Pickerel is a fish of clear waters with abundant aquatic vegetation. Like all members of the pike family it is a highly carnivorous ambush predator with a very large mouth. The shape of the jaws is like a duck bill, and the jaws are equipped with rows of sharp, barracuda-like teeth.	**Natural History:** Inhabits swamps and streams. In smaller creeks it usually is found in quiet pools. This fish likes clear waters and avoids muddy streams. This is the smallest of the pike family and thus feeds on smaller prey. Minnows and other small fish are the principal prey.	**Natural History:** Known as the "Muskie" by fishermen, this largest of the pikes is a prized game fish and one of the most difficult fishes to catch. They live in both man-made lakes and clear water rivers where they favor the deep pools containing boulders, logs, and other types of hiding places.

Family—**Salmonidae** (trout, salmon)

Rainbow Trout *Oncorhynchus mykiss*	**Brown Trout** *Salmo trutta*	**Brook Trout** *Salvelinus fontinalis*

Presumed range in Kentucky	Presumed range in Kentucky	Presumed range in Kentucky
Size: World record 42 pounds 2 ounces.	**Size:** World record 40 pounds 4 ounces.	**Size:** World record 14.5 pounds.
Natural History: The Rainbow Trout was originally native to pacific drainages of the northwest. Today they have been widely introduced across much of America. They require cold, clear waters and thus are very limited in distribution in Kentucky. Several streams and some reservoirs in Kentucky are regularly stocked by the KDFWR.	**Natural History:** Like the Rainbow Trout, this species has been introduced into Kentucky where cool, clear waters allow for its survival. In the most ideal waters, some natural reproduction may occur, but most of the Brown Trout caught by anglers in Kentucky were hatched in one of a handful of fish hatcheries in the state.	**Natural History:** The Brook Trout is the only trout native to the eastern United States, but it likely never occurred in Kentucky as a wild population. Like our other trout species, the Brook Trout of Kentucky are introduced by man. This fish requires cooler water temperatures than our other trouts, and is less tolerant of changes in stream conditions.

Class—**Actinopterygii** (bony fishes)

Order—**Salmoniformes**	Order—**Amiiformes**	Order—**Gadiformes**
Family—**Umbridae** (mudminnows)	Family—**Amiidae** (bowfin)	Family—**Gadidae** (codfish)

Central Mudminnow *Umbra limi*	**Bowfin** *Amia calva*	**Burbot** *Lota lota*

Presumed range in Kentucky 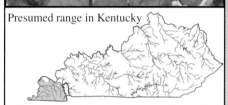	Presumed range in Kentucky 	Presumed range in Kentucky 
Size: Maximum length of 5.25 inches.	**Size:** Record size 21.5 pounds.	**Size:** Record size 18.5 pounds.
Natural History: The Central Mudminnow is the only Kentucky representative of a very small family of fishes found throughout North America and Europe. They live in swamps and still waters of oxbows or slow-flowing lowland creeks. Mainly a northern fish, the Mudminnow ranges southward into the upper Coastal Plain of KY and west TN.	**Natural History:** This is the only surviving species of an ancient family of primitive fishes that dates back to the age of the dinosaurs. Found in swamps and oxbow lakes. In KY they often go by the nickname "Grinnel." These fish are capable of gulping air into the swim bladder to breathe and burrowing into the mud to survive during droughts.	**Natural History:** A relative of the salt water cod, haddock, and pollock, all of which are important food fishes. The Burbot is the single freshwater species of the entire order. They are cold water fish that inhabit large rivers, including the Ohio. They are primarily nocturnal and usually confined to deep waters. This fish is a species of concern in KY.

Order—**Clupeiformes** (sardines, herrings, shad)

Family—**Clupeidae** (herring, shad)

Skipjack Herring *Alosa chrysochloris*	**Gizzard Shad** *Dorosoma cepedianum*	**Threadfin Shad** *Dorosoma petenense*

Presumed range in Kentucky 	Presumed range in Kentucky 	Presumed range in Kentucky 
Size: Up to 3.75 pounds.	**Size:** Up to 3.5 pounds.	**Size:** Maximum of 9 inches.
Natural History: Originally an anadromous species that is now mostly landlocked due to the presence of dams on most major rivers. Although they are sometimes caught by fishermen they are not regarded as good table fare. Their range is restricted mostly to larger rivers and their impoundments.	**Natural History:** Gizzard Shad are plankton feeders that filter tiny organisms from the water through specialized gill rakers. These fish occur in major rivers and their large impoundments throughout the eastern United States, including all the larger rivers in Kentucky. They are an important forage species.	**Natural History:** These small filter feeding fishes occur in large schools and are a major food for many important game fishes in America. They are not very tolerant of cold temperatures and severe winter cold fronts can cause major die-offs. Like other Clupeidae, they occur in major rivers.

Class—**Actinopterygii** (bony fishes)		
Order—**Siluriformes** (catfishes)		
Family—**Ictaluridae** (American catfishes)		

Yellow Bullhead *Ameiurus natalis*	**Black Bullhead** *Ameiurus melas*	**Brown Bullhead** *Ameiurus nebulosus*

Presumed range in Kentucky	Presumed range in Kentucky	Presumed range in Kentucky
Size: Maximum of 19 inches.	**Size:** Maximum length of 24 inches.	**Size:** Maximum length of 21 inches.
Natural History: Widespread, common, and easily caught on hook and line, the Yellow Bullhead is a familiar fish to many Kentuckians. They are often known by the nickname "Mudcat." Ranges from the central Great Plains eastward, including all of Kentucky. Told from other bullheads by yellow colored chin barbels.	**Natural History:** Black Bullheads are mainly nocturnal fishes that do not feed during the day. They live in still-water pools in streams or in natural lakes and man-made impoundments. They can be distinguished from the Yellow Bullhead by their dark chin barbels, and from the Brown Bullhead by the lighter color of the caudal fin.	**Natural History:** Very similar to the Black Bullhead. The least common of the Kentucky's *Ameiurus* catfishes. As with other bullheads, the parent fish stay with the eggs until hatching and the newly hatched young swim in schools near the surface with the mother bullhead in attendance. Found in ponds, lakes, sloughs, creeks, and small rivers.
Channel Catfish *Ictalurus punctatus*	**Blue Catfish** *Ictalurus furcatus*	**Flathead Catfish** *Plylodictus olivaris*

Presumed range in Kentucky	Presumed range in Kentucky	Presumed range in Kentucky
Size: Maximum of about 65 pounds.	**Size:** Maximum size 150 lbs and 5 ft.	**Size:** Maximum of about 100 pounds.
Natural History: Perhaps our best known catfish and a popular game species. Grown commercially as a food fish on fish farms in the south and sold in groceries and restaurants. Specimens in clear water are uniformly dark (as in photo above). Individuals from turbid waters are light gray with black spots.	**Natural History:** This is America's largest catfish and old reports of specimens in excess of 300 pounds exist, though their reliability is questioned. This is an important game fish and also important commercially. Most common in the larger rivers and their impoundments. Both a predator and a scavenger.	**Natural History:** Second in size only to the Blue Catfish. Found mostly in rivers and in impoundments of larger rivers. Adults are mainly nocturnal and spend the day hidden among submerged structure such as logs or rocks. Often hides in caves in steep banks. More predaceous than our other large catfish.

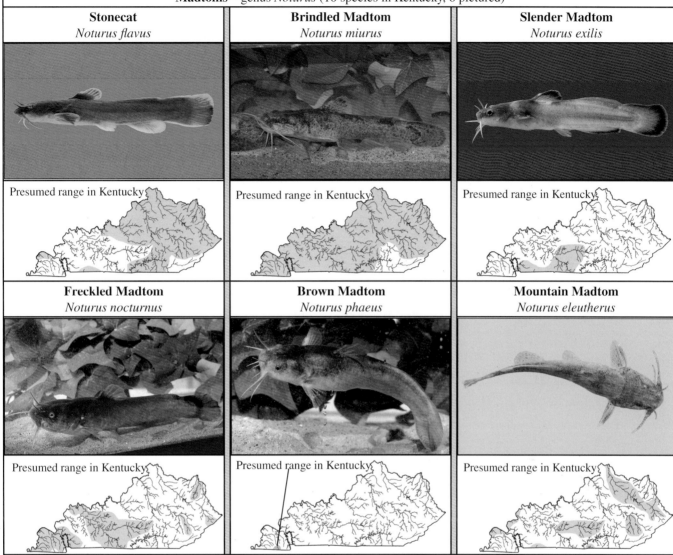

Class—**Actinopterygii** (bony fishes)		
Order—**Siluriformes** (catfishes)		
Family—**Ictaluridae** (American catfishes)		
Madtoms—genus *Noturus* (10 species in Kentucky, 6 pictured)		
Stonecat *Noturus flavus*	**Brindled Madtom** *Noturus miurus*	**Slender Madtom** *Noturus exilis*
Presumed range in Kentucky	Presumed range in Kentucky	Presumed range in Kentucky
Freckled Madtom *Noturus nocturnus*	**Brown Madtom** *Noturus phaeus*	**Mountain Madtom** *Noturus eleutherus*
Presumed range in Kentucky	Presumed range in Kentucky	Presumed range in Kentucky

Size: These are small catfishes. The largest example of the genus is the widespread Stonecat (*N. flavus*), which can reach a length of 12 inches. Most are much smaller. The maximum recorded length for each of Kentucky's madtom species is as follows: Brindled Madtom and Northern Madtom, 5.25 inches; Brown Madtom and Slender Madtom, 5.33 inches; Tadpole Madtom, 5 inches; Elegant Madtom, 3 inches; Freckled Madtom, just under 6 inches; and Mountain Madtom, 5 inches. Kentucky's smallest species is the Least Madtom (*N. hildebrandi*), which grows to a maximum of only 2.5 inches.

Natural History: There are 26 species total in this genus; 10 occur in Kentucky but several of these are rare and limited in distribution in the state. Three species in Kentucky are endangered and another is regarded as a species of special concern. Two of the three endangered Kentucky species (Brown Madtom—*N. phaeus* and Least Madtom—*N. hildebrandi*) are found in Kentucky only in a single drainage in southern Graves County (Terrapin Creek). All Madtoms are secretive and nocturnal, and are thus relatively unknown to the general public. Most Madtom species occur in the eastern portion of America, but a few species range well into the Great Plains and the Stonecat can be found as far west as Wyoming and Montana. Like other American catfishes the Madtoms have spiny dorsal and pectoral fins that produce a mild venom. A puncture from one of these spines can result in a significant amount of pain and swelling, but it is not life-threatening. Like all catfishes, Madtoms have a fleshy fin between the dorsal fin and the tail known as an "adipose fin." In the most Madtoms this fin connects to the caudal (tail) fin, a characteristic that immediately separates Madtoms from the rest of the catfish family. These are predaceous fish that feed on a wide variety of aquatic life consisting of both invertebrates and very small fishes. They feed and are active mostly at night, and spend the days hidden beneath overhanging root wads or burrowed into detritus of deep pools. Shown above are six of the ten Madtom species found in Kentucky. The other Madtom species found in Kentucky are as follows: Elegant Madtom (*N. elegans*); Northern Madtom (*N. stigmosus*); Tadpole Madtom (*N. gyrinus*); and Least Madtom (*N. hildebrandi*).

Class—**Actinopterygii** (bony fishes)

Order—**Acipenseriformes** (primitive fishes)

Family—**Acipenseridae** (sturgeons)

Shovelnose Sturgeon *Scaphirhynchus platorynchus*	**Pallid Sturgeon** *Scaphirhynchus albus*
	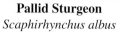
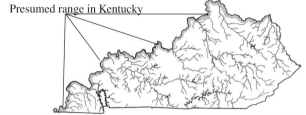Presumed range in Kentucky	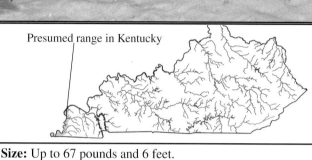Presumed range in Kentucky
Size: Maximum of 43 inches.	**Size:** Up to 67 pounds and 6 feet.
Natural History: Lives in the deep channels of the Mississippi, Ohio, Missouri, Tennessee, Arkansas, and Red rivers. Extirpated from the Rio Grande. The Shovelnose Sturgeon is a fish of flowing water rivers, thus they cannot live in lakes.	**Natural History:** Found only in the deep channels of the Mississippi and Missouri rivers, this is a rare fish throughout its range and especially rare in Kentucky where it is an endangered species.

Family—**Acipenseridae** (sturgeons)	Family—**Polydontidae** (paddlefish)
Lake Sturgeon *Acipenser fulvescens*	**Paddlefish** *Polyodon spathula*

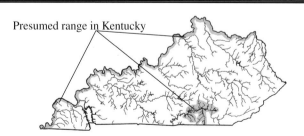Presumed range in Kentucky	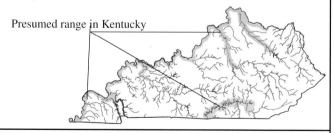Presumed range in Kentucky
Size: Record 310 pounds. Maximum length 8 feet.	**Size:** Can reach at least 180 pounds and over 7 feet.
Natural History: Now highly endangered, the Lake Sturgeon inhabits the deep channels of the large rivers draining the middle of America. Range includes the Mississippi (except near the mouth), the Missouri, the Ohio, the Cumberland, the Arkansas, and the Tennessee rivers as well the Great Lakes. Lives for up to 150 years. Large females will lay up to 3 million eggs. Females attain a greater size than males.	**Natural History:** Paddlefish often go by the name "Spoonbill Catfish," but in fact they are not related to the catfishes. They are a member of a very small, primitive order of fishes that contains only two species (the other is a giant found in China that can reach lengths of over 20 feet). Paddlefish have skeletons that are mostly cartilage. Lives in larger rivers with turbid waters. Flesh is edible and is commercially valuable.

Class—**Actinopterygii** (bony fishes)

Order—**Lepisosteiformes** (gar)

Family—**Lepisosteidae**

Longnose Gar *Lepisosteus osseus*	**Shortnose Gar** *Lepisosteus platostomus*

Presumed range in Kentucky

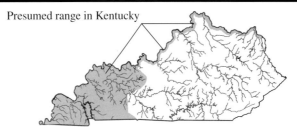

Presumed range in Kentucky

Size: Record 50 pounds (6 feet in length).

Size: Maximum of about 5 lbs and 33 inches.

Natural History: Our most widespread gar species, the Longnose Gar can be found in both large and medium-sized rivers as well as large creeks. Also common in natural lakes and oxbows and in man-made impoundments. Females average larger than males and can live over 20 years. Highly piscivorous, feeding mostly on shad and other forage fishes.

Natural History: An inhabitant of quiet pools and floodplains of rivers and large creeks. Also found in swamps and oxbows and can tolerate waters with high turbidity. During periods of severe drought can survive for days in the mud of drying pools. In addition to fish also eats insects and crayfish.

Spotted Gar *Lepisosteus oculatus*	**Alligator Gar** *Atractosteus spatula*

Presumed range in Kentucky

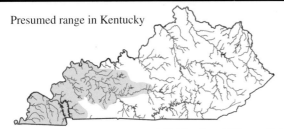

Presumed range in Kentucky

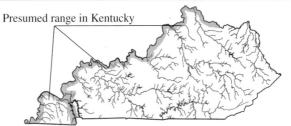

Size: Maximum size about 3.5 feet.

Size: Can reach 10 feet and 300 pounds.

Natural History: Habitat is swamps, sloughs, oxbows, natural lakes, and slow-moving creeks. In Kentucky they are most common in the Coastal Plain region. This gar prefers clearer waters with less siltation than the similar Shortnose Gar. Heavily vegetated waters are preferred. Best differentiated from the Shortnose Gar by the presence of dark spots on the snout. Food is mostly fishes.

Natural History: Alligator Gar once ranged well up the Ohio and Mississippi rivers and their major tributaries into Illinois, Missouri, and southern Indiana and southern Ohio. Today this is a highly endangered fish and efforts to restore the species are being undertaken by the KY Deptartment of Fish and Wildlife. Adult Alligator Gars are highly predaceous and known to eat small mammals and birds as well as fish and even carrion.

Class—**Actinopterygii** (bony fishes)

Order—**Cypriniformes** (minnows, suckers)

Family—**Catostomidae** (suckers)

Largemouth Buffalo *Ictiobus cyprinellus*	**Smallmouth Buffalo** *Ictiobus bubalus*	**Black Buffalo** *Ictiobus niger*

Presumed range in Kentucky	Presumed range in Kentucky	Presumed range in Kentucky
Size: Can reach a maximum of 80 lbs.	**Size:** Maximum probably about 30 lbs.	**Size:** To at least 30 lbs, probably more.
Natural History: Largemouth Buffalo are important commercial food fishes. Found in large rivers and their backwaters and in impoundments and is more accepting of silt-laden waters than others of its genus. Breeds during spring in flooded fields and backwaters. May be negatively impacted in flood controlled rivers and streams.	**Natural History:** A river fish that also thrives in lakes and impoundments. Less likely to be found in turbid water than the Largemouth Buffalo and also is more fond of waters with some current. Feeds on bottom dwelling invertebrates and plants. Like all three of the *Ictiobus* (buffalo fishes), this fish is harvested commercially for human consumption.	**Natural History:** Least common of the Buffalo fishes and regarded as a species of concern in Kentucky. Morphologically somewhat intermediate between the two previous species. In habits, feeding, etc., most similar to the Smallmouth Buffalo. Found in large and medium size rivers throughout much of the Mississippi drainage system.
Blue Sucker *Cycleptus elongatus*	**White Sucker** *Catostomus commersonii*	**Spotted Sucker** *Minytrema melanops*

Presumed range in Kentucky	Presumed range in Kentucky	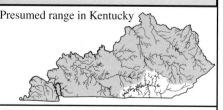Presumed range in Kentucky
Size: Can reach 20 pounds.	**Size:** Maximum 25 inches and 7 pounds.	**Size:** Maximum of about 18 inches.
Natural History: A unique member of the sucker family, the Blue Sucker is the only species of its genus. Although its range includes all of the Mississippi, Ohio, Missouri, and western gulf coastal rivers, this is today a rare fish throughout most of its range. It prefers fast flowing channels over hard bottom. Dams and siltation impact both.	**Natural History:** Name comes from the white belly of the breeding male. They inhabit a wide variety of small rivers and creeks as well as natural and man-made lakes, and are more common in the eastern two-thirds of the state. Although bony, their flesh is quite palatable and they are sought for food and sport in some regions.	**Natural History:** Lives in pools and slow-moving waters of large and small rivers, as well as larger creeks. Moves into smaller creeks in spring to spawn over gravel or rocks. Feeds on small aquatic invertebrates. Although fairly widespread, this is not a common fish and it may be decreasing in much of its range as water quality declines.

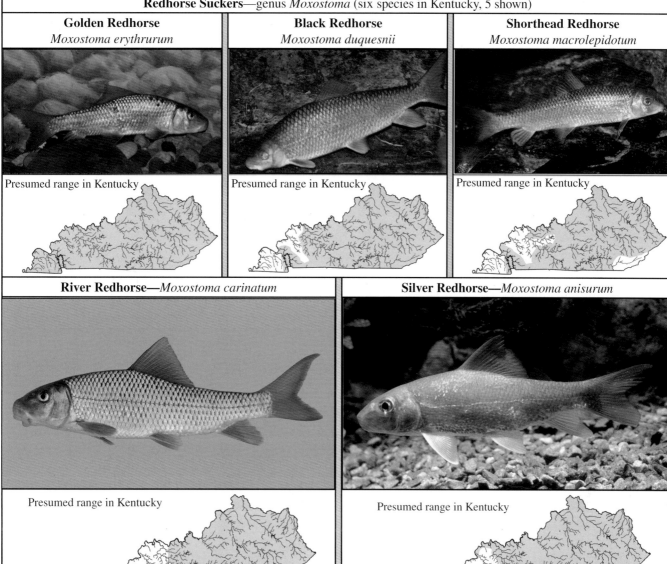

Class—**Actinopterygii** (bony fishes)

Order—**Cypriniformes** (minnows, suckers)

Family—**Catostomidae** (suckers)

Redhorse Suckers—genus *Moxostoma* (six species in Kentucky, 5 shown)

Golden Redhorse *Moxostoma erythrurum*	**Black Redhorse** *Moxostoma duquesnii*	**Shorthead Redhorse** *Moxostoma macrolepidotum*

Presumed range in Kentucky

Presumed range in Kentucky

Presumed range in Kentucky

River Redhorse—*Moxostoma carinatum*

Silver Redhorse—*Moxostoma anisurum*

Presumed range in Kentucky

Presumed range in Kentucky

Size: River Redhorse may reach 10 pounds. Blackfin Redhorse only 6 inches. Others are between 3 and 8 pounds maximum.

Natural History: The Redhorse Suckers are the most diverse group within the sucker family, with 20 species found in North America. The genus ranges across much of the eastern United States and there are six species that range into Kentucky. All are similar in appearance and can be difficult to properly identify. Juveniles often show a pattern of dark blotches. These are stream fishes that are typically found in clear waters. Their flesh is good but bony, and they are sometimes pursued by anglers both for food and sport. In some regions of their range there are "gigging seasons" for these species, and they are hunted at night with lights and gigs from specialized boats. This practice is fairly common in the clear rivers of the Ozark Plateau in Missouri. Some anglers will use bow-fishing techniques for these species as well. A new form of angling that is growing in popularity across the world is known as "rough fishing" and entails the pursuit of the many fish species that are not generally regarded as "game" fishes. For more information on this new angling sport visit www.roughfish.com. Although suckers will persist in reservoirs they always spawn in small to medium-sized streams with gravel substrates. Pictured above are five of Kentucky's *Moxostoma* species. The other species (not shown) is the very rare **Blacktail Redhorse** (*M. poecilurum*) from the Terrapin Creek drainage in Graves County, Kentucky. In addition to all these species, there are at least 18 other *Moxostoma* suckers found in the United States. Finally, there is another very unique sucker species in Kentucky that was once placed in the *Moxostoma* genus but is now in a separate grouping. It is the **Blackfin Sucker**, *Thoburnia atripinnis* (not shown). It is found only in the upper Barren River drainage.

Class—**Actinopterygii** (bony fishes)		
Order—**Cypriniformes** (minnows, suckers)		
Family—**Catostomidae** (suckers)		

Quillback *Carpoides cyprinus*	**Highfin Carpsucker** *Carpoides velifer*	**River Carpsucker** *Carpoides carpio*

Presumed range in Kentucky 	Presumed range in Kentucky 	Presumed range in Kentucky 
Size: Average about 6 pounds but can reach 12 pounds. Maximum length 2 ft.	**Size:** Maximum length about 15 inches and maximum weight about 2 pounds.	**Size:** Maximum length 25 inches. Record weight 10 pounds,
Natural History: Though found statewide, the Quillback is least common in the Coastal Plain. Food is benthic invertebrates sucked from the substrate. Occurs both in rivers and impoundments but may be less tolerant of turbid conditions than its larger cousin the River Carpsucker. Like the River Carpsucker this is a commercial food fish.	**Natural History:** This is the smallest of the Carpsuckers and is therefore not highly valued by commercial fishermen. This species inhabits medium to large rivers and favors clearer waters with some gravel substrates. Highfin Carpsukers are less common than our other two species. Siltation and lake impoundments may be to blame.	**Natural History:** Found in the larger rivers and their reservoirs. Most common in the Ohio and Mississippi rivers and also in the lower reaches of Kentucky's other larger river systems. Food is tiny invertebrates sucked from mud of the bottom of a river or lake. Known to live at least 10 years. Valued as a commercial food fish.
Northern Hogsucker *Hypentelium nigricans*	**Lake Chubsucker** *Erimyzon sucetta*	**Western Creek Chubsucker** *Erimyzon claviformis*

Presumed range in Kentucky 	Presumed range in Kentucky 	Presumed range in Kentucky 
Size: Up to about 2 feet in length.	**Size:** Maximum of about 15.5 inches.	**Size:** Maximum about 15 inches.
Natural History: In Kentucky this species is found mostly in large, clear creeks with rocky or gravel substrates. In the Ozarks region it is common in large rivers. This is a bottom dweller that hugs the substrate and sucks small aquatic invertebrates from sand, gravel, or silt. They are very cryptically patterned and blend in well with rocky or gravel bottoms.	**Natural History:** Lake Chubsucker is threatened in Kentucky and is found in the Coastal Plain and the Shawnee Hills in quite waters. These two very similar species are differentiated by counting dorsal fin rays (see Creek Chubsucker). Although they occur in the same regions of Kentucky, they partition the available habitats. This species prefers still water lowlands, i.e. swamps, oxbow lakes, etc.	**Natural History:** The Creek Chubsucker is widespread throughout the western third of Kentucky. It is fairly common in small and large creeks with sand or gravel substrate. They eat tiny crustaceans, insects, and algae. Very similar in appearance to the Lake Chubsucker, which has 11 or 12 dorsal fin rays as opposed to 9 or 10 in the Creek Chubsucker.

Class—**Actinopterygii** (bony fishes)

Order—**Cypriniformes** (minnows, suckers)

Family—**Cyprinidae** (minnows)

Grass Carp *Ctenopharyngodon idella*	**Silver Carp** *Hypophthalmichthys molitrix*	**Bighead Carp** *Hypophthalmichthys nobilis*

 Presumed range in Kentucky	Presumed range in Kentucky	Presumed range in Kentucky 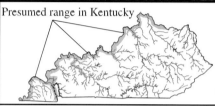
Size: 4 feet and 100 pounds (in Asia).	**Size:** Can reach 60 pounds.	**Size:** Up to 3 feet and 90 pounds.
Natural History: Inhabits pools and backwaters of large rivers and both man-made and natural lakes. Introduced into the United States from Asia to control aquatic plant growth in commercial minnow ponds. As with most alien species, the Grass Carp probably does more harm than good to the environments where it has become established.	**Natural History:** Native to China, the Silver Carp has become established in the larger rivers of the eastern United States. These fish consume tiny zooplankton and algae that is filtered from the flowing water of large river channels. Originally imported into Arkansas along with the Bighead Carp to control algae blooms in fish ponds.	**Natural History:** Like the previous species this fish is native to China. Now widespread in the major rivers of the eastern U.S., this is a filter feeder that inhabits the flowing waters of large river channels. Though both species of *Hypophthalmichthys* were intentionally introduced, they are now regarded as environmentally harmful aliens.
Common Carp *Cyprinus carpio*	**Goldfish** *Carassius auratus*	**Golden Shiner** *Notemigonus crysoleucas*

 Presumed range in Kentucky	Presumed range in Kentucky 	Presumed range in Kentucky 
Size: Angling record is 55 pounds.	**Size:** Maximum 20 inches and 5 pounds.	**Size:** Maximum size 14.5 inches.
Natural History: Many people are surprised to learn that the Common Carp is an invasive species in America. Native to Eurasia, they were first brought to the U.S. in the early 1800s. They are now widespread and common in most aquatic habitats in America. A benthic feeder that "roots" like a hog in muddy bottoms and increases water turbidity.	**Natural History:** Native to Asia, the Goldfish is now widely established across most of North America. The gaudy colors commonly seen in "fish ponds" and pet stores rarely survive in wild populations. Found in most rivers and lakes and can survive in tiny ponds. More tolerant of pollution and siltation than many native species.	**Natural History:** This minnow is well known among fishermen and is sold as a bait fish in many regions of the U.S. In their natural habitat they are fish of still water pools of streams and backwaters of rivers. They will also thrive in impoundments and small farm ponds. Millions are raised commercially each year to be sold in bait stores.

Class—**Actinopterygii** (bony fishes)

Order—**Cypriniformes** (minnows, suckers)

Family—**Cyprinidae** (minnows)

Redside Daces—genus *Clinostomus*	Redbelly Daces—genus *Chrosomus*	Stonerollers—genus *Campostoma*
Rosyside Dace—*C. funduloides* **Redside Dace**—*C. elongatus*	**Southern Redbelly Dace**—*C. erythrogaster* **Blackside Dace**—*C. cumberlandensis*	**Central Stoneroller**—*C. anomalum* **Largescale Stoneroller**—*C. oligolepis*
 Rosyside Dace (Breeding Color)	 Southern Redbelly Dace (Breeding Color)	 Largescale Stoneroller
Presumed range in Kentucky Redside Dace (light gray) Rosyside Dace (dark gray)	Presumed range in Kentucky Southern Redbelly (light gray) Both species (dark gray)	Presumed combined range of Stonerollers in Kentucky
Size: Can reach 4.5 inches.	**Size:** Maximum of 4.5 inches.	**Size:** Maximum of about 11 inches.
Natural History: There are two nearly identical *Clinostomus* Daces in Kentucky. Rosyside Dace occurs in three widely separated populations in the state while the Redside has a contiguous range. Both live in clear water creeks and small, clear rivers with gravel, sand, or rock substrates. Both species tend to inhabit pools and still water areas.	**Natural History:** The two *Chrosomus* species found in Kentucky are very similar. Southern Redbelly Dace (pictured) is the most common. Blackside Dace is a threatened species in Kentucky and only occurs in the Upper Cumberland Watershed. These fish require clear, cold water streams and their diet is mostly insectivorous.	**Natural History:** The two similar Stonerollers in Kentucky are among our most common fishes. Nearly every stream within their range capable of supporting fish life will have a population of Stonerollers. Their name comes from their habit of aggressive bottom feeding in gravelly stream beds, moving small stones in the process.
Striped Shiner *Luxilus chrysocephalus*	**Blacknose Dace**—*Rhinichthys atratulus* **Longnose Dace**—*Rhinichthys cataractae*	**Creek Chub** *Semotilus atromaculatus*
	 Longnose Dace (inset) Blacknose Dace	 Inset—Head of Breeding Male Below—Typical Adult
Presumed range in Kentucky	Presumed range in Kentucky	Presumed range in Kentucky
Size: Maximum length 9 inches.	**Size:** Reaches about 5 inches.	**Size:** Maximum length 12 inches.
Natural History: As with many minnow species, the color and pattern of the Striped Shiner can change with age and significant sexual dimorphism also occurs (shown above is a mature male). Miscellaneous invertebrates including aquatic insect larva are eaten along with algae. Habitat is small creeks with sand or gravel bottoms.	**Natural History:** Widespread and common in the state except for the much of the Coastal Plain and the Shawnee Hills. Found in springs and in small spring-fed creeks. Both species feed on the larva of aquatic flies and other tiny invertebrates. The Longnose Dace, *R. cataractae* (inset photo) occurs in only a few streams in far eastern Kentucky.	**Natural History:** One of the most widespread and common creek fishes in America, the Creek Chub probably inhabits nearly every stream in Kentucky that is capable of supporting fish life. Like many minnows, breeding males develop tubercles on the head and snout, leading to the common nickname "Hornyhead" (see inset photo above).

Class—**Actinopterygii** (bony fishes)

Order—**Cypriniformes** (minnows, suckers)

Family—**Cyprinidae** (minnows)

Bigeye Chub *Hybopsis amblops*	Pugnose Minnow *Opsopoeodus emiliae*	Flathead Chub *Platygobio gracilis*

 Presumed range in Kentucky	 Presumed range in Kentucky	 Presumed range in Kentucky
Size: May reach 4 inches.	**Size:** Maximum of about 2.5 nches.	**Size:** Can reach a foot in length.
Natural History: A fish of small rivers and large creeks. In decline over much of its range, probably due to dams and siltation. A similar species, the Pallid Shiner (*H. amnis*), may also occur in Kentucky. The latter is extremely rare (possibly extirpated) and is regarded as an endangered species in the state.	**Natural History:** This tiny minnow is widespread across the southeast from South Carolina to eastern Texas. It also ranges northward up the Mississippi and Ohio drainages as far as the southern Great Lakes. Habitat is backwaters and pools of low gradient streams having some aquatic vegetation.	**Natural History:** This rare minnow is a species of concern that occurs in Kentucky only in the Mississippi River. A fish of large rivers, it ranges as far north as the Arctic Circle in Canada's Northwest Territories. Although tolerant of high turbidity, it seems to prefer gravel or sand substrates.
Mustache Chubs—genus *Erimystax*	**Silvery Minnows**—*Hybognathus*	**Macrhybopis Chubs**—genus *Macrhybopsis*
Streamline Chub—*E. dissimilis* **Blotched Chub**—*E. insignis*	**Mississippi Silvery Minnow**—*H. nuchalis* **Cypress Minnow**—*H. hayi*	**Shoal Chub**—*M. hyostoma* **Silver Chub**—*M. storeiana*
		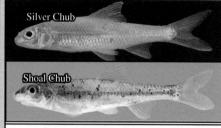
 Presumed range in Kentucky	 Presumed range in Kentucky	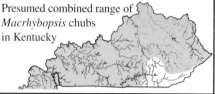 Presumed combined range of *Macrhybopsis* chubs in Kentucky
Size: Maximum about 3.75 inches.	**Size:** 6 inches maximum.	**Size:** From 3 to 9 inches as adults.
Natural History: These small minnows live in small and medium-size rivers in highland regions. They favor flowing water over gravel bottoms. The Streamlined Chub is the most widespread in Kentucky but neither species is common. Blotched Chub is restricted to the Cumberland River drainage and is an endangered species in Kentucky. Food is both algea and invertebrates.	**Natural History:** In Kentucky only the Mississippi Silvery Minnow is common. The Cypress Minnow is an endangered species in the state. A third species of *Hybognathus* minnow, the Plains Minnow (*H. placitus*), barely occurs in Kentucky in the Mississippi River. These fish are bottom feeders that ingest tiny algae and detritus from the silt of sloughs and backwaters.	**Natural History:** This genus inhabits rivers and does not tolerate the still waters generally associated with dams. In addition to the two species listed in the heading above there are two other *Macrhybopsis* chubs that occur in the Mississippi River bordering Kentucky. They are the Sturgeon Chub, (*M. gelida*) and the Sicklefin Chub (*M. meeki*). Both of those are endangered in Kentucky.

Class—**Actinopterygii** (bony fishes)
Order—**Cypriniformes** (minnows, suckers)
Family—**Cyprinidae** (minnows)
Bloodtail Shiners—genus *Lythrurus* (3 species in Kentucky)

Redfin Shiner *Lythrurus umbratilis*	**Ribbon Shiner** *Lythrurus fumeus*	**Scarlet Shiner** *Lythrurus fasciolaris*

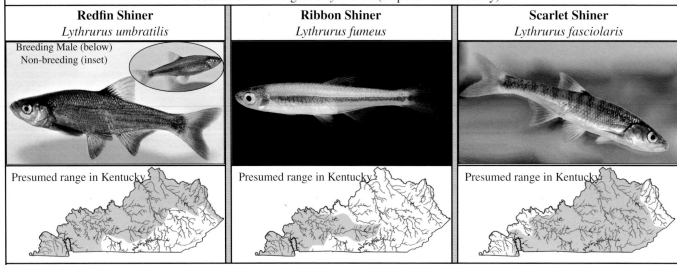

Breeding Male (below)
Non-breeding (inset)

Presumed range in Kentucky

Size: Redfin Shiner and Scarlet Shiner to 3.5 inches. Ribbon Shiner 2.5 inches.

Natural History: These are mostly stream fishes that occur in small to medium size creeks, although the Scarlet Shiner can also be found in large rivers. They are typically a very common genus and populations of at least one of these fishes probably occur in most streams in Kentucky that are capable of supporting fish life. Their reproduction habits are noteworthy due to the fact that they often spawn in the nests of other fish species, often using the nest of one of the sunfishes. Food is small aquatic insect larva such as mayfly and midge nymphs supplemented by filamentous algeas. Habitats include a wide variety of streams from still-water oxbows to fast flowing mountain creeks. Redfin and Ribbon Shiners tolerate both clear and turbid conditions. Longevity for individuals of this genus is short, and most will not survive beyond three years.

River Chubs—genus *Nocomis* (3 species in Kentucky)

River Chub *Nocomis micropogon*	**Hornyhead Chub** *Nocomis biguttatus*	**Redtail Chub** *Nocomis effusus*

Male

Juvenile

Male

Male

Presumed range in Kentucky

Size: River Chub can reach 13 inches. Redtail Chub and Hornyhead Chub are about 10 inches maximum.

Natural History: Habitat is clear creeks and small rivers with gravel bottoms. These large minnows are both herbivorous and invertivorous in diet. Breeding males of all three species have well developed tubercles on the head. Males build elaborate nests by moving pebbles with their mouth. The Redtail Chub prefers smaller streams with gravel bottoms and is most common in the Mississippian Plateau physiographic region. The River Chub will inhabit larger creeks and small rivers in the Appalachian Plateau. The Hornyhead Chub is rare in Kentucky and apparently restricted to the lower Kentucky River drainage in the Bluegrass Region. It is regarded by KDFWR as a species of concern. Large adults are quite carnivorous and feed on small crayfish, snails, and aquatic insects. They will readily take worms on hook and line and many a young fishermen learned their trade by catching River Chubs from nearby rivers and streams. All species of *Nocomis* develop tubercles on the snout and head. These tubercles are especially apparent on the nuptial males, who will also have small tubercles on their pectoral fins. The number and placement of the tubercles are important characteristics used by ichthyologists to identify different species.

Class—**Actinopterygii** (bony fishes)

Order—**Cypriniformes** (minnows, suckers)

Family—**Cyprinidae** (minnows)

Fathead Minnows—genus *Pimephales* (3 species in Kentucky)

Bluntnose Minnow *Pimephales notatus*	**Bullhead Minnow** *Pimephales vigilax*	**Fathead Minnow** *Pimephales promelas*

Presumed range in Kentucky 	Presumed range in Kentucky 	Presumed range in Kentucky 

Size: Four inches is the maximum length for these small minnows. Males are larger than females.

Natural History: These are very common minnows that may be found in rivers, creeks, reservoirs, and even ponds occasionally. They are tough little fishes that can survive warm, low-oxygen waters and waters with high turbidity. Breeding males of all three species have very dark, nearly black heads and tubercles on the snout. Their resilience, rapid reproductive capacity, and ease in rearing in captivity has led to the Bluntnose Minnow and the Fathead Minnow being widely used as a bait minnows, where they are often sold under the nickname "Tuffy." A reddish colored strain of the Fathead Minnow known as "Rosy Red" has also been bred for sale in bait stores. Because of their prolific use for bait, these minnows have become widely established across the United States and Canada and they are today perhaps the most common fish species in North America. These minnows are mostly bottom feeders that eat a variety of tiny invertebrates as well as algae.

Stargazing Minnow *Phenacobius uranops*	**Suckermouth Minnow** *Phenacobius mirabilis*	**Silverjaw Minnow** *Ericymba buccata*

Presumed range in Kentucky 	Presumed range in Kentucky 	Presumed range in Kentucky 
Size: 3 to 3.5 inches as an adult.	**Size:** Maximum length 4.75 inches.	**Size:** About 3.75 inches.
Natural History: This minnow's name comes from the unusual orientation of the eye, which is situated high on the head and directed upward. This minnow is found in the upper Tennessee, Cumberland, and Barren river systems. Habitat is riffles areas of clear rocky or gravelly streams with flowing waters. Stargazing Minnow is a species of concern in Kentucky.	**Natural History:** This minnow is a habitat non-specialist that occurs in both small creeks and large rivers. It is tolerant of a wide variety of conditions from clear flowing waters to still waters with some turbidity. The common name "Suckermouth" is derived from the sub-terminal position of the mouth, which is typical of the sucker family (*Catostomidae*).	**Natural History:** The Silverjaw Minnow is unique among Kentucky minnows in having a series of visible cavities within the upper jaw below the eye. The function of these cavities may be tactile or sensory. Habitat is clear streams with sand or rock substrates. Some ichthyologists place this species in the much larger genus *Notropis*.

Class—**Actinopterygii** (bony fishes)	
Order—**Cypriniformes** (minnows, suckers)	
Family—**Cyprinidae** (minnows)	
True Minnows—genus *Notropis* (18 species in Kentucky, 11 pictured here and on next page)	

Silver Shiner—*Notropis photogenis*	Presumed range in Kentucky

Highland Shiner—*Notropis micropteryx*	Presumed range in Kentucky

Popeye Shiner—*Notropis ariommus*	Presumed range in Kentucky

River Shiner —*Notropis blennius*	Presumed range in Kentucky

Ghost Shiner —*Notropis buchanani*	Presumed range in Kentucky

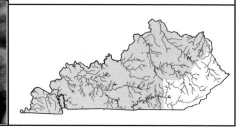

Class—**Actinopterygii** (bony fishes)

Order—**Cypriniformes** (minnows, suckers)

Family—**Cyprinidae** (minnows)

True Minnows—genus *Notropis* (continued)

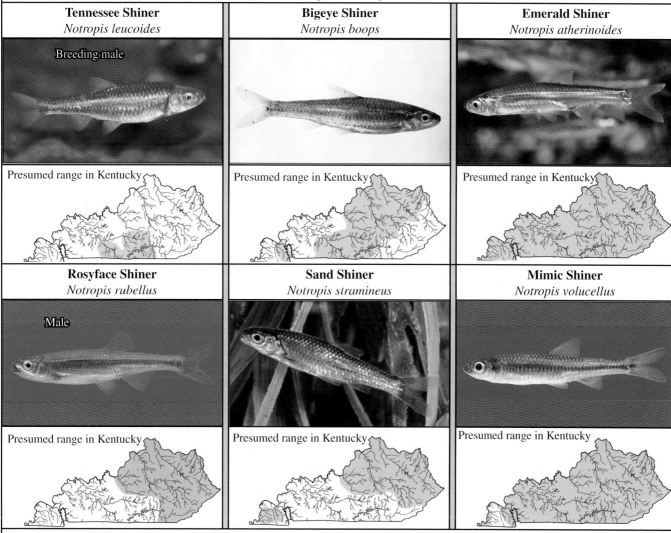

Tennessee Shiner *Notropis leucoides*	Bigeye Shiner *Notropis boops*	Emerald Shiner *Notropis atherinoides*
Breeding male		
Presumed range in Kentucky	Presumed range in Kentucky	Presumed range in Kentucky
Rosyface Shiner *Notropis rubellus*	**Sand Shiner** *Notropis stramineus*	**Mimic Shiner** *Notropis volucellus*
Male		
Presumed range in Kentucky	Presumed range in Kentucky	Presumed range in Kentucky

Size: In the sense that most people think of minnows as being tiny fishes, these are the "true minnows." Members of this genus are among the smallest of Kentucky fishes. Several Kentucky *Notropis* are quite diminutive with a maximum length of only about 2.5 inches. The two smallest species are the Ghost Shiner (*N. buchanani*) and the Sawfin Shiner (*Notropis* species). The largest Kentucky species are the River Shiner (*N. blennius*) and the Silver Shiner (*N. photogenis*), but neither of these will exceed 5.5 inches.

Natural History: *Notropis* is largest genus of minnows in North America with as many as 83 species across the continent. In fact, this is the second largest generic group of fishes in North America, surpassed only by the darters of the *Etheostoma* genus. The exact status some species included in this genus is problematic and taxonomic changes occur frequently within the group, with occasional species being re-assigned to another genus and some being added from other genera. Their distribution is generally east of the Rocky Mountain Continental Divide, and most species occur within the Gulf of Mexico Drainage Basin. At least 18 species are recorded from Kentucky. Many are common, but two, the Palezone Shiner (*N. albizonatus*) and Sawfin Shiner (*Notropis* species) are presently endangered in the state. Another, the Taillight Shiner (*N. maculatus*) is threatened and another is proposed for listing as an endangered species. At least one species has apparently been extirpated from the state. Collectively, the Shiner Minnows are found in virtually all aquatic habitats within the state and their combined ranges encompass all of Kentucky. In addition to the six species pictured and those mentioned above, the following *Notropis* species have also been recorded in the state: Channel Shiner (*N. wickliffi*); Silverband Shiner (*N. shumardi*); Spottail Shiner (*N. hudsonius*); and Telescope Shiner (*N. telescopus*). The breeding males of many *Notropis* species are quite colorful. Even those species that don't acquire significant color on the body will typically acquire yellow, orange, or red color in the fins of nuptial males. At least one species, the Emerald Shiner (pictured above, top right), is widely used as a bait minnow.

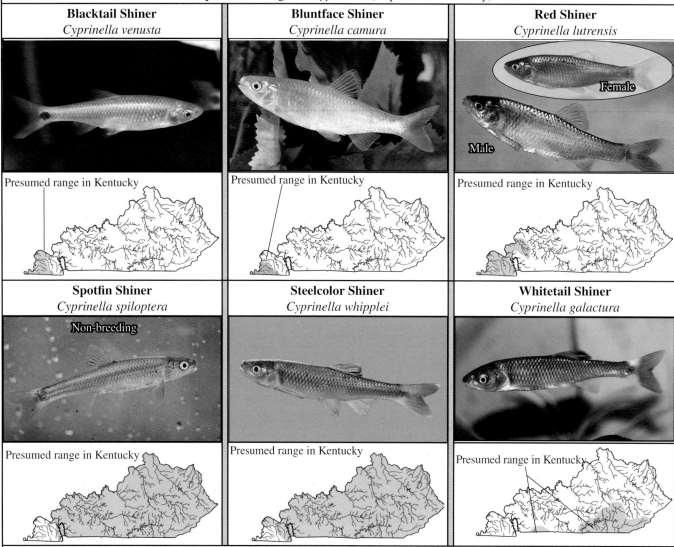

Class—**Actinopterygii** (bony fishes)

Order—**Cypriniformes** (minnows, suckers)

Family—**Cyprinidae** (minnows)

Carp Minnows—genus *Cyprinella* (6 species in Kentucky)

| **Blacktail Shiner** *Cyprinella venusta* | **Bluntface Shiner** *Cyprinella camura* | **Red Shiner** *Cyprinella lutrensis* |
| **Spotfin Shiner** *Cyprinella spiloptera* | **Steelcolor Shiner** *Cyprinella whipplei* | **Whitetail Shiner** *Cyprinella galactura* |

Presumed range in Kentucky

Non-breeding

Female

Male

Size: Members of this genus are typically larger than the similar *Notropis* shiners, and two Kentucky species can reach 6 inches in length (Whitetail Shiner and Bluntface Shiner). The Red Shiner is the smallest at 3.5 inches. Maximum sizes for the other species are as follows: Steelcolor Shiner, 5.5 inches; Blacktail Shiner, 5 inches; Spotfin Shiner, 4.75 inches.

Natural History: These minnows are very similar to the *Notropis* shiners and many species were once included in that group. This is a fairly large genus with 27 total species ranging throughout the eastern half of North America from southern Canada to northern Mexico. The group name "Carp Minnow" comes from the genus name, which translates as "little carp." Like many minnows, immatures and females can pose a difficult identification challenge, especially for non-professionals. The adult males (especially in breeding colors) are usually fairly distinctive in color and morphology and much easier to recognize. The Bluntface Shiner is rare in Kentucky where it is regarded as an endangered species. It, like the Blacktail Shiner (which is a species of concern), is found only in the westernmost tip of the state. Here their preferred habitat of sandy bottomed steams has been greatly reduced by siltation produced by intensive agriculture. The Red Shiner on the other hand is much more tolerant of siltation and water turbidity and is a fairly abundant fish. The Spotfin Shiner and the Steelcolor Shiner are our most common and widespread *Cyprinella*, ranging throughout most of the state east of the Gulf Coastal Plain. These two species are habitat generalists that can exist in a variety of stream conditions. The Whitetail Shiner is a fish of the Cumberland Plateau and the Mississippian Plateau regions where it inhabits relatively cool, clear water streams with gravel or rocky bottoms. All *Cyprinella* are mainly insectivorus but some plant material is also eaten. Some species are quite opportunistic and larger invertebrates or even tiny fish fry are taken on occasion. Hybridization can be common among these minnows where their ranges overlap, adding to the already difficult task of identification.

Class—**Actinopterygii** (bony fishes)

Order—**Cyprinidontiformes** (topminnows, livebearers)

Family—**Fundulidae** (topminnows)

Blackstriped Topminnow *Fundulus notatus*	**Starhead Topminnow** *Fundulus dispar*	**Golden Topminnow** *Fundulus chrysotus*
		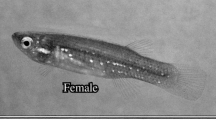
Presumed range in Kentucky	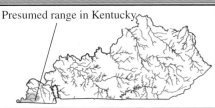Presumed range in Kentucky	Presumed range in Kentucky

Northern Studfish—*Fundulus catenatus*	**Blackspotted Topminnow**—*Fundulus olivaceus*

Presumed range in Kentucky	Presumed range in Kentucky

Size: Blackspotted Topminnow, 3.75 inches maximum. Blackstripe Topminnow, maximum of 3 inches. Golden Topminnow, 2.75 inches maximum. Northern Studfish, may reach nearly 7 inches. Starhead Minnow, has a record length just over 3 inches.

Natural History: The topminnows get their name from the fact that they are always seen right at the water's surface. They feed on both emerging aquatic insects and tiny terrestrial insects that fall or fly onto the water. The characteristic white spot on the top of the head of many species is easily visible as they suspend at the surface. Most species are found in the Mississippi River Basin, and in Kentucky most occur only in the Coastal Plain in the western end of the state. The Blackstripe Topminnow is the most widely distributed *Fundulus* species in Kentucky, being found everywhere *except* for the Appalachian Plateau. It and the Northern Studfish are the only species that occupy upland streams, with the Northern Studfish ranging into most of the Mississippian Plateau. Although found in flowing streams, all topminnows prefer quiet pools and backwaters, including beaver ponds, swamps, and low gradient streams throughout their range. The Starhead minnow and Golden Topminnow are endangered species in Kentucky, the latter being found in Kentucky only in the Reelfoot Lake area of Fulton County.

Family—**Poeciliidae** (livebearers)

Western Mosquitofish—*Gambusia affinis*

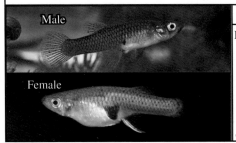

Size: Females 2.5 inches, males 1.25.

Presumed range in Kentucky

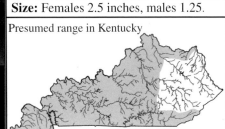

Natural History: True to their name, these tiny fish eat large numbers of mosquito larva. Uniquely among Kentucky fishes, they give birth to fully formed young. They live in the shallows of swamps and backwaters, where they will forage in water less than an inch deep. A close relative of the aquarium Guppy.

Class—**Actinopterygii** (bony fishes)

Order—**Atheriniformes**	Order—**Osteoglossiformes** (bonytongues)	
Family—**Atherinidae** (silversides)	Family—**Hiodontidae** (mooneyes)	

<table>
<tr>
<td>

Brook Silverside—*Labidesthes sicculus*
Mississippi Silverside—*Menidia audens*

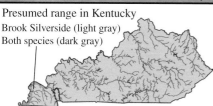

Presumed range in Kentucky
Brook Silverside (light gray)
Both species (dark gray)

Size: About 5 inches for both species.

Natural History: The silversides are related to the famous marine species the Grunnion, which spawns in unfathomable numbers on west coast beaches. Silversides travel in large schools near the surface of lakes and rivers and are important prey for larger fish species, including many game fish.

</td>
<td>

Mooneye
Hiodon tergisus

Presumed range in Kentucky

Size: Maximum 17 inches and 2.5 lbs.

Natural History: The Mooneye is one of only two species in the family Hiodontidae, which is endemic to North America. Their appearance is very similar to their distant relatives the shads and herrings. They live in large rivers and lakes and feed on a wide variety of invertebrate and small vertebrate prey.

</td>
<td>

Goldeye
Hiodon alosoides

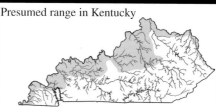

Presumed range in Kentucky

Size: Reaches 20 inches and 3 pounds.

Natural History: Similar to the Mooneye but found in rivers with higher turbidity. Unlike the Mooneye, this species does not thrive in impoundments, but does exist in natural lakes and backwaters of large rivers. It is an important food fish in parts of Canada, where it is eaten smoked.

</td>
</tr>
</table>

Order—**Anguilliformes** (eels)	Order—**Scorpaeniformes** (scorpion fish)	
Family—**Anguillidae** (freshwater eels)	Family—**Cottidae** (sculpins)	

<table>
<tr>
<td>

American Eel
Anguilla rostrata

Presumed range in Kentucky

Size: Can reach 4 feet in length.

Natural History: Eels have one of the most remarkable life cycles of any fish. After hatching far out in the Atlantic Ocean tiny larva migrate to the coast and swim hundreds of miles upstream in inland rivers. After as many as 15 years adults return to the sea to spawn and die. Dams can hinder dispersal and the occurrence of eels today is sporadic.

</td>
<td>

Banded Sculpin
Cottus carolinae

Presumed range in Kentucky

Size: May rarely reach 7 inches.

Natural History: Most of the 250 plus members of this order of fish (Scorpaeniformes) are cold water marine species. About 30 species inhabit freshwater streams in America. Kentucky's two species are among the most common. The Banded Sculpin is a stream fish that favors fast-flowing water and riffle areas of very small to large streams.

</td>
<td>

Mottled Sculpin
Cottus bairdii

Presumed range in Kentucky

Size: Maximum 4.5 inches.

Natural History: Typically a fish of upland streams and spring-fed runs where they inhabit the fast-flowing regions with gravel or rocky substrates. All Sculpins have large mouths that enable them to take larger prey than would be suspected for such a small fish. They are highly cryptic and nearly impossible to see when motionless on stream beds.

</td>
</tr>
</table>

Class—**Actinopterygii** (bony fishes)

Order—**Percopsiformes**

Family—**Amblyopsidae** (cavefish)

Spring Cavefish
Forbesichthys agassizii

Size: Both the Spring Cavefish may reach 3.5 inches maximum. Northern Cavefish can reach 4.5 inches.

Natural History: In addition to the Spring Cavefish shown above, there are two other cavefish found in Kentucky. The **Northern Cavefish** (*Amblyopsis spelaea*) and the **Southern Cavefish** (*Typhlichthys subterraneus*) are both true troglodytes (cave dwellers) and thus lack eyes or pigmentation in the skin. The Spring Cavefish lives in the mouths of caves and in springs emanating from underground waterways and is thus heavily pigmented and has small eyes. All members of this family in Kentucky are uncommon to rare, and the Northern and Southern Cavefish are both regarded as species of concern.

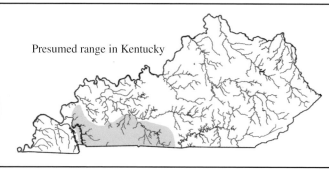

Presumed range in Kentucky

Family—**Aphredoderidae** (pirate perch)

Pirate Perch
Aphredoderus sayanus

Presumed range in Kentucky

Size: Maximum 5.5 inches.

Natural History: The Pirate Perch is endemic to North America. It lives in swamps and spring-fed wetlands among heavy aquatic vegetation. May also be found in backwaters of large creeks and small rivers. Although they are small fishes, they have rather large mouths and they are quite predaceous on insects, crustaceans, and small fishes. This is a fairly common fish in the lowlands of westernmost Kentucky.

Family—**Percopsidae** (trout perch)

Trout Perch
Percopsis omiscomaycus

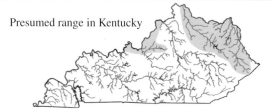

Presumed range in Kentucky

Size: Adults are about 6 inches.

Natural History: The Trout Perch lives in lakes and quiet pools of larger streams. It feeds on insects, crustaceans, and small fish. Mainly nocturnal, it spends the day in deep water and moves into the shallows at night to feed. This is a species of high latitudes that reaches the southernmost limits of its range in Kentucky, where it is uncommon and a species of concern.

REFERENCES

Chapters 1, 2, and 8

Print

Bailey, Robert G. 2009. *Ecosystem Geography, From Ecoregions to Sites.* Springer Science & Business Media, New York, NY.

Hunt, Charles B. 1974. *Natural Regions of the United States and Canada.* W.H. Freeman and Company, San Francisco, CA.

Ricketts, Taylor, H., Eric Dinerstein, David M. Olson, and Colby J. Loucks, et al. 1999. *Terrestrial Ecoregions of North America.* World Wildlife Fund and Island Press, Washington, DC.

Internet

Kentucky Department of Environmental Protection, Division of Water—www.water.ky.gov

Kentucky State Nature Preserves Commission—www.naturepreserves.ky.gov

U.S. Environmental Protection Agency / Ecoregions of North America—www.epa.gov/wed/pages/ecoregions.htm

The Encyclopedia of Earth—www.eoearth.org

USGS—www.usgs/science/geology/regions

Commission for Environmental Cooperation—www.cec.org

Mammal References

Print

Barbour, Roger W. and Wayne Davis. 1974. *Mammals of Kentucky.* University Press of Kentucky, Lexington, KY.

Bowers, Nora, Rick Bowers, and Kenn Kafuman. 2004. *Mammals of North America.* Houghton Mifflin Company, New York, NY.

Campbell, Joshua W., Micheal T. Mengak, Steven B. Castleberry, and Jason D. Mejia. 2010. *Distribution and Status of Uncommon Mammals in the Southern Appalachian Mountains.* Southeastern Naturalist 9(2) 275–302.

Kays, Roland W. and Don. E. Wilson. 2009. *Mammals of North America.* Princeton University Press, Princeton, NJ.

Sole, Jeffrey D. 1999. *Distribution and Habitat of Appalachian Cottontails in Kentucky.* Proceedings of the Annual Conference, Southeastern Association of Fish and Wildlife Agencies.

Trani, Margaret K., Mark Ford, and Brian R. Chapman. 2007. *The Land Manager's Guide to Mammals of the South.* The Nature Conservancy, Southeast Region, Durham, NC.

Walker, E.P. 1983. *Walkers Mammals of the World.* The John's Hopkins University Press, Baltimore, MD.

Whitaker, John O. Jr. and W. J. Hamilton Jr. 1998. *Mammals of the Eastern United States.* Cornell University Press, Ithaca, NY.

Wilson, Don E. and Sue Ruff. 1999. *North American Mammals.* Smithsonian Institution, Washington, DC.

Internet

Kentucky Department of Fish and Wildlife Resources—www.kdfwr.state.ky.us

Kentucky Bat Working Group—www.biology.eku.edu/bats

International Union of Concerned Naturalists—www.iucnredlist.org

Nature Serve Explorer—www.natureserve.org

Smithsonian National Museum of Natural History—www.mnh.si.edu

Mammalian Species, American Society of Mammologists species accounts—www.science.smith.edu

Print

Clark, William S. and Brian K. Wheeler. 1987. *A Field Guide to Hawks—North America.* Peterson Field Guides, Houghton Mifflin Co., Boston, MA.

Dunn, John L., Kimball Garret, Thomas Shultz, and Cindy House. *A Field Guide to Warblers of North America.* Peterson Field Guides, Houghton Mifflin Co., Boston, MA.

Farrand, John, Jr. 1998. *An Audubon Handbook, Eastern Birds.* McGraw Hill Book Co., New York, NY.

Floyd, Ted. 2008. *Smithsonian Field Guide to the Birds of North America.* Harper Collins Publishers. New York, NY.

Johnsgard, Paul A. 1988. *North American Owls, Biology and Natural History.* Smithsonian Institution Press, Washington, DC.

Kaufman, Ken. 2000. *The Birds of North America.* Houghton Mifflin Co., New York, NY.

Mengel, Robert M. 1965. *The Birds of Kentucky.* American Ornithologist's Union Monogram, no. 3. The Allen Press, Lawrence, KS.

Palmer-Ball, Brainard. *The Kentucky Breeding Bird Atlas.* The University Press of Kentucky, Lexington, KY.

Palmer-Ball, Brainard. 2003. *Annotated Checklist of the Birds of Kentucky.* Kentucky Ornithological Society, Louisville, KY

Peterson, Roger T. 1980. *A Field Guide to the Birds, Eastern Birds.* Houghton Mifflin Co., Boston, MA.

Vanner, Micheal. 2003. *The Encyclopedia of North American Birds.* Parragon Publishing, Bath, UK.

Internet

Cornell University Lab of Ornithology—Birds of North America Online—http://birds.bna.cornell.edu.bna/species.

Ebird—www.ebird.org

Environment Canada—www.ec.gc.ca

Kentucky Department of Fish and Wildlife Resources—www.kdfwr.state.ky.us

Kentucky Ornithological Society—www.kybirdrecords.org

McGill Bird Observatory—www.migrationresearch.org

NatureServe Explorer—www.natureserve.org

Waterfowl Hunting Management in North America—www.flyways.us

Turtle References

Print

Buhlmann, Kurt, Tracey Tuberville, and Whit Gibbons. 2008. *Turtles of the Southeast.* The University of Georgia Press, Athens, GA.

Collins, Joseph T. and Travis W. Taggart. 2009. *Standard Common and Scientific Names for North American Amphibians, Turtles, Reptiles & Crocodilians.* The Center for North American Herpetology, Hays, KS.

Conant, Roger, and Joseph T. Collins. 1998. *Reptiles and Amphibians of Eastern/Central North America.* Houghton

Mifflin Co., Boston, MA.

Ernst, Carl H., Jeffrey E. Lovich, and Roger W. Barbour. 1994. *Turtles of the United States and Canada.* Smithsonian Institution Press, Washington, DC.

Niemiller, Matthew L., R. Graham Reynolds, and Brian T. Miller. 2013. *The Reptiles of Tennessee.* The University of Tennessee Press, Knoxville, TN.

Trauth, Stanley E., Henry W. Robison, and Michael V. Plummer. 2004. *The Amphibians and Reptiles of Arkansas.* The University of Arkansas Press, Fayetteville, AR.

Internet

Kentucky Department of Fish and Wildlife Resources—www.kdfwr.state.ky.us

NatureServe Explorer—www.natureserve.org

Reptile References

Print

Collins, Joseph T. and Travis W. Taggart. 2009. *Standard Common and Scientific Names for North American Amphibians, Turtles, Reptiles & Crocodilians.* The Center for North American Herpetology, Hays, KS.

Conant, Roger, and Joseph T. Collins. 1998. *Reptiles and Amphibians of Eastern/Central North America.* Houghton Mifflin Co., Boston, MA.

Meade, Les. 2005. *Kentucky Snakes. Their Identification, Variation, and Distribution.* Kentucky State Nature Preserves Commission.

Niemiller, Matthew L., R. Graham Reynolds, and Brian T. Miller. 2013. *The Reptiles of Tennessee.* The University of Tennessee Press, Knoxville, TN.

Shupe, Scott. 2005. *U.S. Guide to Venomous Snakes and Their Mimics.* Skyhorse Publishing, New York, NY.

Trauth, Stanley E., Henry W. Robison, and Michael V. Plummer. 2004. *The Amphibians and Reptiles of Arkansas.* The University of Arkansas Press, Fayetteville, AR.

Internet

Kentucky Department of Fish and Wildlife Resources—www.kdfwr.state.ky.us

The Center for North American Herpetology—www.naherpetology.org

NatureServe Explorer—www.natureserve.org

Amphibian References

Print

Collins, Joseph T. and Travis W. Taggart. 2009. *Standard Common and Scientific Names for North American Amphibians, Turtles, Reptiles & Crocodilians.* The Center for North American Herpetology, Hays, KS.

Conant Roger, and Joseph T. Collins. 1998. *Reptiles and Amphibians of Eastern/Central North America.* Houghton Mifflin Co., Boston, MA.

Niemiller, Matthew L. and R. Graham Reynolds. 2011. *The Amphibians of Tennessee.* University of Tennessee Press, Knoxville, TN.

Trauth, Stanley E., Henry W. Robison, and Michael V. Plummer. 2004. *The Amphibians and Reptiles of Arkansas.* The University of Arkansas Press, Fayetteville, AR.

Dodd, C. Kenneth. 2013. *Frogs of the United States and Canada.* Johns Hopkins University Press, Baltimore, MD.

Internet

Kentucky Department of Fish and Wildlife Resources—www.kdfwr.state.ky.us

The Center for North American Herpetology—www.naherpetology.org

International Union of Concerned Naturalists—www.iucnredlist.org

NatureServe Explorer—www.natureserve.org

Fish References

Print

Burr, Brooks M. and Melvin L. Warren, Jr. 1986. *A Distributional Atlas of Kentucky Fishes.* Kentucky Nature Preserves Commission.

Clay, William M. 1974. *The Fishes of Kentucky.* Kentucky Department of Fish and Wildlife Resources, Frankfort, KY.

Eddy, Samuel. 1969. *How to Know the Fresh Water Fishes.* Wm. C. Brown Company Publishers, Dubuque, IA.

Etnier, David A. and Wayne C. Starnes. 1993. *The Fishes of Tennessee.* The University of Tennessee Press, Knoxville, TN.

Goldstein, Robert J. with Rodney Harper and Ridchard Edwards. 2000. *American Aquarium Fishes.* Texas A&M University Press, College Station, TX.

Miller, Rudolph J. 2004. *The Fishes of Oklahoma.* The University of Oklahoma Press, Norman, OK.

Page, Lawrence M. and Brooks M. Burr. 2011. *Peterson Field Guide to Freshwater Fishes of North America North of Mexico.* Houghton Mifflin Harcourt, Boston, MA.

Pflieger, William L. 1975. *The Fishes of Missouri.* Missouri Department of Conservation, Springfield, MO.

Internet

Kentucky Creeks.com—www.kycreeks.com

FishBase—www.fishbase.org

North American Native Fish Association—www.nanfa.org

National Fish Habitat Action Plan—www.fishhabitat.org

NatureServe Explorer—www.natureserve.org

USGS Fact Sheets—www.search.usgs.gov

International Union of Concerned Naturalists—www.iucnredlist.org

Kentucky Department of Fish and Wildlife Resources—www.kdfwr.state.ky.us

Encyclopedia of Life—www.eol.org

GLOSSARY

Aestivate / Aestivation	Dormant state of inactivity usually brought on by hot, dry conditions. The opposite of hibernation, which is a wintertime dormancy.
Amphipod	A crustacean of the order Amphipoda. Includes the freshwater shrimps.
Anadromous	Ascending into freshwater rivers to spawn.
Annelid / Annalida	A class of invertebrate organisms commonly known as worms.
Anuran	A member of the amphibian order Anura (the frogs and toads).
Arboreal	Pertaining to trees.
Arthropod	A member of the invertebrate phylum Arthropoda.
Aspen Parkland	An open or semi-open area in the high mountains where the dominant trees are aspen.
Aut021my	A defensive response in which the tail is vountarily broken off. Occurs in many salamanders and most lizards.
Barbel	A long "whisker-like" appendage orginating near the mouth of fishes, often sensory.
Barrens	Open areas within normally forested or brushy habitats.
Benthic	Pertaining to the bottom of a stream or lake.
Bivalve	An organism of the phylum Molluska (mollusks) or Branchiopoda having a shell consisting of two halves.
Boreal	Northern.
Borrow Pit	Shallow ditches and ponds created by road construction when earth is "borrowed" from a nearby area to build up road beds.
Buteo	A hawk belonging to the genus *Buteo*. Also known as the "Broad-winged Hawks."
Cache	The act of storing or hiding food for future use.
Carapace	The top half of the shell of a turtle.
Carnivore	A meat eater.
Caudal	Pertaining to the tail.
Chromosone	Long strand of proteins and DNA found within the nucleus of a cell.
Circumpolar	Literally, around the poles. Usually used in reference to the geographic range of an organism, that is found throughout the northern hemisphere.
Cloaca	A common opening for reproductive and excretory functions in an organism. Typical for all animals except mammals.
Congeneric	Belonging to the same genus.
Conspecific	Belonging to the same species.
Contiguous	In contact with or adjoining.
Copepod	A group of tiny crustaceans belonging to the suborder Copapoda. Many are microscopic and aquatic and are important food for tiny fishes and other small aquatic organisms.
Crustacean	A member of the class Crustacea. A class of Arthropod organisms that includes the crayfish, lobsters, crabs, shrimps, barnacles, copepods, and water fleas.

Cryptic	Pertaining to concealment.
Dessicate / Dessication	Dry out.
Dipteran	An insect of the order Diptera. Includes flies, mosquitos, gnats, and midges.
Disjunct	Not attached to or not adjoining.
Diurnal	Pertaining to day. Being active by day.
Dorsal	The top or back of an organism.
Dorsoventral	The region between the side and the belly of an organism, or along the lower side adjacent to the belly.
Echolocate / Echolocation	The use of sound waves to navigate or move about. As in bats.
Ecoregion	A large unit of land or water containing a geographically distinct assemblage of species, natural communities, and environmental conditions.
Ecotone	The region where one or more habitats converge.
Embryo	A young animal that is developing from a fertilized egg. Embryonic stage ends at birth or hatching.
Endemic	Native to a particular area.
Ephemeral	Fleeting. Temporary.
Extirpated	No longer found within a given area.
Fecund / Fecundity	The capacity to produce large numbers of offspring.
Fin rays	The bony structures that support the membranes of a fish's fin.
Fossorial	Burrowing or living in underground burrows.
Gastropod	A class of the animal phylum Molluska. Includes snails and slugs.
Herbaceous	A type of flowering plant which does not develop woody tissue.
Holarctic	The circumpolar region that includes North America, Europe, and Asia.
Homogeneous	Of the same kind.
Insectivorus	Insect eating.
Intergrade	An organism that possess morphological characteristics that are intermediate between two distinctly different forms.
Irruptive	The sudden movement of animals from one portion of their range to another, often very distant portion of their range. As in when Snowy Owls occasionally move down from the Arctic region into the southern half of North America.
Isopod	An order of Crustaceans that includes the familiar pillbugs.
KDFWR	Kentucky Department of Fish and Wildlife Resources.
Mandible	The lower jaw of an animal or the bill of a bird.
Marine	Pertaining to living in a salt water environment.
Mast	Seeds produced by plants in a deciduous forest. Usually means the cumulative production of acorns, nuts, berries, seeds, etc., which are widely utilized by wildlife as food.
Melanistic	A predominance of the dark pigment known as melanin. The opposite of Albinistic.
Mesic	Damp or moist.
Metabolic / Metabolism	The sum of the chemical activity that occurs within a living organism. Usually relates to the digestion of food and utilization of food compounds within the body.
Metamorphose	Change of the body. Usually refers to the change from an immature stage to a more mature stage (as in a tadpole to a frog).
Metamorphosis	Abrupt physical change of body form.

Millinery Trade	Refers to the creation of women's hats for sale, which used to involve use of bird feathers.
Molt	The shedding of and renewal (replacement) of skin, hair, or feathers.
Morphology	The study of the body form, shape, and structure of organisms, including colors or patterns.
Muskeg	A sphagnum bog occurring the boreal (northern) regions of North America.
Neotropical	Pertaining to the tropical regions of the western hemisphere.
Nuptial	Pertaining to breeding.
Obligate	In biology means occurring within a restricted environment.
Omnivore	Eats both plant and animal matter.
Ontogenetic	Related to the development or age of an organism.
Opercle flap	The bony structure on the side of a fishes head that covers the gills. Also sometimes called gill cover.
Organism	A living thing.
Orthopteran	A member of the insect order Orthoptera. Includes such well know insects as crickets and grasshoppers.
Ovoviparous	A condition in which developing embryos are nurished by a yolk sac but the young develop within the mother's body and are born fully developed.
Palearctic	The geographic region that includes Europe and northern Asia.
Parthenogenesis	The development of an ovum (egg) without fertilization.
Passage Migrant	Refers to birds that merely migrate through an area without staying any appreciable amount of time.
Pelage	Fur.
Phylogeny	The evolutionary relationships and/or evolutionary history of organisms.
Physiography	Refers to the natural features of a landscape, i.e. mountians, rivers, plains, etc.
Piscivorous	Fish eating.
Plastron	The ventral (bottom) portion of a turtle's shell.
Plumage	The feathers of a bird.
Polychaete worms	Annelid worms (phylum Annelida) belonging to the class Polychaeta. Mostly marine but some are freshwater.
Precocial	Being highly precocious.
Precocious	Having adult (or highly developed) characteristics in the young.
Predaceous	Feeding on other animals, being a predator.
Piscivorous	Fish eating.
Prehensile	Grasping. As in a prehensile tail that is able to wrap around and grasp a tree limb.
Puddle Duck	Ducks belonging to the genus *Anas*.
Regenerative	Refers to the ability to repair or replace damage or destroyed tissues or structures.
Riparian	Pertaining to the bank of a stream or river.
Sexual Dimorphism	Morphological differences between the sexes.
Successional Woodlands / Areas	Landscape areas (usually woodlands) that are undergoing change from an early stage of development to an older stage. As in woodlands regenerating following logging operations.
Sympatrically	A condition where more than one species occurs in the same or overlapping area or habitat.

Taiga	A type of forest occurring in the far north. Usually dominated by dwarfed spruces.
Topography	The configuration of the land surface. Literally, "the lay of the land."
Troglodyte	Cave dwelling. Usually refers to organisms that live in caves.
Turbid	Water that is opaque due to the high amount of suspended silt particles.
Tympanum	The circular ear structure on the side of the head of frogs and toads.
USFWS	Acronym for the United States Fish and Wildlfie Service.
Ventral	Pertaining to the belly or bottom side of an organism.
Vernal	Pertaining to spring. Also frequently used to describe temporary ponds and pools that hold water only during the wet season.
Vestigial	A rudimentary structure. Usually a remnant, degenerative structure that was once (in the evolutionary history of the organism) a fully functioning structure.
Xeric	Dry.
Zygote	A fertilized egg that has not yet begun to divide.

INDEX OF COMMON NAMES

PHOTO CREDITS

Matthew R. Thomas

Eastern Sand Darter, Blackside Darter, Frecklebelly Darter, Slenderhead Darter, Fantail Darter (M & F) Speckled Darter (M & F), Slough Darter, Emerald Darter, Cypress Darter (M & F), Mud Darter, Bluntnose Darter, Teardrop Darter, Harlequin Darter, Headwater Darter, Varigate Darter, Banded Darter, Skipjack Herring, Threadfin Shad, Stonecat, Slender Madtom, Spotted Sucker, Pugnose Miinow, Streamlined Chub, Blotched Chub, Mississippi Silvery Minnow, Shoal Chub, Silver Chub, Redtail Chub, Bullhead Minnow, Stargazing Minnow, Suckermouth Minnow, Silver Shiner, Highland Shiner, Rosyface Shiner, Mimic Shiner, Starhead Minnow, Goldeye, Spring Cavefish, River Redhorse, Quillback.

John R. MacGregor

Least Weasel, Spotted Skunk, Allegheny Woodrat, Golden Mouse, Cotton Mouse, Southern Red-backed Vole, Southern Bog Lemming, Meadow Jumping Mouse, Masked Shrew, Eastern Red Bat, Eastern Small-footed Bat, Gray Bat, Hoary Bat, Rafinesque's Big-eared Bat, Silver-haired Bat, Eastern Slender Glass Lizard, Four-toed Salamander, Hellbender, Green Salamander, Wehrle's Salamander, Black Mountain Salamander, Northern Redback Salamander, Plains Leopard Frog.

David Speiser, www.lillibirds.com

Wilson's Warbler (M), Golden-winged Warbler, Mourning Warbler, Connecticut Warbler, Buff-breasted Sandpiper, Long-tailed Duck (M & F), Surf Scoter, Black Scoter, Alder Flycatcher, Yellow-bellied Flycatcher.

Don Martin Bird Photography

Willow Flycatcher, Henslow's Sparrow, LeConte's Sparrow, Piping Plover, Ruby-crowned Kinglet (M), Least Flycatcher, Olive-sided Flycatcher, Wilson's Warbler (M).

Konrad Schimdt

Flathead Chub, Ghost Shiner, River Shiner, Mooneye, Trout Perch, Silver Redhorse.

Brian Zimmerman

Popeye Shiner, Saffron Darter, Splendid Darter, Cumberland Darter, Highfin Carpsucker, Lake Chubsucker.

James Kiser

Evening Bat, Northern Short-tailed Shrew, Bluebreast Darter.

T. Travis Brown

Mottled Sculpin, Striped Darter, Cumberland Plateau Darter.

Phil Myers
Meadow Vole, Smokey Shrew.

Cheryl Tanner
Eastern Harvest Mouse

Kevin Lawson
Cooper's Hawk

Kris Light
Appalachian Cottontail

Kate Slankard
Short-eared Owl

Dave Neely
Ribbon Shiner

Don Brockmeir
Blue Grosbeak (F)

Sterling Daniels
Hairy-tailed Mole

Jeffrey Offerman,
www.flickr.com/photos/jeff_offerman *Long-tailed Weasel*

David Haggard
Green Treefrog (rare blue morph)

Uland Thomas
Mooneye

*All other photographs by Scott Shupe.

ABOUT THE AUTHOR

Naturalist Scott Shupe began his professional career in 1971 at the famed Ross Allen Reptile Institute and Venom Laboratory in Silver Springs, Florida. He later worked at the St. Augustine Alligator Farm in St. Augustine, Florida, and with Reptile Gardens in Rapid City, South Dakota. From 1992 to 2002 he enjoyed an association with the Knight & Hale Game Call company in Cadiz, Kentucky, where he served as director of the Woods and Wetlands Wildlife Center, a private zoo/nature center. He is the founder and original owner of the Natural History Educational Company, an organization of professional naturalists that provided live-animal wildlife education programs to thousands of schools throughout the United States.

He has served as a host and narrator for wildlife-related television programming (*In the Wild*-Outdoor Channel), produced educational life science videos, and has appeared as a guest naturalist on a number of public television

programs and satellite networks. He has been recognized for his contributions to conservation education by the U.S. Fish and Wildlife Service, named naturalist of the year by the Kentucky Society of Naturalists, awarded the Jesse Stuart Media Award for his educational video productions, and received the Environmental Stewardship Award from the Kentucky Environmental Quality Commission. Since 1987 he has contracted annually with the Kentucky Department of Parks to provide naturalist programming in state parks across Kentucky.

He has written for outdoor and nature periodicals and scientific journals and his wildlife photographs have appeared in dozens of nature magazines and books. This is his fourth book on nature and wildlife and his third book for Skyhorse Publishing. He also authored *U.S. Guide to Venomous Snakes and their Mimics*, *Venomous Snakes of the World: A Handbook for Use by U.S. Amphibious Forces*, and *Life List of North American Birds*. A freelance naturalist with nearly forty years' experience in a wide array of nature interpretation, wildlife tourism, education, zoological exhibits administration, writing, and wildlife photography and videography.

Contact Scott Shupe at: kscottshupe@gmail.com.